BILL OF FARE

NOW SERVING FOOD WHERE PRICES APPEAR

FRUITS, ETC.

Orange Juice	10¢	Tomato Juice	10¢
Grapefruit Juice	10¢	Fruit Salad	15¢
Baked Apple	10¢	Half Grapefruit	15¢

TOAST AND CEREALS

Dry or Buttered Toast	10¢	Oatmeal, Cream	15¢
Milk Toast	25¢	Oatmeal, Milk	10¢
French Toast	35¢	Grape Nuts	15¢
Cakes and Coffee	10¢	Corn Flakes	15¢
Doughnuts	05¢	Bran	15¢
Coffee, with above orders	05¢	Muffins	05¢

SOUPS TO ORDER

Chicken	15¢	Vegetable	15¢
Tomato	15¢	Chili Con Carne	

STEAKS, CHOPS, ETC.

Small Steak		Lamb Chops	50¢
Club Steak		Veal Chops	45¢
T-Bone Sirloin Steak		Fried Ham or Bacon	45¢
Porterhouse Steak		Fried Onions with the above orders.	
Beef Tenderloin Steak	50¢	Extra with above orders:	
Pork Tenderloin		Mushrooms	10¢
Hamburger Steak	35¢	Breaded, extra	
Pork Chops	45¢	Tomato or Spanish Sauce, extra	10¢
Veal Cutlets			

EGGS AND OMELETTES

Two Eggs Fried or Boiled	35¢	Onion Omelette	35¢
Three Eggs Fried or Boiled	45¢	Tomato Omelette	40¢
Two Poached Eggs on Toast	35¢	Bacon or Ham Omelette	45¢
Three Poached Eggs on Toast	45¢	Cheese Omelette	40¢
Ham and Eggs	45¢	Spanish Omelette	50¢
Bacon and Eggs	40¢	Mushroom Omelette	50¢
Minced Ham and Scrambled Eggs	40¢	Jelly Omelette	40¢
Plain Omelette	35¢	Toast & Coffee with above orders.	

PRINTED IN THE U.S.A.
FIRST EDITION
BOOK & COVER DESIGN: *Martha Blowen / Soleil Press, Lisbon Falls, Maine*
　　　　　■ *It's been an honor to work with you, Emily! — M.B.*

DISTRIBUTION: Contact Soleil Press, 95 Gould Road, Lisbon Falls, ME 04252
207-353-5454 ✪ barjo@turningmemories.com ✪ www.turningmemories.com

PUBLISHER'S CATALOGUING IN PUBLICATION DATA:

Foster, J. Emily
　The Legend of Barjo Restaurant / the Life of Josephine McAllister Stone / J. Emily Foster.
1. Foster, J. Emily, 1939—. 2. Women—Biography—20th century. 3. Maine—Family life. 4. Conduct of life. 5. 20th Century—Maine—History. 6. Food Service—Maine—20th Century.
ISBN 0-9619373-8-6
LC # 133490

ACKNOWLEDGEMENTS:
The author acknowledges the following sources for historical information:
　　■ *Bound By Memories' Ties*, by Father Donald McAllister, 1988, Norway, ME.
　　■ *The Oxford Hills*, by Diane and Jack Barnes, 1995, Arcadia Publishing, Dover, NH.
　　■ *The History of Norway, Maine*, by William B. Lapham, 1886, reprinted 1986,
　　　　New England History Press, Somersworth, NH.
　　■ articles by Mary Delameter, reporter, Lewiston *Sun-Journal*, Lewiston, ME.
　　■ articles and photographs by Jack Quinn, reporter, Portland *Press Herald*,
　　　　Portland, ME.
　　■ articles by Bob Gardner, reporter, Portland *Press Herald*, Portland, ME.
　　■ *The Congressional Record*, March 9, 1990, article by Senator William Cohen.
　　■ the Norway Memorial Library.
　　■ the Norway Historical Society.

Photographs not otherwise credited are from Josephine Stone's personal collection.

SPECIAL THANKS:
　　■ *to Jo's younger sister, Grace, who told me the stories about Jo as a kid in East Stoneham. Many times, Grace enlightened me with details Jo had omitted in her version. Thanks, Grace, for your insights.*

　　■ *to Jo's nephew, Donnie, for guidance with dates from the family genealogy and for the information used from your book,* Bound by Memories' Ties.

　　■ *to Denis Ledoux and Martha Blowen of Soleil Press, Lisbon Falls, Maine, for the many hours they have spent guiding me through "Turning Memories into Memoirs." Without your help, this project might never have been completed. MANY THANKS!*
　—J.E.F.

Jo Stone

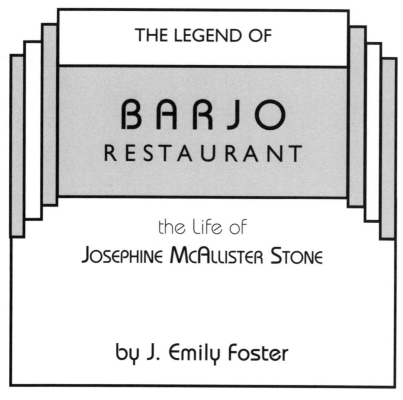

THE LEGEND OF

BARJO
RESTAURANT

the Life of
JOSEPHINE McALLISTER STONE

by J. Emily Foster

Best Wishes,

J. Emily Foster

McJeffEmy Editions
NORWAY, MAINE
SOLEIL PRESS

TO MARGARET MCALLISTER

who was one of my greatest supporters,

and whose dream was to be a writer.

"God is my refuge and strength,
a very present help in time of trouble."
Psalms 46:1, KJV

— TABLE OF CONTENTS —

— FOREWORD —

This book includes some yarns about "Jo," as she prefers to be called—some good, some not so good, and some just plain funny.

We have been together for a long time, ever since my sophomore year in high school. Jo has been just like a mother to me and seen me through many good years and many hard times. We have always overcome the many turns and twists in the road of life through our faith and by the leadership of Our Heavenly Father, and His Son, Jesus, with much guidance from the Holy Spirit.

Today, Jo is still going strong at age 96. She has as much vim and vigor as though she were still behind the grill in Barjo's kitchen, where she spent her waking hours for over sixty years.

I hope you will enjoy these stories and will grow to appreciate Jo as much as I have. Her love of people and her generosity have touched many, many people from all walks of life.

"She is truly a great lady!"

—Emily Foster
Norway, Maine
Summer 2000

— SECTION ONE —

PART I

Jo's Childhood and Adolescence

Josephine McAllister, 1909,
(center, front row, with white pinafore and hairbow,)
with classmates at the East Stoneham School

from the East Stoneham Hills

Near the Maine-New Hampshire border, in the western foothills of Oxford County, is located the town of East Stoneham, Maine. Off Main Street across a granite-slab bridge which spans Cold Brook sits a set of farm buildings once owned by Charles Frederick Small. This is where Jo Stone was born in 1903 and lived up to the age of fourteen. On the same side of the brook, at that time, a footpath led to Virgil Littlefield's long-lumber mill yard, where Jo's father, Leslie McAllister worked for many years. Just beyond were the cooper shop and the blacksmith shop. In the center of the town was the First Congregational Church and the general store owned by Melvin Bartlett.

In the forests around East Stoneham, red oaks, white birches, poplars, beeches, and white pines grew abundantly, making lumbering the main source of employment for the community. Jonathan Bartlett & Pete Kilgore ran the Spool Mill where spools were made from white birch. "Jock" Bartlett's long-lumber mill in Bartlettboro, a part of East Stoneham, provided the white birch, sawed into four-foot lengths that were to be used at the Spool Mill. Shingles for the homes were also made locally, as well as "shook," the stock for barrel staves.

Water from the numerous rivers and streams in the area was harnessed to furnish power for these mills. In the spring of each year, the local men took part in the log drives on the Songo River and the Five Kezars lakes in Lovell.

At the turn of the nineteenth century, horse-drawn wagons were the standard mode of transportation. In Washington, the Republican Party under the guidance of President "Teddy" Roosevelt controlled the country. The State of Maine was a Republican stronghold and continued to be until the election of Edmund Muskie, the state's first Democrat governor, in 1954.

In small Maine towns, the focus of daily life was the home. In most families, the mother stayed at home to take care of the family, while the father worked to earn a living. Much of the entertainment centered on family activities at school and church.

In the early 1900's, the family doctor would come to the home to deliver the babies. A family member acting as midwife helped him. Usually, this was a grandmother or an aunt of the child.

On a cold December 26, 1903, it was Tena's cousin, Minnie Littlefield, who assisted Dr. Coolidge with the birth of Josephine Arlene. The baby was born in the front room of her grandfather's home. Her parents, Leslie and Tena Small McAllister already had two children, Gerald, (or Jim as he preferred to be called) born May 24, 1895, and Helen, born July 14, 1897. Jo would be joined by three younger children, Donald, born July 1, 1906, Margaret, born December 8, 1908, and Grace, born July 13, 1911.

The house where Jo was born and her family lived in East Stoneham belonged to her maternal grandfather, Charles Frederick Small. He and their grandmother, Jane Whitehouse,[1] had been married in 1871 and had had three daughters, Nettie, Maude and Tena.

Fred, as his neighbors called him, and Jane had been married eighteen years when they divorced on October 23, 1889. Jane got the divorce on grounds of cruel and abusive treatment[2] This was common for divorce in those days, although Fred's drinking habits could certainly have been considered a factor. He had many drinking buddies hanging around and swigging on his stock of hard cider. Strange as it may seem, the only charge in the actual court documents was that Fred had made Jane "chop and carry in all the wood."

When she divorced, Jane left East Stoneham and went to work at the Elm House, a hotel in Norway, taking Nettie, 17, and Maude, 15, with her. Jane was a strong willed individual and wanted to gain her independence by earning her own income. While at the Elm House, they all worked either waiting on tables or helping with the housekeeping duties.

Jo's mother, Tena, however, was only 13 years old, not old enough to work. Tena decided to stay in East Stoneham and keep house for her father. Knowing that Virg and Georgia Littlefield and their other relatives that lived nearby would keep an eye on her, Jane agreed to this arrangement.

In 1892, Jane Whitehouse Small married Frank Moody, her second husband, and moved back to East Stoneham to his farm. Frank Moody and Fred Small were cousins and good friends, so the children were welcome in both homes. The McAllister kids called their step-grandfather "Uncle Frank."

In 1894, when Tena was 19, she married Leslie McAllister. The newly-weds lived at her father's home and took care of him.

By the time Grampa Small died in 1909, they had established their family. Jo was 6 years old and all but Grace, who would come along two years later, were part of a growing household. It had not been easy for Tena to raise her family in her father's house. Grampa Small always had too many friends hanging around as drinking buddies. Because Tena disliked how her father's friends behaved after having several drinks of hard cider, she vowed she would never stock any barrels of cider in her own cellar. When Grampa Small died, Tena inherited the house and never allowed a drop of liquor to enter there. She instilled this attitude in her children, too. When Jo and her younger sister, Margaret, grew up, both had an intense dislike for liquor or for anyone who had been drinking.

Small in stature, Grammie Moody, as Jo and her sisters and brothers called her, had a lot of "get-up and go," planting and harvesting her garden by herself. Because she had Indian heritage,3 she was used to hard work. She mowed the fields with a scythe and raked them with a hand rake. In the early 1900's, no modern equipment was available to cut down on manual labor. An immaculate housekeeper, she kept her home spotless.

As one of Jo's important mentors, Grammie Moody taught her how to work hard and to be sure she finished anything she started to the best of her ability. Jo never forgot these lessons, as her many long days of work at Barjo's Restaurant would show.

The McAllister children called their father "Pa." That's what Maine Yankees used for Father, instead of "Dad" or "Daddy." Pa was a strapping man, about six feet tall, with the healthy complexion of an active outdoorsman.

Jo's father was a woodsman who could figure a board foot of lumber in his head, a useful skill in his trade. Pa worked for Virgil Littlefield, Tena's cousin, as a sawyer running either his long lumber or short lumber mills. Working as a woodsman in the winter months, he had to load the logs on the horse-drawn sleds with a bolt hook to bring the logs to the lumber mill. This work required him to be strong and physically fit. Jo stated many times over the years that she was sure he could have licked John L. Sullivan, the famous prizefighter.

With a keen sense of humor and a good disposition, Pa got along well with everyone he worked with. In many ways, Jo was like him. They were both outgoing and loved people.

Jo's mother, Tena, whom the children always called Mother, was a strong figure in the lives of her husband and children. She had never gone to high school and she was determined her children would each have a high-school education.

When Pa was gone during the week, working to support his family, Mother was the disciplinarian and as Jo describes her, "the power behind the throne." She taught her children from a very early age to depend on God and to pray to Him for guidance.

Because there were no modern conveniences, mothers had a full-time job of caring for the family, washing and cleaning. Mother was no exception and, as a result, she was always there for the family when they came home from school or work.

Kerosene lamps provided light for the homes. Every morning, Mother had to clean the chimneys, trim the wicks, and then fill the lamps with kerosene for use in the evening.

Like all women during this era, Jo's mother did all her own cooking and baking on a wood stove. Everything was made "from scratch" with no mixes or anything of that sort. A staple for the McAllister family, as for most families, was steaming-hot biscuits. Biscuits were served at every meal and required a hot, constant heat to bake well. The temperature in the oven was regulated by how much or how little wood was put in the firebox of the kitchen stove. In this way, Jo's mother kept the oven temperature even while doing her baking.

In the early 1900's, canning was a necessity. Every pantry and vegetable cellar was well stocked with provisions against the winter snows. The McAllister home was no exception. Mother worked over the stove for hours, canning vegetables and fruits for the winter's supply.

On Monday, the family wash day, Jo's mother heated large kettles of water for the washing, which she would do in a large washtub with a scrub board. Doing laundry was an all-day procedure by the time she had finished hanging out all the clothes.

This same wash tub was used for the children's baths. Water, for that, too, was heated on the wood stove. When the children were small, Mother gave them their baths in front of the wood stove in the kitchen, so they wouldn't catch cold.

By the time Jo was four years old, she was allowed to take her bath alone in the shed attached to the house, where her parents and the older children took theirs. Getting out of the tub in the winter was a challenge. Shivering in the chilly air of the unheated shed, she would waste no time wrapping up in a big towel and hurry to the house by the wood stove to get warm.

Because Jo was the oldest of the four younger children, she assumed the role early on of helping her mother. Her brother, Jim, who was nine years older, was already working at the mill and Jo felt she should do her part to help with the daily household chores. In 1908, soon after she turned five, her first chore on a typical day was keeping the wood-box full. Because there was no hand-pump inside the house, Jo's next chore was going outdoors to the well to draw a bucket of water for her mother to use in the house.

A rope attached to the bucket was used to lower it into the well. Once it was filled with water, Jo would pull the full bucket out of the well with the rope. In the winter, it was very icy around the well. With the weight of a full bucket of water in hand, Jo could easily have had an accident.

Every morning before she went outside, Jo's mother would warn her, "Be careful, you don't fall in!"

"At the time, I didn't know that others in the neighborhood used a hand-pump by the kitchen sink to get their water," Jo explained. "I thought everybody went to the well to get their water. I didn't realize that we were poor. Pa and Mother showed us a lot of love and that was all that really counted."

Having a large family to supervise, Mother encouraged her young children to play in front of the house where she could watch them easily. She was afraid the kids would go near the road that ran through the center of East Stoneham, or fall in the brook that meandered by their home. Since the other neighborhood children came to play with them, her children were close to the house. So successful was Mother in encouraging them to play nearby that the front yard had very little grass.

The first one up in the morning, Pa got himself a hearty breakfast before going to work at Virgil Littlefield's lumber mill, or outdoors, to cut logs in the woods. Pa's breakfast often included fried potatoes. "Up with the birds," Jo would often share some of his fried potatoes before the rest of the family came down. Always an early riser, Jo enjoyed her father's companionship as they ate breakfast together. It was a special time for both of them.

Jo's sister Helen tells this story, one of her most vivid memories, about one of Jo's antics involving Pa on a bitter cold winter day when Jo was about five.

Her father came home and ate lunch. Getting ready to leave, he said, "Jo, have you seen my hat?" She kept quiet. The family scoured the house to no avail. Finally, putting on a summer hat, he left for work in the woods. In the spring, they found the woolen hat hidden in Jo's bureau drawer under a lot of papers.

"Jo hid the hat," Helen explained. "She loved Pa and wanted him to stay home. She thought this would prevent him from going back out into the extreme cold."

One afternoon, the McAllister family was to have their pictures taken by one of their neighbors. Jo was a very bashful, shy child who thought she was too homely to be photographed. She was scared to death of the camera. When Mother told Jo to go out in the yard to have her picture taken, she refused and hid instead.

"Mother made me go to my room and stay in bed for the rest of the day," Jo said. "That was the worst punishment I could have had. I loved the outdoors and staying in the house would have been bad enough but staying in bed was horrible."

To this day, if Jo sees someone with a camera, she will cover her face or try to hide so they won't be able to take her picture.

Mother's cousin, Virgil Littlefield, whom the McAllister kids called Uncle "Virg" and his wife, Aunt "Georgie", were very kind to the kids as they were growing up. They included Jo and her sisters and brothers in whatever was going on. The Littlefield children, Harlan, Catherine, and Thaxter, had many good times with their McAllister cousins.

"On weekends, Uncle Virg and Aunt Georgie would invite us to go with them to picnics by the lake," Jo said. "Aunt Georgie often invited me to stay overnight with Catherine. She let us sleep in the guest room, a big thrill for me. At home, I shared a bedroom with my sisters."

Every year, the Andrews family, proprietors of Andrews Stables in Norway, made a special trip to the West to buy Western workhorses which were distinguished by their unusual strength and endurance. These were important qualities to Maine people who used the animals in the woods hauling logs and on the farms for plowing the fields and harvesting their crops.

Jo's father bought a team of Western horses, Kit and Nell, from the Andrews Stables in Norway. They were gentle animals and dear to Jo's heart. Every morning after the animals had been fed and watered, next on the agenda was harnessing and getting the workhorses ready for their day's work hauling logs in the woods. Even though the stately animals towered over her, never did Jo have any fear they would hurt her or try to bolt from the barn when she was attending to them. She always had a confidence with horses beyond her years.

The area around East Stoneham was beginning to be developed around a chain of lakes in that region known as the "Five Kezars." Summer camps and cottages were in demand. Uncle Virg furnished the lumber for all the new cottages. Pa was working for him at his sawmill where the sawed timber was made into boards to be used by the carpenters. The lumber was loaded in the mill-yard right next door to Jo's home. Then it was delivered to his many customers at the shore front locations by Uncle Virg's teams of horses.

One day, when the drivers got ready to deliver a load to Center Lovell about five miles away, they called out to Jo.

"We're all loaded and ready to go to Center Lovell. Come on and you can drive the horses," they said.

As Jo headed out the door toward the mill-yard, Helen hollered to her, "Jo, you come right back in here and wipe the dishes."

"Wait for me," Jo shouted to her friends. "I'll only be a minute."

"We'll wait," the men replied.

The teamsters knew that she loved to drive the four giant workhorses, so they waited patiently in the mill yard for her to finish helping Helen. This kind of incident happened frequently. Helen was older than Jo. She didn't think Jo should be going off with the drivers, even though she knew that Jo had their parents' permission and would much rather be outdoors.

In the first decade of the 1900's when Jo started school, most small Maine towns had a one-room school with one teacher for all the children from the first grade to the eighth. In East Stoneham, the schoolhouse was often used as the town meeting house as well. Election Day meant a day off for the local school children, so the balloting could be held at the schoolhouse.

In 1910, Jo went to school with her older siblings, Jim and Helen, and her younger brother, Donald. Alice Perry, the teacher in the East Stoneham school, made a big difference in Jo's life.

"I felt like I was the dumbest kid in East Stoneham when it came to learning to write my name," Jo said. "I never will know why they named me Josephine. It took me forever to learn how to spell my own name. If it hadn't been for Miss Perry, I never would have gotten on the ball!"

Miss Perry taught the children a lot about God by reading daily from the Bible and by having a prayer with them every morning at the start of the school day. She taught them to memorize many of the Psalms and Proverbs.

With the faith in God that Tena had instilled in her, Jo was an eager student and wanted to learn how to read and write. Never forgetting the lessons of her childhood, it would be Jo's strong faith in God that sustained her throughout her whole life.

When Pa worked for Uncle Virg, he also drove the stagecoach which carried the United States Mail and passengers from Norway to East Stoneham. Jo used to walk to North Waterford to meet the stage. Then her father would let her drive the four-horse team back to East Stoneham.

It was during this time that she got acquainted with Freeland Howe who often rode the stage to visit friends in Center Lovell. Jo was an unusual child, driving her father's horses with confidence and spirit. It's no wonder that an accomplished and talented man like Freeland Howe took note of her.

Freeland worked as an engineer for the public works department in a city in upstate New York. He was an active trader in the stock market. He was a noted naturalist and bacteriologist who often pondered the true meaning of life. After he returned to Maine to live, many people called him the Sage of Norway.

Later, after her family moved next to him in Norway, Jo came to know him well. He was one of those who taught her about the financial world. This included the Dow Jones Industrial Average and interpreting the stock quotes in the daily paper.

In the early 1900's, he was considered to be a very successful businessman. He was the proprietor of the "Howe Music Store" on Main Street in Norway. The music store was next door to a store owned by Alonzo Nevers, whose son, Percy, or "Uncle Pert" as the kids called him, had married Jo's Aunt Nettie.

Freeland's father, a dynamic businessman, owned the Howe Insurance Agency that was also on Main Street in Norway. His brother, George, was a noted geologist and mineralogist. He found an abundance of Maine gems in the local area,[3] including the area surrounding East Stoneham.

Uncle Virg also had a cooper shop where his crew made barrels. Fred McKeen and Moses Grover ran the shop. The red oak "shook," or barrel staves, was at first made by hand and later by circular saws. A movable table mounted on a track was run past the saw blade, which was slightly curved so the staves were sawed narrower at the ends than in the middle. This made the bulge in the hogshead barrels. To make a hogshead, the wood had to be heated by steam so it would bend before the barrel could be shaped. Sometimes, when the men heated the shook to shape the barrels, Jo and her brother, Donald, got right into the center of the barrel. Holding the shook together with temporary rings, the men built the barrel around them. After the barrel was completed, the permanent iron rings or bands as they were sometimes called, were put on to hold the staves in place.

"What great fun," said Jo, "having Fred and Moses build a barrel around us! Don and I thought we were something special."

A summer attraction for the children was the organ grinder with his monkey. He toured the town, singing everywhere he went. The monkey, dressed up in a fancy hat, sat on the organ grinder's hurdy-gurdy (music box). The summer visitors from around the lakes in the area would come into town to see him.

"During his annual visits, the monkey captivated the attention of all the neighborhood kids. We followed the organ grinder all over town as he played his hurdy-gurdy and sang, while the monkey performed for us," Jo said. "The tiny red hat and jacket with gold braid fascinated us. We'd never seen an animal dressed in clothes before."

In the summer, all the children in the village swam at Lake Keewaydin.

The fields of East Stoneham were the playgrounds for the McAllister kids and their friends. Hiking the hills behind their home, playing games in the pastures, and fishing in the millpond by Uncle Virg's mill yard were some of their favorite pastimes.

Another summer activity for Jo was going berrying with Grammie Moody. Grammie Moody had a hidden place, deep in the woods on her own farm, where wild berries grew in abundance. The only one she ever invited to go with her on these excursions was Jo.

"Come with me, Jo," her grandmother would say. "Hitch up the horse and we'll go get a batch of blueberries. Then I can make you kids a pie."

When they returned home, she used some of the berries to make the family a tantalizing dessert. Some of the berries she made into jams and jellies or canned them to be used when the winter snows were blowing.

At Thanksgiving and for other special occasions, Grammie Moody often surprised the McAllister family with a freshly baked pie. Often, she used some of the berries that Jo had helped her pick in the summer. She was a wonderful pastry cook.

Often, it snowed by Thanksgiving Day, so Pa would harness the horses to the sleigh and go get Grammie Moody and Uncle Frank for Thanksgiving Dinner. The whole family—all the McAllisters, Grampa Small while he was living, Grammie Moody and Uncle Frank—enjoyed the holiday dinner together.

Although Grampa Small and Grammie Moody had divorced, they maintained a friendly relationship. One year, the McAllisters had Thanksgiving at home and Christmas dinner at Grammie Moody's. The next year, they reversed the order.

Every year, Grammie Moody's pumpkin pie graced the McAllister's holiday dinner table. Everybody looked forward to the family's favorite dessert.

"That pumpkin pie would just melt in your mouth!" said Jo.

It was even better than their mother's, and the kids thought their mother was the best cook in the whole world.

On Thanksgiving Day, when the kids visited at Grammie Moody's house, she would let them go into the parlor to look at pictures through the stereopticon. A unique piece of equipment, it fascinated them for hours at a time. It was a treat to the kids to view pictures looked three-dimensional. They'd never seen anything like it before. The children weren't allowed in the parlor any other day in the year, so this was a special occasion for them.

A special treat at Christmas for the McAllister children was to find an orange as one of their gifts. This was a luxury they only received at Christmas.

"It wasn't until after I grew up that I knew Pa loved oranges," Jo said. "The fruit was expensive, and he had only enough money to buy them for us. Pa and Mother went without."

In the winter, the numerous hills in East Stoneham provided Jo, her family and friends, with plenty of places to go sliding. Using anything they could find, from pieces of cardboard to homemade sleds, the kids spent the days outdoors on the snow-covered fields surrounding their home. One hill, Butters Hill, located on the outskirts of town, was several miles long and a great place to go sliding.

"When we went sliding on Butters Hill, Uncle Virg loaned us a pair of his steers and one of the sleds used at his lumber mill," Jo said. "This sled was large enough so all of us could slide down the hill together. The teamster was his son, Thaxter. He looked after the steers and met us at the bottom of the hill. He guided the animals while they pulled the sled back to the top so we could go for another slide."

Skating on the Mill Pond near the village, Jo had a wonderful time. Not many had lace-up shoe skates, but the kids found many ways to have good time with what they did have.

"We didn't have fancy ice skates, just some that strapped onto the bottom of our boots," Jo said. " We enjoyed slipping and slid-ing over the ice, playing games. You could hear us laughing and singing all the way to the village. We had a ball."

Because Helen and Gerald were much older and involved in other activities, the responsibility for helping to care for the young children became Jo's as she got older. She knew how much her mother depended on her, so she shouldered well the trust her mother had put in her.

One task Jo took on to help provide for the family was to take Don, Grace and Margaret berrying with her, just as Grammie Moody had taken her. She took the family horse to old aban-doned farms in Stoneham to pick wild strawberries, raspberries, blueberries and blackberries as the summer went on. Berry brushes grew in abundance around old stonewalls. Blueberries grew near slashings where timber had been cut.

Grace, 4, Margaret, 6, and Don, 8, thought Jo was a little too strict when she insisted they fill up their berry buckets before eat-ing any. But she knew how important it was that every berry picked be taken home for their mother to use in the cooking and canning. Sometimes the kids took their cousin, Catherine Littlefield, along. Catherine was about Jo' s age but she wasn't ambitious. To hurry her up, Jo helped her fill her berry bucket.

"She was so slow picking berries, I thought we'd be there all day, if I didn't help her," Jo said.

Margaret, Grace and Donald thought Jo wasn't fair by helping Catherine. Jo insisted they each pick a bucketful of berries without any help.

"No leaves or green ones, either, and no eating the berries!" Jo said to the kids.

Jo also came to be known as a prankster in her family. Jo and the younger McAllister kids felt Gerald and Helen didn't share with them or include them in the things they were doing. Gerald was working for Uncle Virg at his mill, so he had some money of his own and felt independent from the younger kids. Being the leader of the pack, Jo was always looking for ways to tease him and Helen. Both of them had to be on the lookout if they didn't want to be the brunt of some of Jo's pranks.

Jo remembers one time when the kids all went berrying. By the time they got home, the horse was too exhausted from traveling over the rough terrain to do anything else. Tiring the horse out in the daytime was one of Jo's favorite pastimes.

Later in the evening, Gerald wanted to take out a girlfriend and expected to use the horse. But Old Jack was good only for an evening's relaxation in the barn. Gerald didn't think Jo's prank the least bit funny. Lying down on the hay in his stall, Jack wasn't interested in pulling the wagon another inch, girlfriend or not.

"I didn't think my taking the horse out in the daytime was really any of Gerald's business," Jo said. "I was trying to help Mother by picking berries for her to can, and it was too far for us to walk. All he wanted Old Jack for was to have a good time with his girl friend. I thought what I was doing was more important even though I was younger!"

The children's cousin, Winnie McKeen, often came to their house to visit Helen. Winnie always tried to act very prim and proper, which made the younger children feel uncomfortable. Being teenagers, Helen and Winnie ignored the younger kids.

One time Jo decided to take them down a peg or two. She went out to the barn and got some "lamb ticks"[4] and put them on Winnie's back. Winnie wasn't aware of what Jo was doing, but should have been paying attention when Jo was quiet. Silence usually meant Jo was up to some prank, as she always loved to play a practical joke on someone.

Turning to the younger children, Jo whispered to them, "I wondered how soon it will be before she notices what I did. Next time, I think she will be nicer to us."

Another time, Jo found a gigantic horse-blanket pin,[5] commonly used to keep the blankets around the workhorses. She walked behind Winnie until she got the chance to fasten it to the back of her dress.

Talking to Helen, Winnie had no idea what Jo was up to. She didn't discover the huge horse-blanket pin until she got to Norway High that day. Mortified when one of her friends ask her about it, she realized that Jo had, once again, outwitted her.

"Why Winnie always acted so stuck-up, I'll never know," Jo said. "All of us went to school together, but she tried to make us younger kids feel unhappy every time she came to visit Helen."

Jo wasn't always the originator of a tease. Sometimes that role fell to her younger sisters, Grace and Margaret. Jo expected, at some point, that her brothers and sisters would make her pay for "raising hell" with them, but she didn't know when. They soon figured out a way that they could torment her.

Grace and Margaret knew Jo was afraid of the dark. The three girls all slept together in an upstairs bedroom, with no heat or lights. As night fell, if Jo had been teasing and tormenting her brothers and sisters, Margaret and Grace would say in unison, "You have to sleep in the bedroom alone tonight, Jo!"

"Please don't do that to me. Come on upstairs with me," she cried to her younger sisters. Sometimes they did, but not always, depending on what Jo had been doing to them during the day.

When Grace and Margaret went to bed without Jo, she'd wait until they went to sleep, then crawl right in beside them. The girls didn't wake-up and didn't know that she had outwitted them until morning.

When Helen, Jo's older sister, was going with Perley Grover, he enjoyed showing off his high-stepping driving horse and fancy carriage. Perley liked to think he was an excellent driver and that no one had a horse as good as his.

One Sunday afternoon, Jo and Don decided to show Perley that their horse, Jack, could beat his horse. But to get from Main Street to their home, the kids had to a make a sharp turn and go over the bridge on Cold Brook to get to their front yard.

Driving their horse down the dusty dirt road, Jo saw Perley and Helen coming. When Jo pulled up beside them, Helen was mad enough to wring Jo's neck.

"How about a race?" Jo hollered to Perley.

Jo knew that her sister would be upset by her challenge.

Helen was trying to impress Perley and wanted no part of her younger sister and brother interfering with her afternoon drive.

"Don't you dare race Perley," Helen hollered at Jo, knowing full well what the kids were up to. She was trying to impress Perley and wasn't sure of his reaction to Jo's challenge.

Helen thought to herself, "What are they trying to do, break us up? Jo knows I worked all afternoon cleaning and dusting the parlor to have everything perfect when Perley got there. Don't those brats realize I don't like to have Perley race with them."

"The only time Helen ever did any polishing of the furniture was when she was entertaining Perley," Jo commented."I thought it was time that things changes just a bit."

But it was too late. Perley had taken Jo's challenge and the race was on. Jo was already tugging on Jack's reins. The sand began to fly from the hooves of the horses as they started off neck to neck along the dirt road.

"Hang on tight, Don. Here we go!" Jo hollered to him, as she encouraged Jack to go faster and faster.

Unable to make the sharp turn in the road, Jo drove Jack, non-stop, through Cold Brook, icy water splashing over the wagon wheels, and reached the house before Helen and Perley.

After defeating Perley, Jo looked at Don and said, "Well, Don, we proved our point. Maybe Perley will show us some respect. And just maybe, Helen will stop calling us 'the brats'!"

Being outdoors much of the time, Jo had a radiant complexion sprinkled with freckles when she was young. She was small, but wiry. She had light brown, red-tinted hair and bright blue eyes that sparkled when she laughed. She enjoyed her young life to its fullest.

In an era so different from today, Jo's was a happy childhood. Being outdoors, driving horses, and watching after the younger children, she had accepted the responsibilities her mother expected of her. Jo showed many leadership qualities that would come to the fore in her adult life.

---

[1] *Jane Whitehouse's mother, Sally Horne, was a full-blooded Penobscot Indian. She married John Whitehouse who was part Indian. The Indian village was about a half mile due west of Jockey Cap, (or Peqwocket as the Indians called the mountain), near Fryeburg and just several miles from East Stoneham.*

[2] *Today, it would probably have been called a case of "irreconcilable differences."*

[3] *The observatory at Oxford Hills High School is named for George Howe. His mineral collection, worth thousands of dollars, is on display at the Norway Historical Society*

[4] Similar to wood ticks, which clung to the sheep's wool while they were in the fields grazing.

[5] Today, jewelry is made similar to the old-fashioned horse-blanket pins, but in the early 1900's, it would have been a disgrace to be seen with one attached to your clothes. Using a horse blanket pin to hold your clothes together meant you were too poor to have properly mended clothes.

McAllister sisters, 1909
Josephine, age 5, and Helen, age 12.

Jo attended Sunday School at the East Stoneham Congregational Church as a child.

Activities at the church played a big part in the family's life.

CHAPTER 2

Growing Up

In 1909, the same year Grandpa Small died, another person made her way into the McAllister family's life through Tena's Uncle Will, who was Charles Frederick Small's younger bachelor brother. This woman would prove to be a blessing beyond Mother's wildest dreams.

Jessie Grace Ricker and Tena's uncle, Will Small, met on the train to Portland. Being a gentleman, he had offered her his seat on the train, impressing her with his courteous manner. Uncle Will was on his way home from Boston, and Jessie was traveling from St. Louis, Missouri, to be with her family who were visiting relatives in Maine. With many family ties to the state, the Rickers spent their summers at the Lafayette Hotel in Portland.

Jessie's grandfather was a farmer in Falmouth, and her father, Robert E. Ricker, was a Colonel in the Civil War. When the Union Army took over the railways, Colonel Robert Ricker was named the Commandant[6] of the Indiana, Ohio and Illinois Railway.

Colonel Robert Ricker was a nephew of Hiram Ricker, who owned the Poland Spring complex that included the Poland Spring House, the Mansion House and the Poland Spring water-works, all located in Poland, Maine. Jessie's mother was Ellen Margaret Sawyer of Otisfield. Jessie had one older sister, Ellen.

After the Civil War, in 1865, when he went to work as a civil engineer for Westinghouse, Colonel Ricker moved his family to St. Louis, Missouri. He invented the Westinghouse air brake for the Iron Mountain Railway[7] that traveled to the peak of Mount Washington in New Hampshire. For his invention, Jessie's father received a substantial amount of Westinghouse stock, which became the foundation of the family fortune.

Shortly after her husband's death in 1894, Mrs. Ricker moved her two daughters to the Southern Hotel in St. Louis. Why Mrs. Ricker and her two daughters left their family home to live in hotels the rest of their lives remains, to this day, a mystery to Jo and her family. The Ricker family's suite included one whole floor at the Southern Hotel. In 1912, when the Southern Hotel closed, they moved to the Planter's Hotel and in 1922 moved again, this time to the Jefferson Hotel. All three hotels were located in St. Louis. From the late 1890's, the Ricker family also retained a suite at the Lafayette Hotel in Portland where they stayed when visiting with relatives in Maine.

After their first meeting on the train, Uncle Will and Jessie Ricker became friends. When they married in 1910, Jessie moved with Will Small to Newry, a very small village approximately eighty miles northwest of Portland. Being from a well to do family and able to afford the construction costs, Aunt Jessie built them a new home. Shortly after, Uncle Will introduced her to his niece, Tena McAllister and her young family. Mother was delighted with Aunt Jessie and they became good friends despite the differences in their lifestyles.

With her charm and graceful manner, Aunt Jessie made a big impression on Jo. She was fascinated by the world Aunt Jessie lived in. The generosity and the kindness Aunt Jessie showed to the whole family overwhelmed Jo. To a farm girl from East Stoneham, it seemed like a dream to have a complete stranger come into her life. She was amazed to be treated as an equal by someone of Aunt Jessie's wealth and experience in the world.

One afternoon, Aunt Jessie came to visit Mother. During the course of the conversation, she said to her, "When I found out where Newry, Maine,[8] was, I was ready to pack my bags and get right on the train to go back home. I thought I was in the middle of nowhere, but I decided I'd try to make the best of it. I really appreciate your kindness to me."

Tena's kindness was returned, many times over. Aunt Jessie used her money to help provide Mother with many things to make her life easier. She also assisted her by making it possible for Helen to have a high school education, and later, by giving Mother furniture for her home.

When she moved to East Stoneham from Newry to be nearer to Tena's family, she built a second home in the center of the village. This house had some unique features. In the parlor, the fireplace was made of aquamarine tile, instead of bricks. Above it was a mirror framed in golden oak On the first floor, in addition to the parlor, were the dining room, the kitchen, the bathroom, and a large room where Uncle Will had his gun shop. Aunt Jessie's furniture was golden oak, including the dining room set and rockers throughout her home. Up the winding stairway, there were four bedrooms featuring brass bedroom sets. One room had a bed that folded back into the wall in the daytime to look like a handsome piece of furniture with a mirror at the top.

Even though she had built a new home, Aunt Jessie retained her suite at the Lafayette Hotel in Portland and continued to travel between the two places.

Aunt Jessie was one of the few people who owned a car at that time. Because neither she nor Uncle Will could drive her Stanley Steamer[9] she hired a chauffeur, Mr. Plummer. When driving for her, he always wore a linen duster. Frequently, she invited the McAllister family to go with her for a ride. This was a special treat, especially to the kids.

Stanley Steamers were powered by steam, so frequent stops had to be made to replenish the water supply. It was similar to stopping at a gas station.

When she was visiting in Portland, Aunt Jessie invited Helen to come for several visits at her suite in the Lafayette Hotel. Because Helen was the oldest girl, Aunt Jessie wanted to give her a bigger view of what the world was like in a big city. What an extraordinary excursion it was for a teenager from a small town!

Later, Mother, Margaret and Grace were invited. The night before they were to go, the younger children were so excited they never slept a wink. Hearing Helen's description of the hotel, they just couldn't imagine having someone serve you dinner, or what the bedrooms were going to look like.

"Never having had the opportunity to go to Portland, they were filled with excitement. Their eyes were as big as saucers when they got home," Jo said. "Margaret and Grace couldn't wait to tell the rest of us what they had seen and done. From the experience of eating in a hotel dining room, to going to see the ocean for the first time, they just couldn't talk fast enough."

"I never was able to explain why Aunt Jessie never invited me or the boys to visit in Portland," Jo said. "I knew how much she liked me, so it did seem strange that I never went to Portland. It must have been because she felt I was too young to go with Helen and by the time she invited the younger girls, I was helping my folks at the farm."

Eager to enjoy Aunt Jessie's companionship, Jo often ran errands for her when she was staying in East Stoneham.

Every September, the big event for all the surrounding towns was the "World's Fair" at North Waterford, Maine. At first, it was held on the Common in front of the North Waterford Church. Later, it was moved to the hillside on the road, beyond the church. In the Exhibition Hall, local farmers entered their best specimens from the garden to be judged by the Fair Association officials. The ladies entered specially prepared preserves and home-canned fruits and vegetables. Many exhibited crocheted and knitted handiwork. Numerous organizations—the Grange, Masonic Lodges, 4-H clubs, Girl and Boy Scouts and veterans organizations—submitted exhibits from their various projects.

The pulling ring was a favorite of the fair. Local men brought their teams of oxen and horses for competition. They delighted in showing the strength of their animals, and how well they, the teamsters, could handle them.

In the numerous weight classes, the Fair Association awarded prizes for the ability of the drivers and the power shown by the animals when pulling different size tonnage across the pulling ring. A grandstand, made from hardwood planks, was provided for spectators to sit on, as they watched the animals with their drivers compete for first prize.

Being the high point of the fall season, the fair attracted everybody in the community. Schools were closed for the day so the children could share in the excitement.

Going to the fair was something Tena was all in favor of—as long as Jo wore shoes. All summer the kids had played outdoors, barefooted. Putting on shoes was not something Jo enjoyed or wanted to do, much less wearing them all day at the fair.

"Why do we have to put on new shoes?" Jo complained to her mother. "My feet will be hurting all day!"

"Just get ready and stop complaining or we'll be late for the fair!" her mother told her. "Put on your shoes right now, or you will have to stay home alone."

"O.K., I suppose so," Jo replied. " I'm *not* staying home!"

They all jumped in the wagon and headed for North Waterford. Forgetting all about her shoes, Jo tossed her head and shouted to the other kids, "Hurray, we're off to the fair for a hot dog!"

A special treat at fair-time was "eating-out." It was the only time of year they had anything but their mother's home-cooked meals. The McAllister kids thought they were in seventh heaven, eating a hot dog and washing it down with a Hires root beer.

One of Jo's early experiences at the fair became a family story. It tells a lot about how secluded New England was then from issues we now recognize as racism. It also tells a lot about Jo and her compassion for others.

At the fair was a ball-toss game that was both racist and mean. Most people didn't realize that then, but Jo did. The target was, as they said then, a "colored" man, whose head stuck through a hole in a painted canvas. It was very unusual in those days, in Maine, to see black people at all. Whoever the target was it seemed mean to Jo. In awe, Jo watched as the men threw the balls, trying to hit him.

Always having a compassion for others, Jo asked. "Poor man, I hope those balls aren't going to hurt him. Are the balls soft ones? How can the men win a prize without hurting him?"

Trying to drag her to some other event being held, Helen said to her, "I don't see what fun you are having, just standing there watching those men. Don't you know how many other things there are to do at the fair? Come on with me and I'll show you."

All day, if the family missed Jo, they all knew where they could find her: right back at the concession where the balls were being thrown. Something about having balls thrown at a person bothered Jo. Even at that early age, she was concerned for the welfare of others.

When Jo's older brother, Gerald entered high school in Norway in 1911, Pa lost his helper for doing the chores and feeding the animals. Jo knew Pa would need some assistance in the barn, so she volunteered.

"Well, Jo, do you think you can handle the job?" Pa asked her.

"Sure can," she replied. "I am just like you and I know how tough and rugged you are."

Off to the barn Pa headed, with a lantern in hand to light the way, Jo at his side. Feeding and caring for the horses was a special part of Jo's day, and she enjoyed Pa's companionship.

"I loved the outdoors," Jo says. "I was a regular tomboy. I would rather help Pa than stay in the house and do housework. Many times, Helen chased me around the mill-yard, trying to get me to help with the dishes. She wanted me to help Mother instead of going with Pa or playing outside with my friends."

One day, Jo was outdoors helping her father with the chores when Willis Learned, a local cattleman, came by to buy a cow. Pa told him all about the animal, and when Mr. Learned was ready to make the deal, Pa walked down to the barn to fetch it.

At this moment Jo decided to put in *her* two-cents worth about this cow. She said to Mr. Learned, "You'll just love this cow. Why, do you know, I think she can *jump* over the Moon!"

(When a cow was frisky and jumped the fence too often, the farmers considered it a poor buy because it gave little milk.)

By the time Pa had returned with the cow, Mr. Learned was walking away down the road. Pa had been counting on the sale to help out with the family finances. Though he never said a word to Jo about this incident, she knew by his expression that this was to be the first, last, and only time she would be allowed participate when he was talking business.

In 1911, Jo was seven when Gerald (or "Jim" as the family called him) started high school. He stayed in Norway with the Edwards family where his roommate was Bert Melvin. Working during the school year at the Carroll-Jellerson Shoe Shop and during summer vacations for Uncle Virg, he paid his own expenses, including his board.

The next year, 1912, Helen entered Norway High School. Aunt Jessie made it possible for Helen to stay in Norway by paying her expenses at a boarding house on Green Street. This allowed Helen to be free of work so she could concentrate on her studies. Aunt Jessie also furnished her with spending money. This was an uncommon luxury for a McAllister since Jim was at this same time earning all his expenses.

Gerald graduated from Norway High School in 1914 and moved to Auburn to board with his grandparents, the Austin McAllisters. Jim worked at Gross Wholesale Grocers,[10] while working his way through Bliss Business College in Lewiston. Talented in mathematics, he could figure out problems in his head, a skill both confusing and irritating to some of his teachers who reprimanded him for not using a pencil and paper to decipher his mathematics. Given a problem to solve, Jim would give the teacher the answer before she had time to write out on the blackboard how it was to be solved.

During the teens and early twenties, much of the freight was shipped by boxcars or by boat. Everything came in bulk. Jim was a wiry man who could carry a barrel of flour, sugar or molasses on his shoulder with an ease that few of his co-workers possessed. These were the days before forklifts or conveyor belts that are commonly used today for loading and unloading freight. Everything then was done with manual labor.

Jo was nine when her mother was taken very ill, hemorrhaging and having unbearable headaches. She was not expected to live. By God's grace, her life was saved. During her illness, Pa stayed with her at the hospital in Lewiston much of the time.

The hired man, who was supposed to keep up Pa's work, was always late. Anxious to do her part, Jo fed the horses, Nell and Kit, herself. Then, climbing up on the grain box so she could reach over their backs, she would put on their harnesses. She loved those big workhorses and they loved her, so they stood very still. Then, she would drive Nell and Kit out to the lake, near North Lovell, to meet the hired man.

Even at this early age, Jo had no tolerance for someone being late for work, no matter what was happening. She knew the hired man was late even when Pa was at home. But she was determined that the horses would be at work on time, even though he wasn't.

Using an excuse such as "I overslept because I was tired," was just as bad in Jo's book. "Tired" is a word she has never used about herself or let anyone that worked for her say.

After Jim and Helen entered Norway High School, Margaret and Grace replaced them at the local one-room school. Once again, four children from the McAllister family were enrolled in the same school.

In the winter of 1913, Pa took a logging job from Ernest Bartlett in West Stoneham. Work was scarce in the area and this was an opportunity for Pa to have work all winter. The family moved there from Grampa Small's house. It was the first time Pa had worked for anyone but Uncle Virg.

Ernest Bartlett's farm in West Stoneham was too far away from the school for Don, who was 7, and Jo, who was 10, to attend classes. It was a big, old, rambling farmhouse with large barns where the animals were kept. Mother, still determined that all her children would get their high school diplomas, wasn't pleased to have her children miss school. But, the family needed the money, so she accepted Pa's decision.

Jim, then a senior and nine years older than Jo, stayed out of school for one whole term to help Pa in the woods. In the spring, he returned to Norway High School, made up his work and graduated in 1914, with his class.

Because Pa was working in the woods all day, Jo and Don took care of 48 head of two-year-old steers and 60 head of sheep for Mr. Bartlett.

"Grace and Margaret were too little to help us," Jo said. "We had one old bull that could be a problem, but Don and I taught him to respect us. We kept him in a separate pen, feeding and watering him alone."

When Pa finished his logging job, the family moved back to Grampa Small's farm in East Stoneham. Ernest Bartlett gave Jo and Don one of his sheep, a highbred ewe they named Belle. She was their pay for taking care of his animals that winter.

"We thought we were in seventh heaven," Jo said. "Belle loved us just as much as we loved her. In the spring, Belle gave birth to a strong and healthy lamb we named 'Manny'."

One day, Donald had a toothache, so Pa took him to the dentist. All the way to Norway, Donald cried because his tooth was paining him so much.

On their way to the dentist, they met the antique dealer, Andrew Eastman's father. He said, " Don't cry, Don. When you get home, I will give you two lambs for your lamb, Manny."

"O.K.!" Don agreed.

Pa nodded, agreeing to the deal. At this point, he was willing to do anything to stop Donald from crying. He knew the lambs would be pets for the children, but he also knew Manny was much more valuable than the two other lambs together.

Mr. Eastman knew he had made a smart deal. Manny was a registered pure bred and the lambs he exchanged for Manny were plain sheep. Being a kid, Don thought two for one was the best bargain. The kids taught the two lambs to pull them around in a cart and had a lot of fun with them.

Several years later, the children were saddened when Belle, with whom they played and whom they trained to do many things, got sick. One day, Jo went to Norway on the stage to take her music lesson and didn't return home until evening. While Jo was gone, Old Belle passed away.

"Grace, don't you dare Jo tell about Old Belle when she gets home," Mother warned her. Mother thought Jo would be too upset to eat any supper.

Naturally, the first thing that Grace said to Jo was, "I know something you don't know about Old Belle! She's gone."

In disbelief, Jo exclaimed. "I am going down to the barn and see if you are telling me the truth!"

Mother was right. Jo didn't eat any supper, but went directly to the barn to make sure that Old Belle had really passed away. She was upset about losing her beloved pet, whom she had cared for since she was a baby lamb. Because they cherished her so much, the kids had a special funeral for Belle.[11]

On Sunday morning, part of the ritual in the McAllister family was going to Sunday school and attending the service at the East Stoneham Church. The children were all dressed in their Sunday best and walked to the church for the services.

When Jo was small, one special dress was worn to Sunday school and other clothes were worn only to school. When they came home from either school or church, their mother expected the kids to go directly to their room and change into old clothes.

After Church, the family ate dinner together. In the afternoon, only quiet activities were allowed. Because Sunday was God's day, no card games or anything of that kind could be played.

Easter, Thanksgiving, and Christmas were very special occasions for the family. The McAllisters, along with the rest of the community, joined in many activities at the church and at home.

Jo's older sister, Helen, and her friend, Edna Allen, went to Lewiston every year to buy presents for the East Stoneham Children's Church Christmas Tree. The presents and decorations for the community Christmas tree were bought with a donation from Aunt Jessie Small. Then, at Christmas, there was a pageant at the church. Then, the presents bought with the money gift were passed out to all the children in the community.

"We thought it was something, " Jo said, "for Helen to be chosen to go to the city! Aunt Jessie loved her adopted community and made it possible for all of us to have a wonderful Christmas."

In 1915, Helen graduated from Norway High School. She was sixteen. Afterwards, she taught at Hunt's Corner School in Albany, Maine, and boarded with the Cummings family.[12]

When Helen was able to come home on weekends, Jo went with Pa to get her. Jo's first question was, "Pa, are you going to let me drive the horse today?"

Most of the time, he let her, but Pa made sure that Jo didn't take any unnecessary chances. Hunt's Corner was near the top of a steep hill. The winding road had many sharp curves. Extra caution was needed when guiding the horse up or down the hill, so as not to tip the wagon over.

After leaving the Hunt's Corner school, Helen taught in the Waterford school system until her retirement at 70. After her retirement, she continued to tutor students at Fryeburg Academy.

One of her former students made this comment, "Mrs. Grover was the best teacher we ever had. We all loved her. She taught us how to apply ourselves to our studies, make good use of our time in the classroom and always show respect to our teachers."

When Helen married Perley Grover, they rented a house owned by Pete Kilgore in North Waterford. In 1922, they purchased Aunt Jessie's home in East Stoneham where Helen brought up her three boys, Keith, Rodney and Dwight and her daughter, Joyce. Helen lived there until her death at the age of 96 on September 24, 1993.

In 1916, Pa was offered a job as a sawyer at C. B. Cummings & Sons in Norway for a lot more money than he was earning in East Stoneham. Traveling eighteen miles to Norway everyday by horse and wagon was unthinkable in the early part of the century. The new job meant that Pa would have to board in Norway during the week, returning home only on the weekend. He rented a room at Harriman's Boarding House on the corner of Main and Whitman Streets, almost across the street from the mill. Even though he would have to pay for his board, he still would have twice as much money to support his family.

Mother let Jo, then 12, with her two younger sisters, Margaret, 7, and Grace, 5, make the eighteen mile trip with their horse, Jack, to pick up Pa at his job on Saturdays. On the way from East Stoneham, Jo had to drive the horse through a long stretch of woods. For many miles, there were no houses.

"On the trip home," Jo said. "The road seem a lot shorter with Pa next to us. I don't know whether we were just tired or felt safer knowing he was in the wagon with us."

In the winter of 1917-18, the focus of the family's lives had shifted from East Stoneham into Norway, eighteen miles away. Pa was working at C. B. Cummings & Sons in Norway, coming home only on weekends. The two oldest children, Jim and Helen, had graduated from Norway High School. Jim was living in Lewiston, and Helen was teaching school. Jo was about to enter high school and would be followed by Don, Margaret and Grace. Transporting four children out of East Stoneham everyday would pose a huge challenge. Having them all stay in Norway and paying board was out of the question.

"What should the family do?" Mother wondered.

Aunt Jessie was living in Portland, at her suite in the Lafayette Hotel, much of the time. When Mother asked her for advice, Aunt Jessie told her that moving to Norway made a lot of sense. When going back and forth to East Stoneham from Portland, she would still come and visit with her. Aunt Jessie knew Mother and her family would always make her welcome.

After her talk with Aunt Jessie, Mother felt the best solution was to leave her family home. Praying to God for guidance, she decided to sell her father's farm. She knew that pulling up stakes and moving to the village would create a whole new environment for her family.

With Mother's decision, more changes were ahead for Jo. Her happy country childhood was coming to an end. She would start high school in Norway, meet new friends, and meet the challenges of working in a factory.

She was fast maturing into a young woman. She was now nearly five feet tall, no longer a child, and had the healthy complexion of someone who had spent many hours outdoors. Being ready for any challenge, she knew she would try hard in school to accomplish her goals. Now it was time for her to look to the future and to prepare for what she might do with her life.

---

[6] This is the title listed in St. Louis, Missouri, court documents at the time of Aunt Jessie's death.

7 It was better known as the Cog Railway.

8 In 1910, Newry was desolate mountain country. Now it is the home of the international acclaimed Sunday River Skiway that is a four-season resort.

9 Twin brothers, Francis and Freeland Stanley, born in Kingfield, Maine, who were inventors, built the steam-powered car in 1897. They operated the Stanley Motor Co. from 1902-1917 and produced the "Stanley Steamers" which broke the world's record for the fastest mile (28.2 seconds) in a steam car in 1906.

10 Later sold to Milliken, Tomlinson Co. where Jim worked until his retirement at the age of sixty-five.

11 On Jo's 95th birthday in 1998, she received a package from Kammie, Grace's daughter, who lives in Florida. In the package were a little fluffy white lamb and this poem.

> *A long time ago,*
> *When life was more slow,*
> *And chickens cheeped*
> *With secrets to keep,*
>
> *Grace promised not to tell*
> *What happened to Olde Belle.*
> *But with today's DNA,*
> *Olde Belle is back to stay*
>
> *She's returned to Jo's home*
> *As Baby Belle—the Clone!*
> *(please squeeze me!!!)*

To Jo's surprise, when she squeezed the little lamb it sounded just like her favorite pet from her childhood days. "Many thanks, Kammie," Jo exclaimed.

12 In 1915, the only requirement to be a teacher was a high school diploma. Later, Helen took summer classes and night courses and earned both a bachelor's and a master's degree in education.

Norway's Main Street as the town looked in 1918.

Celebrated fiddle player Mellie Dunham and his wife, "Gram," returning on the 'Dummy' from their Keith-Albee Vaudeville Tour.

The 1894 fire devastated Norway's central business and residential district.

CHAPTER 3

Moving to Norway, Maine

In 1894, a destructive fire became the most devastating event in Norway's town history. Remarkably, no one was killed and only two people sustained serious injuries.

On May 9, 1894, at 2:00 p.m., an employee of C. B. Cummings & Sons Mill discovered a fire on the second floor of the "pancake house,"[13] in which were housed open containers of lacquers used at the mill. He sounded the fire alarm, then went for help. By the time he returned with a crew, the entire building was engulfed in flames fed by the fumes of the open lacquer canisters.

The fire jumped across the Mill Stream, over to Main Street, engulfing the Opera House Block, which had been constructed entirely of wood, as were all the buildings on Main Street. On that tragic day in May, a strong, blustery wind carried the embers to the twelve year-old opera house building and beyond. Quickly, the fire engulfed over ninety buildings, leaving one hundred and fifty families homeless. Though fortunately there were no deaths, the fire devastated this small town.

From Stone's Drug Store down, all buildings on the south side of the street were destroyed including Horne's Tannery at Snow Falls. Burning shingles and firebrands were carried over five miles by the power of the hot air cyclone created by the fire. Some were found as far away as Oxford village.

When it became apparent that the Norway fire department needed help, Mrs. Laura Sanborn of the Advertiser office telegraphed both Lewiston and Portland for help. Lewiston's Steamer Unit arrived in thirty-three minutes and Portland's Steamer and Hose No. 6 arrived in one hour and fourteen minutes. Both of these companies came to the village on railroad flatbed cars to the Norway Station of the Grand Trunk Line. Fire companies from South Paris and Bethel assisted as well.

After the fire, neighbors helped neighbors in any way they could. Some even exchanged house lots to recreate the neighborhoods. They provided each other with food and shelter and helped each other in building their new homes.

After the fire, the Horne Tannery complex was shut down, leaving 150 people unemployed. It was the only major business that wasn't reconstructed after the fire.

By 1918, when the McAllisters moved to town, Main Street had recovered. There were many new store fronts. A new brick opera house with stores on the first floor and a clock tower above was built. Beautiful elm trees shaded the dusty, unpaved Main Street, down the center of which ran trolley-car tracks. The trolley provided transportation between Norway and South Paris.

Hitching posts were prevalent, as horses were still the usual mode of transportation. In back of Beal's Tavern on Temple Street, the Starbird Stables provided horses for the stage and others who needed them. Many people left their animals at the stables, to rest, while they did their shopping.

On the north side of Main Street, were Verenis Fruit Store and a general store owned by Alonzo J. Nevers. At the corner of Lynn and Main was the Carroll-Jellerson Shoe Shop.

At the other end of town, on the corner of Main and Paris Streets, was Norway High School, a three-story wooden building with a tower to house the school bell. Originally called Norway Liberal Institute, it had been a private school where students paid tuition. In 1865, the town had taken over the school, changing its name to Norway High School. When the school burned in the fire of 1894, Charles Adams, a contractor, replaced it.

Across the street on the opposite corner was the Second Congregational Church. Its original building was also a casualty of the fire. The church's pastor, Rev. Bates Rideout, was one of two people seriously injured that day.

At the foot of Lake Pennesseewassee was the Norway Ice Company, owned by Eugene Millett. In the winter months, the ice was harvested from the lake using horses. It was stored in a large building by packing it in sawdust. Throughout the year, a horse-drawn wagon delivered ice to local businesses, as well as to homes. In the summer, people at the cottages around the lake were serviced, too. With several changes in ownership, this business continued until 1954, when the service was no longer needed because of the prevalence of electric refrigerators.

In the early 1900's, Norway attained the title of "Snowshoe Capital of the World." It was a local "character," Mellie Dunham, who contributed to this distinction. He made a diamond-weave snowshoe with craftsmanship so superior that Commodore Robert E. Perry made a special trip to his home on Crockett Ridge. Commodore Perry ordered sixty pairs of these snowshoes for his expedition to the North Pole in 1909. Today, some of these snowshoes, with his initials burned into them, are on exhibit at the Smithsonian Institute Museum, Washington, D.C. Others are displayed at the Norway Historical Society.

At times during the winter, from the end of World War I, in 1918, to the 1950's, Main Street would be closed off for snowshoe contests. One winter, there was no snow. Sawdust was hauled from the huge pile at the C. B. Cummings Mill and spread thickly along Main Street. This sawdust carpet made it possible for the International Snowshoe Races to be held in Norway that year despite lack of cooperation from the weather.

Snowshoes weren't the only things that made Mellie Dunham famous—the other thing was his fiddle. An accomplished musician, he always preferred to be called a "fiddler" rather than a "violinist." In 1926, Mellie entered the fiddlers' contest at the Eastern States Expo in Springfield, Massachusetts. Winning that competition led to a famous friendship.

Returning home, Mellie found a letter in the mail from Henry Ford, one of the wealthiest men in America. Ford had learned of his win at the competition and invited him to play for him.

Alanson "Mellie" Dunham and his wife, "Gram" (Emma Richardson Dunham), were the honored guests of Henry Ford and entertained the Fords and Michigan's other elite at a dance at the Ford Engineering Laboratory. For this performance, Dunham didn't dress up like the rich crowd but wore the plaid flannel shirt and khaki pants he did for barn dances in his own hometown. The highlight of the busy evening was Dunham's performance of his favorite tune, "The Rippling Wave Waltz" followed by many other New England dance tunes. Although Ford offered Mellie a generous amount of money for playing, he refused to accept anything more than his usual performance fee of $3.

Mellie's friendship with Ford led him to greater fame on the Keith-Albee Vaudeville Circuit, and he appeared in 19 US cities in 22 weeks. For each of these performances, he accepted $100. This was big money at that time. Later, he ended up in New York City where he instructed young dancers in the "old barn dances" of their parents and grandparents.

Even before his friendship with Ford, Mellie Dunham had a famous acquaintance. He corresponded regularly with the writer, Jack London. Although he was an avid outdoorsman, Mellie had not had as many adventures as London who had travelled in the Yukon. Dunham enjoyed the vicarious experiences Jack London's writings brought him.

Despite his adventures with the upper classes, Mellie returned to his hometown, Norway. To show appreciation for their favorite fiddler, a group of Mellie's friends got together and constructed a gigantic fiddle as a gift for him. The fiddle was six feet long, two feet wide and was made from rare "pumpkin pine."

"What a day that was," Jo exclaimed. "Everyone in town turned out to greet Mellie and Gram as they pulled into the Norway station on the "Dummy."[14] Having been on tour hadn't changed them a bit."

A huge celebration was held to welcome home the town's own celebrity. As the evening progressed, someone in the crowd shouted, "How about a tune, Mellie?"

With a broad grin and a wave of his hand, Mellie tucked his fiddle under his chin, stamped his feet and hollered "Let 'er rip!" This was the way he had started off an evening of barn dancing at the Heywood Club on Crockett Ridge for years.

In April 1918, Jo's mother sold the house in East Stoneham she had inherited from Grampa Small. Mother knew that the farm would soon need major repairs. Selling it and moving to an apartment in Norway nearer to Leslie's work and to the children's high school was a smart move.

Mother moved her family to Norway into an apartment over Alonzo J. Nevers' Store. His son, Percy, whom the McAllister children called Uncle Pert, had married Mother's sister, Nettie.

For the first time, Jo's family enjoyed indoor plumbing. In East Stoneham, baths were taken in the washtub in an unheated shed and the toilet was an outhouse at the end of the walk out back. On a cold winter night, using it was a chilling experience. Having both functions indoors was a real treat of town living!

Another big change was having electric lights. In their East Stoneham home, one of the morning chores had been to clean the glass chimneys, trim the wicks, and fill the kerosene lamps for use in the evening. Now, the McAllister family could flip a switch and enjoy bright lights. No longer did Mother have to fear that someone would tip over a lamp and cause a fire.

"Homework was no longer an eye-straining chore," Jo said. "We were so happy to have all these new conveniences. After living on the farm, we thought we were in seventh heaven."

The living room, which ran across the front of the second floor apartment, faced Main Street. From its several windows, the kids could see both up and down the street. This, too, was a treat and a change from the farm-life they had known.

During winter days, they were fascinated by teams of horses pulling a huge snowroller to pack down the snow on the Main Street.[15] The sidewalks were shoveled by hand. When there was a bad storm, it could be a week before the streets were passable.

Hardwood floors throughout the apartment were a nice change from the worn-out wood floors in their East Stoneham home. There were three bedrooms. One had double beds where Jo, Grace and Margaret slept. The second was for Ma and Pa, and the third was a guest room. An additional small room, probably at one time a pantry, was where Donald slept. The kitchen was at the back of the house with a porch that faced the Starbird Livery Stables. Jo loved horses and she enjoyed seeing the animals come and go as the drivers made pick-ups and deliveries.

The building the McAllisters lived in was right next door to the Rices, who ran a rooming house in Freeland Howe's former home. (Freeland Howe was Jo's stagecoach friend and, later on, would play a bigger part in Jo's life.) Freeland Howe had married and built a new home on Pleasant Street. He was working at the time as an engineer, designing the waterworks for a city in upstate New York. The next building down on Main Street was Howe's Music Store.

After the open, quiet spaces of the country, being in the village where something was always going on was quite a change for the McAllister kids. The noises of the busy town were different from the farm sounds they had been accustomed to. Jo liked the hour chime of the town clock and found it a great comfort to her in the years to come.

Aunt Nettie Nevers, Mother's sister, and her family welcomed the McAllisters whole-heartedly, easing their move to Norway. The boy cousins, Harold, Percy and Paul, and their sister, Irene, introduced the newcomers to the community. Aunt Nettie was a great community worker. She planned senior class suppers for the Norway High School and chaired many events for the Second Congregational Church.

It didn't take long for Jo to get acquainted with many people. Some would become life-long friends. She missed her East Stoneham home, but she was anticipating entering high school. She knew her Mother had made the decision to move to Norway with the best interest of her children in mind. She did not want them to have to stay in a boarding house during the week in order to go to high school as the older kids had had to.

Jo's best friend, Verna, from East Stoneham days, wasn't so fortunate. Staying at a rooming house on Cottage Street in Norway, she was able to attend high school, but she had very little to eat—often just a few biscuits and one pint jar of baked beans for the whole week.

"When Mother made a pie, she cut it into six pieces, one for each of us," Jo said.

Wanting to help Verna, Jo saved her piece. She went without dessert at lunch, so she could give the wedge to Verna.

"I loved dessert, but I knew Verna needed that pie more than I did," Jo said. She shared her food with her friend during all four years at Norway High School.

As the church had always been a big part of their life in East Stoneham, the family joined Aunt Nettie's church where they were made to feel welcome. With its imposing bell tower, the new church built after the fire of 1894 was much larger than the one Jo and her family had known in East Stoneham. Behind the sanctuary was a large pipe organ, an instrument quite different from the one at the simple little church in East Stoneham.

Hearing the majestic pipe organ for the first time, Jo recalls, "I thought the music was divine. What a beautiful church it was, with its chestnut pews and wall-to-wall carpets. It was a big change from the little church in East Stoneham."

In the basement was a dining room and kitchen from which church suppers were served. Many of the youth activities of the church were held here as well. The McAllister children participated in Christian Endeavor, Sunday School and many other events. Over the next few years, Jo would spend many happy hours participating in these activities.

Aunt Jessie had also paid high school expenses for Helen. Gerald, however, had earned his own way. Now, Jo felt it her responsibility to follow Gerald's example and do the same. She did not want to depend on Aunt Jessie's generosity.

When the family moved to Norway, Pa no longer had to pay for his board at a rooming house. This saved the family some money. With the sale of the farm, finances eased a bit for Mother and Pa. But the family was large and expenses in town continued to add up. Jo knew that Mother worked hard to meet the rent and buy their clothes and food. She didn't want to add to the burden with school expenses when she could add a paycheck by working. Even though the high school was a public school, books, school supplies and sports equipment still needed to be paid for. Jo knew Mother's goal was for all her children to graduate from high school so she decided to do both high school and a real job. She knew Mother had made a big sacrifice when she sold her home in East Stoneham so her children could have a high school education. By helping with the family expenses, Jo felt she could show how much she appreciated Mother's decision.

Even at this early age, Jo wanted to be self-sufficient. This trait would be a factor visible in Jo throughout her life. She always wanted to support herself rather than depend on others.

In 1918, Jo began working during school vacations and in the summer. Because of the child labor laws, high school kids weren't allowed to work in the factories during the school week. Because Jo was only fourteen, she had to have a work permit that was obtained through the school superintendent's office. From that time on, she paid her mother for her board and room.

She worked at the Carroll-Jellerson Shoe Company. It manufactured ladies shoes. Garfield Walker was the boss of the packing room where Jo worked. As the styles changed from year to year or from season to season, the production staff readjusted the factory to produce new designs.

Many of the full-time workers at the factory resented having a high school student working there. In order to hold onto her job, Jo had to prove to them that she was capable of doing adult work. Because it involved being part of a production force, Jo had to show that she was efficient and rugged enough to handle the packing cases used in that part of the factory.

At the shoe shop, her job was sizing and pack the shoes. A "runner" brought a rack of finished shoes to the packing room from the finishing department. Jo laid the shoes out on the bench with the largest size at one end and the smallest at the other. Then she paired each shoe with one of the same size and style. The pair was then packed in a box and placed in a large shipping crate.

"During vacations, I worked from 7:00 a.m. to 6:00 p.m. five days a week and Saturday mornings," Jo said. "It was hard work, but it taught me to appreciate my opportunity to get a high school education."

After Jo's first summer of work, the assistant superintendent, Joe Terrio, would be watching in the late spring for her to come down Lynn Street. As she passed by, Jo would hear an insistent tapping on the office window. Looking up, she'd see Joe Terrio signaling for her to come in. She'd know immediately that he had a summer job waiting for her.

"Mr. Terrio would ask me when I would be out for summer vacation," Jo explained, "and then tell me when he expected me to come in to work."

One summer, the woman working beside her was pregnant and her eyes were affected. She was finding it difficult to size her shoes. Jo knew that she needed her work to support her family.

"I wanted to help her all I could. I helped her size her shoes all that summer so she could keep her job," Jo said.

As soon as he was old enough, Donald got a job at the A & P store, working for Mr. Hood, and paid his board, too. With more money coming in, Mother was able to have a few extras.

One of these was a set of lace curtains for the front windows. These lovely curtains were something she had long dreamed of having, but had never been able to afford.

One day, Pa's brother and his wife and three sons came from Lewiston to visit and one of the boys chewed a *hole* in Mother's lace curtains. She bit her lip to stop herself from exploding with anger. She could have *wrung his neck*.

Turning on her heel and heading for the kitchen, Mother said, "Let's all have dinner now, I think you boys must be very *hungry* because one of you just chewed up my new lace curtains!"

"After that, we always called these Lewiston cousins 'the *curtain eaters*'!" Jo exclaimed.

The Verenis family were neighbors who lived in an apartment over their fruit store, next door to Alonzo Nevers' store where the McAllisters lived on the second floor. Their son, George, age four, loved to come over for the homemade cookie or doughnut Mother always gave him.

He would ask her, "May I have a 'tookie'?" When his father missed him, he always came to the McAllisters' first.

"Now Georgie," his father would say. "You can't just run away. I told you to stay at home today."

Mr. Verenis brought a little stick with him to make George think he was going to spank him all the way home. He never hurt him—only frightened him, so his memory of the "punishment" was very short lived. In fact, the next day, George would be back for another "tookie."

Next door on the other side, were Donald Rice and his family, who lived in Freeland's house. They had moved from North Waterford, near East Stoneham, so the kids knew each other from having participated in both school and church events together.

One night after supper while doing the dishes, Jo and the others looked out the window just in time to see Lila, Don's mother, throw an entire pot of baked beans, pot and all, out the back door.

"Did you just see what I saw?" Grace asked Jo.

"Yes, I did," she replied. "What do you suppose is going on over there?"

In a few minutes, Will, Donald's father, came running out the back door and around the house. Lila stood in the back door shouting at his fleeing figure as he ran down Main Street.

"We never did find out what happened, "Jo said. "But we never forgot what a sight it was to see that "flying bean pot."

Two of Jo's friends, Elizabeth Bartlett, from East Stoneham, and Alice, from Norway, were cousins. Frequently, they came to visit the McAllister girls and have supper with them. They had a crush on Donald Rice and, shouting out the open kitchen window, they would flirt with him. Getting an invitation to come down and play croquet with Donald Rice was really what Elizabeth had come to visit the McAllisters for.

Alice was a tomboy and wrestling with Jo's brother, Don, was another favorite sport of hers. Even though she tried to make Jo and Elizabeth think it was Donald Rice she was interested in, Jo's brother seems not to have been all that unattractive to her.

Whenever they'd start to scuffle on the floor, Alice would say to Don, "Stop a minute, I have to take the 'coots' out of my hair."[16]

Because Mother didn't like to have the kids wrestling in the house, she warned them to be careful. Of course, she didn't want them to get hurt, but she also didn't want them to break any of her furniture. At this point, the family had very little furniture, and she couldn't afford to replace it.

Norway High School had three floors of classrooms. Each room was dedicated to the instruction of a separate subject. A different teacher for each subject was a whole new concept for Jo. After the one-room school in East Stoneham, where one teacher taught all eight grades, Jo was uncomfortable at first. Whereas before she had to relate to only one person, now she had many she needed to understand. Always a people person, Jo took it seriously to know and meet each teacher's expectations.

While she was at Norway High School, Jo had an extraordinary principal, Professor Albert C. Parker. He was also her arithmetic and geometry teacher.

"Professor Parker was a special part of my high school years," Jo said. "No matter how busy he was, he always had time to listen to us. Whether it was helping us with our lessons or supporting us on some other project."

He was also one of Jo's Sunday School teachers at the Second Congregational Church, helping organize special events on the weekends and after school.

Other teachers included Lee Luce who taught history and Miss Anna B. Longfellow who taught Latin and French. Miss Longfellow was also the girls' basketball coach.

Miss Katherine Moses (later married to Henry Rolfe) was Jo's English teacher. She later became a close friend. Until after her ninetieth birthday, Katherine Moses Rolfe visited Jo's restaurant often. She enjoyed telling stories about how much her days at Norway High School had meant to her, and about her former students in the class of 1923. One of Jo's classmates, Gwen Lord Pike, who lived in Bridgton near their former teacher, often came with her to Barjo's.

Miss Edith Knight headed the Commercial Department. With Miss Catherine Martin, she taught shorthand, bookkeeping, typing and other business-related subjects. Enrolled in the commercial course, Jo received many awards for her accuracy in shorthand and typing. Her business preparatory would prove to be a great asset later when she went into the restaurant business.

In the fall of 1918, soldiers returned home from World War I via the South Paris station of the Grand Trunk Line. Harry Twitchell, Albert Thompson and many of Jo's other friends were among the returning soldiers.

The local bands played "The Star Spangled Banner" and the streets were lined with people cheering. Pounding on tin pans and anything else they could find to make noise, the community welcomed its returning sons. The Welcome Home parade stretched from Market Square in South Paris to Advertiser Square at the head of Main Street in Norway.

The whole McAllister family joined in the celebrations. Jo was awestruck by the soldiers and all their medals and impressed with what they had lived through. Many were only several years older than she. These young men—many would become lifelong friends—had seen the horrors of the war. What they had lived through was almost more than she could comprehend.

The three Fogg brothers, one of whom would play an important role later in Jo's life, served in the European Theater during the war but were not in the first contingent to arrive home. Percy, who was known as P. Y., served in the Occupation of France immediately following World War I and returned a year later.

Jo's older brother, Jim, served in the border conflict with Mexico so he wasn't directly involved in World War I. At the time Jim served in the Army, the US wasn't yet actively involved in World War I. Many felt the Mexican conflict was a direct result of the Germans' promise to the head of the Mexican government that if the Mexicans could defeat the United States Army, Germany would give Mexico all the land west of the Mississippi River as their reward. The Mexican Army was soundly defeated.

Shortly after World War I, tragedy struck the local area. In the fall of 1918, the Spanish Flu Epidemic took many victims. Suffering seemed to spare no family, sometimes taking every member in its wake. Only three doctors, Dr. Beal F. Bradbury, Dr.

Herman Bartlett and Dr. Barker were available in Norway to care for the hundreds of sick and dying people. The nearest hospital was in Lewiston, so the Norway Grange Hall and the Opera House were pressed into service as makeshift hospitals. Many volunteers helped to deliver food for their suffering neighbors, to the homes and to places where they were being cared for.

The Rices, next door, furnished some of the food for the people at the Grange Hall on Whitman Street. Everyone pitched in to help in anyway they could.

Lila Rice said to Don, "Will you deliver some of the meals to the Grange Hall, if I pay you twenty-five cents per meal?"

To a twelve year-old, that seemed an awful lot of money for doing an errand. He had no idea what a risk he was taking. When Mother found out what Don had agreed to do, she made him stop. Mother didn't want her whole family to come down with the Spanish Flu as so many others had. She felt there were other things to be done involving less risk to her children.

With World War I behind them, Americans were going into the "Roaring Twenties" with a lot of enthusiasm for the future. Everyone was looking forward to peace and prosperity. The town of Norway was no exception.

In 1920, an annual event for Norway was the Clerk's Ball. Held at the Opera House every year, all the clerks and business owners from all the stores dressed in evening gowns and tuxedos and spent the evening dancing to an orchestra. Students from class of 1923 were chosen to serve the refreshments.

One of the high school students chosen was Jo. Fascinated by the excitement of the evening, she almost forgot she was supposed to be serving punch and snacks. To a country girl, it was a beautiful and distracting sight to see the elegant gowns and watch the couples waltz and polka across the ballroom to some of the most beautiful music she had ever heard.

Just a few years later, Jo would be a part of this grownup world where everyone celebrated their prosperity with elegance and style. Jo would quickly learn to dance to the music of the polka and the ballroom waltz. Jazz and Ragtime were just becoming popular. By the mid 1920's, everybody would also be swinging to the "Charleston" and the "Haymaker's Jig." Jo was a fast learner and would soon be dancing these popular dances.

[13] So-called because of the large, pancake-like containers of lacquer stored there for use in painting the dowels made in the mill.

[14] This was what the engine of the Norway Branch Railroad was called. It transported passengers from the South Paris station of the Grand Trunk Station to Norway.

[15] In Maine, horse-drawn snowrollers were used to clear the streets until 1927. This method packed the snow down, rather than removing it.

[16] A popular style of the 1920's, artificial hair called "coots" could be worn added to your own hair and then the hair combed over them. The effect was similar to the bouffant style of the 1960's.

A giant snowroller was drawn by teams of horses to pack down the snow and make the roads passable for sleighs.

Aunt Jessie generously gave her furniture to Jo's mother, Tena, when she sold her home.

Today some pieces are on display at the Norway Historical Society; this golden oak diningroom set remains in the house where Jo lives today.

CHAPTER 4

A New Home on Deering Street

After living in an apartment for two years, Mother and Pa decided it was time to look for a permanent house for their family. Renting had been the only thing they could afford when they first moved to Norway. Now, with Jo and Donald paying board, they could afford to buy a home. The children were growing up and needed to each have rooms of their own.

In 1920, they bought a house at 26 Deering Street, Norway. It had been built by Dr. Harry Jones for his sister. Dr. Jones was a conscientious businessman and had made certain that the house was well constructed. It was a good investment for the McAllisters. Mother, Pa and Margaret were to live there for the rest of their lives.

Twenty-six Deering Street had three floors and a basement. It had a parlor, a sitting room, a dining room and a kitchen on the first floor. There was a pleasant hall at the front entrance where an open, winding stairway led to the second floor. The bathroom was on the second floor, along with three large bedrooms and a large attic in the back. There were two more bedrooms on the third floor. Now, the children could each have a bedroom.

By 1920, Aunt Jessie and Uncle Will's marriage was not going well. The differences in their lifestyles caused a lot of conflict. Uncle Will was living in another part of East Stoneham. Even though Aunt Jessie had a home in the village, she preferred city life. She had been brought up living in hotels; being a farmer's wife wasn't something she enjoyed. On the other hand, Uncle Will didn't like going to the opera nor did he enjoy her high style of living. After realizing how different Uncle Will's lifestyle in the country was from her own, Aunt Jessie kept her suite at the Lafayette Hotel in Portland and stayed there most of the time. Whenever she returned to East Stoneham, she stopped in Norway to visit with Tena and her family.

Aunt Jessie had provided Uncle Will with the money to start his gun shop business. He operated this venture from their home. After the McAllister family moved to Norway, Uncle Will often came to town to visit while Aunt Jessie was in Portland. Often, he had supper with the family.

In 1922, after thirteen years of marriage, Aunt Jessie divorced Uncle Will. Though the marriage had been turbulent at times, Aunt Jessie had stayed in Maine because she was eager to see Mother have a better life. Now the McAllisters were beginning to get on their feet, and she felt satisfied she had made a difference in Mother's life.

After the divorce, Aunt Jessie closed her East Stoneham house and gave Mother all of her golden oak furniture. She then moved back to St. Louis to be with her only sister, Ellen, but she still kept her suite at the Lafayette Hotel in Portland and kept in touch with Mother. She came to Norway whenever she was in Maine to visit with her Ricker relatives.

Aunt Jessie's pieces of furniture were the first nice ones the McAllisters had ever owned. Now, their new home also had beautiful furniture. Aunt Jessie's draperies, made of rich damask that looked and felt like velvet, tied back with thick golden cords, were hung between the parlor and the sitting room. The brass beds and numerous rockers gave their bedrooms a distinctive look, as did Aunt Jessie's wicker furniture.

The ornate dining table, ladder-back chairs, elegantly carved sideboard with exquisite mirror, and the hutch with its Haviland china imported from France, graced the dining room. Mother only used this china on special holidays like Thanksgiving and Christmas when she entertained the whole family. Jo still has Aunt Jessie's dining room furniture in her home.

In the front hall was a golden oak hall-tree, a unique piece. It had a large mirror at the top, with brass hooks to hang coats and hats. On a seat that tipped back to reveal a storage space, one could sit to put on or take off winter boots.

In the parlor was a Victrola, mounted in a golden oak cabinet with a drawer of recordings of classical music. A Grandfather clock with imported works beautified the sitting room, while another antique clock sat on the mantle in the dining room.[17]

After they moved into their new home in 1920, helping Mother keep the house spotless was one of Jo's priorities. She treasured the lovely furniture and the polished hard wood floors and couldn't bear to have a speck of dust on any of them.

In 1921, on Jo's eighteenth birthday, Aunt Jessie gave her an exquisite dinner ring made of brilliant turquoise surrounded by four sparkling diamonds. Jo's December birthstone is turquoise. Margaret had a December birthday, too, so her birthstone was also turquoise. The dinner ring Aunt Jessie gave Margaret was a similar turquoise one, but she planned to have the diamonds added on Margaret's eighteenth birthday.

"We never had seen such beautiful rings," Jo said. "Much less hoped to own one. Because Aunt Jessie had them made as special presents for us, we will treasure them for the rest of our lives."

After the McAllister family moved to Deering Street, Mother become acquainted with Eva Fogg and they became good friends. She lived around the corner on Summer Street with her son, Percy. Later, Percy would play an important part in Jo's life. Eva Fogg and Nettie Nevers encouraged Mother to join several organizations, the Daughters of Veterans and the Norway chapter of the Pythian Sisters. Now she was able to enjoy a little social life, something she hadn't had the time or the opportunity to do in East Stoneham with six children to care for. Even though she had joined the East Stoneham chapter of the Pythian Sisters, Mother had been unable to share in many of the activities.

"One year, though, she had accepted the ladies' invitation to play the lead in the Pythian Sisters' annual play," Jo said. "This was quite an event in East Stoneham and we felt honored that she was playing such an important part. We kids thought she was the most beautiful woman in the whole production. It was the only time I can remember that she took part in any of the activities of the lodge until we moved to town."

Mother had enjoyed the play and looked forward to being active now that she lived in town and had more time.

Meanwhile, Jo was no longer a brand new worker at the shoe shop. In the summer of 1922, she and one of her classmates decided they needed a raise, so they got up their courage to go together to see Garfield Walker, the boss of the packing room. He was a real gentleman, and Jo felt it was worth the risk to approach him, especially with a friend for moral support.

"What may I do for you girls?" he asked as they entered his office.

"Well," they said, looking at each other for encouragement, "we came to ask you for a raise."

After standing in awkward silence for several minutes waiting for a reply, Jo and her friend made a quick exit back to work. The boss hadn't answered or given them any indication whether or not he would grant them a raise.

Looking at each other as they left his office, Jo remarked to her girlfriend, "I don't think we had better try that again. He might have answered that he didn't need us any more, and we'd have been without a job altogether."

Later in the day, Mr. Walker came, unnoticed, into the packing room and stopped behind the other girl's bench. She was relaxing, her chair tipped back, her hands in back of her head and her feet on the bench. He tapped her on the shoulder and said, "I thought you were the girl who wanted a raise."

Then Mr. Walker continued on down the length of the room, until he reached Jo's bench. She was busily arranging the shoes that she had been sizing and was getting ready to pack them in boxes. Her boss picked up a shoe as if to inspect it and at the same time said to Jo, "The next time you want a raise, don't bring anyone with you."

When she received her next paycheck, she found that Garfield Walker had granted her request for a raise.

"Garfield Walker taught me to stand on my own two feet," Jo said, "to speak for myself and let the others do the same. I didn't need a friend for support. The quality of the work I did was all the support I needed. That was a valuable lesson!"

During their high school years, Don, Grace and Jo played on the basketball teams at Norway High School.

In the 1920's, girls' basketball rules didn't allow the guards to score. They and their opposing forwards had to play on one-half of the court. The only players allowed to play on both sides of the court were the two opposing centers.

Jo's team included Alice Montpelier as center, Helen Purington and Florence Hadley as forwards, and Dorothy Newcomb and Jo as guards. Miss Longfellow was their coach. They traveled to other schools to play—by train to some and to Bridgton Academy by horses and pung.[18]

"When we went to play at Bridgton Academy, the boys' team rode in one pung and our team rode in the second one. We laughed, sang songs and threw snowballs at each other on the way over to the game," Jo stated. "We were much quieter on the way home. I don't know whether it was because we were tired out or because of how we had played that evening."

The Norway High basketball teams played all their home games at the Norway Opera House because there was no gym at the high school. The Opera House had a balcony for the spectators, making it possible to remove the seats from the main floor for basketball games or for dances. The folding seats were stored at back of the building for future use. The Opera House building was heated with piped-in steam heat from the C. B. Cummings mill. The visiting teams weren't used to playing in that kind of heat, so it proved to be a big advantage to the local players.

"By half-time, our opponents were sweating and tired out

from the heat!" Jo exclaimed. "We had them on the run for the rest of the game."

Often, when the distances were great enough, the basketball team traveled by train to the towns where the game was to be held and stayed overnight at the homes of the local team members. Usually, these evenings were easy enough, but one occasion proved a real challenge to Jo.

In 1922, the team traveled to the town of Mexico and Jo had dinner at the home of the principal of the high school. That year, the school had produced Maine's Championship girls' basketball player. The principal was understandably proud of her accomplishments. At the supper table, all the talk was about what an outstanding player she was.

Faced with this challenge, Jo was determined to beat the odds. She knew that she could play as well if not better than the champion could. This determination was a trait that would later serve her well as the restaurateur.

At the game that night, Jo played guard to Mexico's champion player. Although Jo was only five foot two, she never let her opponent get near enough to the basket to score a single point. Norway High School's team won the game by a score of 28 to 6.

As luck would have it, after the game, Jo and Ida Lapham, her substitute guard, learned that they were to spend the night at the home of Mexico's star player.

"Boy, did I hate the thought of spending the night at her home after that game!" Jo exclaimed. "But it wasn't half as unpleasant as I had thought it was going to be."

The other girl's parents made Jo and Ida feel right at home. Even though they had been tough opponents on the basketball court, the three girls talked about what they were doing in school and about sports. The next morning, the rivalry of the night before had been forgotten, and Norway's team was on its way back to the train station for the ride home.

In the 1923 Norway High yearbook, *The Caduceus*, there is a mention of the season's last game for the girls' basketball team.

Berlin, New Hampshire, had played Norway three times during the 1922-1923 season, and had lost all three games. The New Hampshire State Champion player was a forward on that team. When the Norway girls went to Berlin, they were greeted by school officials and team members and taken on a tour of the Berlin textile mills. Just before game time, one of the referees asked which player was Jo McAllister.

"When he asked which one I was, I knew I was in trouble," Jo said. "It was the last game of the season, and the New Hampshire fans wanted their star to have an outstanding game. We had played three other times against them that season and in each one I played her guard. I hadn't let her get a basket once."

The two teams had been on the floor less than two minutes when the referees threw Jo out of the game, claiming she had fouled out. The Berlin star scored all but one of her team's baskets. Berlin won the game by a score of 15-8.

After the game, knowing that the Norway team was very upset by the way that Jo had been treated, the Berlin officials offered to replay the game. The Norway team showed that they were the best sports team, by refusing to play again and accepting the defeat. Jo knew the five fouls had been unfair calls, done to stop her from guarding their star. While sitting at the end of the bench, she had watched her team, with a substitute guard, go down in defeat. After the game, the Berlin team gave the Norway girls a party and all the antagonism was forgotten.

It was a bitter pill to take, but Jo had learned a lesson. No matter how hard you try to do the right thing, sometimes life isn't fair. To rise above the adversity and move on takes a lot more courage than to complain and whine about being misused. Jo chose to rise above the situation and move on.

In June 1923, thirty-three young men and women graduated from Norway High School. With her parents in the audience, Josephine Arlene McAllister received her diploma. It had been one of Leslie and Tena McAllister's goals for Jo to have a high school education. In the 1920's, unless children came from well-to-do families, few students went on to college, so a high school diploma was considered an important achievement.

A rugged young woman, with steel blue eyes and reddish brown hair, Jo had a beautiful complexion. Having been brought up on a farm and having played basketball through her high school years, she was physically fit and ready for any challenge that might arise in her life. With her sunny personality and love of people, she was looking forward to the future.

Jo's dreams to be a nurse and later to be a pharmacist were, however, never to be realized. Little did she know what life had in store for her or that she would enter an entirely different field, the food service industry.

With knowledge of business fundamentals from her high school commercial courses, Jo was ready to begin a new phase of her life. A self-reliant young woman with her childhood years behind her, Jo was ready to join the business world.

[17] *Many of these period pieces are now on loan by the McAllister family to the Norway Historical Society.*

[18] *A pung is an open sleigh drawn by a team of horses.*

Norway High School Girls Basketball team 1922-23

standing: Marita Cushman, Alice Lewis, Miss Longfellow, coach, Josephine McAllister
sitting: Elizabeth Hall, Helen Richardson, Dorothy Newcomb, Florence Hadley.

PART II

Jo Gets Her Bearings

*Jo's graduation photograph,
Norway High School,
Class of 1923.*

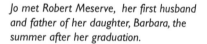

Jo met Robert Meserve, her first husband
and father of her daughter, Barbara, the
summer after her graduation.

*McAllister Family Picnic, 1929
Kneeling front : Pa (Leslie McAllister) with
Dwight Grover, Rodney Grover, Helen's hus-
band Perley Grover.
Second row: Mother (Tena Small McAllister),
Keith Grover holding Barbara Meserve, Ovis
McAllister (Jim's daughter), Jo holding
Freddie (Donald's son), Robert Meserve.
Behind Jo are Mildred and Donald. At the
back: Flora and Jim (Gerald) McAllister.*

CHAPTER 5

Out on Her Own

By 1923, Jo had seen many changes during her five years in Norway. The Norway-Paris trolley that ran through the Main Street had been discontinued. With more automobiles appearing on the scene, its services weren't needed.

The Prince sisters' dry goods store at the corner of Cottage and Main Streets had been bought by Zeb and Marguerite Merchant, who moved it across the street to the Abbott Building. It became known as the Merchant Block and they continued in business at this location for over fifty years.

After the sale of the Prince sisters' business, Frank Beck ran a bazaar store at their corner location, but the Norway National Bank soon bought the property. The building was moved to a location beside Beal's Tavern. Plans for a new two-story brick bank building in the vacated lot would soon become a reality.

On Deering Street, changes were in progress as well. Dr. Harry Jones, a local dentist, had just sold an apple orchard at the corner of Deering and Pearl Street to Edwin Cummings. As Jo walked past this orchard on her way to school and work, she watched with interest as the new home for Mr. Cummings, and his wife, Kate, and their children, Elliot and George, was being built. This house would mean much more to Jo in future years.

Having worked at the shoe shop each summer of her high school years, Jo was ready for a change. Working in a factory had given her little opportunity to meet new people or to stretch her horizons. In that summer of 1923, little did Jo realize that her summer employment would be a stepping stone to her future, both in business and in her private life.

After she graduated from high school, Jo and her friend Addie applied for a summer job at Chute's Homestead, a summer resort on Sebago Lake in nearby Naples. Addie's father was L. M. Longley, the owner of L. M. Longley & Son, a plumbing and hardware store on Main Street. He had done some work for Mr. Chute and used his connection to help the girls get jobs.

Naples was a hot spot in the summer. There were boat tours

around the lake and through the Songo Locks on the Songo River. Tourists from every state in the nation came to enjoy the beautiful scenery of the White Mountain Range reflected in the bright-blue waters of Sebago Lake. Sebago is the second largest lake in Maine and provides the water source for the city of Portland and other towns in the surrounding area. Boating, canoeing, fishing and swimming at the several public beaches were very popular. There were many summer recreational camps for children and privately-owned cottages around the lake.

The clientele at Chute's Homestead came from all over the United States. Many people stayed for the entire summer season in those days. The main house, or hotel, as it was called, was located on the hillside on the upper side of the road, while cabins were right on the shore of Sebago Lake. All the employees lived in tents on the hillside by the main buildings.

Arriving in Naples, Jo and Addie were introduced to some of the other young people working at Chute's. One of them was Robert Meserve, a carpenter. He was a handsome young man with curly black hair and beautiful brown eyes. He was two years older than Jo. At first, it seemed he was interested in Addie, but before long it was Jo who had won his heart.

One day, the parents of two teen-age boys who had just been asked to leave one of summer camps came to see Mr. Chute. The two boys were courteous, intelligent kids but they were high-spirited and loved a practical joke. Because the teenagers had disobeyed some of the camp rules, the counselors had asked them to leave. The parents inquired whether or not the boys could spend the rest of the summer at Chute's Homestead. Because their parents who lived out of state had once been guests at the hotel, Mr. Chute agreed, as a favor to them, that the boys could stay, but only if they were under his watchful eye.

When the boys arrived, they asked if they could choose their waitress from the crew. They chose the most beautiful one, Miriam, a girl from Portland, but she was stiff and distant. She preferred to wait on older people who would leave her tips, not rowdy teenagers who liked to fool around and play tricks on her.

In less than a week, the boys realized that looks weren't everything and they had made a mistake. Could they have Jo instead? Perhaps Jo wasn't the prettiest, but she gave them much better service. Her outgoing personality was more what they liked, and they became best of friends. For the rest of the summer, when Addie and Jo had free time in the afternoons, the two boys went swimming or wrestled with them on the beach.

In the 1920's, the popularity of swing and jazz music was

spreading across the country at a rapid pace. Pioneered by Duke Ellington, Louie Armstrong and Paul Whiteman, many of the local bands were playing this new style of rhythm.

The town of Edes Falls, a short distance from Naples, held a dance every Saturday night with a local band playing. After working hard all week, Jo looked forward to spending her only night off at the dance. She loved music and enjoyed dancing. It wasn't long before Jo was swinging to the Charleston, the polka, and many of the square dances, like the "Lady of the Lake" and the "Haymaker's Jig."

"Robert, had a car, so Saturday nights he drove us to Edes Falls to dance," Jo said. "We invited people from work to go with us, including the two camp boys."

The young people also enjoyed canoeing on Sebago Lake. Many times, the girls and their friends ventured right out to the center of the lake. If they had tipped over the canoe, a very easy thing to do, returning safely to shore might have been impossible for the others. Jo was a strong swimmer, but Addie wasn't at all, so a tragic accident might have occurred—but luckily didn't.

Looking back, Jo said, "How young and foolish we were to think we could ever have swum back to shore! At some points, we must have been over a half a mile from the beach."

One afternoon, Addie and Jo thought they would like to go for a ride, so they borrowed Robert's Model A Ford. In those days, drivers' licenses were a more casual thing and it was common for unlicensed drivers to be on the road. They decided to go to Harrison, over ten miles away. Jo didn't drive. Growing up on a farm, her passion had been for horses. Addie had driven a little bit, so she served as the chauffeur.

In the 1920's, very few cars went over twenty-five miles an hour. Being inexperienced, Addie drove very slowly, not going over ten miles an hour. The brakes were worn out and didn't work, so Addie had to use the clutch to slow the car down.

Going down a long hill, they were horrified to see a runaway team of horses pulling a huge wooden hay-rake that nearly filled the road at the bottom of the hill. There was no driver in sight. Jo jumped out of the car and ran to grab the reins, trying to calm the frightened animals. The horses were just as scared of the automobile as the girls were that they might bolt and run directly into them. Meanwhile, Addie was having problems of her own, trying to maneuver the car around the nervous horses. Finally, Jo was able to steer the horses to the side and Addie drove around them.

"The clutch had burned out by the time we got back to Naples, but we made it in time to serve supper at Chute's

Homestead," Jo added to the story.

When Robert was told what had happened, he wasn't pleased with the condition of his car.

Jo said to him, "If the brakes had worked, Addie wouldn't have had to use the clutch so much. Why didn't you tell us before we left?" Robert made no comment, but the girls knew better than to ask to borrow the car again.

Back in Norway after the summer was over, Jo went to work at Ashton's Drug Store for Lester Ashton. Len Sessions was the pharmacist there.

Thinking that Robert Meserve had forgotten all about the fun they had during the summer, Jo was surprised when he came to see her in town.

"When Robert drove up in front of the house, I was amazed that he had found out where I lived," Jo said in an excited voice. "I didn't remember ever telling him myself. I was thrilled to think he wanted to invite me out for an evening."

As the month of September flew by, Robert became more attentive with each passing day. During the last weekend of the month, after asking for her parents' permission, he proposed to Jo. An October 4th wedding was set.

"When he proposed to me," Jo said, "I could just imagine what a wonderful thing it was going to be to have my own home and to have a loving husband to provide for me."

Robert Meserve had graduated from Bridgton Academy. He was one of four children. He had a brother, Arthur, and two sisters, Addie and Marion. Their father, John L. Meserve, was active in the town government in Naples as a selectman as well as in several other offices. Their uncles, too, were well-known in their fields: Edwin was a contractor/builder in the Greater Portland area and Albert was the head of the Kennebunk Waterworks.

John Meserve had been a strict disciplinarian. After their mother's death on May 4, 1919, and their father's death on July 21, 1921, the children thought it was time for them to have some enjoyment out of life. Having been held down by a strict father, they hadn't been to dances or enjoyed many of the other things their friends did. The children had been left an inheritance, but didn't understand how to handle it. Consequently, Robert, his sisters and brother spent much of their money without looking to the future. Robert had told Jo that he had $2000 in savings. In fact, he had $6000 in outstanding obligations.

On the afternoon of October 4, 1923, Pa drove Jo and Robert

to South Paris to be married. Jo wore an attractive, deep crimson dress with matching shoes, while Robert was dressed in a navy blue serge suit, white shirt with a matching tie and shiny black dress shoes. Mother stayed at home to cook a special dinner for their return.

At the rectory, Rev. Wilburn Miller, with whom they had made their wedding arrangements, had been unexpectedly called away for the day. So Pa stopped at a local car dealership to get directions to the home of the Congregational minister, Rev. Fred Bannister, who was filling in for him.

After waiting for Pa in the car for what seemed like an eternity, Jo said to Robert, "I think you'd better go in and find out why it's taking Pa so long to find out where the minister lives."

Robert found that the salesman was trying to sell Pa a new car. Pa was looking the car over and talking with the man about financial details. He had forgotten all about getting the directions to the minister's home. The minute Robert came though the door, Pa knew why Jo had sent him in. He hurried back to the car with Robert and off they went—at last—to be married. Pa and the minister's wife stood up with Jo and Robert and signed the marriage certificate as witnesses.

Jo and Robert's first home was on Whitman Street in Norway. After her marriage, Jo gave up her job at Ashton's Drug Store, expecting Robert to support them as was common in those days.

The first week of their marriage, they pooled their paychecks, but that was the last time they did so. Married life with Robert was not what Jo had dreamed it would be.[19]

In the first week of their marriage, when she was getting ready to go grocery shopping, Jo found out that Robert had already spent all their money.

She asked him, "Robert, what did you do with our paychecks? I gave you mine and you were going to cash both checks so we could go shopping for our week's groceries and pay the rent. Where did the money go?"

He didn't answer, nor did he explain what he had done with their money. With no savings to rely on, Jo and Robert gave up the Whitman Street house. Swallowing her pride, she asked her parents if they could move back to Deering Street. In the second week of October 1923, Jo went back to work in the shoe shop.

The fact that they moved in with Jo's parents didn't seem to bother Robert in the least. Jo paid their board and room from her wages and took on all the housework for her mother.

Robert was such a friendly, likable guy she had taken for

granted that he was the man for her. Now she realized she ought to have looked into his finances and his attitude more carefully. Her parents liked Robert, so living with them was not difficult. But Jo was hurt and disappointed that her dream of independent married life was so short-lived. The reality wasn't much like her expectation. But by praying to God for guidance, she made the best of a bad situation. She never let anyone know how upset she was, nor what had transpired. This trait of making the best of it would sustain her through many more difficulties in her life.

Robert went to work for Blake Lumber Company (later Diamond National) on Cottage Street in Norway. Then he became a shoe cutter at Jellerson-Rafter Shoe Company with Percy Nevers, Jo's uncle, as his boss.

In the fall of 1923, Jo and Robert took a trip to Canada with their friends, Rusty Herrick and his mother. The foliage was at its peak, with brilliant reds, oranges and yellows mixed in with the green of the firs and pines. It wasn't really a honeymoon, but it was the only trip Jo would ever take outside of the United States.

It was Jo's first time out of the state of Maine, too, and the beautiful scenery thrilled her. They had a wonderful time sight-seeing. She was surprised to find that people in Quebec lived much like folks in Maine. The Canadian people were very friendly and made their visitors feel right at home.

Robert was a member of the Oriental Lodge, F. & A.M. of Bridgton, and the Oxford Royal Arch Chapter and Ark Mariners of Norway. Several evenings a week, he went to the lodge and played pool with fellow lodge members.

Having a wonderful time at country dances had been a special part of Jo's summer in Naples. The dances at Edes Falls near Robert's former home in Naples continued to be a part of their Saturday night entertainment. Because Jo was often busy helping Mother take care of the house in addition to her full-time job, an evening out was a special occasion to her.

Jo realized it was time for her to do her civic duty and register to vote. The McAllister family were staunch Republicans and encouraged her to enroll in the Republican party. Attending town meeting, she voted in the local elections as well. The first president Jo cast her ballot for was Calvin Coolidge. He had succeeded Warren Harding who died in office in 1922. From that day on, she never missed doing her civic duty to vote in local and state elections and has participated in all the presidential elections for over seventy years.

In 1924, Margaret started having convulsions. These episodes developed into a seizure disorder. Suffering from a nervous breakdown as well, she had to leave high school in her junior year and was unable to return.

"What a disappointment this was to Mother. Her intent had been for us all to graduate from high school," said Jo with sadness in her voice.

Margaret's illness made these dark days at 26 Deering Street. At the supper table, no more conversations about school activities or any sports were allowed. Margaret had been an excellent student in English and enjoyed writing. Now Mother warned the other children repeatedly never to mention school for fear of upsetting Margaret and causing more seizures. She was afraid that the competition at school had brought on Margaret's nervous breakdown. Margaret lost all self-confidence and was afraid to go out of the house. For over two years, she rarely left her bed.

Helen had taught Mother how to read and comprehend what she read. During this terrible time for the family, the Bible was Mother's constant companion. She also read the religious tracts called *The Upper Room*. During the years that Margaret was confined at home, Mother prayed constantly to God for her recovery.

By then, Jo had learned how quickly things could change. Her marriage to Robert Meserve taught her that life was more than having a good time. Now, she understood that being responsible for her own finances was a key to her independence and that she could not rely on anyone else to be in charge of this important feature of her life. During her years in business, she never forgot that principle of self-reliance.

Margaret's sickness had shown her how the family had to pull together when one of them became sick or disabled. Her mother's prayers for her family made a lasting impression on her. Looking to the future, Jo realized what a big part God was playing in her life.

---

[19] *Margaret's version of this story is a little bit different. She feels Jo's impulsiveness and eagerness to please were as much to blame as Robert's lack of responsibility.*

"Jo, you know you said 'yes,' and then you didn't have the guts to say 'no!'" said Margaret. "No matter what anyone asks you to do, I think the word 'no' is simply not in your vocabulary. This time, I think you should have done a lot more thinking about what you were getting yourself into before saying 'yes.'"

Two views of Stone's Drug Store on Main Street, Norway, where Jo worked from 1925 to 1932.

CHAPTER 6

Stone's Drug Store Days

The shoe shop where Jo worked was unbelievably hot in the summer, and her work in the packing room was not much of a challenge. In 1925, a clerk's position opened at Stone's Drug Store where Margie Bowser's father, Giles Frost, was the manager. When Margie learned of the opening, she urged Jo to apply. Jo applied right away, and Giles Frost hired her immediately.

"Working in a store would be more like Chute's, where I had enjoyed meeting some wonderful folks," Jo said. "I would be greeting people, talking with them and helping them."

Stone's Drug Store was a prominent local establishment. Entering from Main Street, customers saw a soda fountain on the right. It had stools and its own cash register. Local people came to enjoy an ice-cream soda or buy an ice-cream cone. The news of the day—politics, town affairs or some business deals—were often discussed, while the customers relaxed over a Coca-Cola.

Beyond the fountain was the cigar case which contained many different varieties of cigars and cigarettes. Because it had its own cash register, the clerk could ring in the sales without leaving the counter.

Across the back of the store, the pharmacist filled prescriptions from small drawers where all the herbs and other drugs were stored. (Later, Jo would find out these drawers were also used for another purpose.)

In the front of the pharmacy was a large display case where fishing tackle of all kinds and varieties was sold. This part of the business was later moved to its own building.[20]

On the left side of the entrance was the showcase for "toiletries" (today we call them cosmetics). Beyond, was the case where all candy was sold in bulk and weighed to order by a clerk. During the holiday season, elaborately decorated boxes of chocolates were displayed. A third register was located there.

The end of the candy counter was used as a first-aid station. In the 1920's, Norway had no hospital, so Mr. Stone provided this health-care service to the community. Often, mill workers came in to have cuts and bruises cared for.

In the center of the floor were several tiers of shelves where magazines and newspapers were displayed. In those days, service was personal in a store like Stone's Drug Store. Regular buyers had newspapers reserved for them. When they came in, often on their noon-hour break, the clerk met them at the door, greeted them, and hand delivered a newspaper marked with their name.

F. P. Stone and Giles Frost ran the drugstore with the help of only one other employee. Jo, therefore, found herself in a position to assume responsibility and to observe first hand all the workings of a small business.

Having come from the country and still being young, she was still quite shy at times when it came to greeting strangers and helping them find the remedies they needed. Working at the drug store gave Jo more confidence to greet the public, one on one. Unlike Chute's Homestead where there was a daily job pattern, at Stone's, she had to help the people who shared their problems with her and asked for personal assistance.

An interim minister at the Universalist Church who came to the drugstore daily shared many insights about handling the public. He impressed on her "to make eye contact with customers when they enter the door."

"Always say 'hello' and 'good-bye'," he said. "One of the most memorable things you can do for people is to notice them. They'll be back, if you show them respect and kindness."

Advice like this would help her become a successful business owner. Some customers she would serve with special attention at the drug store would later give her a helping hand when she decided to open her own business . Others would become her regular clientele.

Working at a drug store during the twenties was much different than it is today. When the clerks worked behind the counter or made ice cream, they wore long black rubber aprons. In the summer, there were no air conditioners or any cooling systems such as we know today. Fans were used to cool the rooms. The fans, however inadequate, were a big improvement for Jo over the oppressive heat of the shoe shop.

A big summer seller was ice cream that was frozen right in the basement, and it was part of Jo's new job to make it. Cakes of ice were delivered daily by Norway Ice Company and stored in a large oaken tub with thick sides. Two containers were used to make ice cream. The larger one was the freezer pail where the ice and salt were placed. The smaller, inside one was for the cream.

First, Jo used an ice pick to chip ice off the block. Then she transferred the chips to the freezer pail. Next, she filled the smaller container two-thirds full with the cream mixture. (The empty space was to allow for "swell."[21]) She then placed it inside the freezer pail of ice and added salt to the ice. Jo was careful not to let the ice and salt cover the top of the inner container. If the salt worked its way into the cream during the mixing and freezing process, the whole batch would be spoiled and have to be discarded. Inside the cream container, a paddle whipped the cream vigorously. It had to be checked frequently, during the twenty minutes it took to freeze a batch, to assure that it was freezing properly. The freezer was run by electricity.

The flavorings for the ice cream were made at the drug store. For instance, a pound of coffee had to be cooked down with sugar and water added to make coffee syrup. By the evaporation of the water as it boiled, Jo could control how thick or thin the syrup would be. Cooking down unsweetened chocolate squares using the same procedure made chocolate syrup. The berries used were picked by the McAllister sisters.

In the summer heat, the ice cream would become soft by the time it was served and drip off the cones. This was natural soft-serve ice cream before such a thing had been invented!

F. P. Stone recognized Jo's potential and taught her how to help him do the buying. He let her buy supplies and drugs from J. E. Gould; Cook, Everett and Pennell; and Loring, Short & Harmon, all business wholesalers from Portland. With this responsibility, Jo learned the importance of knowing how much inventory the drug store needed. Little did he realize, but F. P. Stone was teaching Jo some significant aspects of the business world that would benefit her greatly in the future.

During the early 1900's, house and chimney fires were common in rural areas, sometimes several occurring in one day. This was because everyone burned wood for cooking and heating.

"Giles Frost was the Norway Fire Chief, with Station One located near Stone's Drug Store," Jo remembers. "Whenever I heard the fire whistle, from the clock tower of the Opera House, I knew Giles had to go to a fire. If I wasn't already at work, I'd go back to the drug store to take his place until the fire had been put out."

One afternoon, in 1926, as Jo came into the house after a day's work at the drug store, her mother said to her, "Margaret has a bad toothache. What can we do?"

It was assumed that Margaret wouldn't be able to go out to a dentist because of her illness. And dentists, of course, didn't make house calls. Because of her confinement during her illness, Margaret hadn't been to the dentist for some time. She needed quite a bit of work done on her teeth.

Jo responded by going into Margaret's room. "Come on, Margaret. I am going to take you to see Dr. Hayden. He can fix your tooth and stop this pain. I'll help you get dressed."

Though Jo was matter-of-fact, Mother was horrified because Margaret's seizures were difficult for the whole family and she was afraid, if Margaret left the security of her home, she would have another attack. Whenever anything happened at home during her illness, Mother had always been there to help.

As she knew, it's hazardous to touch someone who is having a seizure. While unconscious, she can swallow her tongue and choke. The violent flailing of the arms and legs can hurt a bystander and is shocking for others in the room. It was also a dangerous experience when Margaret passed out and fell.

With Jo at her side, off Margaret went to Dr. Hayden's office on Main Street. There were no difficulties, after all. Dr. Hayden fixed her tooth and encouraged her to have the rest restored. While he was doing this dental work, they became great friends.

Initially, many of Margaret's seizures had been triggered by her fear of failure. After the humiliation of suffering seizures at school, Margaret had feared going outside her own home. Between them, Jo and the dentist helped her to regain her self-confidence. Because the dentist was kind and gentle to her, Margaret no longer feared meeting the public.

It was Jo who encouraged her to take that first step of crossing the threshold and walking up Main Street. Mother had not believed it could be accomplished. But with God's guidance, Mother's prayers and Jo's will and determination that her sister would succeed, Margaret did overcome her fears.

In the fall of 1926, while in St. Louis, Aunt Jessie became ill. She had promised and planned to add diamonds to Margaret's turquoise dinner ring for her eighteenth birthday (December 8, 1926), but other than Aunt Jessie, only Margaret and her family knew of this.

Aunt Jessie died at the Jefferson Hotel in St. Louis, Missouri, in January 1927,[22] without a will and without descendants. Two years earlier, in 1924, Uncle Will had died of consumption in East Stoneham. Her sister, Ellen Ricker, inherited Jessie's entire fortune, valued at $350,000. This was quite a sum of money for those days. The majority was in General Electric stocks and bonds.

Disappointingly, Margaret never received her diamonds.

In early 1927, Jo learned that she was pregnant. Margaret offered to take her place at Stone's Drug Store. By holding Jo's job, Margaret would make it possible for her to go back to work after the baby was born. Margaret was still living at home and Mother was sure she wouldn't be able to work every day. Margaret proved the whole family wrong. It was another important step for Margaret as she assumed a more active life.

Jo and Robert became the proud parents of a baby girl on November 26, 1927. They named her Barbara Jean. Because they were still living at 26 Deering Street, Mother took care of Barbara when Jo and Robert were working. Pa adored his new grand-daughter and she would soon become his constant companion. Besides Jo and her young family, Margaret and Grace were still sharing the large house with Mother and Pa.

Margaret had done such a good job that after Jo went back to work, Mr. Stone asked her to stay on. It was the first time he had had hired two girls. Giles Frost continued as drug-store manager.

When Margaret had the afternoon off, she'd dress up baby Barbara and bring her upstreet in the carriage. Looking out the drug store window, Giles Frost would say to Jo, "Here comes Marg with the baby."

In the evenings, Jo often worked a shift at the drug store. When Robert went out with his fellow lodge members, he would ask Mother to take care of Barbara. Jo never worried about Barbara when her mother was taking care of her since she was her grandmother's pride and joy. Mother shooed everybody out of the kitchen when she gave Barbara a bath because she was afraid drafts coming from around the doors would give the baby a cold. With a wood stove, Mother couldn't regulate the heat as it now can be done with a furnace.

The excellent care given Barbara by her grandmother was plain to see. She was a healthy, happy child, eager to be a part of things in their home. As Barbara grew, she loved to help Jo with the housework.

"One thing Barbara enjoyed was dusting the floors at Mother's," Jo said. "Often, when I was dusting, I'd turn around to see her smelling the dust cloth. I wasn't sure which part she like best, the smell of the furniture polish, crawling on her knees while polishing the hardwood floors, or helping dust the stairs."

Margaret was not to be the only McAllister girl Mr. Stone added to his crew. While still in Norway High School, Grace came to work at Stone's Drug Store. With three girls now working, Mr. Stone felt he needed one of them to be "boss," so he placed Jo in charge.

All three girls worked together taking inventory at the drug store. Jo thought of herself as the dumbest one in the family. She has no reason to feel this way, but this is a trait she never has overcome. Somehow, over the years, her self-esteem has never risen to match the level of all her accomplishments. In her own mind, she still thinks she is that little girl in East Stoneham struggling to spell "Josephine." Jo thought Grace was much smarter than she so when it came to spelling the names of the different drugs, Grace was elected to be the scribe. Feeling outdone by her youngest sister, she realized that if Grace could, she could also. Jo soon learned to spell the long names of prescription drugs herself.

Mr. Stone encouraged Grace to further her education after she graduated from high school in June 1929. She went to Gorham Normal School and completed the two-year course that earned her a teaching certificate in 1931.[23]

At the turn of the century, people had begun to build summer cottages around Lake Pennesseewassee, also known as Norway Lake. The lake is located to the northwest of Norway with the outlet, called Pennesseewassee Stream, winding through the village. The water from the stream was used to provide power for C. B. Cummings mill and several other businesses located in Norway. The waterway empties into the Little Androscoggin River below Snow Falls at the lower end of the village.

Since there were no roads, the lake was used for transportation. People would dock their boats at the bridge at the head of Main Street and walk into town to do their shopping. Many people from out of state—New York, Pennsylvania and New Jersey, etc.—were regular customers at Stone's Drug Store.

From 1907 to 1931, cottage owners could use the services of Captain Eddie Ames and his side-wheeler steamboat, *The Pennesseewassee*. From the landing at the head of Main Street, he made regular trips around the lake, watching for a flag hung out to signal that the cottage owner needed groceries or a ride to town. Stopping at their dock, he would pick up the grocery list and delivery the groceries on his next trip around the lake. The steamboat captain conducted guided tours as well.

"The first time I saw the steamboat as a young girl, I was fascinated by the sidewheel on it. I loved to watch Captain Ames pull into the dock," Jo said. "After I went to work at Stone's, Captain Eddie Ames and his family became my good friends."

With the introduction of private motor boats on the lake,

Captain Ames' services were no longer in demand. *The Pennesseewassee* was taken to Harrison and used on Long Lake.

"At Stone's, we knew all the customers by name," Jo said. "If people failed to come in for their paper or to get their medicine at their usual time, we asked their friends if they were sick. To us, all our customers were an important part of our day's work."

Among the summer clientele at Stone's Drug Store were Dr. C. A. Stephens. In addition to being a writer for *Youth's Companion*, a nationally popular journal for young people, he was a doctor and a scientist with a passion for the study of longevity and the basic cell structure of the human body. His wife, Madame Scalar, was an opera singer. Their mansion at Norway Lake village, called *The Laboratory*, was a unique piece of architecture with its copper dome (weighing three ton) that sat seventy-five feet in the air. Much secrecy had surrounded the building of this enormous forty-room house in 1888. Later, he envisioned his home becoming Norway's hospital, but this was never realized. Stephens Memorial Hospital, located on Norway's Main Street, was, however, named in his honor.

Another summer visitor was Walter Winchell, the newspaperman from New York City, and his wife. Often while Walter Winchell talked over the latest news stories with the local businessmen, Jo helped his wife make a decision about the latest shades in cosmetics that Stone's had to offer.

The Brewsters were summer customers who took a special interest in Jo and what she was doing. As owners of Birch Rock Camp on McWain Pond, in East Waterford, the Chief and Onie[24] saw a lot of young people and they spotted leadership potential in Jo. Both remained loyal customers to Jo throughout her business career. In later years, they brought their entire group of campers to the restaurant to eat many times during the summer.

Jo came to know her public well. She was friendly and warm with every customer whether summer people or local folks, and this attitude, born of her natural love for people, made her a confident business woman, even though her nature was shy and matter-of-fact.[25]

One year, during the annual Firemen's Carnival week, the McAllister sisters decorated a convertible to represent Stone's Drug Store in the Grand Parade. Ralph Sturges, the owner of the local Chevrolet dealership, lent them the car. Margaret was very artistic and with the help of Jo and Grace, she created a "masterpiece." The whole car was covered with woven strips of green and yellow crepe paper creating a basket-weave appearance. Being very innovative, Margaret covered the hubcaps of the wheels with finely cut crepe paper to create a shaggy effect. With the addition of paper carnations around the entire top of the car, the automobile was a work of art. Dedicating every spare minute they could find, the girls had their car ready for Saturday morning's Grand Parade. All three rode in the parade, while Giles and Mr. Stone ran the drug store.

In 1919, laws had been passed prohibiting the sale of liquor in the United States. One afternoon, Mr. Stone told Jo some stories about himself and activities of his that were decidedly illegal during that Prohibition era.[26]

Rumors circulated around town, that he was selling bootleg liquor. Being a prominent citizen in the community, he denied it whenever he was challenged.

"Of course, I had heard these rumors but I had thought them to be all false," Jo commented. "If he hadn't been in failing health, which made him more trusting, I don't think Mr. Stone would ever have confided in me. He was seventy years old when I went to work for him."

Deke Decoster, the sheriff of Oxford County, lived across the street from Mr. Stone on Pike's Hill. One day, Decoster got word that F. P. Stone was on his way to Canada on a train to pick up a shipment. Sure that the rumor was true, Sheriff Decoster caught the next train and followed his neighbor to the Canadian border.

"I outwitted him," Mr. Stone confided to Jo. "Deke never was able to prove a thing," he said with a smile, seeming, thereby, to confirm that he had, indeed, been involved with bootlegging.

"I never told a soul what he said to me. I really had a hard time believing he had been involved in anything illegal," Jo said.

Mr. Stone went on to surprise Jo by telling her that he had false bottoms in his prescription medicine drawers. Putting a lot of faith in her, he showed her these drawers.

"Some of his customers would come into the drugstore, write their own prescriptions, and pass them to him," Jo said. "When he filled them, he did so not with medicine, but with liquor."

Several months later, Mr. Stone revealed one more secret, this time to all three McAllister girls who worked for him. In the back of the store, there was a hidden stairway. If he heard government inspectors were in town, he could leave the building with his bootleg liquor. No one could see him as this stairway was only accessible from a hidden door in a back room where the girls changed their uniforms.

In 1923, the year that Jo had graduated from high school, the Weary Club had been organized. Several gentlemen had formerly congregated on the porch at Beal's Tavern, but Mrs. Seavey, the new owner, objected to their whittling on her porch. The name for the club came from the idea that "many were weary of their wives" and needed a place to congregate with their friends for card games, jackknife whittling (a pastime of that era), and storytelling. At the time of the club's inception,the charter stated that clear cedar should be available at all times for whittling. The ability to produce a cedar shaving light enough to float was a requirement for membership in their special circle. Many of the club's members were Jo's friends and customers, such as her former boss at the shoe shop, Garfield Walker, Sheriff Deke Decoster, and many other local businessmen.

In 1927, after the building the club had been renting was sold to the Norway National Bank[27] and torn down, Fred Sanborn, the owner of the *Advertiser*, Norway's local newspaper, came to the club's rescue. He bought a portion on the northern end of the lot and had a new building constructed.

The new meeting house was called the Weary Club Building and was located on Norway's Main Street. Fred Sanborn turned this building over to the club organization on a ninety-nine year lease. When he died in 1938, he provided a trust fund of twenty thousand dollars for the club in his will. It was to be invested at a local bank at interest. The trust stipulated that a sum of forty dollars be paid to the club treasurer. Annual Christmas remembrances were to be given to children in the vicinity who were under ten years of age. This fund was to be known as the Sanborn-Weary Club Trust Fund and is still in existence.

Fred Sanborn and his wife, Laura, were some of Jo's good friends and customers at the drug store. They set an example for her of what community spirit really meant. From them, Jo learned never to give up. She learned that where there is a will there is a way. They demonstrated, too, that there is always some child in need of help. Jo has maintained this awareness throughout her life. Soon after knowing them at Stone's Drug Store, Jo followed in their footsteps with her own style of giving.

Some of the local businessmen—Judge Jones, Ed Cummings, one of the owners of C. B. Cummings & Sons, Bert Stearns, a local lawyer, Shavy Noyes, Garfield Walker, and Sheriff Deke Decoster —used to play cards at the Weary Club, across the street from the drugstore. The loser had to buy the other players a Coke from the fountain at Stone's, after the game was finished.

Garfield Walker, Jo's former boss at the shoe shop, would

knock on the drug store window. He knew hard feelings existed between Mr. Stone and the sheriff and was trying to avoid trouble. Jo and Garfield Walker had established this communication so not to draw any unnecessary attention to the predicament.

Knowing what the knock meant, Jo would look around the store and then go out back. Often, she found Mr. Stone, sleeping in the back room.

"Jo, is it all right to bring Deke in?" Mr. Walker would ask.

"The coast is clear," she'd reply.

When the men entered the drug store, they sat at the counter, had a Coke, and discussed affairs of the day. Hearing the men's voices, out of the back room Mr. Stone would come, looking like a thundercloud. Going behind the fountain, he would glare at his old adversary, Deke Decoster. This was about the only time he ever came in back of the fountain. The rest of the time he stayed in the prescription department, or talked with customers in some other part of the store.

"I am his neighbor for heaven's sake!" Mr. Stone said to Jo. "What was Deke doing trying to nab me and prove I was guilty?"

Mr. Stone held the grudge which stemmed from the chase to Canada. Even though Sheriff Decoster had proven nothing and Mr. Stone had outwitted him, he still felt there was "bad blood" between them. Convinced the sheriff should have had consideration for his neighbor instead of doing his job, Mr. Stone maintained both his innocence and his indignation.

In the late 1890's, Herbert Walker, whose grand-daughter was to play a prominent role in Jo's life, had brought his seven younger siblings to the United States. His father, Thomas Walker was an Englishman who owned a general store (or trading post as they were often called) in Saint Patrick, Quebec, near the Saint Lawrence River. Because the younger children had grown up in Quebec, they spoke French with a smattering of English mixed in.

At first, the family had worked the hotel circuit, at The Weirs in New Hampshire in the summer and at warm-weather resorts in California in the winter. Around the turn of the century, the Walker family settled locally. Herbert lived in East Waterford. Garfield, Billy, Arthur, and their sister Katherine, in Norway, while the others moved to other areas. Garfield had been Jo's boss at the shoe shop, where Katherine, Arthur and Billy also worked. Billy had become one of Norway's colorful characters.

One afternoon, Billy Walker, who was the youngest, came into Stone's Drugstore. Billy spoke broken English, but was very good at getting his point across.

He had been to Paris Manufacturing in South Paris, earlier in the day, and had bought a pair of skis. Before coming in, he stood his newly purchased skis in the middle of the display in front of the drug store.

"I see you are selling skis. Come out and tell me the prices on them, Jo," he said to her.

"I'll be right with you, Billy," Jo replied. Together, they went out to the sidewalk where the skis and sleds from Paris Manufacturing were displayed.

Jo told him the prices of all the skis and sleds and thought she had made a sale. She looked into the drugstore to see if the other customers were being waited on and then turned around to finish the deal. At that moment, Billy Walker picked up a pair of skis, put them over his shoulder, and walked up Main Street toward home.

"Where are you going, Billy?!" Jo asked.

"What's the problem, Jo?" Billy asked. "I just wanted to see if you knew the prices. These skis here I bought in South Paris this morning. See you later!"

Suddenly, Jo realized Billy Walker had fooled her with his prank. She ought to have known exactly how many skis were in stock in the drug store display and he had proved she didn't.

"From that time on," Jo said, "I stayed on the ball. I made sure no one would ever able to trick me again and that I always knew exactly how much inventory we had."

Billy Walker had shown how easy it was for someone to be deceived. He had also taught her never to take anything for granted, no matter how well you know the person. This lesson, she never forgot.

20 It was then called Woodman's Sporting Goods Store and was next door to the Opera House block. Originally, that building had been Norway's Fire Station One.

21 The "swell" was air that was worked into the cream by turning a paddle in the container by a crank mounted on the cover.

22 Jessie Ricker Small died in 1927 and is buried in Evergreen Cemetery, Portland, Maine, with her father Robert Ricker who died in 1894, her mother who died in 1914 and her sister who died in 1946.

23 The whole family, including Jo, celebrated Grace's college graduation. Having her youngest sister join the teaching profession seemed to Jo quite an accomplishment. Now there were two teachers in the family: Helen in the Waterford school system and Grace in the Oxford school system.

24 The nicknames their campers had given them.

25 *Over the years, she considered every customer a part of the "Barjo Family," a name she always used whenever speaking of her clientele at the restaurant.*

26 *These laws were repealed on December 5, 1933.*

27 *When the new bank building was completed, one of the tellers at the old Norway National Bank, P. Y. Fogg, moved all the bank securities in a wastebasket from the old bank in the Opera House block to the new! No one gave it a thought that this was an imprudent thing to do!*

Young Percy Y. Fogg (P.Y.), left, was a waiter at Poland Spring House. An avid and life-long outdoorsman, he enjoyed entertaining his friends at his cottage on Lake Pennesseewassee.

Below: a successful hunting trip with friends, 1935 included Percy, Fay Blake, Vernon Edminster, and Norman Greenlaw, each with a trophy.

CHAPTER 7

The Roaring Twenties Come to an End

In 1929, the United States had been setting itself up for an economic crash for some time. Many people were buying stocks and bonds "on the margin," by putting a small percentage down (as low as 10%) and paying the broker the rest of the money as the stocks went up in value.

The stock market crash of 1929 happened on the last Monday of October of that year. All trading records were broken with a turnover of 16,410,000 shares on the New York Stock Exchange and 7,096,300 shares on the New York Curb Market.

By the end of year, the New York Stock Exchange had dropped 40% of its value and losses were estimated at forty billion dollars. That is why October 29 is called "Black Monday."

This unfortunate market crash sent the country into a deep depression with banks closing everywhere and business shutdowns occurring daily. Before the year came to an end, thousands of people were out of work and jobs were next to impossible to find. It would be a decade before many people were able to regain any form of stability in their lives.

Even in Norway, the stock market crash had a devastating effect on some of the people who were close to Jo. Her old friend, Freeland Howe, had been working as an engineer for a city in upstate New York, where he had done all the planning for the city water works. While in New York, he had been married and had bought a home of his own on Pleasant Street in Norway.

In the stock market crash of 1929, he lost a substantial amount of money and moved back home to live. He lost all his money and his real estate including his home. His wife divorced him. Needing a place to live, he built a tiny tarpaper shack on a corner of the Pleasant Street property. He lived there until he became sick and was moved to a nursing home.

"I never was quite sure if he had been able to save that tiny piece of land for himself," Jo said. "Or whether he had just assumed squatter's rights to it. He never did tell me."

At the time, Freeland said to her, "I'll never do another day's work. What is there to be gained by working?"

And he never did. Instead, he depended on the kindness of his friends for his living.

Jo remained a good friend to Freeland for the rest of his life, but it was hard to see her former mentor in his declining years.

One of his neighbors, Anna Dubey, who lived on Pleasant Street, felt sorry for Freeland so she did his laundry, but she was not above making catty remarks that Jo didn't care for.

One day, she came in the store and said, "See what I have here!" as she held up a pair of long johns (a one-piece union suit).

"Look at all the holes in this, Jo!" she went on. When she held the long johns up to the light, they were perforated with holes.

If Freeland had known Anna had shown his union suit to Jo, he would have been mortified. He thought Anna was his friend. Mending the underwear and keeping quiet about what she had done would have been a better way, in Jo's opinion, to show friendship. Anna's way did not appeal to her The less people knew about what she had done for them, the happier Jo was.

Jo's brother, Donald, was also effected by the stock market crash. After he had graduated from Norway High School in 1925, Mr. Hood, the manager of the A&P store where Don had worked, got him a job at the First Auburn Trust Bank in Auburn.

Don did well at the bank. Soon, the bankers offered to help him make some investments in the expansive market. With their help, he was successful, making money on his stocks. Then he decided to try investing on his own. This time, the stocks he chose lost money and Donald lost everything he had invested.

Several years later, Donald became the manager for the Morris Plan Bank, in Auburn. He married Mildred Oberg on February 25, 1928. She had graduated from the Maine School of Commerce and planned to have a career in teaching commercial courses at the high-school level.

Investments weren't the only challenges in Donald's life. In the late fall of that year, Donald and Mildred had a son, Frederick, who was born a "blue baby."[28] Many medical procedures that can be done now weren't available in the late 1920's. It was soon discovered that he couldn't hear or talk and had trouble learning to walk. Because it was hard for his mother to accept that her son would never be a normal child, she withdrew from him. All his care became Donald's, who had to depend on the help of hired caregivers rather than Mildred. One of these caregivers was Elizabeth Walker whose uncles, Garfield and Billy, were some of Jo's friends. She taught Freddie how to tie his shoes, to help set the table and to button his clothes. Her daughter, Emily, would later become close to Jo and to the rest of the McAllister family.

Over the next several years, Don and Mildred had three more children, all girls. One lived to be just over a year old, one was stillborn and the third died soon after birth. Family life included a lot of sadness for Donald and Mildred.

The years after the stock market crash, the 1930's, proved to be a very hard time for Jo. Robert, Barbara and Jo were still living with her parents on Deering Street. She was the backbone of the family, paying their board every week to her mother. Jo had busy days, taking care of Barbara when she had time off and doing housework for her mother. By now, Robert was working as a shoe cutter at Jellson-Rafter Shoe Company with Percy Nevers, Jo's uncle, as his boss.

Barbara was an active child who loved her grandparents dearly. While Jo was working, Barbara was Pa's shadow. An inquisitive two year old, she kept her Pa and her Nana (as she called Jo's parents) busy trying the keep up with her.

Just before Robert and Jo's seventh wedding anniversary, he was taken seriously ill with a ruptured appendix. He was in the Central Maine General Hospital, in Lewiston, for over six weeks. For those desperate weeks, Jo went to the hospital daily. Because she didn't have a driver's license, she had to depend on the kindness of her friend, "Shorty" Phanus, who had a business on Main Street to drive her to and from the hospital. Robert had terrible hiccups and was burning up with fever. The poison from the ruptured appendix had gone through his whole system. None of the miracle drugs, common place today, existed in those days.

"I fanned him by the hour to give him, at the very least, some comfort from his extreme fever. It was living hell to see him die this way and to know there wasn't a thing I could do to save his life," Jo said with a deep sadness in her voice.

Their daughter was almost three years old at the time her father became ill. She stayed with her grandparents while her mother was visiting him in the hospital. He grew worse daily. Robert, Jo's husband of seven years, died on November 2, 1930. He was 29 years old. Three weeks later, Barbara had her third birthday on November 26, 1930.

Many of Jo's relatives came to the funeral service held at Spiller's Funeral Home on Main Street in Norway, where the Oxford Lodge of Masons, F. & A. M., conducted the burial service. The bearers at his funeral were his brother, Arthur Meserve, Jo's brothers, Gerald and Donald, and family friend, P. Y. Fogg.

Robert's two sisters, Addie Ridlon, with her family, from

Naples, Maine and Marion Hoyt, with her family, from Watertown, Massachusetts, and his brother, Arthur, as well as his uncles, Edwin Meserve from Portland, and Albert from Kennebunk, also attended the service. Jo's Aunt Nettie had charge of arranging the flowers for the service and helped Jo obtain a cemetery lot near her own, at Norway Pine Grove Cemetery. Robert was interred there on November 5, 1930.

Losing her husband when she was 26, Jo knew she had a life of hard work ahead of her with a small child to support.

"I had my health and my strength," Jo said. "With God's guidance, I knew He would show me how to support Barbara. She would be my priority in life, and I wanted to do everything I could to see that she was well taken care of."

Even in the midst of her tragedy, Jo knew that she was fortunate to have a job that was not threatened by the Depression. In fact, about six months after Robert's death, Jo received a raise and was now earning $20 a week at the drug store, the most money she had ever earned. She paid her mother $12 a week for Barbara and herself for room and board.

Having been neighbors since the McAllister family moved to their Deering Street home, Jo and P. Y. Fogg often walked to work together. His family's home had been located around the corner on Summer Street. Jo enjoyed talking with him about the impact the financial world was causing on the local community.

He had lost his money in the stock market crash of 1929. Because of this, in 1931, Jo paid $5 a week to Anna Stone's Boarding House for her good friend, P. Y. Fogg's meals. With his knowledge of the market, he was able to save his stocks in several local industries. But, it would be a while before these stocks would have any monetary value. Jo was glad to help him out. He was a businessman who recognized in Jo a kindred spirit.

In April 1931, Jo's employer, F .P. Stone, died suddenly. He was a great fan of baseball, and had been to a local game. When he came home from the game, his head was fire-red. His family believed that he had become too emotionally involved in the baseball game and urged him to rest. Shortly after returning home, he had a stroke and died several days later.

Stone's Drug Store was left with no druggist. The Stone family enlisted the aid of Cook, Everett and Pennell, one of the wholesale firms with whom they did business, to help them find a pharmacist. The firm found Mr. Cole who became the new druggist. He continued to operate in much the same way as F. P. Stone had. Before coming to work at Stone's Drug Store, he had been involved in an automobile accident. After a short time, Mr.

Cole had to go into the hospital for surgery on his feet. At the time, he thought he would be able to return, but it wasn't to be.

A young man from the pharmaceutical house came to take Mr. Cole's place and immediately began to change things. He reorganized the whole store. His ideas of how services should be provided clashed with all the methods Mr. Stone had used. Just out of college, he thought the way things were being done at Stone's was old-fashioned. What he didn't realize was that he was in a small town. The local people were accustomed to the service they were receiving and preferred the old ways. Soon, the regulars began asking questions of Jo, Margaret and the other help. The customers made it very plain: they still wanted to be served as they had been for years.

Dissatisfied with the changes at work, Jo and Margaret started discussing the possibility of opening their own business. Customers encouraged them to do so. They told Jo and Margaret they would patronize them in whatever kind of business the girls decided to go into. Don was working at the Morris Plan Bank in Auburn and came home on weekends. He offered to help his sisters get the financing they would need to start a new venture. He advised them first to make wholesale connections with the suppliers. This they were able to do.

With the encouragement of customers and the assurance that wholesalers would deal with them, Jo and Margaret decided to make their move. Now they needed a place to rent and a specific business idea.

The J. J. Newberry Co. had just built a new store on Main Street and had some additional retail space available for rent. Jo, Margaret and Don went down to the store and talked with the Newberry people about renting part of the building. They came to an agreement to lease a small section for their new venture.

After the decision was made on the location, they decided to have a restaurant. Because the restaurant would be in part of the J. J. Newberry store, Jo thought many people would stop for lunch while doing their shopping.

Though Jo had never before considered the food business, she realized she could expand on her experience and understanding of running the soda fountain at Stone's Drug Store. She already knew how to make ice cream, so that would be an important part of their menu. The menu would include homemade ice cream specialties and a limited number of sandwiches.

Jo felt the local people who already knew her and had offered their support could become a major part of their clientele. She knew that she and Margaret had the customer service background, the determination, and the willingness to work hard that the restaurant would require to be a success.

The three siblings opened their new business in the Newberry Block on Main Street in April 1932, as equal partners. Their arrangement was agreed to in a conversation. Jo and Margaret would handle the daily operations, while Donald would do the bookkeeping, handle the finances and pay all the bills. The three partners also agreed to name their restaurant "McAllister's."

McAllister's Restaurant was in one side of J. J. Newberry's building and had its own entrance. Because it ran the length of the building, it was a small, narrow store. Along the sidewall were narrow booths and tables with inlaid tops. It featured a fountain with stools on the other wall. The kitchen area at the back. Norman Greenlaw made all the hand-crafted mahogany cabinets and benches for them.

It was a beautiful little restaurant and special to them because it was their own. Jo and Margaret were full of excitement about their future as business owners and restauranteurs. They were prepared to work hard to make a success of this joint venture with Donald.

They served homemade ice cream and sandwiches. One of the featured sandwiches was hot chicken, a suggestion from a friend, Archie Goodwin, a local farmer. Mrs. Onie Brewster, a friend from Stone's Drug Store and owner of Birch Rock camp, helped them get connections so they could sell the Boston newspapers at the restaurant.

Jo continued to make all her own ice cream at McAllister's. She used rich cream from local farmers to make the ice cream a special treat. People came from miles around to enjoy it. Because McAllister's Restaurant was a different style of business, Jo didn't feel that she was a competitor of Stone's Drug Store.

In May 1932, McAllister's hired their first kitchen employee, Myron Lovejoy, a high school student who washed dishes, helped with cleaning and prep work. They teased him by calling him their "sanitary engineer."

It wasn't long before Jo and Margaret realized that something was wrong with the partnership. The restaurant bills were piling up. Jo and Margaret, knowing how important it was to have good credit, were puzzled. Why wasn't Donald paying the bills on time? Jo was determined to find out.

When she asked, he answered, "Just give me some time and I'll straighten everything out." He refused to explain more.

To complicate matters, Donald hadn't had the legal papers made out, as the sisters understood he would. Because he was their brother, both Jo and Margaret let the matter slide. Repeatedly, when asked, he would say the paperwork was still in the process. Rather than tell them why he hadn't kept his end of the bargain, he evaded the issue.

"I was disappointed and discouraged," Jo said. "Margaret and I were working long hours to make the business a success and now this."

What Jo and Margaret didn't know was that his wife, a graduate of Maine School of Commerce, felt the girls weren't as knowledgeable as Donald in the financial matters of the restaurant. She was urging him to keep the financial status of the business from them.

Finally, the truth came out. Donald wasn't paying the restaurant's bills with the income that Jo and Margaret were working so hard to generate during that spring and summer. Instead, he was using the positive cash flow they were creating to pay off notes he had co-signed for his clients at the Morris Plan Bank. Because of conditions in the country caused by the Great Depression of the 1930's, many of the people he had trusted had defaulted on their notes and Donald was paying them back himself.

Jo was stunned. Her dream of owning her own business was being comprised by her brother's poor judgment and lack of honest communication. The restaurant's credit was being destroyed. Business wholesalers had trusted Jo because it was she they had dealt with at the drug store. Now her credibility, as well as her credit, was being ruined and she was being humiliated. She grew more discouraged each day because Don wasn't keeping his word and paying the bills when they came due.

Unhappily, Mother and Pa got involved, too. Their parents thought Jo and Margaret were in the wrong by requesting that the legal paperwork be completed. This lack of openness on Donald's part and the hurt caused by her parents not believing she had the ability to operate a business bewildered Jo.

Mother had been protective of Donald, when he had lost money in his previous venture. Now, more than ever, Mother and Pa not only wanted Donald to succeed, but they believed he was on the way to success! They couldn't seem to see the situation from Jo and Margaret's point of view, that Donald was taking advantage of his sisters.

They felt that the concerns over the legal technicalities of the restaurant business cast a shadow on Donald's reputation. Pa and Mother were upset. Instead of letting Jo, Margaret, and Don settle their differences and work out a businesslike agreement, their parents insisted the girls themselves leave the partnership.

Because they didn't think the girls were capable of taking care of a business, they thought Jo and Margaret should stay out of the restaurant and let Donald have it.

In late January 1933, matters were going from bad to worse. Finally, one afternoon, Jo confronted Donald. Neither did he offer any excuses for what he was doing nor did he explain why Jo and Margaret hadn't received legal papers to show they were part owners in the restaurant. There was little Jo could do. In early February 1933, Jo and Margaret both left McAllister's Restaurant.

After Pa and Mother found out that Jo had challenged Donald and questioned his ability to run the restaurant, they told her she was no longer welcome in their house. She would have to move out. They were willing for Margaret to still live at home. Knowing how their parents felt about Jo, Margaret realized that she couldn't voice her opinion or support Jo if she wanted to stay there. She chose to keep quiet and soon went to work at Ashton's Drug Store. The only family member to stand by Jo during this sad and difficult time was Aunt Nettie.

Because the family were on the outs with her, Jo wondered what to do about child-care, for she would have to find a job. Jo had no place for her and Barbara to live. It was a huge challenge. Mother was still willing take care of her granddaughter, so Jo accepted her offer. Barbara stayed at the Deering Street house with her grandparents when Jo moved out. There didn't seem to be any other choice. Jo paid weekly board and room for her.

In 1920, the Foggs and the McAllisters had become friends after Mother and Pa bought their Deering Street house. P. Y., as Percy preferred to be called, occasionally walked to work with Jo. As a bachelor, he lived with his mother while both his brothers, Lewis and Linwood, married and had homes of their own. After his mother's death in the late 1920's, P. Y. moved to an apartment over Cook's barbershop on Main Street.

In 1932, before any problems had arisen at McAllister's, Jo's parents had objected to her seeing P. Y. Mother had the idea that Margaret, who was single, not Jo, who had already been married, should go out with P. Y. Now Mother and Pa were more upset than ever knowing that Jo was seeing him. They were afraid she would confide in him about the mistakes Donald had made in banking and they worried about Donald's reputation. While her growing friendship with him only increased the tension between Jo and her parents, P. Y. offered her something she sorely lacked.

"When P. Y. came into my life, I needed a lot of support and guidance. He was extra kind to Barbara during those hard times and that meant the world to me," Jo said.

P. Y. had a summer home on the lake. He was a great sportsman who loved to hunt and fish with his friends, Vern Edminister, Hugh Bethel, Norman Greenlaw, Ray Eastman and several others. His cottage had a cupola with a dormer window in the living room, from which you could see the whole length of Lake Pennesseewassee. The field stone fireplace made the cottage a perfect place for him to relax with his friends. They could go hunting in the surrounding woods, or fishing on the lake. Many evenings were spent having dinner and relaxing after a day's work by the fire.

P. Y. had graduated from Norway High School in 1910 and from Bryant & Stratton College of Business Administration two years later. He was a veteran of World War I and served in France with Headquarters Co. 90th Division seeing action in the battles of St. Mihiel and Meuse Argonnes. His division of the army served as the Army of Occupation in France from July 8, 1918, until June 7, 1919. He was well known in the Masonic circles, since he was a Shriner and a 32nd degree Mason and held several important state positions.

Remembering the kindness Jo had shown him in 1931 when she paid for his meals, P. Y. offered her his apartment at 225 Main Street. Jo and Barbara moved to the Barbershop Building where he was living and P. Y. found himself a room elsewhere.

Soon after Jo moved into the apartment, Barbara became severely ill with scarlet fever. Mother told Jo that it was her responsibility to care for Barbara during her illness, so for six weeks Jo held her in her arms much of the time. In those days when anyone had scarlet fever, the whole family was quarantined by the local doctor and couldn't leave the house. Because Barbara had become sick, Jo was unable to look for work. Consequently, Jo and Barbara had little money to live on.

In the months following the rupture with her family in 1933, Jo and P. Y. became close friends. Because he was available to help and advise her when her own family had turned their backs on her, there quickly grew an intimacy between them. He was twelve years older than she was, but the age difference wasn't important to her. What was important was how kind he was to her and her little daughter during this hard time in their lives.

In the early 1920's, Pa had become Norway's police officer and night watchman. On his beat, he met many people. When questioned about the restaurant's problems, he didn't hesitate to share his opinion that Jo was at fault. She had no right, he maintained, to question Donald's ability to run the restaurant since he had experience in the banking field.

"I felt like I was a 'black sheep'," Jo said sadly. "It was hard to ask anyone for work under these conditions."

There were few jobs anywhere because of the Depression. The combination of these two factors was devastating to Jo. After Barbara recovered, Jo found a job working for Jim and Gladys Applin at their restaurant, the Norway Cafe. Jim was a meat cutter for the A & P store next door and Gladys ran the restaurant.

Remembering how Mr. Stone handled his situation, she had some insight into how she should handle any incident that involved illegal liquor.

Jo had heard rumors about the Norway Café before she went to work there. The talk of the street was Gladys Applin was selling bootleg liquor. Jo had hated liquor since she was a small child in East Stoneham living with her grandfather. She also realized how dangerous it was for Gladys to risk involving the business. But during the 1930's work was very scarce and Jo was willing to "look the other way." She remembered Mr. Stone's indignant denial that he was violating the law and realized that she could do the same. It was worth risking being implicated in bootlegging, in order to provide a living for Barbara and herself.

She soon found out the rumor was true when word came about a bootleg delivery that had been made. One of the girls who worked at the Norway Cafe went to Welchville with her uncle to a hidden drop-off where they picked up the contraband liquor. The "rum runners" had left it there for the Applins. The teenager had no idea what was in the boxes, only that she wasn't to tell where she found them. The girl's uncle, a pillar of the church, would never have taken her to Welchville, had he known what was going on.

The Applins had worked out a unique way to conceal liquor at the restaurant when the need arose. When they got word the restaurant was going to be raided by inspectors, the girls took all the liquor upstairs and hid it under the beds in the upstairs rooms which were rented out to boarders.

"You know what Glad is doing," P. Y. warned Jo. "If you get caught in one of those raids, don't call *me* to bail you out of jail."

"P. Y.'s fears never materialized, but they were indeed well-founded!" Jo said. "Luckily, even though we had many inspections, I never was present when the men came."

In her heart, Jo knew P. Y. was right. Gladys Applin sold all the liquor herself, on the sly, to local businessmen. She was careful not to involve employees directly in this part of her business. But, by telling them not to reveal what she was doing, she was really involving them in a conspiracy to break the law.

The Prohibition period was an attempt by a part of society to impose its religious and cultural values on all of society. It was neither popular nor respected by many who did not feel any great need to uphold Prohibition on moral grounds. The public felt, however, a concern to protect themselves from persecution by the Federal authorities and P. Y. was concerned about that aspect as well.

The friendship between Jo and P. Y. continued to grow. By the spring of 1933, it was clear to both of them that their mutual regard should lead to marriage.

On the national scene that spring, a money panic was spreading rapidly across the country. On Friday afternoon, March 5, 1933, the day after he was sworn in as president, Franklin Delano Roosevelt declared a Bank Holiday to stop the panic. This closed all the banks in the country.

The only local bank to survive the Bank Holiday of 1933 was the Norway Savings Bank. Established in 1868, it had always been a strong financial institution.

The directors of the Norway National Bank, however, were unable to save the bank from disaster and P. Y. Fogg lost all his securities. He was out of town on a fishing trip when the bank crash came and had no knowledge of the Bank Holiday. He was unable to save any of his bank stocks. When the Norway National Bank closed March 5, 1933, P. Y. Fogg was out of work.

"In 1932, when I started going with P. Y., he was worth $30,000," Jo said. "When I married him, in April, 1933, he owed $15,000. In 1931, we had been just neighbors when he had lost money in the stock market crash."

Feeling sorry for his situation, Jo had paid his board at Anna Stone's Boarding house until he was able to get back on his feet. Now with the bank failures Jo and P. Y. were experiencing more financial problems, only this time together.

"It was a difficult time," Jo said. "With his business knowledge, P. Y. was able to raise enough money to save the cottage by enlisting the help of some of his business associates. I paid off the mortgage on the cottage after his death."

Jo and P. Y. planned to get married the first week of April. But P. Y. was deeply involved in town affairs and many issues of importance to the town needed to be taken care of. Having Norway's best interests at heart, P. Y. felt he needed to attend the Town Meeting. Since they were planning only a small wedding, they postponed the date in order to attend the meeting.

At that time, many of the local people who wanted to get

married went to Conway, NH. It was a nice ride and allowed them to enjoy a little more privacy. Because it was only a little over fifty miles away, Jo and P. Y. decided to go there, too.

"When we went into the minister's home and into his study, we were struck by what a beautiful setting it was for a wedding. We had already made the arrangements and had the necessary paperwork with us. We were married that afternoon," Jo said. "It was a lovely wedding with Rev. Charles H. Morrhouse[29] performing the service."

Estranged from her family by the continuing bad feelings over McAllister's Restaurant, Jo told none of her family that they were going to Conway, to get married on the afternoon of April 30, 1933. After their marriage, P. Y. moved back to the apartment at 225 Main Street from the room he had been renting. Barbara continued to live mainly with Mother and Pa on Deering Street.

In 1934, P. Y. went to work for Howard Sanborn as the accountant and treasurer of Sanborn's Motor Express, where he worked until his death. He was Howard Sanborn's right-hand man and handled the daily operations of the express-trucking business, while at the same time doing all the bookkeeping.

Several months after her marriage, while Jo was still working at the Norway Cafe, she experienced a humorous incident that involved a "missing piece of roast pork." At the time, though, she didn't think it was the least bit funny.

When Jo went to get the roast pork from the storage shelf to serve for supper, it was nowhere to be found. Because meat was scarce during the Depression, many people were living on eggs, chicken, and vegetables. Jo was, therefore, understandably afraid that Gladys might think she had stolen the pork to feed herself and Barbara. In an effort to save her job and her good standing with Gladys, she undertook a frenzied search of the entire restaurant. The roast was nowhere to be found! Surely she would be blamed and fired from the job she so desperately needed. Finally, looking under the kitchen bench, she saw the missing piece of roast pork. A rat had dragged it from the counter and was attempting to take it to his hole in the floor!

"What a relief to have found it," Jo said. "Now, Gladys would never need to know that the meat was missing! We could go on serving our supper special."

Jo washed the meat thoroughly and continued the preparations for supper. No one was any the wiser.

Donald and Mildred moved back to Norway from Auburn and lived on Deering Street in an apartment house behind the

Norway National Bank building. On August 21, 1933, Donald Leslie McAllister was born. For several months prior to his birth, the doctor had put Mildred to bed to assure a successful delivery. Donnie was a healthy, rugged little fellow with a shock of red hair. Because they had lost three little girls and their oldest child, Freddie was ill, Donnie seemed to be a miracle to his parents.

A happy baby from the beginning, as he grew older, he became his cousin Barbara's shadow. Often, Barbara brought Donnie to visit with Jo. Both children spent a lot of time with their grandparents and grew up more like brother and sister than like cousins. Even though there were still hard feelings between Jo and Donald, their children were never involved. When the kids visited at their grandmother's, Barbara helped take care of Freddie and Donnie was her constant companion.

One Sunday in the fall of 1934, P. Y. took Jo for a trip to Azicohos Dam located in the western mountains of Maine. This was a place near the Rangley Lakes region where he had gone fishing with his friends.

"I had never been to this part of Maine," Jo commented. "I was overwhelmed by the beauty of the lakes and mountains. There was the brilliant blue of the vast waterways offset by the white snow of the capped mountains. I could easily see why P. Y. loved this place. We only went for the day, but P. Y. and his friends usually spent a week there fishing."

Even though Jo had grown-up in the foothills of the White Mountains, this was a new experience for her—her only other trip into the mountains had been to marry in Conway. She found going by car to the Rangley Lakes region a thrilling adventure. The brilliant blue of the vast waterways was offset by the white snow-capped mountains.

In their early fifties now, Pa and Mother hadn't been able to achieve peace of mind over the family conflict that had occurred at McAllister's Restaurant. They hadn't forgiven Jo for challenging Don and still weren't speaking to her. Mother saw P. Y. as an adversary of Donald's and thought Jo had made a huge mistake by marrying him.

Occasionally, when Barbara came back home to have supper with Jo and P. Y., Pa and Mother sent a nasty note with some sarcastic remark in it. Barbara loved her grandparents and never spoke about the notes. It was hard for her to be pulled in two directions. Jo encouraged Barbara to love Pa and Nana. She told Barbara to ignore all the unpleasant things that she knew they must have been saying in front of her.

But, there was a deep relationship between Barbara and her

grandparents. Often when Pa was going out for the afternoon, Barbara would tease to go, too. Winding her grandfather around her little finger was her favorite pastime. He often invited her to go with him. Before leaving the house, however, she would ask, "Are you going to the Selectmen's office, Pa?" This was the only place she didn't like to go. She got bored when the men got to talking. She thought that he stayed too long, shooting the breeze.

On winter days, Barbara often talked Pa into taking her to school on a sled so she wouldn't have to walk. If it was raining, he walked with her, covering her up with a big umbrella so she wouldn't get wet. He would get drenched. Barbara could do no wrong in her grandfather's eyes because he loved her so much.

These years were difficult ones for Jo. She endured the distance between her and her parents and suffered the loss of closeness with her daughter. But she supported them both through hard work and remained true to her nature—determined, outspoken, and hard working. Yet there were more challenges ahead for her. She would have to face many more important decisions that would shape her life in the years ahead. Many of the lessons she had learned at work, in business, and with people would help sustain her through the many changes she was about to face.

Her honesty was a virtue that would follow Jo throughout her entire life and lead to her success in the business world. Whether it was money, how much food was served to her customer or what she had to say about another person, Jo never waived from the truth.

Eventually, she would be the sole owner of her own business and become a leader in the national food service industry.

---

[28] *His parents' blood involved an incompatible Rh factor. Today, a blood exchange would prevent some of the complications Freddie suffered.*

[29] *This is the spelling as it appears on their marriage certificate.*

PART III

Jo in Full Stride!

Mother and Margaret, right.

Pa in his constable's uniform.

P.Y.'s cottage on Lake Pennesseewassee, where he continued to invite friends to join him in hunting, fishing, and long evenings of storytelling, was also the place he went to stay in order to demonstrate his opposition to Jo's decision to go back into business with her siblings.

CHAPTER 8

The Beginning Restaurant Years

In the early 1930's, economic conditions in the United States had steadily worsened. Many people had lost their life's savings and mortgages went unpaid. Businesses and factories had to close their doors leaving thousands without work. Bread lines increased as more people became unemployed. The President promised many new programs to help the country, but few were passed by Congress and brought into existence.

In the fall of 1934, the J.J. Newberry Store began an expansion project and needed the space occupied by McAllister's Restaurant. Donald moved his business from the Newberry Block to a two-and-one-half-story building at 210 Main Street. This building, the former Brooks Brother Grocery Store[30] was owned by Louis Brooks. Donald signed a lease for the building.

One winter day in 1935, Jo's older brother, Jim, came to see her at The Norway Café where she was working. Jim, a delivery man with Milliken, Tomlinson & Co., wholesale grocers from Lewiston, delivered groceries to the restaurant on a regular basis.

He told Jo, "You need to go back to work at McAllister's. I deliver there and I can see that Don needs some help."

P. Y. was dead-set against Jo ever having anything to do with the restaurant after the way the family had used her. Mother and Pa had tried to convince her that she wasn't smart enough to run a business. Jo had been discouraged and hurt because her parents had somehow forgotten that they had depended on her help when she was just a child in East Stoneham and that it was she who had helped Margaret to put her illness behind her.

Jo's first response to Jim was,"Why don't you go help him if you think things are that bad?"

Much older than Jo, Jim hadn't been involved in the family dispute.[31] He was living in Auburn and had a family of his own, yet having trouble in the family bothered him. Jim thought he could patch things up and bring about a peaceful solution if only he could talk Jo into going back to the restaurant to help Donald.

For several weeks Jo thought about Jim's suggestion. In the

end, her interest in being a business owner won out over the ache in her heart and the anxiety and the hurt she felt over Donald and the rest of her family.

She knew she had much more experience both in serving the public and in ordering supplies than Donald did. He had worked with numbers as a banker but had never been involved in the daily operations of a business.

In addition to her experience, Jo had contacts. As the buyer for Stone's Drug Store, she was a known quantity to many of the salesmen who also supplied the restaurant. Because she felt they trusted her, she guessed they might be willing to consider payment schedules for the restaurant's existing debts.

If she could get Margaret's help, Jo thought, they could make the restaurant show a profit. Together, with God's guidance, she felt they could succeed. By now, she was ready to ask Margaret to come into business with her.

"You know," Jo said, "we're the ones the suppliers did business with. Maybe Jim is right—we should talk with Donald."

Margaret agreed to join her.

When Jo told P.Y. Fogg what she and Margaret had decided, he told her, "Jo, I am against your getting involved. You know what's happened in the past in your family. If you insist on going back to the restaurant, I will go stay at the cottage."

He thought if he held fast to his challenge, Jo would reconsider. But Jo did not back down. Determined to be a success in the restaurant business, she stuck to her plan. Against P. Y.'s wishes, Jo approached Don.

When she entered the restaurant for the first time in two years, she couldn't believe her eyes. The beautiful inlaid wood tables were nearly destroyed. It was hard to set down a cup of coffee or a bowl of soup without spilling it. Playing cards with the high school kids, the help hadn't watched to see what was being done to the furniture. Customers had carved initials in the tops of the tables, damaging the surface. Though these kids weren't malicious—they were just killing time—many of the tables now wobbled and needed to be repaired or replaced. Various display cases were damaged, also, and the equipment in the kitchen needed much more than soap and water could do. The grease was caked onto the fry pots and grill.

In her early 30's, Jo was ready for a challenge! She was ready to risk everything, to "make something of herself." She was determined to make the move, no matter what obstacles she might face. In fact, perhaps it was the challenge to turn the business around and to prove herself that enabled Jo to overcome the hostility of her family and to disregard her husband's advice.

The girls found the financial situation was much worse than Jim had guessed. E. F. Jackson from Auburn, who held the mortgage on the business including the furniture and fixtures, had already put a lien on the restaurant and was ready to foreclose.

As a first step, Jo and Margaret talked with him. He was willing to give them an extension. Then the girls talked to each of the suppliers. The business people were willing to give them time to pay off the outstanding bills—under one condition: only if they became the owners of McAllister's Restaurant.

Jo made arrangements with her lawyer, Robert Dow, whose law office was on the second floor of the Stone's Drug Store, just opposite the restaurant. It would take almost a year to get the legal papers in order for the girls to buy the restaurant. In the meantime, Jo and Margaret went to work trying to straighten out all the errors that had been made at McAllister's.

"One afternoon after I had returned, I looked out the front window, just in time to see Pa going up the stairs to Robert Dow's office," Jo said. "It didn't take me but a minute to run across the street and up those stairs myself."

Flinging open the door, she demanded, "Bob Dow, who are you working for, Pa or me?!"

Jo made it plain to both of them, *"No negotiations* about the restaurant are to be held behind my back!"

"Pa, I don't want you interfering or trying to talk to my lawyer unless I am present," she said. She felt this time around she needed to be clear about what she would and would not tolerate from her parents. They might mean well, but they had shown they didn't always have her best interests at heart.

It took until May 18,1936, before all the details for final legal papers were worked out and signed. Jo and Margaret bought McAllister's Restaurant from Donald. Jo paid the sum of $100 to finalize the sale. The rest of the agreement stated that Jo and Margaret would assume all of the outstanding obligations of McAllister's Restaurant.

The restaurant was so far in debt that by paying off the mortgage and all the outstanding debts, the girls were paying far more for it than the original start-up costs would have been. The outstanding debt was over $5000 and the restaurant had accounts receivable from its customers totaling only slightly over $200. Credit had been extended because many people were out of work but still needed a place to eat. These receivables were placed with Frank Bjorklund, an attorney, for collection.

In the 1930's, this imbalance represented an enormous financial burden for any business. The banks were unstable, making it impossible to borrow money even if the restaurant had been able to present a good financial statement.

During the Depression, the idea of starting a new business instead of taking over McAllister's didn't enter Jo's head. She knew the restaurant had a good customer base and she knew all the suppliers. It was just a matter of showing the public that she could earn their trust.

True to his word, when Jo and Margaret bought the restaurant, P. Y. went to reside at his cottage on Lake Pennesseewassee in Norway. P. Y. had a lot of respect for Jo and admired her ability to work, but he felt she was making a terrible mistake. He was willing to support and guide her, but he didn't feel the restaurant deserved any kind of assistance.

Jo was so sure of her choice and of her need to be a success at the family business that she was willing to risk her marriage to P. Y. In the end, both choices proved right. Jo's determination paid off and in June, P. Y. realized Jo was intent on making the restaurant a success. After six weeks, he came back home and became a great help to Jo by using his banking experience to help her straighten out the legal and financial tangles of the restaurant.

To give themselves a new starting point, on August 23, 1936, Jo and Margaret changed the name to "Marjo's," a combination of their two names.

Jo had worked at the shoe shop and Stone's Drug Store and had built up a cash reserve on her life insurance policy. She borrowed $300 from her Metropolitan Life Insurance policy to use for working capital. The only decorations on the walls were some Camel, Old Gold, and Chesterfield posters, which were the popular cigarettes of that era. Having no extra money to buy new booths, Jo picked up good used items wherever she could. Nothing matched, but neither did anything wobble and every surface was scrubbed and spotless.

Doing all her own cleaning was a practice Jo continued throughout her restaurant career. Margaret, too, was consistent about cleaning and insisted that all the help come to work with polished white shoes and neat, clean uniforms.

While still a girl in East Stoneham, when her mother was ill, Jo had done much of the cooking. As an adult, she had continued to cook both at The Norway Café and at home. She became an experienced cook. Doing the cooking at the restaurant became her responsibility. Margaret managed the dining room and ran the cash register. Mother, who had made all the pies and done the baking for the restaurant at home, agreed to continue.

"P. Y. made a business woman out of me," Jo said. "He was strict with me where the financial end of the restaurant business was involved. He taught me bookkeeping, cost control and the legal aspects of owning a business. In our original store, neither Marg nor I knew a thing about that part of owning our own business. That was one of the reasons we were so naive about what Donald was doing."

Even though P. Y. taught Jo how to handle the finances, he wanted no part of the daily operations of the restaurant. He stayed on as the accountant and treasurer for Sanborn's Motor Express.

Every day, he checked to see how Jo was doing and how she was following his instructions in regards to handling the banking. P. Y. taught Jo how to reconcile the restaurant checking account. Having worked in the bank, he stressed how important it was to balance the books right to the last penny. He told her, one penny is just as important as though you had made a mistake of one hundred dollars. She never forgot that lesson.

Watching how much she was buying, he stressed to her how important it was to know *exactly* how many servings she would get out of each item ordered. She must know *exactly* what a serving on the menu cost and which items were profitable to serve.

One day, for instance, P. Y. came into the dining room and observed one of the waitresses dipping ice cream. She gave the customer a double scoop on her cone—much more than he paid for. P. Y. went directly into the kitchen through the swinging doors.

"Jo," he said, after explaining what had happened. "You would have been better off if that customer hadn't come into the restaurant."

It was this art of mentoring on P. Y.'s part that helped Jo learn to excel at her business.

"P. Y. didn't know much about food preparation, but he did know how to evaluate how much each serving cost," Jo said. "By always having the best interests of the business at heart, he served my best interests."

The two sisters were anxious to prove to their creditors that they deserved the trust that was being given them. Jo and Margaret labored together to pay off all the bills Donald owed to the creditors. They arrived early in the morning and worked until late in the evening to make a success of their venture.

In the fall of 1936, Ralph Stone[32] was looking for work. After he graduated from South Paris High School in 1932, he found work to be very scarce. His father was a teamster, so Ralph was able to hire out to work in the logging camps in Northern Maine.

There he learned to cook. Wanting to return to the Norway-Paris area, he had gotten a job at Beal's Tavern. Mrs. Seavey, the owner, was very strict as to how the food was prepared and how many ingredients could be put into it. Stony (as Ralph Stone preferred to be called) was unhappy. He was expected to always scrimp and to work with no stock on hand. He wanted to have more freedom in what he prepared.

Many crews of workers from the power companies, telephone companies and construction crews had become regulars at Marjo's. With business increasing, the restaurant needed more staff. Margaret had already hired additional waitresses in the dining room. Jo agreed that they needed more help in the kitchen, too. When Stony came by, complaining about cooking at Beal's Tavern, Margaret hired him on the spot. This was the first time that Jo had an assistant cook. Up to this time, the only other kitchen employee was a high school kid who washed dishes.

At first, Jo and Stony clashed over how the kitchen was to be run. Many of the entrees served at the hotel were prepared quite differently from the restaurant's style.

For example, just before Stony came to work at the restaurant, he said to Jo, "I am going to make a cake and bring it to the restaurant to show you how my pastries look."

To prove to him that she had better quality ingredients and would provide them for his baking, Jo hurried around and made a cake herself. When Stony showed up with his cake, she had hers sitting on the counter.

"His cake wasn't very thick." Jo said. "But I knew why. Mrs. Seavey only let him use one egg in his and I used six in mine."

Stony was furious because he thought Jo was trying to show him up. It wasn't long after going to work at the restaurant that he realized what she actually had been doing. She had been trying to show him what a difference it made when you had first-class groceries to work with.

Jo bought quality products to be used for dinner specials and baking. In the logging camps, the men had expected good hearty food. Jo was providing him with the same kind of ingredients for his cooking and baking as he had known in the logging camps.

"No matter how good it *looks*, if it doesn't *taste* good, no one is going to eat it," was his philosophy. Now, he would be able to cook the same way he had for the men.

As long as Jo was in business, excellence in the food she served was her priority. She believed, also, that an adequate inventory was a necessary part of her business and that her customers deserved the finest money could buy.

If Margaret hadn't been Jo's partner after Donald left the restaurant, Mother probably wouldn't have continued baking the pies. She had never gotten over believing that Jo was responsible for the difficulty at McAllister's.

When she found out the girls had hired a cook, she said to Jo with sarcasm in her voice, "You don't need to have me do the baking anymore. Your cook can do it."

"It didn't make things any easier to have Mother so difficult," Jo said sadly. "After that, she never did any baking for us."

After her graduation from Gorham Normal School in 1931, Jo's youngest sister, Grace taught in the Oxford Elementary School for three years and then taught in the Norway school system for three more years. During vacation from teaching school, Grace worked several summers at the restaurant. She was going with Elliot Cummings and wanted to learn to cook. She knew Elliot would expect her to stay home and raise their family.

"Jo, can't I help you cook that order. You know Mother never let me do any cooking at home and how am I ever going to be able to cook for Elliott, if you don't show me." Grace pleaded with Jo, every time an order came into the kitchen.

"It was kind of funny to me," Jo said with a laugh. "Grace was so insistent on learning to cook that she bugged me constantly. Sometimes almost to the point of being a real pest."

With Jo's help, Grace became an excellent cook. In September, 1936, she married Elliot Cummings, stopped teaching, and devoted herself to raising her family.

Before long, other things would surface in Jo's life that would change her whole concept of the restaurant business.

Hiring Stony had been Margaret's idea not Jo's, but in the future he would play a much greater role in her life. Not only would he prove to be an asset at the restaurant, but he would play a part in her personal life as well.

---

[30] *The oldest building in Advertiser Square, it was built in 1804 as a law office for Levi Whitman. At a later date, it would be listed on the National Register of Historic Places, and become a part of Norway's Historical District. The original stone foundation made the building eligible for this designation.*

[31] *Jo's sister, Helen, hadn't been involved either. She was teaching in the Waterford School system and raising her four children in East Stoneham.*

[32] *No relationship to the Stones at Stone's Drug Store.*

Barbara, clockwise from top left: 10 months old; with Jo at age 18 months; outside Barjo's at age 10; teenage Barbara with Bryant Gurney; performing at WCOU with the Pearl Kilborn Marimba Band (Jimmy Goodwin behind her) at age 8; with Jo at Nana's house; and center, waiting for Pa to come home from work (wearing his cap) at age 3.

CHAPTER 9

Jo as a Mother

Another tragedy struck the McAllister family in 1935. On February 19, at the age of fifty-nine, Pa died suddenly. For ten days, he had had a bad case of the flu that turned into double pneumonia. He had always been healthy and robust, doing hard physical work for most of his life. It was a terrible shock.

"I don't remember Pa ever having a sick day in his life," Jo said. "Mother had been the one we worried about, never Pa."

Several weeks before, in January, Jo and Pa had been in contact concerning his visit to the lawyer's office. Jo had seen him going into her lawyer Robert Dow's office during her negotiations to buy the restaurant. Now his sudden death seemed almost like a bad dream to her. She had no idea whether Mother would allow her in the house or what kind of a reception she would receive from the rest of the family.

Before the funeral, Jo went to her parents' home for the first time in three years. Going into the house with some doubts, she was pleasantly surprised. Mother acted as though nothing had ever happened. Jo helped clean the house from the attic to the cellar to get ready for the funeral.

The entire time Pa's casket was at the house, Barbara played around it, as if he was sleeping and she was waiting for him to wake up. She had been his shadow. At seven, she didn't understand what death meant, though she had lost her father at three.

Pa's funeral was held at home on Deering Street.

"Mother thought the emotional strain would be too much for Margaret," Jo said. "Taking Barbara with her, Marg spent the day at Aunt Nettie's."

Pa was buried at Hillside Cemetery in East Stoneham.

"Shortly after Pa's death, I thought Barbara needed some activity to help her recover from losing her grandfather," Jo said. "I enrolled her in a dance class. Her teacher came to Norway from Lewiston once a week to give lessons to the local children."

Barbara's dancing partner was Jimmy Goodwin. He was a handsome blonde-haired, blue-eyed boy who was about her height. Having dark hair and unusual dark brown eyes, Barbara looked good dancing with Jimmy. They made an adorable team. At their recital, he wore a top hat and tails, while she wore a pretty pink organdy dance outfit. The youngest dancers on the program, they performed their routine without a flaw.

After Pa's death, Grammie Moody came to stay with Mother and Margaret. Since the death of Uncle Frank in 1932, Grammie Moody had continued to live alone on the farm in East Stoneham. After she suffered a stroke, it became apparent that she could no longer stay alone. She wasn't eating properly and was no longer able to care for herself.

Barbara was still staying full-time with her grandmother on Deering Street, but she was finding it hard. She missed her grandfather and all the good times they had had together.

Although Barbara could only sense it without being able to understand why, there continued to be tension between Mother and Jo, coming mostly from Mother. For instance, Barbara was sometimes asked to deliver notes to Jo from her Nana. She didn't understand what the notes were all about. Because she had little time off at the restaurant, Jo felt it was important to have Mother continue to take care of her daughter.

When Barbara was with Jo and P. Y., he called their relationship the "Club of Three" to try to ease the stress.

By this time, Donnie had become an active child. He was the darling of the whole McAllister family for a long time because he was the youngest.

He and Barbara never played an active role in the problems involving their parents. Because Barbara was an only child and Donnie's brother was sickly, they spent many hours together and always remained close.

Donald and Mildred both worked, so the children were taken care of during the day by a hired caregiver. Freddie occupied much of his parents' free time. As a result, Jo often invited Donnie to come to the restaurant to play with Barbara.

Because Jo was working long hours at the restaurant, Don and Mildred, too, often invited Barbara to have a family meal at their home. Mildred cooked Barbara's favorite vegetables: boiled onions, boiled cabbage and turnip. Mother, too, had both children at her house often. They had many good times with their Nana including every holiday.

"Whenever I had off, I went to get Barbara at Mother's," Jo said. "P. Y. and I managed to have her eat supper with us every night. If I had the afternoon off, I did something special with her."

Still, Pa's death weighed on her and Grammie Moody's sickness demanded much of Nana's attention. Barbara grew unhappy. While she loved her Nana, she had been very close to Pa and being at Deering Street seemed to remind her of her loss. She was finding it hard to adjust.

One day, as Jo and P. Y. were sitting down to dinner at their home on Main Street, Barbara walked in the door to join them. By now, she was eight and her grandmother's home was only a short distance from Jo's apartment, so she had walked over by herself.

After entering the door, she sat down on the floor in front of the refrigerator. With tears in her eyes, she cried out, "I'm not going back to stay with Nana again while you are working!"

"What's the matter Barb?" P. Y. asked. "I thought you were part of our 'Club of Three'."

"Well, what I really want to do is stay with you and Mother all the time," she said. "I know Nana loves me and I love her lots, but I want to stay here with you."

"Barbara, I'll try to find someone to watch you," Jo said to her. "If you want to stay here full-time with us, of course, you can. Please don't cry. You know how much I love you. Tomorrow morning, I'll look for someone to be here when I'm at work."

Barbara had never complained about having someone sick around, but it was apparent that was a big part of the problem. The next day, Jo hired Mrs. Adams to take care of Barbara so she could stay at home all the time. Being with Jo and P. Y. made her feel loved and protected once again.

After Barbara moved home with her mother, she found out that Jo looked under her bed with a flashlight every night before going to bed. She thought this was a strange thing for a grownup to do. Jo had never overcome her childhood fear of the dark or what might be lurking around the corner. Every night, Barbara peeked at her mother from the other side of the bed to try to frighten her and teach her that there was nothing under there.[33]

When Barbara was small, P. Y. would take her to the cottage with him and together they would go fishing and boating.

One Sunday morning, Barbara and one of her young friends came home from Sunday School and asked if they could go fishing at the cottage. P. Y. willingly obliged.

She was fishing from the wharf when she hollered excitedly, "I've got a *bastard!*"

She had hooked a small-mouth black bass, the first fish she ever caught. P. Y. hurried to her rescue and found the other little girl holding onto Barbara for dear life. Her arms were wrapped around Barbara's waist so she wouldn't fall into the lake with her fish. P. Y. helped her reel in her prize catch—and then he correct-ed her language.[34]

Shortly after moving back with Jo at 225 Main Street, Barbara started taking marimba lessons. Pearl Cook Kilborn had her music studio on the first floor of the Cook Barbershop building where they lived. Her teacher was also the bandleader for the Norway Community Marching Band. Jo bought Barbara her own marimba and Pearl Kilborn taught her how to assemble it. For an eight year, that was quite a challenge.

Playing in Pearl Kilborn's Marimba Band, Barbara became an accomplished musician.

Barbara's dancing partner, Jimmy Goodwin, also played in the marimba band. On one occasion, the marimba band was invited to play at the radio station, WCOU, in Lewiston. Playing live on the air was a whole new experience for them.

"I wondered how they would perform," Jo said. "I shouldn't have worried. Barbara and Jimmy never let on there was a microphone right above their heads. Pearl took them to the stu-dio and play with the band herself. None of them missed a beat."

For the rest of Barbara's childhood, Jo and Barbara were never separated no matter what transpired. Knowing that Mother would be hurt because Barbara had decided not to stay with her all the time, Jo made sure that her daughter visited often. Jo also knew that Mother needed the money that she had been paying her for Barbara's board to help support the family. She gave Barbara money to give her Nana on a regular basis. Barbara still continued to spend a lot of time with the rest of the McAllister family at 26 Deering Street especially on Thanksgiving, Christmas and other special occasions.

---

[33] *Not very successfully, I might add, because she still looks under her bed now at the age of 96! —J.E.F.*

[34] *Though others used this kind of language frequently, never in her life has Barbara uttered a word of this sort. This is why it has remained a family story to chuckle over for many years.*

CHAPTER 10

More Trouble Ahead!

In the spring of 1937, a year and a half after they had resumed working together, it became apparent that the two sisters had different ideas as to how the business should be run.

"Margaret thought all the money should be applied directly to paying off the outstanding bills. She was running the dining room, but I was doing the cooking and buying," Jo said. "I knew that to operate the business successfully, the inventory had to be replaced as it was used. I had learned how to buy from F. P. Stone at Stone's Drugstore. Saving on inventory to pay the bills didn't seem to right way to go."

The sisters had many clashes over their differing points of view. Jo was willing to take a risk to make the business a success. Margaret was much more conservative, believing that unnecessary chances should not be taken.

At the time, Margaret was still living at home. When she and Jo disagreed, it was only natural for Mother and the rest of the family to side with her. Mother hadn't approved, but she had come to accept that Margaret and Jo had taken over the restaurant.

Whenever Margaret or any of the waitresses wanted some time off, they consulted with Mother instead of Jo. This caused a lot of friction between the sisters. Jo was scheduling the hours for each employee. She expected them to come to work on time and not skip their shifts. She felt that Mother had no right to interfere in the daily operation of the restaurant. Because this had happened before at McAllister's, Jo was determined that it wasn't going to happen again.

Many years before in East Stoneham, Jo had learned how important it was for everyone to do his or her share of the work. Even as a child, Jo had taken the responsibility to see that the workhorses were at work on time when her mother had been in the hospital, even if the man Pa had hired to help him was late.

It was apparent that her family still couldn't accept or perhaps understand the fact that Jo had the will, the determination, and the ability to run a successful business.

This time, other parties outside the family were involved in the dispute. Margaret's boyfriend, Frank Bjorklund, who had his law office on the second floor of the restaurant building was giving her advice as to what the next legal steps should be. He was encouraging Margaret to take Jo to court. He drew up all the legal papers and filed them in court. Needless to say, the partnership between Jo and Margaret was deteriorating rapidly.

Frank suggested to Margaret that she have Jo buy out her share. Both Jo and Margaret knew neither one of them had the cash or the desire to do this. Jo also knew that pressure was being put on Margaret to close Marjo's, but Jo wanted no part of that. Frank included a clause in the legal papers stating that Jo had refused Margaret's offer for a solution to their problems.

"I just couldn't believe Marg was listening to Frank. I didn't understand how she could do this to me," Jo confessed.

"We had both been trying so hard to make the restaurant a success. Both of us had been working many long hours to accomplish our goal. I thought Margaret wanted the restaurant just as much as I did, but I guess I was mistaken about her priorities."

Jo was learning a bitter lesson. She could see that if she was going to be successful, she would have to be the sole owner. A partnership, no matter how well she thought she knew the other person, would never work out. She held this as a fundamental belief for the rest of her business career.

In early June, Margaret left the restaurant. Then, on June 12, 1937, Margaret had civil papers served on Jo to begin the receivership proceedings against her. At this point, Jo had already loaned the business over $700. This included money she had borrowed from her life insurance policy.

On the day the case was heard in Superior Court in South Paris, Jo and Margaret were assigned to separate rooms. Neither was allowed in the courtroom when the other was testifying.

On June 17, 1937, Jo won the court case, dissolving the partnership. She became the sole proprietor of the restaurant. The judge also ruled the restaurant was to be in her husband, P. Y. Fogg's name as a receiver of the court.[35] The restaurant remained in his name until his death on December 1, 1940. P. Y. wanted no part of the restaurant business and was only acting as the Superior Court's designated receiver to pay off the bills from the partnership.

It would still be several days before all the final papers were completed. To Jo it seems like an eternity. As the Superior Court proceedings in South Paris were winding down, some final papers needed to be signed at the federal courthouse in Portland by Judge Beliveau. P. Y. Fogg drove to Portland with court papers in hand to speed up the process, so the restaurant could be reopened. When he arrived at the courthouse, the clerk told him that Judge Beliveau had just left for Rumford. P. Y. was determined to close this matter, so he raced up Route 26, passed through Norway, and continued north to the Judge's home in Rumford. When P. Y. arrived there, hours after he had started, Judge Beliveau quickly signed the necessary legal documents.

Meanwhile, Jo waited impatiently at their apartment at 225 Main Street across from the restaurant, for word from P. Y. to find out if he had found the judge.

"The second I received the call that everything was signed and the restaurant was mine," Jo said, "I was off and running."

She hurried across the street and up the alley between the buildings. Then, she climbed through the bathroom window, and once in the restaurant, she began baking pies and rolls and preparing the specials for the day. Before long the smell of food cooking wafted in the air outside the restaurant as Jo prepared dinner. By noontime, she had the doors open and was back serving her customers.

By June 20, 1937, with all the necessary legal documents signed, Jo changed the name to "Barjo Restaurant" a combination of her name and Barbara's. This name was used throughout the rest of her business days on Main Street.

For the next six weeks, the restaurant was allowed to operate with two attorneys as referees and P. Y. Fogg as the receiver for the court. Frank Bjorklund represented Margaret. Robert Dow represented Jo. The attorneys came to the restaurant every day, did the cashing up, and subject to P. Y. Fogg's supervision as the Superior Court's representative, paid the bills.

As part of the receivership transactions, all the canned goods had to be brought from the basement storeroom and displayed in the restaurant dining room for the attorneys to have for a public auction. Jo hired Guy McAlister[36] who helped out at the restaurant to carry the groceries into the dining room of the restaurant for the sale. The produce and meat were being bought on a daily basis from local farmers, so the perishables were not involved.

By the end of July, the final accounting had been made and the bills either paid off or transferred to the Barjo Restaurant account. Because the judge ruled in Jo's favor, no cash payment to Margaret was needed to dissolve the partnership.

By now, Jo had learned that the ones who would come to her aid in time of trouble weren't her family, but her many friends and business associates. Her clientele and the wholesalers had supported her throughout the entire litigation proceeding.

It took many months, but by paying five dollars a week to each creditor, Jo saw to it that they all got the money owed them. To cope with her debt, Jo needed a larger cash inflow. She decided to change the menu to feature ice cream and to include breakfast and full-course meals. P. Y. approved and continued to encourage her to use the cost control methods he had taught her.

After Jo gained control of the daily operations of the restaurant, she featured a fountain to serve homemade ice cream. Making her own ice cream, which had been the foundation of their original restaurant menu, seemed to be a wise move. By promoting over twenty flavors at a time and serving many ice cream specialties, she hoped to would complement her expanded menu. The ice cream was frozen on the premises. Jo used the old-fashioned method of salt, ice and a crank freezer. All the cream was bought from local farmers, Harlan Whitman and the Thurstons. Many of the fruits used in the ice cream were picked in the area. All the syrups were made by cooking down the ingredients such as coffee and chocolate.

"To serve the public better, we needed to serve more than ice cream and sandwiches," Jo said. "Many depended on Barjo's for all their meals, and I wanted to be able to help them. The expanded menu served two purposes: it helped me to pay off the bills and to serve my clientele three meals a day."

After the court case was settled, Margaret went back to work for Lester Ashton at Ashton's Drug Store. Margaret was living with her mother on Deering Street and her income helped to provide a living for Mother, Grammie Moody and herself. Even though Mother and the rest of the family were not speaking to her, Jo continued to send money to Mother on a regular basis to replace Barbara's board.

Needing some extra income, Mother herself had started a doughnut business from her home. She called it "McAllister's Doughnuts." Her doughnuts were sold at local stores and restaurants. Many people came to her home to pick up the doughnuts themselves. Mother continued the doughnut business from 1935 until after World War II.

After Margaret left the restaurant, Jo kept on selling "McAllister's Doughnuts" at the restaurant and encouraged people to buy them and continued to supply her mother with the ingredients to make the doughnuts. Jo could get these wholesale. Their relationship remained uneasy, nonetheless.

Even with Margaret's help and her own effort with McAllister's Doughnuts, Mother was having a hard time to pay her bills. Without Pa's salary and with the cost of Grammie Moody's sickness, she needed the extra help that Jo's support gave her.

In 1938, Grammie Moody died at home at 26 Deering Street.

Jo had learned many things from her trials and tribulations. One was to overcome her hurt and be loyal to her family while insisting on her own independence. Another was how to serve her public. "Give them good, wholesome food and plenty of it, and they'll come back" was the motto she adopted early in her restaurant career and always believed in. People from every state in the Union have eaten at Barjo's, many being the second, third, and fourth generation in their family to do so.

---

35 *This court proceeding was similar to today's Chapter 11 bankruptcy laws in which a court administrator handles the finances of a business.*

36 *All the McAllisters were related in some way, although their names were occasionally spelled differently.*

Jo posed for this photo with her first electric refrigerator in 1942 .

For many years, a sign in the shape of a giant snowshoe proclaimed Norway the 'Snowshoe Capital of the World.'

Other Things Were Happening in Norway

While Jo was busy with the early stages of creating a successful restaurant in the mid 1930's, the town of Norway, too, was experiencing many changes and attracted some interesting people and events.

In the fall of 1935, the town of Norway needed a new central fire station. For many years, the Norway Fire Department had three stations, Station One located near Stone's Drug Store, Number Two in the middle of the village, and Number Three in Ward Eight at the lower end of town.

A piece of land was selected below the shoe shop on Main Street for a new one-story building. But, the fire department was having a hard time to raise money to build its new station.

Learning about the fund-raising difficulties, Victorine Blanchard, a wealthy widow who had moved to Norway from Worcester, Massachusetts, only several years earlier, offered to finance the project. Her offer was quickly accepted. Her generosity not only helped hasten the construction of the station, but it permitted the department to erect a two-story rather than a one-story brick building. The new station could accommodate four fire-trucks. It was a big improvement for the town.

"The fire station wasn't Victorine Blanchard's only contribution to her adopted town. For the American Legion, she had the Stone-Smart Legion Post built on lower Main Street and during the War, she bought an ambulance for the Oxford County Red Cross," Jo said. "She was one of Norway's original benefactors, contributing to the town in many ways."

One of the peculiar things Jo remembered about Victorine Blanchard was her butler walking her two small dogs up and down the street every afternoon. He wore a long black coat and top hat. This was an odd sight in a small working-class town.

The Town of Norway commemorated its sesquicentennial in 1936. Every store in the town was decorated with bunting for the special celebration of 150 years of existence.

The special events started on Sunday, August 16, with all the area churches participating in special services. One evening, there was a concert at the Norway Fair Grounds by the Inter-Church Orchestra of Portland with Allister Grant as conductor.

Meeting many new people during the festivities, Jo was anxious to please them and to encourage them to return to the restaurant as regulars. Jo and Margaret recognized the parade as an occasion to take their fledgling company in front of the public and attract new clientele. Their presentation would help them establish a reputation as a solid business.

On the morning of Monday, August 17, the float parade was held. Lloyd Flanders, Jo's friend who was a logging contractor, let her borrow his horses, his driver, Mr. Monk, and his logging vehicle. Margaret took charge of decorating the float, which was large enough for all the restaurant crew plus some of the local kids to ride on.

"The huge work-horses were magnificent and the float Marg created was a masterpiece," Jo said. "It was a thrill to watch those beautiful animals pulling our float in the parade."

"What can we do to make the restaurant special so all these people will want to return?" Jo said to Margaret. "Maybe I can find something unusual for decorations."

One of the bosses from the Norway Shoe Shop, who had been transferred to Brazil, had brought home a mammoth snakeskin when he came for a visit. To dress-up the dining room, he let Jo borrow it for the festivities. The enormous snakeskin was so long that it was attached to a beam in the center of the room.

"The South American boa constrictor skin stretched from one wall to the other. What a lot of comments and questions we got about it. It was some conversation piece," Jo said.

In the afternoon, the Pine Tree League baseball team from Norway played Dixfield. The local baseball players had a successful week, winning all their games.

"Many of the boys who played in the Pine Tree League were our friends and neighbors," Jo said. "At the restaurant, we got acquainted with a lot of boys from the visiting teams."

At 8:30 p.m., a Pops Concert performance was enjoyed at the Norway Opera House. Many people came from the surrounding towns to hear the music.

Tuesday was Carnival Day at the Norway Country Club with free golf all day for everyone. During the evening, games of every description, dancing and music were provided. A Chevrolet car, courtesy of Ralph Sturges, was given away.

Wednesday was a day to reminisce about the "Good Old Days." Group pictures were taken at 10:00 a.m. and the rest of the day was given to renewing old friendships.

"Some of my friends from high school days came back to visit," Jo said. "At Marjo's, many of our customers from Stone's Drug Store came in to say hello and have lunch at the restaurant."

Baseball at 5:30 p.m., featured Norway vs. Lisbon Falls at the Fair Grounds. In the evening, a stage production, *Smilin' Through*, was presented at the Norway Opera House across the street from Marjo's by the Pennesseewassee Players.

Thursday, August 20 included an Old Time Fiddlers' Contest and a Costume Barn Dance at the Opera House. Norway's own celebrity, Mellie Dunham, was featured.

"Mellie was right at home with his fiddle," Jo said. "His granddaughter, Cherry Noble, played the piano for him. She was one of my high-school classmates."

Friday, August 21 was set aside as "Summer Residents Day" with Governor Louis J. Brann serving as host. There were foot and bicycle races, swimming, canoeing, and other water events.

"The summer people thought it was a great idea to include them in all the festivities," Jo said. "Being a part of everything made them feel like Norway was their hometown, too."

At 8:00 p.m., Major Bowes Amateur Hour entertained at the Fair Grounds. Many of the local people performed in the show.

Saturday was the Grand Finale for the events of the week. At 7:00 p.m. a "Horribles" Parade was held on Main Street, followed by a Street Dance. Dancing was permitted on Main Street from Whitman Street to Deering Street. This was right in front of the restaurant, so the dining room was packed most of the evening.

"We could skip out for a dance then go back to work," Jo said. "I loved to dance and had a wonderful time that evening. Everyone in Norway joined in the fun at the festivities."

Some people came in to have dinner, while others came in to have a coke or an ice cream soda to cool off.

Rudy Vallee was one of those people. He was an actor, writer, and composer from Maine who made it big in Hollywood in the 1930's. His most famous song was the "Maine Stein Song" which was adopted by the University of Maine as their school song. Rudy Vallee entertained many famous guests at the cottage he bought on Lake Kezar in Lovell. Among these guest was Alice Faye, a popular Hollywood actress and film star. Often at his parties, his guests enjoyed a sampling of McAllister's Doughnuts and home made ice cream from Barjo's.

Not as famous, but more intimate with Jo in those days, were the Vivians, the Naschkees, the Schebners, the Kleslers, the Schmidlins, and the Brushes who owned cottages on Lake

Pennesseewassee. Other summer resident friends and acquaintances stayed in different places—Lakeside Inn, Shepard's Camps, and Papoose Pond Camps. Others came from the surrounding area of the Oxford Hills as many lakes abounded in this region of Maine. The Shepards, who owned Shepard's Camps, were year-round customers as well.

Peter and Viola George, Antoinette Pacent and her sons, as well as many other families came regularly.

Bill Kreidler and his family were also summer residents. Jo became acquainted with him, when Bill came on fishing trips to Maine from out of state.

"After Bill and his friends came back from a fishing trip, I cooked the fish they had caught. They were a nice bunch of guys, and I had a good time doing it," Jo said. "They always ate at the restaurant when they came for a visit or brought their families."

Bill bought a home on Paris Hill where he came with his family in the summer. After he retired, he made it their year-round home. The Kreidlers have remained Jo's good friends.

While summering in the area, many people went to the Band-Box Dance Pavilion at Lake Pennesseewassee. It was a popular attraction featuring many big-name bands. Many local folks and summer visitors came to dance the night away. After the dance, people of all ages would head for Barjo's for a late night treat before going home.

Knowing how many people attended these dances, Jo realized that, if she kept open longer hours, she would attract the late-night clientele. Jo was growing beyond being just a cook into being a business person. She was ready to accept the challenge to promote new business for her restaurant.

"Everybody at the restaurant looked forward to the dance rushes," Jo said. " From 12:00 a.m. to 2:00 a.m., the store was jampacked with people from all the area dances. Booths for four often had eight or more seated in them. Barjo's was like a second home to all the local young people, coming in for a midnight snack. Many of them called me their "Saturday-Night Mother."

In the late 1930's, one of Jo's friends, Lloyd Flanders, a local lumberman, and his wife, advertised for a child to take care of. They were loving people and wanted to be foster-parents to a young child. Their own two were growing up and would soon be leaving home. The response they had was surprising.

One day, a chauffeur-driven Packard limousine with out-of-state plates drove into their yard. Inside was an elderly gentleman, a young woman and a small boy. The man was J. P. Morgan, the famous financier. The woman was his daughter and the little boy was her son and Morgan's grandson, John.

A tiny, timid child, John stepped from the car and was awe-struck by the team of enormous horses standing in the yard ready for their next trip into the woods for logs. He wore a flimsy knitted romper, and shoes with no socks. The elegantly-dressed gentleman and the child's mother came into the Flanders home and stayed fewer than ten minutes.

"It looked as though they were trying to avoid any conversation that would require any promises to the child," Lloyd Flanders' son, Frank, said.

The little boy might as well have been homeless, for these people showed no affection for him. These well-to-do people had brought no clothes for him to wear or toys for him to play with. With no apparent remorse, they got back into the limousine and drove off, leaving the frightened little boy with the Flanders.

"John was scared to death by the horses," Frank recalled. "He stood in the middle of the floor, petrified and not knowing what was happening to him. It must have been a scary situation for him, not knowing any of us."

John Morgan was loved and nurtured by his new family, even though his own family never returned to see him. Lloyd Flanders and his wife brought him up as their foster son and put him through high school. It was a case similar to many we see today, when people seem to think children are a hindrance to their plans and they want no part in raising them.

When it was time for him to go into the service, Mr. and Mrs. Flanders contacted his mother in New York so that he could see her before going off to War.

"Lloyd told me," Jo said, "that John needed to see his family before he faced the front lines. They hadn't looked after him as they should, but the Flanders felt John needed to know who his birth family was and where they live."

When John finished his tour of duty, the Flanders again arranged a meeting of mother and son. This was the last time John ever saw his mother. Neither he nor the Flanders received a nickel from his family for his care over all those the years.

John grew up to be a very caring person. He became active in many civic organizations, especially the local and national Veterans organizations. At the present time, he works at the U.S. Post Office in Norway.

During the Depression of the 1930's, the Civilian Conservation Corp was put into place by President Franklin Delano Roosevelt to help the country get back on its feet. Members built roads and bridges and helped to rebuild the infrastructure of the country.

Eddie Ames, who suffered from tuberculosis, was working for the C. C. C. He had to work because there were no government programs then to help and everyone had it hard. In those days, no work meant no money to live on.

Jo felt very sorry for Eddie Ames because he really was too sick to work and didn't have half enough to eat. She packed a lunch for him so he would have some food in his stomach to give him strength to continue at his job. Eddie Ames was the first person that Jo gave a free meal to at Barjo's restaurant—and he wouldn't be the last.[37] Although she was learning to be a businesswoman, Jo was not forgetting to put love and kindness first.

Snocraft of Norway received an order for 1,278 pairs of snowshoes from the Civilian Conservation Corps of New England for use at some of their job sites. The price agreed upon was $6.18 per pair. This order helped provide work for many in the area. One man could weave about 12 pairs of snowshoes a day. It took 168 feet of cow's hide to weave the body of just one snowshoe. The nine-foot strip of ash used for the frame had to be steamed three-quarters of an hour to make it pliable enough to bend.

A giant snowshoe, crafted by Charles Aldrich, the owner of Snocraft, stood at the entrance of Norway, on Route 26 by the bridge. It weighed fifty pounds, stood sixteen feet tall by four feet wide and contained the leather from two and a half steers. A sign was attached to the snowshoe proclaiming Norway, the "Snowshoe Capital of the World." It also gave a list of the businesses in Norway, the population (at the time 2,873), and pointed out the fact that Norway was half way between the Equator and the North Pole.

During the late 1930's, many high school kids made Barjo's their second home before school in the morning and after school in the afternoon. The surrounding towns paid tuition for the pupils at Norway High School but there were no school buses. The students came into town when their parents drove to work. At lunchtime, many came to the restaurant. Some had brought their food with them, while others bought their lunch. Jo would give all the kids big bowls of French fries to go with their sandwiches. She did this regardless of whether they had bought a meal or brought their own lunch.

One fall day in 1937, a young man from East Stoneham came into Barjo's for the first time. He was with Jo's nephews, Rodney and Keith Grover, and their friends. They all had a sandwich and a Coke on the house.

"How are you doing today, boys?" Jo asked as she visited

with the schoolkids. "Are you all having a good day at school? What about lunch, did you have enough to eat?"

She especially enjoyed this part of her day. She wanted to look after the kids and to be sure the waitresses were, too.

After having some french fries with his sandwich, the new kid looked at Jo and said, "Would you like to have me bring you a peanut butter and jelly sandwich tomorrow?" He wanted to show his appreciation for her kindness to him.

"Sure," Jo replied, "I'd love one when you come in tomorrow."

The next day, in came the boy with a delighted expression on his face and Jo's sandwich in his hand. He passed it to her and said. "I'm so glad you accepted. When I told my mother how nice you were to all of us, she could hardly believe it."

Jo didn't like peanut butter and jelly sandwiches, but she didn't want to hurt the youngster's feeling when she accepted his offer. He never found this out.

Very early on, Jo realized that it was not just high school kids she wanted to give her food to. She fed many hundreds of wanderers, or tramps, as they were called, who didn't know where their next meal was coming from. If she spied them on the street, she invited them in for the same kind of hot meal with dessert as she was serving her clientele. Often, this would be a roast beef dinner with all the fixings, apple pie with ice cream and a steaming hot cup of coffee. The tramps had a regular route with different places marked to go. Barjo's was one of them.

"I never could tell you why I started giving to others," Jo said. "I guess I just wanted everybody to have a good hot meal. I remembered how poor we had been as children, and how hard it had been for Mother to feed our family with very little income, I never turned away anyone that was hungry."

Dr. Nelson, a local family doctor, would send a tramp to the restaurant to eat. Afterwards he always came by himself to pay for the tramp's dinner. He did not give the man money because the tramp might spend the money for "Canned Heat,"[38] which he would drink rather than for a square meal. One man in Norway was known to have died from drinking it. Many of the tramps and local drunks drank anything that had alcohol it, from vanilla extract, cheap perfume, Lydia Pinkham medicine, rubbing alcohol, oxbeef-iron tonic to "Canned Heat".

One colorful tramp wore a coonskin coat with all the fur worn off and had just one tooth. He claimed he had a brother who was a chef in Paris, France.

Jo went out often to visit with the tramps because they fascinated her. Many of the fellows had seen much of the world. Some had traveled from coast to coast by hiding in the boxcars of the trains or jumping on the caboose as the train pulled out from a station. Others had hiked and camped out in hobo jungles, often under bridges or near riverbanks, all over Europe.

The whole community knew Jo was a soft touch when misfortune was uppermost. But she was a most determined woman when it came to concealing what she did to help the unfortunate. She always preferred to stay in the background. If possible, she preferred to keep it from the person she had assisted.

"P. Y. thought I was foolish to feed them but I got a big thrill out of listening to their stories about their escapades all over the country," Jo exclaimed.

One afternoon, after Jo had gone home to rest, a waitress refused to serve a tramp. When he found out, P. Y. went down street, caught up with him and brought him back for some dinner. By then, Jo had taught P. Y. that giving to others was important, too. He had learned to have a little humility and show some hospitality to others.

But even with Jo's generosity, it was Vermont and not Norway that the tramps liked to go for the winter.

"They told me that they planned to break some small law," Jo said. "Nothing big, just enough to get a sentence of 30 to 90 days in the County Jail. Otherwise, the towns were only required to keep them overnight. The next day they had to move on."

The tramps liked to stay in the jails in Vermont because the facilities were better than in the jails in the other New England states. During those years, the town officials had to take people in, if they had no place to eat or sleep.

In the fall of 1937, another occurrence was about to happen that would go down in the history books as the event of the century for the Oxford Hills area. At Barjo Restaurant, Jo would become the beneficiary of a large increase in business as a result of this tragic incident.

---

37 *Jo's philosophy was based on Matthew 25:35 — "For I was hungry and you gave Me food; for I was thirsty and you gave Me drink; I was a stranger and you took Me in." and Matthew 25:40 — And Jesus answered, saying to the them, "…inasmuch as you did it unto the least of these my brethren, you did it unto me." KJV Loving Jesus, Jo, in her own way, was able to help others through Him.*

38 *This was similar to "Sterno" that is used today for camping equipment.*

CHAPTER 12

The Big Trial

In 1937, for the first time in the history of Oxford County, two violent murders took place. This brought shock waves of horror to the area. Television had not yet established its instantaneous on-the-scene reporting, but print media and network radio provided details of what had violated the peace and quiet of this sheltered community. Their accounts shocked the entire nation.

In North Arlington, New Jersey, on October 16, a few hours past dawn, patrolling police noticed a Buick sedan with Maine license plates parked at the side of the highway. The driver, who was asleep and appeared to be young, was unshaved. His foot was propped up on the dashboard. The police could see a hole in the bottom of his shoe. His disheveled appearance simply did not jibe with the expensive car he was driving. Suspecting him of vagrancy and possibly theft, the officers brought him to the police station for questioning. He was identified as Paul Dwyer of Paris Hill, Maine. Paul was taken inside while the officers examined the car further.

In the back seat, covered with clothing and luggage, an elderly woman's body, fully dressed, was crumpled on the floor. Paul Dwyer identified the body as that of Lydia Littlefield of South Paris. He told the startled police chief that the body of her husband, Dr. James G. Littlefield, bludgeoned and strangled, could be found in the trunk of the car. He was not the murderer, he said.

Paul Dwyer was a slightly-built boy, nineteen years old, who lived on Paris Hill with his mother. Jo knew him well.

"He was a quiet boy, who loved to dance and was well-liked by his classmates," Jo said. "I couldn't imagine Paul being involved in such a terrible crime. I felt he had been used as a pawn to cover the tracks of someone else who had really committed the murders."

Jo had also known the doctor and his wife well. They had been her customers, both at Barjo's and at Stone's Drug Store.

"No one could believe that our beloved Doctor Littlefield could possibly have died in such a horrible way. There seemed to

Regional newspaper clippings recount the details and chronicle the sensation caused by what came to be known as "the big trial."

be no rhyme or reason for the terrible things that happened," she comments with sadness even now after all these years.

There were many conflicting theories about the crime. Many thought it was a drug deal gone horribly wrong. Some neighbors mentioned having seen a Lincoln-Towne car that they thought was owned by drug dealers. A young man from Bryant Pond was reputed to be making deliveries in the area for the drug ring.

Another rumor had it that two young men from a prominent Norway family were involved. A bloody trench coat found buried in the area seemed to support that link.

Still another rumor pointed to a deep conspiracy involving the sheriff's department. Another possible suspect was at a card game at the home of a local druggist that night. Francis Carroll, an Oxford County deputy, had left that game suddenly at 7:30 p.m. and never returned to his friend's home. Where had he gone? People wanted to know.

However, Paul Dwyer was pointing the finger directly to himself. When the officers were returning him to Oxford County, Paul Dwyer signaled to a remote spot in New Gloucester near Crystal Lake where he claimed to have choked Mrs. Littlefield to death. On October 18, Paul Dwyer was arraigned in Cumberland County court and charged with murder for Mrs. Littlefield's death. The next day, he was returned to Oxford County where he was arraigned for Doctor Littlefield's murder. He pleaded guilty to both charges.

The trial date was set for November 30, 1937. In the meantime, Paul Dwyer began telling his attorneys quite a different story and changed his plea to innocent.

According to Dwyer, in the late summer of 1937, at the fairgrounds in Norway, he had confronted Francis Carroll, the Oxford County deputy. Paul told him that Carroll's daughter, Barbara, had written him letters accusing her father of sexually molesting her. Barbara and Paul Dwyer had gone together through their high school days. Dwyer had then revealed the sexual abuse charge to the doctor. To protect himself against public disclosure, Carroll had killed Dr. Littlefield. On the witness stand, Dwyer declared he loved Barbara and always would.

After three days, Dwyer retracted this plea and again pleaded guilty to the murder of Dr. Littlefield. In minutes, he was sentenced to the state prison in Thomaston at hard labor for life.

Three months later, in the safety and seclusion of his cell at the state prison, Dwyer now believed he could tell what he said was the truth. He wrote a seventeen-page statement and submitted it to the Prison Warden, John C. Welch. Meanwhile on the outside, rumors of a new development in the Doctor Littlefield murder case raised further doubt as to Dwyer's guilt.

On May 27, 1938, the most sensational phase of the Littlefield murder began with the arrest of the 43-year-old ex-deputy sheriff, Francis Carroll on a charge of incest.

By the time Carroll was arraigned in the Superior Court of Oxford County, on June 24th, he had been indicted for the murder of Doctor Littlefield as well. The question of who murdered Mrs. Littlefield was not included in the indictment. No one has ever been indicted for her murder.

At Carroll's trial, Paul Dwyer was the star witness. This is the story he told. When Paul confronted Carroll about Barbara's charge of incest, the deputy accused Paul of getting his daughter pregnant. He told Paul that he had made arrangements for Barbara to be examined by Doctor Littlefield. On October 13, they would all meet at Dwyer's home on Paris Hill at seven-thirty p.m. and go to the doctor's together. On that day, Dwyer caught up with the busy doctor at his office and they drove together to Dwyer's home. Carroll arrived ten minutes later.

Dwyer testified at the trial that Carroll said this to the doctor.

"What the hell are you doing here, Littlefield?" And Carroll turned to him and asked, "Is this a trap?"

"Where is Barbara?" the doctor asked.

"In the car," was his reply.

"Bring her in, I'll examine her upstairs," said the doctor.

Dwyer testified that Dr. Littlefield then walked to the foot of the stairs carrying on a conversation with Carroll. As the two men walked up the stairs together, the doctor threatened to drive Carroll out of the community.

"I suppose you know that this boy has got my girl in trouble," said Carroll.

The next thing Dwyer said he remembered was Dr. Littlefield at the top of the stairs doubled over with pain, his hands between his legs and Carroll standing over him. He saw Carroll strike the doctor two or three times on the head with a hammer. The doctor fell to the floor. Dwyer went to the second floor to assist his friend but the doctor was a large man, and Paul Dwyer was unable to move him. And Dwyer was forced to defend himself from Carroll's onslaught.

"Are you trying to kill him?" Dwyer said he asked Carroll.

"I didn't kill him! I'll go out to the car and get some whiskey to revive him," Carroll said, his voice thick from too much liquor.

"When he came back he didn't have whiskey, he had an automatic," Dwyer stated.

Describing the horror that transpired next, Dwyer stated that Carroll gripped the barrel of the gun and beat the doctor unconscious. Next, he ordered Dwyer to take off his belt and tighten it around the doctor's neck. Dwyer refused. Roughly, Carroll pulled off his own belt and did the job himself while Paul Dwyer held the doctor's head helplessly in his hands.

Carroll was halfway down the stairs dragging the body, when Dwyer caught up with him. Carroll ordered him to take the body and put it in the trunk of the doctor's Buick or be prepared to meet the same fate.

"I told him I couldn't do it alone and asked him to help me," Dwyer said. "He said, 'Roll him up in a blanket first.' I picked up the doctor's feet and Carroll took the head and shoulders. We carried the body to the trunk of the car."

"I argued with him," Dwyer said, "and told him Mrs. Littlefield knew where the doctor was. Finally I agreed to take the doctor's body and dispose of it."

As instructed by Carroll, later that same night, Dwyer picked up Mrs. Littlefield, telling her the doctor had had a car accident. He said the doctor had run down two men, panicked and then left town. Dr. Littlefield needed her, he told her.

Dwyer's mother was a nurse at the Hebron Sanitarium and had been a family friend of the Littlefields. Lydia Littlefield knew Paul well. Paul Dwyer had often chauffeured the Littlefields, so she was not surprised the doctor had sent him for her.

Dwyer drove to the Eagle Hotel, Concord, New Hampshire, where they registered at four a.m. Dwyer registered as Philip Davis and Mrs. Littlefield used her maiden name of Cummings. After driving most of the next day, ending up just outside of Boston, Massachusetts, he finally told Mrs. Littlefield that her husband had been killed. All the while, his body was just a few feet away in the trunk of the car.

Paul Dwyer was scared to death and had no idea which way to turn. Hoping that he could save Mrs. Littlefield's life, he drove back to South Paris by the shortest route possible. Thinking that maybe Carroll had realized what a mistake this had all been, Dwyer parked in front of a small store in front of Carroll's home on High Street.

It was late and the night was dark and forbidding as Carroll came to the door, gun in hand. He told Dwyer to drive to Turkey Hill, a short distance from the house. Before Paul Dwyer reached his destination, Carroll stopped him on Prospect Avenue.

"You know too much, old woman. I can't have you blabbing your mouth," Carroll said to Mrs. Littlefield.

Carroll came around to the front seat and strangled Mrs. Littlefield with his bare hands.

"Paul, you know what I told you. Now get out of town or you'll have to pay the consequences."

Carroll left and walked back to his home.

Overwhelmed, Paul Dwyer dragged Mrs. Littlefield's body to the back seat and covered her with any thing he could find. Not having any idea what to do next, he got into the driver's seat and drove until he could drive no longer. That was when the New Jersey police found him.

Inside the courtroom that June and July of 1938, men sweltered and ladies on the back benches dipped contentedly into small boxes of ice cream while the grisly details were recited. It was a Roman holiday, providing entertainment for everyone except the unfortunate elderly couple who had provided it.

Many people in Norway and South Paris benefited from the business the Littlefield trial brought to the community. Barjo's became the headquarters for many of the visiting press. One reporter from the Boston Post set up shop in the back booth at the restaurant. Because rumors flew left and right, he interviewed anyone who would talk to him trying to get a scoop for his paper. Barjo's business increased dramatically and the trial proved to be a bonanza for Jo's struggling restaurant enterprise.

Beal's Tavern (later to be Hotel Stone) was filled to capacity with spectators and reporters from out-of-town. The local merchants sold souvenirs and mementos to the many visitors who had come to hear the gory details of the Littlefield murders.

An enterprising teenager set up a newsstand at the corner of Cottage and Main Street. One afternoon, Barbara who was 9 came running into Barjo's to ask her mother, "Can I help Walter sell newspapers? He told me I could help him if you agreed."

"O.K.," Jo said to her. "But remember don't stay too long. I want you back here in an hour."

Ashley Bean and "Chinny" Briggs set up a hot dog stand near the court house in South Paris, where spectators jammed the courtroom. They sold hot dogs, sandwiches and cold drinks to the public attending the trial.[39]

For ten grim days, a parade of witnesses arrived and departed. Several, including Carroll's daughter and one of his fellow deputies, were never allowed on the witness stand. Carroll was convicted of Doctor Littlefield's murder in July 1938, but again no charges were made in Mrs. Littlefield's death.

Francis Carroll joined Paul Dwyer who was serving a life sentence at the state prison at Thomaston.

Barbara Carroll was a good student, but at the trial her father told the court she wasn't physically or mentally capable to testify. One of the deputies involved had moved out of state. Because of the interference by the sheriff, he was never allowed to come any nearer than Waterville, Maine. His testimony could have cleared up many of the unanswered questions and discrepancies in the testimony at the trial.

"I knew that deputy well," Jo commented. "Later, he told me how he had been stopped from returning to town on several occasions. He was well aware why. He knew too much and could have exposed the corruption that existed in the area at the time."[40]

On September 20, 1950, Francis Carroll was released on a "writ of habeas corpus," after serving twelve years in prison. His attorneys stated that the state had committed an illegal act by convicting two men for the same murder, making this fact the basis for his discharge from prison.

For years, two of Jo's friends, Ruth Cushman and Ruth Twitchell, who were schoolteachers, wrote letters to the Governor and the legislatures and hired lawyers to prove Paul's innocence. The only thing they asked of him was to have dinner with them when he was paroled. After the two women's hard work, Paul Dwyer was released in 1959 after serving twenty-one years for a crime he may or may not have committed. But he refused to keep his promise to them.

When Paul Dwyer was paroled, he had no place to go. The prison claimed he was trained to be an accountant, but no one was willing to hire him. Many of the local people didn't want him to return but he had a lot of supporters, too. One of them was Jo.

"My friends came to me and asked me if I would give Paul a job when he left prison," Jo said. "This was the only time in her life that Barbara questioned something I was going to do. She didn't think Paul Dwyer should work for us."

Upon Paul Dwyer's release from Maine State Prison, Jo and Stony gave him a job at Hotel Stone. Jo had a lot of faith that Paul would tell the truth and disclose what had actually happened that October night.

"He was just a good everyday kid and had many friends. He was in the restaurant all the time," Jo commented. "Ruth Cushman came to me and asked me to be careful what I said to the parole officer when he checked on Paul. The joke was on the girls. His parole officer had been a basketball referee when I played basketball. I knew him well."

Paul Dwyer never did tell anyone what really happened, even though the general public asked many questions. Parade

Magazine did a story on his life, but he revealed no new insight into why he had been willing to serve a good part of his life for the crime. When the parole officer found out about his interview with Parade, the publication was forbidden to print the rest of Paul Dwyer's story.

"I never knew whether he was too scared to tell the truth because he was guilty or whether someone had threatened to kill him if he did tell the truth," Jo said.

Two books, "New England Gothic" and "Thunder over South Parrish" by Adamerson Allen have been written about this trial. The first, a hard cover edition, is probably the most accurate. The second book, a paperback edition, is the more colorful of the two, but both are based on the facts of the case using fictitious names and settings. Both books are in the local libraries.

Many thought Paul Dwyer was neither able nor had good reason to commit the crimes.

Paul Dwyer married Caroline Pinkos but the marriage didn't last. After leaving Norway, he married for a second time and had a son. He has since passed away. None of the people who were directly involved in the murders are now living, so the mystery of Doctor Littlefield's murder and that of his wife, Lydia, will never be known.

It was a long time before the local people stopped talking about the "Trial of the Century." To this day, hearsay and rumors float around about what and who were or might have been involved in the murders.

As the 1930's came to a close, Norway was beginning to recover from the "Great Depression." At the restaurant, Jo was beginning to get better organized and had expanded her menu to include breakfast. With a larger menu, the restaurant business was growing. She was becoming adept at her career in the business world and was showing that she had the making of a sharp businesswoman.

---

[39] *After the trial, this venture would grow into "Bean's Restaurant" on Main Street, South Paris. When the boys were first learning the restaurant business, they came to Barjo's where Jo and Stony, her cook, taught them a lot about restaurant cooking and how to make many dishes.*

[40] *In 1998, the last person who had been a part of the Oxford County Sheriff's Department in 1937 passed away. None of the principals in the Doctor Littlefield case ever revealed what they knew and now it will always remain a mystery.*

CHAPTER 13

What to Do Now?

Many other things were happening in 1938: the war was heating up in Europe, World's Fairs were being planned for New York and San Francisco, and in the town of Norway, a new public library was being built.

The town already had a library, but space was limited. In 1885, a group of citizens had organized the Norway Library Association and started a subscription library in the old Reformers' Hall. Interest was keen from the start with a nucleus of two hundred members.

In 1892, the town voted to take over the library, now officially named the Norway Public Library. Two rooms over the L. M. Longley & Son store on Main Street served as the library's home. By the mid-1930's, the books were stacked from floor to ceiling in those two rooms. It was very crowded.

Then Mrs. Maude Kammerling came into the picture. Her family roots in Norway dated back well before the Civil War. Maude Kammerling's grandparents were Jonathan and Elizabeth Blake. (Elizabeth Blake had been a Crockett after whom Crockett Ridge in Norway was named.) Her parents were Albert and Mary Blake Thompson. Thompson family interests included the lumber and mining industry in the local area.

Maude Kammerling had studied music in Paris, France, and gave up a promising music career to come back to the United States in order to manage the family businesses after the death of her father and brother.

In the winter, she lived in Stark, New Hampshire. Because of her roots in Norway, she came to her adopted town to spend her summers. She was a regular summer visitor at both Stone's Drug Store and, later, at Barjo's. She wore large hats that Jo had only seen worn by actresses in movies. Jo was also struck by Mrs. Kammerling's grace and style and by her generosity to the town.

A world traveler, Mrs. Kammerling had acquired mannerisms that also fascinated Jo. For instance, as she walked down Norway's Main Street, she smoked a cigarette in an elegant, long-

Norway Public Library was established in 1885. The new facility, which still serves the town today, was built in 1938.

Fire damage to Barjo's upper stories is evident in this 1940 photo.

Donnie, left: at age 6, dressed for work; right: with Barbara's bike in front of Barjo's.

stemmed holder. This was an unusual sight in a country town, as women did not smoke in public in those days.

Recognizing the town of Norway needed a larger library, Mrs. Kammerling decided a new facility would be a perfect memorial to her parents and her brother. She let it be known that if the town would provide a suitable location, she would fund a new building and equip it. Even before the town had accepted her offer, she researched library building styles to find one suitable for Norway.

A lot at the corner of Main Street and Greenleaf Avenue was obtained from Miss Isabelle Whitcomb who agreed to donate the property in exchange for $2,242.77 owed in back taxes and a stipulation that the lot must be used for a public building. The original building owned by her father, W. H. Whitcomb, had been destroyed in the fire of 1894 and never replaced. Trees and bushes had grown where their home once stood.

Library officials were pleased with the new site, but they were concerned with having an adequate endowment to maintain the institution. They wired Mrs. Kammerling, suggesting that once the library had been constructed, it be endowed. She cabled from Europe "increased upkeep guaranteed."

Returning to the United States, she hired the architect, William B. Coffin of Boston. The library would be a two-story brick building of Colonial design with majestic columns at the front entrance. Philip D. Wright of Norway submitted a low construction bid of $31,190 (fifty years ago that must have looked like a misprint since the figure would have been considered large). In May 1938, the construction began and was completed in December of the same year.

The Norway Memorial Library was dedicated to the memory of Mrs. Kammerling's parents, Albert and Mary Blake Thompson, on December 18, 1938. Winnie McKeen Bickford,[41] Jo's cousin, became Norway's Librarian in January 1938. Under her direction, 9000 books were moved from the L. M. Longley building to the new library. It was a massive undertaking. In the past, no matter what anyone was looking for, whether for research or just for enjoyment, Winnie Bickford had a knack of finding the right book in the crowded stacks. What a relief it was to her to be able, for the first time, to properly store all the books on the new library shelves. Winnie Bickford continued as Norway's Librarian for over twenty-five years.

In addition to funding the library, Maude Kammerling was a generous benefactor of the Universalist Church and later, made a major contribution to the new hospital building fund.

On April 4, 1938, Jo made the final payment on the mortgage for the restaurant's fixtures and equipment. It was held by E.F. Jackson's in Auburn. This mortgage had been incurred by her brother, Donald in 1934 and had been one of the obligations that Jo had incurred in 1937 at the dissolution of the Marjo's partnership. For the first time, Jo had a clear title to Barjo's. By court order, the restaurant was still in P. Y.'s name, even though both their names were on the final discharge papers. With P. Y.'s financial expertise and guidance, Jo had finally paid off all the outstanding obligations. For the last three years, ever since Jo had come back to work at McAllister's in 1935, that mortgage had been a constant reminder of the past. Now, she would be able move on and look to the future. Being able to apply the profits from the restaurant to making some improvements at Barjo's, Jo felt she was now truly on her own.

"What a relief that was!" Jo exclaimed. "Now I could concentrate on the daily operation of the restaurant and know that all I owed were current bills for my own business."

On February 19, 1940, Jo bought the restaurant building at 210 Main Street, where she and Barjo's would be for the next six decades. It was a two and one-half story building with Frank Bjorklund's law office and an apartment on the second floor.

She obtained a mortgage for $2,500 from Norway National Bank to finance buying the building and real estate from Louis Brooks. No longer would Jo have to worry about a lease or having to pay rent. Since her business was now showing a profit, she felt the purchase was a good investment.

It wasn't long before misfortune struck. On a Sunday night in late March, on the eve before a new diner was to open in town, the Barjo's restaurant building caught fire. Jo was working in the kitchen preparing food to be sure she was ready for the next day's business. Told that the upstairs of the building was on fire, she had so much faith in the fire department that she ignored their warnings and kept right on baking. Finally, when danger of the whole building becoming engulfed in flames seemed imminent, the firemen forced her to leave.

After the Norway Fire Department put the fire out, the lights didn't work and the ceiling was hanging down in spots. Fifteen minutes after the fire whistle in the clock tower of the Opera House block blew the "all out," the firemen rigged the restaurant up with some Christmas lights and hoisted up the soggy, sagging ceiling with two-by-four beams. They just sort of built it up around the customers. Not a customer left, and Jo only missed serving breakfast Monday morning.

The fire caused all the ice cream in the fountain to begin melting. Jo went out on the street and found all the children she could and treated them all to free ice cream. As was her way, she felt someone should get the good out of the ice cream before it melted and couldn't be used. Walter Bennett was one of those kids and, to this day, he never fails to mention how much all the children appreciated her kindness.

Interviewing Jo later, a reporter asked, "What about that new diner that opened the day of the fire? What happened to it?"

The diner had lasted for only several months before closing. But, it had been a threat Jo had been concerned about on the night of the fire.

Jo successfully met the challenge posed by the fire. She assured her loyal customers she would continue to serve them. She had established a solid and stable business and didn't want to lose their trust. She knew that this was another crisis that she would have to overcome. With God's guidance, she knew that she would be able to. P. Y.'s support would help her rebuild.

With the many challenges they had faced together, P. Y. and Jo had mutual respect for each other's ability. Jo admired P. Y. for all the guidance he had given her and his expertise in the financial world. While he respected Jo for her ability to accept adversity, use her common sense, aim for a higher goal, and then work hard to accomplish it.

Jo had only a minimum amount of insurance. How was she to raise enough money to rebuild, she wondered as she looked at her newly acquired building? In 1940, the Depression was still felt and money was tight. A loan seemed out of the question.

P. Y. contacted Phil Wright and got an estimate for renovations and rebuilding. When the insurance money came in, he applied it to the purchase of materials. What P. Y. didn't tell Jo was that he was studying the situation further and was making other arrangements to secure financing. He went to the directors of the Norway National Bank and asked them to refinance the original mortgage obtained on February 19, 1940, for the land and buildings. Through this process he was able to obtain an additional $2,000. On June 4, a new real estate mortgage was written for $4,500.

After a talk with his good friend, Ed Cummings, P. Y. decided to engage the help of their friends to raise the rest of the money. On June 11, P. Y. enlisted Phil Wright, Ray Eastman, David Klain, Stuart Goodwin, James Favor, Ed Cummings and

Charles Cummings, who signed two notes. One of the notes was on P. Y.'s cottage and the other was on the furniture and fixtures, each for $1,500—to back up a master note at Norway National Bank for $3,000. This additional money took care of the remainder of the renovations. Jo was able to pay off the two mortgages at the Norway National Bank in July 1943.

Philip Wright did all the renovations on the restaurant building. Jo decided not to have any more apartments on the second floor. It was in one of the apartments in the original building that the fire had started. She didn't want to have to worry about that happening again. The building was rebuilt to one and one half stories with the second floor used as storage.

Prior to the fire, George Hill, who owned a car dealership on one side of Barjo's, and E.B.Jackson, who owned the grocery store on the other side, had tried to prove that Jo owned less property than the recorded deeds showed, including a right-of-way between the two buildings.

"When the men realized that I had bought the building," Jo commented, "they were determined to squeeze me on both sides by telling me that I owned very little land. Later, when the building burned, they were sure they had succeeded. But they had underestimated P. Y.'s legal mind and my determination."

To straighten out the legal tangles, P. Y. insisted that the Barjo property be surveyed in the summer of 1940. This proved that it was George Hill's building that sat on the restaurant's property line. The survey also showed that Jo owned one half of the alley between Barjo's and Jackson's Market, making it clearly illegal for Jackson to block off the alley between their buildings.

In the fall of 1940, P. Y. was worried that the United States was going to get involved in World War II. Hitler had already invaded his European neighbors and was threatening Great Britain. It looked like it would only be a matter of time before the United States became involved. The United States was just beginning to get back on its feet after the Depression.

P. Y. was concerned with the effect war would have on the business community and the state of Maine. Many of the summer customers at Barjo's were from out of state. Would they still vacation in Maine or would this source of income for the restaurant dry up? He knew that Jo was going to need all the income the restaurant could generate to pay off the debts from the fire.

P. Y. was taken seriously ill in November 1940. He had injured his back on a hunting trip and never fully recovered. At first, he was hospitalized at the Maine General Hospital, but he suffered complications from his sugar diabetes, which stalls the healing process. When the Portland hospital felt they done all that they could for him, he was sent to Deaconess Hospital in Boston.

One of her friends drove Jo to Boston to see him. She borrowed $200 from Stony so she would have ready cash in her pocket if some emergency arose while they were in Boston. When Jo arrived, the doctors told her there was no hope for P. Y.'s recovery. All the medical procedures they had tried to save him had failed. Nothing more could be done.

On December first, P. Y. died.

The next day was a cold, bleak December day. Jo waited at the South Paris station for the train to arrive bringing P. Y. Fogg's body home from Boston. In the distance, the mournful, wailing sound of the train whistle hung in the air as the train pulled into the station. To this day, when Jo hears a train whistle, it reminds her of that very sad day in her life.

There followed one of the darkest times in Jo's life, when she really didn't know which way to turn. P. Y. had been there for her when her family had turned their backs on her. He had given her business and financial advice and guided her through two major turning points in her life. At the restaurant, he had helped her to establish her business and her self-confidence.

Now he was gone.

During these difficult years, the only family members who had stood by her were Aunt Nettie and her family. Still by Jo's side, Aunt Nettie was the only family member who attended P. Y. Fogg's funeral.

It was only with God's guidance that Jo was able to carry on. From the time she was a small child, Mother had taught her to pray to God. Although it was hard for her to understand, God was shaping her future in many ways. Praying to Him at night and when she awoke in the morning, the solution to her problems had seemed to be clear. Now, in her grief, Jo prayed even harder to do God's Will in her business and asked Him to help her cope with the problems with her family.

Although she had just become a widow for the second time in ten years, Jo's first concern was for Barbara. P. Y. had always been very kind and considerate, guiding Barbara through the loss of her father and grandfather. Now he, too, was gone.

After P. Y.'s death, finding a babysitter was hard, but Jo was able to hire Mrs. Adams once again so that Barbara could stay at home. Barbara had just turned thirteen and Donnie was seven. Even though Donald and Jo still hadn't resolved their difference, the two cousins became closer than ever.

The next summer, Barbara, Donnie and Mrs. Adams stayed at the cottage for the summer. They came down Lake Pennesseewassee in a row boat. To come to the village, Barbara would row to the head of Main Street, a distance of over a mile. They stopped at the boat landing by the bridge and walk down to Barjo's for lunch. When Jo asked what they would like, Donnie always said, "I'll have a ham sandwich."

Ask him what he would like today, fifty years later, and he will say the same thing, "I'll have a ham sandwich."

"The kids loved it at the cottage," Jo said. "Without Mrs. Adams, I wouldn't have dared to let them go. Barbara loved to swim and so did Donnie. P. Y. had taught her to be careful around the water. His boat and fishing equipment were still there, so they could go fishing when they wanted to. It helped her overcome her sadness about his death, doing things at the lake that they had done together."

From the time Jo met Stony, in 1936, she realized what a good worker he was. During Jo's time of crisis after P. Y.'s death, they grew closer. Stony volunteered to help her in many ways and they worked together much of the time at the restaurant. Soon a bond began to form between them. Stony was kind to Barbara, which meant a lot to Jo. Jo didn't drive, so Stony often volunteered to take them to Naples to see Barbara's Meserve aunts or to some other social event.

In 1941, roller-skating was all the rage. The roller-rink in Oxford was where the kids went for a good time.

"Barbara wanted to learn to skate, so I got Stony to drive us to the roller-rink. The first people we met were my cousins, 'The Curtain Eaters'. Even though they were a lot older than Barbara, they offered to teach us how to skate," Jo said.

After accepting their offer for a lesson, Barbara turned to her mother and said, "You hadn't better learn to skate. You might break a leg and you're the only one who can support us."

"Losing her father and P. Y. had made her think twice about what I should do," Jo said.

Even though the relationship between Jo and her family was still strained, Barbara had continued to visit with her grandmother and Margaret at their Deering Street home. Donnie's parents, Donald and Mildred, had continued their practice of inviting Barbara for an occasion dinner at their home on Water Street.

Being cared for by hired women was hard for Donnie. Both

his mother and father worked during the day. Because of the limitations placed on the family by Freddie's illness, Donnie's social life centered on Barjo's. Aunt Jo and Cousin Barbara became the ones who helped him to entertain his friends. Wherever Barbara went, he wanted to go, too. She always took him along, whether to the movies or some other thing they could do together.

His personality was, in many ways, a reflection of Jo's own. He, too, loved to be with people and he knew all the clerks in the stores on Main Street and the customers at the restaurant. His experience as a child proved to be a foundation for his work in later life as Norway's historian.

On his fourth birthday, Jo organized a birthday party for him at Barjo's. She told him to invite all his friends. When the youngsters didn't come because they were afraid his brother, Freddie, would be there, Jo went out on Main Street and invited everyone she knew. The party was a huge success, thanks to his Aunt Jo.

"It really didn't make any difference to Donnie whether they were four or ninety-four," Jo said. "He made friends easily because of his outgoing personality."

Being part of the restaurant family was a big part of Donnie's life. At eight, he was too young to be much help, but Jo made him feel like one of the crew. He loved to come to Barjo's where the girls dressed him up in their headbands and aprons.

"Occasionally, Donnie asked if he could wait on tables," Jo said. "Sometimes he stayed a half hour, other times, longer."

Being observant, Donnie noticed a customer had put two teaspoons of sugar in his coffee.

Donnie said to him, "Mister, aren't you afraid you'll get sugar diabetes? Wasn't that a mistake to put extra sugar in your coffee?"

"The man gave him a smile and thanked him for his concern," Jo said with a laugh. "I told him not to say anything next time."

Jo kept an eagle eye on him to see that he paid attention to his customers. Making sure of he was up to was a full-time job.

"I never was quite sure what he was going to do next," she said. "He liked to help the girls, but he was easily distracted. He might decide to go visiting downstreet in the middle of a rush hour, instead of waiting on the customers."

One afternoon, Barbara had gone to Lewiston with her friends and Donnie was lonesome. He went off to see the office girls at C. B. Cummings & Sons mill and then downstreet visiting with everybody in the stores. Returning to the restaurant, he found Jo in the kitchen. She had just finished serving lunch.

"Aunt Jo, would you go to the movies with me this afternoon," he asked. "I don't know what to do with myself."

She agreed. Donnie went home to change his clothes. Back he came all dressed up in his white shirt, sports jacket, flashy tie and gray, felt hat with a feather in the hatband.

Ready for his big date, Donnie asked, "Why didn't you change your clothes, Aunt Jo?"

"I didn't have time," Jo said. "I knew you would be disappointed, but I have to come right back to work."

As they were walking down Main Street to the Rex Theater for the afternoon matinee, he looked up at her.

"Aunt Jo," he said, "did you remember to bring your Tums?"

"This was a personal joke between us," she said. "You know the old slogan, 'Tums for your Tummy'. Sometime before, I had said to him, 'Don't eat too much popcorn at the movies. You'll have a tummy-ache'."

Every time there was a parade, the crew at Barjo's would go out on the front steps to watch it go by. Harley Stevens and his beautiful high-stepping horse that kept time to the music led Norway's parades. Next were the color guards from several organizations carrying the flags. Donnie loved the rhythm of the band. He felt honored to march along behind them with his Scout troop, in military precision to the music. During the 1940's, all the young people in town, including Donnie, thought being in a parade behind the marching band was a big deal.

One Memorial Day as Donnie went by, Jo teased him with cheering and loud laughter and shouts of encouragement.

"You're doing a tremendous job, Donnie! Keep up the good work!" she shouted.

"Don't you ever come out and holler at me again! Don't you know my scout leader is a minister," Donnie later scolded his aunt. "Don't you know I just joined the Scouts and the scout master doesn't know you are my aunt."

After the Memorial Day parade, the American Legion gave the kids ice cream tickets as a reward for marching. Donnie and his friends cashed theirs in at Barjo's because he thought his aunt would give them a double scoop. Barbara went to Ashton's Drug Store with her friends.

"To me," Barbara said, "it wasn't a treat at Barjo's, so I went to Ashton's, where Aunt Marg was working. She always treated me with special attention. If I went Barjo's, I knew that I would probably have to get my own ice cream or help Mother dip cones for the other kids."

During that era, fireworks were legal and one of the big events of the summer was the Fourth of July. The three local drug stores in town sold fireworks. Later, Barjo's also sold them. The

Town of Norway was ablaze with all kinds, sizes, and descriptions of brilliant displays. Everyone in town stayed up all night to enjoy the fun. A variety of fireworks were shot the whole length of Main Street. The kids had Norway's police officer, Frank Lafrance, beside himself trying to keep up with their antics.

Fireworks were popular, too, with people who owned cottages around Norway Lake, as well with the owners of the boys' and girls' camps on the lakes in the area. Mrs. Brewster from Birch Rock Camp on McWain Pond in East Waterford, was one who bought fireworks to shoot off over the lake for her campers.

Donnie was going to help sell fireworks one year, but he decided that shooting off "rockets" with the other boys would be a lot more fun. One of the rockets misfired and ended up in the office of Frank Bjorklund, on the second floor of the restaurant. That accident caused no major damage, but gave all the kids a good scare. Selling the fireworks ended up being Stony's job, while Donnie and the other boys had a ball. With many bangs and blasts of other rockets, the night sky was aglow.

During Firemen's Carnival Week in the middle of July, there was a parade every night. It was a big week for the kids in town. Donnie was no exception. He wanted to be in every parade.

Because his parents were both working, one of his neighbors, "Mama Card" as Donnie called her, helped him with his costumes. If it was the bicycle parade, she helped him decorate the wheels with crepe paper and made him a costume to match.

If it was the Horribles parade, she dressed him up in a pair of red baggy pants three sizes too big or something equally ridiculous. Old-fashioned bright yellow suspenders held up his pants. His shirt was made from an old burlap grain bag with all kinds of medals hanging from it. She made him a black stovepipe hat from cardboard, with a bright ribbon for a hatband, sticking in some yellow flowers for decorations.

"Donnie didn't care if he won a prize," Jo said. "He just enjoyed marching to the fairgrounds with the other kids."

One afternoon, Donnie felt sad because Barbara went to Lewiston to do her Christmas shopping with her friends and didn't invite him.

"Aunt Jo, what can I do? Maybe I could go Christmas shopping downstreet, if you could give me some change?" he sighed.

Jo gave him some money to spend. He asked her to change the bills to pennies. He shopped all day on Main Street, making the merchants wait while he count out his pennies.

Wanting to share his secrets with someone when he came

home, he sat down with one of the girls at Barjo's.

"Guess what I have been doing all afternoon," he said to her excitedly. "I've been buying Christmas presents for all my friends. Let me show you what I got."

It was the first time he had done his shopping alone and he was thrilled. Christmas seemed to him to be too long to wait to share his gifts.

Attending Sunday School and church with Barbara was an important part of Donnie's childhood. Both his parents worked for the church, preparing food for church suppers and participating in the events of the Second Congregational Church Circle.

One day after church, Judge A. J. Stearns and the minister were talking when they noticed that Donnie was still there.

They turned around and noticed Donnie standing at the back of the church. Wondering why he was still there when everyone else had gone, the minister said to him, "Donnie is there something we can do for you?"

"Well, gentlemen, I have been thinking whether I want to become a minister or a lawyer," Donnie told them quite seriously. "I have decided to be a minister because all I would have to buy is a Bible."

Little did Donnie know how right he was and that there would be even greater things to come in his life as a clergyman.

In 1941, Jo was about to see all P. Y.'s predictions come true about the war and the economy. But the impact on her business would be much different than the scenario that P. Y. had foreseen. The conditions in the country were to take a dramatic turn. Barjo's would benefit from many of these changes.

---

41 *Winnie McKeen Bickford was Jo's cousin who chummed with her sister, Helen. Jo had played many practical jokes on Winnie when they were living in East Stoneham.*

PART IV

The War Years

Ralph Stone in the Barjo's kitchen, 1941

Stony, home on leave, and Jo, 1943

The Barjo's Crew, 1944

*L—R: Jo, Barbara, Margaret, Jack Smith, Gina Olson, Susie Olmstead,
Roland Curtis, Barbara McAllister (Lawrence).*

CHAPTER 14

The Beginning of World War II

After the attack on Pearl Harbor on December 7, 1941, the United States became involved in World War II. Because most of the young men were drafted, there were fewer workers left at home. To make up for the lack of numbers, those who were left, whether teenagers or older people, had to work day and night. Everybody put up willingly with hardships for the good of the country and the love for their fellows. Interestingly enough as a result of this hard work, many people were able to start saving money for the first time since 1930.

The first hint of World War II in Norway came when the government sent a unit of U.S. Army troops to guard the bridge at the head of Main Street. Maine, being the nearest point to Europe, was considered vulnerable to attack from the Germans. Many such divisions of the Army were used to guard the infrastructure of the United States.

The construction of the Norway Armory had been completed, but the food facilities there had not. The soldiers slept at the Armory and local people took turns cooking for them.

The Norway National Guard, "Company C," was called to service. Some went to Europe and fought in the Battle of the Bulge and the March through the Black Forest under the Command of Gen. George C. Patton. Others went to the South Pacific: Midway Island, Wake Island, the Marshall Islands, North Marianas, and Japan. Some of the officers from Norway were Harry Twitchell, Lowell Henley, Lewis Olmstead and Frank Thompson.

Because there were few places high school kids could work, many Norway-area boys worked at Barjo's. When they went to enlist, they cited either Barjo's Restaurant or Josephine Stone as a previous employer on the government service forms.

After a while, the Army recruiter in Portland began to say to the enlistees from the Norway area, "Please don't tell me that you worked at Barjo Restaurant or for Josephine Stone!"

"I don't know why the recruiter was so amazed," Jo commented with a wry smile. "There weren't many places for high school boys to work so lots of them had worked for me."

During the Omaha Beach campaign under Gen. Patton, Jo's nephew, Helen's son, Keith Grover, was killed. Sarah Grover and her husband, Keith's aunt and uncle lost two sons at the same time. The loss of these young men and of many of their friends saddened the community.

"Keith was going to the University of Maine when he was called to serve his country," Jo said. "Before he left, he went to see all his relatives to say good-bye. It was kind of eerie. Looking back, I think, in his own mind, he thought it was the last time that he would ever see us. I don't think Helen ever got over his loss."

Keith's brothers, Rodney and Dwight, served in the South Pacific and returned home safely.

Many times, letters from home failed to reach the young soldiers because of the pace of their assault on the Germans. They never knew how much they were missed by family and friends.

The towns had many blackouts during the war years. These were for training in the event that the enemy attacked. The firemen and the Norway Women's Relief Corps (WRC), a branch of the American Red Cross, patrolled the streets to be sure the laws were obeyed. The members of the WRC drove an ambulance, a gift from Victorine Blanchard. They checked that all lights had been turned out or the windows covered with black cloth. Among those on the WRC patrol was Jo's sister, Margaret.

"Marg was the last one in the family that you would have expected to go out at night walking around the dark streets," Jo said. "Because of her sickness when she was in her teens, it took a lot of courage for her to risk her health to volunteer to serve her country in this way."

Others in the family served in their own ways. Grace's husband, Elliot Cummings, his father, Edwin, and other members of their family owned C. B. Cummings & Sons in Norway. At the machine shop of the mill, Eliot designed a part for submarines. This part had to be perfected to 1/1000 of an inch. The mill was able to perform this fine work with the help of Virginia Luce, a local woman, who did the measuring.

Many from Norway and the surrounding towns worked at Bath Iron Works in Bath and the shipyard in South Portland. They did work for the Department of Defense on United States ships and submarines. Jo's brother Donald worked at the shipyard in South Portland all during World War II, traveling back and forth daily to South Portland with some others from Norway.

While Don was working there, he developed a hearing problem from all the noise. The machinery that was used at the shipyard caused many people to go deaf.

In January 1942, Stony enlisted in the Army Air Force,[42] and served until January 1946. As mess sergeant, he ran the food facilities in officers clubs at bases in Florida, Indiana, New Hampshire and at the "Base under the Ice" in Iceland.

The local company, Snocraft,[43] furnished the snowshoes and toboggans used at that base. The company also made a snowshoe called the "Bear Paw," that was used on the rugged terrain of the Arctic. American soldiers used Snocraft toboggans to haul supplies and weapons, both in the Arctic and in Europe.

Jo had waited on Fred Foster and his family many times at Stone's Drugstore and Barjo's. Fred was one of the weavers at Snocraft during the war. He used strips of rawhide that had been soaked in a vat for several hours to soften it. It was then woven into a white ash frame to form the main part of the snowshoes. His young daughter, Emily, was fascinating by how fast his fingers flew as he twisted and tied the rawhide to the snowshoe.

It was really hard for Jo with Stony gone. Two fellows worked for her, Bob in the kitchen and Allie in the dining room. Allie had lost one arm in an industrial accident. Although he had only one arm, he could dip ice cream as well with one arm as someone who had both. He anchored the cone in a milk bottle with his hook and then dipped the ice cream with his good hand.

He and Bob didn't get along and were constantly trying to do something to make the other one look bad. One afternoon, Jo went home for a few minutes. When she got back, one of them had put something in the batches of ice cream she was ready to freeze. The cream was curdled and had to be thrown away. She let them both go shortly after that incident.

After P. Y.'s death, Jo's mother seemed to reconcile to the fact that Jo was making a success of the restaurant.

"I got the feeling that P. Y.'s death had solved some of my problems with the family. I never had understood why Mother and Pa had been so against my friendship and then my marriage to P. Y.," Jo said. "It was as though their feelings were so resolute that anything he did to help me establish the restaurant and make it profitable was all wrong in their eyes."

When Stony left for the war, Jo took over the entire operation of the kitchen as well as the dining room. She knew that Margaret would never have left the restaurant in the first place, if their parents hadn't interfered. The two sisters, Jo and Margaret, had worked together at Stone's Drug Store and had never had an unhappy moments there.

Jo took it upon herself to be sure that that everyone who

entered Barjo's was made to feel welcome. Customers enjoyed having someone to talk with who cared about them. With all the tragedy of the war, people needed a listening ear.

Because Margaret was still working on Main Street at Ashton's, customers did not forget her. Many remembered when Jo and Margaret had worked together, first at Stone's Drug Store and later at McAllister's Restaurant and Marjo's.

With Stony in the military service, Jo could see she needed Margaret to help her run the restaurant. Jo came to the decision during "Oxford County Fair Week" in September 1942. With Margaret's ability to handle the help and run the cash register, Jo felt she would be able to return full time to the kitchen to run it more efficiently. Jo sent Barbara down to Margaret's home on her bicycle.

"Please ask your Aunt Marg if she would come back to work at the restaurant," she said to Barbara.

"I'll go ask her, but I don't think she'll come," Barbara said.

When she came back, Margaret was with her.

When Margaret came in, Jo exclaimed, "Hurray, here you are! Marg, I really need your help. With Stony gone, it is impossible for me to be in two places at once. If you will manage the dining room for me, I'll do the cooking."

"I'll help out all I can, but I have to work a two week notice for Lester Ashton," Margaret explained to Jo. "After that I will be back to help you full-time."

Barbara handed Margaret an order book and showed her where the silverware was. Then she said to Margaret, "Here you are, Aunt Marg, I'll see you later. I'm going to the Fair."

Wanting to do something more for Margaret and Mother, Jo gave Margaret $1,000 to deposit in her savings account to help run their home. Margaret refused to accept the money—saying the tellers would wonder how she had gotten the money. She finally accepted the money under the condition that Barbara was to go to the bank with her when she made the deposit.

"Margaret was afraid someone would think she had stolen the money," Jo said. "Nobody would say that, but I couldn't convince her. Margaret was the most honest person in the world. With Barbara at her side, she finally agreed to take the money."

In the spring of 1943, Jo wanted Marg to have a nice suit, hat and shoes for Easter. As a result of her generosity, however, Jo couldn't afford to buy a new Easter outfit for herself, too, so she bought just one—for Margaret.

"She loved to dress up, so I sent her to Ward Brothers in Lewiston to pick out her outfit," Jo said. "When Margaret was young, she hadn't been able to go out as much as the rest of us because of her sickness. I wanted to make up for that for her."

Margaret worked for Jo for the next fifty years and retired only when she had back surgery and was no longer able to come to the restaurant. She handled the cash, the bookkeeping and the payroll as well as managed the dining room.

After leaving the restaurant, Allie began selling liquor on the side. Norway was a "dry" town. There was a State of Maine liquor store, but no other stores or restaurants sold or served liquor. Allie went around to all the business people on Main Street and borrowed $5 on Friday afternoon. With that money, he bought liquor and sold it on the sly over the weekend, when the State Liquor Store was closed. Sunday night, when Jo and Margaret were cashing up the receipts for the restaurant, he came in off the street and sat on the opposite side of the room. When Allie cashed up his money from selling liquor, there were many times when he had more money than they did.

Shortly after Stony went into the service, Bryant Gurney lost his grandmother with whom he had been living. He asked Jo if he could live with Barbara and her while he finished high school.

He was the first of many young people to whom Jo served as a foster mother. Jo never considered herself the mothering type, but she had compassion to help everyone. She always came to the rescue when she saw a kid having a difficult time. Margaret helped out at the restaurant by teaching the kids how to work and how to handle the public.

"Bryant," Jo said, "You can live with us, but I will expect you to get up on your own and go to school every day just the same as Barbara does."

He agreed.

Bryant worked at Barjo's in the kitchen and also in the dining room, waiting on tables. In later years, his daughter, Jane, also was a waitress at the restaurant.

One day, Margaret sent him to the Norway National Bank to get change for the dining room. When he had been gone longer that she felt he should have been, she went looking for him. Bryant had taken a detour to the poolroom on Cottage Street for a game. He was having a great time until he spotted Margaret coming through the door. She was the last person in the world he ever expected to see in the pool hall.

"Bryant," she said sternly, "there will be no more games of pool when I sent you on an errand."

When Stony came home on leave in January 1943, Jo and he were married. On January 30, Rensel Colby, a South Paris minister, performed the ceremony at his home. With time a big factor because Stony had to return to his base in New Boston, New Hampshire the next day, none of Jo's family were present. The minister went out on the street and asked two passersby to come in to be witnesses to the marriage.

"Getting married seemed to be the right decision. He was nine years younger than I was, but we didn't think anything about it at the time," Jo said. "P. Y. had been twelve years old than I was, so age made no difference to me."

After taking Stony back to his base in New Boston, New Hampshire, Jo laid her hat down on her bed while she finished undressing. When she turned around, her dog, "Susie," had pulled the hat off the bed and chewed the fur pompom off.

"Susie, what did you do that for? You have never acted like this when I've left you before," Jo said to her pet in a disgusted voice. "You know better than that!"

A small dog with short brown hair, Susie was upset at being left alone all day at the apartment. She liked to ride and Jo usually took her along. Her mild mannered dog made Jo pay a good price for her trip this time.

One afternoon, shortly after Jo and Stony were married, Donnie, looked Jo in the face and said, "Aunt Jo, you can't get married again, people will start talking about you. Remember this is the third time, 1923, 1933, and 1943."

The summer of 1943 was a good one for the restaurant. That fall of that same year she could not afford an Easter suit for both herself and Margaret, Jo went with her sister into Lewiston to shop for new outfits. They picked out a jacket of the latest fashion from the collection at Murphy Furriers. They had never had a fur coat before, and Jo decided to splurge. She bought a silver fox jacket and a black hat with a silver fox pompom on top for each of them.

When Stony came home on leave, he would take Jo to the dances at the Norway Grange Hall, located on Whitman Street, the street in back of Barjo's. Stony was an especially good dancer and enjoyed taking her to the dance.

"Stony and I loved to do the polka. He was a large man, but he was light as a feather on his feet as we danced," Jo said.

One Saturday night after she had finished serving supper, Jo went across the street to her apartment to get ready to go to the dance. When she left, Barbara was cooking and Bryant was waiting on tables in the dining room.

"When Stony and I went by the restaurant door on the way to the dance, things didn't look just right," Jo said. "I should have been suspicious because Barbara and Bryant had changed positions. She was in the dining room. He was in the kitchen. We were only gone about two hours. When I went back into the restaurant to close up, Bryant had the sixty-three year old woman who was helping in the kitchen, sitting on a stool. It seems that his evening project had been to teach her how to smoke a cigarette instead of waiting on tables as he was suppose to."

"From then on, I made it perfectly clear, I wanted Barbara to do the cooking and *no* changing places with *anyone*," Jo said with a voice of authority.

Looking forward to the day when Stony would be discharged from the service, Jo worked harder than ever at the restaurant. Once he got home, she felt that they would able to organize the hours more efficiently. For now, she knew long hours were the only way that she could keep the restaurant going.

"Stony was a good cook and an asset to Barjo's," Jo said. "He had learned to decorate cakes from the baker at Norway Home Bakery. When we catered to weddings and special functions, he made beautiful wedding cakes and other fancy desserts. We worked together making fancy sandwiches and other distinctive dishes for the buffets."

Dressing up the dining room for the holidays was something else Stony enjoyed. Each year, he saved all the pine cones, balls and other ornaments from the table centerpieces to decorate the walls the following year.

Business was booming in Norway during the War years. In 1942, Portland Pipeline began laying a pipeline from Portland to Montreal. It would carry oil from tankers in Portland harbor to Canada. The company brought in crews of construction workers from the oil fields of Texas. Hiring local people, too, they trained them on the job to weld and fit the pipes. Much of the heavy equipment used for the project was shipped in from the South.

Because Maine was the nearest point to Europe, observation towers were created the whole length of the pipeline and manned by local people from their respective towns. These people were called "National Observers" and were part of a volunteer force of the United States government, dedicated to helping their country. By serving in this way, people who were too old to enlist for military duty could still do their part for freedom.

To honor the soldiers, Barjo's waitresses dressed in uniforms designed in military style, complete with jaunty overseas caps.

With Stony in the service, Barbara wanted to do her part for the war effort, too. She got up at 4:00 a.m. and helped her mother cook until she had to go to school. She helped measured the ingredients for 36 cream pies, while Jo did the baking. Jo served breakfast, while Barbara waited on tables.

"At breakfast, Barbara waited on the rugged oil men from Texas and Oklahoma who were working on the pipeline and all the other construction workers. They all showed her a lot of respect," Jo said with admiration in her voice. "They were a wild bunch, but never did any of them give her a bit of trouble."

During the war years, the high school had a shortened session. Coming to the restaurant from her classes at Norway High School, Barbara helped Jo serve lunch during her lunch hour.

"Many days, Barb headed back to school with a cheeseburger in her hand, while her friends had all enjoyed lunch in the dining room. She treated her friends at noon-time, but none of them ever offered to help so she could sit down and enjoy hers," Jo said.

After school, Barbara came right to the restaurant with her homework under her arm. She helped serve supper and did the short-order cooking, while Jo did the baking for the next day.

Every night, for over a year and a half, Jo and Barbara put up three hundred lunches for the workers from Central Maine Power Co., New England Telephone Co., Portland Pipeline and the Cornell Construction crew. The workers had breakfast and dinner at the restaurant.

Barbara said to her mother, "Don't put too much filling in the sandwiches because if you do, we won't make any money!" She got this idea right from P. Y., who was always trying to make a businesswoman out of Jo and to teach her cost-control.

Recalling one of the most unusual events at the restaurant, Jo tells the story about an incident in the 1940's involving several of the pipeline workers.

Two men were eating together when an argument between them turned bitter. Their quarrel over money had started at the rooming house. The men moved out to the alley between Jackson's Market and Barjo's where one of them was beaten unmercifully and dragged through the dirt. Blood gushed from his head. He was gasping for breath when he was carried into Barjo's kitchen. Suffocating from the dirt he inhaled, he died on the kitchen floor before any medical doctor could be reached.

"The fellow who had given him that awful beating got off with a small fine," Jo exclaimed. "I couldn't believe what a small value the courts had put on that man's life. If the boss of the crew had listened to me when I told him that trouble was brewing, it never would have happened. Just imagine how I felt to see him gasping for breath on my kitchen floor! I was horrified."

During World War II, all food and baking supplies were scarce. The government, to insure that food would be available for troops here and overseas, controlled supplies by issuing ration books of stamps for food and gasoline to every person.

All the people in the surrounding towns, East Stoneham, Waterford, Harrison, Oxford, South Paris and Norway, rode together and paid each other with gas ration stamps instead of cash. This was a necessity at the time to make the ration stamps go further. This was the beginning of car pooling to go to work, which is done today for a completely different reason.

Because of the government rationing, many products were in limited supply. Many people grew their own vegetables in "Victory gardens." Beef was shipped overseas to feed the troops, so much of the beef available in this country was sold on the blackmarket. Many people raised their own chickens, providing both eggs and meat for their neighbors.

At Barjo's, Jo served chicken prepared in many different ways. She had to be creative to provide her customers with different choices on her menu. Many items were made using a cream sauce to stretch the little meat that was available.

One afternoon, Jo received a call from one of her friends telling her that he had a side of blackmarket beef to sell. She agreed to buy it, but he didn't dare deliver it to the her. After dark that evening, Jo and Margaret walked to Pleasant Street to meet him. The beef was in a large basket with two handles.

"As we were walking down the street, I must have been pushing Margaret to the side of the road. When I looked over, she was almost in the ditch," Jo said with a hearty laugh. "I thought it was funny, but Marg didn't."

"When I agreed to help you, I didn't know we'd have to carry 150 pounds of meat for over a mile!" Margaret complained to Jo.

"I probably weighed about 30 pounds more that she did," Jo said. "We sat the basket down and changed sides. By the time we got to the restaurant, I'm sure we both were sick of our bargain. Never again did we agree to haul a beef creature that distance. If the seller couldn't deliver, we didn't buy."

U. S. Government agents carried out surprise inspections to check for hoarding of rationed goods. One day, Jo got word the inspectors were in the Oxford County area.

A man she knew called and told her that Barjo's was on the

list for an inspection the next day. Guy McAllister was working for her as a handyman at Barjo's. To protect her stock, she had him take the groceries from the cellar storeroom of the restaurant to the basement of the building where she was living. When the inspectors arrived, the only food visible was what was being used to prepare for the day's business.

Later, the inspector who had called her said to Jo, "I know I gave you advance warning, but I expected you'd have a few groceries in the cellar. You did quite a job concealing your stock!"

"Well, you didn't expect me to show your men what I really had on hand," Jo said. "I knew they would either confiscate the groceries or fine me!"

Sometime later, the U.S. Government inspectors came to check again. This time they called on Mother's doughnut business. Working out of her own kitchen, Mother fried the doughnuts using two huge iron frying pans filled with lard on top of the wood stove. Dozens of plain, chocolate and molasses doughnuts were sold everyday at Barjo's. She had many customers who also came to her Deering Street home to buy directly from her.

During the inspection, one of the men asked where she had gotten her sugar,[44] to make the doughnuts.

She answered, "I have no problem getting anything I need. My daughter, Jo, gets it for me."

After the war, this same inspector went to work as a salesman for Sunshine Biscuits from whom Barjo Restaurant bought.

He said, "You know, Jo, I could have reported you to the government for furnishing Mrs. McAllister with groceries."

"I thanked him," Jo said quietly. Thinking to herself, "if he only knew how many things I'd gotten for her, he probably would have had me in Federal prison. Mother had no idea what rationing was or how hard I had to work to get her supplies."

During the war years, many of Jo's salesmen were a great help to her. Through her brother, Jim, who working for Milliken, Tomlinson Co., she met Mr. Fogg (no relation to P. Y.), who preferred to be called "Foggie." He helped Jo set up her menus. After his talk with Jo about the menu for the week, he would go to the cellar stockroom and take his own order.

"Foggie never let me run out of anything," Jo said. "I trusted him to order what I needed, but not to overstock me with unnecessary items. He never did, and we became best of friends."

During the early war years, Jo was able to save $2,000. But Jo's good fortune wouldn't end there. By 1945, she had $30,000 in savings.

"When I finally had accumulated $2,000, I didn't think I ever would need another penny," Jo said. "It seemed so good to know that at last I had some money to fall back on."

She kept the day's receipts in paper bags in the living room of her apartment. After she had time to do the bookkeeping, she put the currency in her safe.

"Every night, Barbara and I got the money out and made a paper carpet with it on the living room floor. After I finished the bookkeeping, I banked the bills and kept the change. This money was used to renovate the restaurant after the war."

On May 22, 1944, Jo bought the Barbershop building at 225 Main Street at bid from the Kimball Estate. She and Barbara had rented from Mrs. Kimball during Barbara's childhood days (from 1933 on) when they lived in the apartment upstairs over Cook's Barbershop on the main floor. They were to stay in that apartment until 1949.

After the war, Donald finished his work at the shipyard in South Portland. By this time, their mother was in her seventies and no longer physically able to run her doughnut business. Donald took it over, still calling it, "McAllister's Doughnuts." Even though Donald was now going to make the doughnuts, Mother refused to let him have the iron frying pans. Jo bought him two fry pots. He had Kimball and Leavitt make special inserts to turn over the doughnuts, to speed up the production.

Now running the business from his Pleasant Street home, he was also able to spend more time with Freddie and Donnie. Mildred was teaching in the Commercial Department at Norway High School. Because of his illness, Freddie wasn't able go out much, but he loved to ride. Donald took the boys with him when he peddled the doughnuts from house to house. Doughnuts were sold to the stores and schools, as well.

Always there to help others, Jo attributed her accomplishments during these years to her loyal clientele. Many knew other factors were involved as well. Hard work, hearty portions of good food, and a spotless restaurant contributed to her success.

With Margaret at her side, she made everyone that came through the restaurant doors feel like they were a part of the Barjo family. Everybody was made welcome; the very young, the elderly, families with children, summer visitors, or anyone who needed a hot meal but had no money to pay for it.

Repeat business was a large part of Jo's achievements at Barjo's. Planning to have sufficient stock of hand, she was able to provide her customers with the same quality food everyday. She was never one to serve her customers anything but first-class food. She believed this was the key to building repeat business.

[42] *As it was called at the time, later to become the United States Air Force.*

[43] *Norway was called the Snowshoe Capital of the World.*

[44] *Sugar was one of the many rationed products.*

CHAPTER 15

Finally—Renovations at Barjo's

In 1945, another person was about to come into Jo and Barbara's lives. He would become a very important part of their immediate family.

The restaurant needed a dishwasher. One afternoon, into the restaurant kitchen came Henry Paradis, a young boy from Buckfield, who needed a job. He was in his early teens and very bashful. Jo hired him to help in the kitchen. He broke so many dishes the first day that she decided to train him to cook.

Jo laughed as she commented, "Henry tells everybody that Barbara, not me, taught him how to cook. But that's O.K. What difference does it really make. He turned out to be a much better cook than he ever was a dishwasher."

As time went on, Henry would become much more that an employee, he would become Barbara's husband. He would also work for Jo for over twenty years and become involved in real estate with her. Later, after their children arrived, he and Barbara would own a restaurant of their own.

While Stony was in the military, from 1942 to 1946, he became familiar with a magazine called *Restaurant Management*. Thinking Jo might get new ideas from it, he bought her a subscription.

"Stony had told me about the military kitchens in which he worked," Jo said. "He described to me the decor of some of the Officers' Clubs dining rooms. I wanted to surprise him when he returned home. From the magazine, I was able to glean many ideas for more modern equipment and new ideas for my menus."

After the fire in 1940, with materials unavailable and a limited amount of money, Jo had repaired the outside of the restaurant. With mismatched booths and few other decorations, the interior still needed a face-lift.

The customers had enjoyed being part of Jo's plans for the restaurant when she rebuilt after the fire. When she began to tell people how she wanted to renovate Barjo's, they asked, "You don't plan to close while the work is being done, do you? We want to be part of the project."

In 1946, as materials became available, Jo hired John Jacobsen, a local contractor, to do all the remodeling. He and his crew dug out the whole basement, reinforcing walls and ceiling with new beams. Additional storage space would now be available for more groceries. All the electrical wiring was run through conduit pipes under the kitchen floor. New beam-work was added to make them sturdy enough to support a terrazzo floor.

"That was something to see!" Jo exclaimed. "They dug up half the floor at once to replace beams underneath. We had to go down one ladder to the storeroom and up another to the kitchen."

Without closing the restaurant, she had a tan, mosaic terrazzo floor made of multi-colored crushed marble laid in the dining room. It was the first of its kind in Norway. Maine Tile Company. of Portland installed genuine rose tile with a black tile border from the floor to a height of four feet on all the walls of the dining room and in the bathrooms. The rest of the wall was covered with bluish-green Marlite.

When the fellows laying the terrazzo floor finished work for the day, Jo filled the jukebox with quarters. The men danced with the waitresses and the customers. The restaurant was open every day while the renovations were being done. The customers and employees alike had a wonderful time. No one seemed the least bit disturbed by the construction work going on all around.

Electricity was just coming into its own in the state of Maine as a source for cooking. Central Maine Power Company engineered an All-Electric kitchen layout. Jo's was the first All-Electric restaurant kitchen in the State of Maine. Central Maine Power Co. had the project written up with picture, in the magazine *Food Service*, a national magazine for the food service industry.

"It was hard for me to believe that I could turn on a switch and have heat for my grill and fry-pots. No more lighting pilots lights or worrying about an open flame," Jo said. "I always have had a fear of fire."

Soule Glass of Portland installed a two-toned green glass tile front with a glass tile sign that said, "All-Electric Cooked Food," "Home Made Ice Cream," "Barjo Restaurant." The original glass-tile front was the first in the area in that style.

Making big changes in the dining room as well, Jo had new light green Naugahyde booths with solid oak frames installed. Before, some booths had high backs, others had coat racks and none of them were alike. Some of them were rickety and others were torn with the stuffing falling out.

"For the first time since going into business," Jo said, "I finally had a restaurant with booths that matched. What an improvement it made in the appearance of the room."

When the CMP engineers designed the new Barjo's kitchen, Jo decided to move the ice cream room to the basement of 225 Main Street. For the first time, the ice cream was frozen using an electric freezer. No longer was ice chopped from a large block with salt added. A cabinet was installed in the new ice cream room, capable of holding forty gallons of ice cream. Before, Jo had used a holding cabinet in the cellar at the restaurant, holding six five-gallon containers of ice cream. When cellar capacity was added to the freezer space in the dining room fountain, she was now able to stock twenty-four five-gallon containers of ice cream at a time. Her new freezer used 24% butterfat ice cream mix (the highest percent available from H. P. Hood, her supplier) instead of raw cream, making freezing the ice cream much easier.

After the new walls were completed in the dining room, a local artist, Vivian Akers, hung many of his oil paintings on them. Included were many portraits. Chief Justice Earl Warren's portrait, displayed at Barjo's, had taken V. Akers to Washington. There, Warren had done several sittings while the artist painted his portrait. Akers' portraits of people looked as if the person could speak to you. Many scenic paintings, for which the artist was also famous, graced the dining walls. In the summer, he was often seen with his station wagon full of paints and brushes, sitting at some scenic spot, capturing a vivid sunset or a rushing brook on his canvas. The dining room at Barjo's was the first place where many of his works were shown. Jo and Margaret helped him sell many of his paintings.

The Vivians who had a summer home on Lake Pennesseewassee took a special interest in Akers' work and paid his way to study in Europe. The Western Maine Art Society has promoted his work though their organization. His oil paintings are now famous around the world with many in private collections, such as the Sanborn Collection. Some are on display at the Norway Historical Society and others are at the Smithsonian Institute in Washington, D.C.

In 1946, Jo bought a house on Crescent Street owned by Len Sessions who lived on the second floor. He had been the pharmacist at Ashton's Drug store where Jo worked in 1923. Len was a real "character" who liked to do things his own way. When the sale was completed, he had no idea of moving to another place.

"I didn't know how to get the point across to Len that the house was no longer his and he needed to move on," Jo stated. "He just didn't think it made any difference who owned it. He had made money off the sale and wanted the comfort of staying put. It took me over a year to get him to find a different place to live."

Len Sessions had another habit that made him a real pain in the neck. He would go to the garden of the people who lived downstairs in the house and pick some of their tomatoes. He brought them to the restaurant with one thing in mind and it wasn't to be nice to Jo.

"When I saw him coming, I knew what he had up his sleeve!" Jo exclaimed.

"I brought some tomatoes for you, Jo," Len said displaying the tomatoes.

"Don't you dare swap your tomatoes for mine today, Len," Jo said to him in a stern voice.

He went right over to the refrigerator and if he thought her tomatoes were better looking, did exactly what she had asked him not to. He swapped the tomatoes, so the neighbors wouldn't know that he had raided their garden.

During fair week, Len came into the restaurant, went into the kitchen and put on an apron as if he was going to help. Clearing a few dishes from the tables, he expected Jo to pay him. That same morning she had already treated him to his breakfast.

When he got ready to go home, he approached Jo and asked, "Well, aren't you going to pay me?"

"For what?" she asked him.

"Well, didn't you notice how much I helped you?! I just cleared off two tables for the girls!"

Even though he was an eccentric character, Jo fed him everyday because she knew he had no one to cook for him.

In January 1946, Ralph Stone came home from the service after spending four years in the military. One week later, Henry, who had been helping Jo in the kitchen, enlisted in the U. S. Air Force and was gone from 1946 until 1948.

When Stony came back to cook at the restaurant, he brought two fellows with him. In the service he had had a large crew working under him and he had gotten used to it. Just a dishwasher seemed too little help to him. Having the two extra assistant cooks was a short-lived experience for Jo.

Shortly after Stony came home, he and Jo had gone home to rest one day. When they came back, the cooks had let all of the grease out of the fry pots and had forgotten to put a bucket under the release valves. All the grease had poured out over the kitchen floor. To make matters worse, the men had gone to Jackson's Market, next door, and gotten sawdust to absorb it. Stony took one look at the kitchen, which looked like a disaster area, and walked away through the back door. The two fellows left, too, never to return. She was dressed in her white uniform—not exactly the proper attire for cleaning up, but Jo got to work. Jo cleaned up the liquid lard from the kitchen floor before someone had an accident and fell. Then she prepared and served dinner.

"That was the first and last time that Stony hired any kitchen help," Jo said. "He knew how I felt about having inexperienced help and that episode was a perfect example."

Barbara graduated from Norway High School in June 1946. Jo bought her a car as a graduation gift. That fall, Barbara began college at Mt. Ida in Massachusetts. Margaret and the rest of the family wanted her to try a different field of work than the restaurant. Barbara enrolled in an airline stewardess course, but never used the training she received to work for an airline. However, she was required to take some courses which were helpful to her in her own restaurant career.

Some of the other girls at Mt. Ida came from the city and knew little about life in the country. They asked Barbara, "What is Maine like? We've never been there."

The next weekend Barbara asked her mother what she should tell them.

"Well, let's see. Why don't you tell them the grass grows right in the middle of Main Street and the black bears roam all over town!" Jo said with a hearty laugh, one of her trademarks.

"Mother, guess what, all the girls at college believed me," Barbara told Jo, when she came home the following week, referring to their little joke about the town.

In 1946, Stony was taken sick shortly after he returned from the service. Jo needed Barbara's help to keep the restaurant open. Because Barbara had a car while she was at Mt. Ida College, she was able to come home every weekend to help. Arriving late Friday night, Barbara worked with her mother all weekend and returned to school late Sunday afternoon.

Many times, Jo has said, "It was only through our prayers to God for guidance that Barbara was able to graduate from Norway High School and Mt. Ida College. I give all the credit to God for His help and for giving us good health and strength."

Barbara worked many long hours at the restaurant during her high school and college years. Jo had working 18 to 20 hour days while Stony was in the service. Now with his sickness, she still had to work many long hours.

Because Jo was busy running the restaurant, Margaret went alone to Barbara's graduation at Mt. Ida College in June 1948.

Shortly after Stony came home, Jo noticed he was having trouble with his skin and then his arms and legs started to swell. This swelling progressed to his entire body and he began to have trouble with his eyes.

Jo knew that he had had sugar diabetes as a teenager, but the doctor had claimed he had cured him by using Karo syrup. When he was given his physical to go in the service, there was no mention of diabetes. Because it was wartime, people had been pushed through with inadequate medical examinations. Stony saw numerous doctors, but none could find a cause for his medical problems.

One day, a customer came to the serving window at the restaurant and said to Jo, "If you don't get help for that man soon, the swelling will make him blind or worse still—he'll lose his mind!"

Everyday for weeks Jo would run across the street to their apartment and pack Stony's body with medicated hot packs. The medicine that she used ate all the finish off the bathtub, but didn't seem to give Stony any relief. The doctors kept trying different medications for months. To Jo it seemed like forever.

"I had bought ultra-violet lights for the walk-in refrigerator because the salesman told me it would keep the food fresher. Stony had told me about all the new things he encountered in military kitchens. I wanted mine to be just as modern and I wanted to surprise him. I had no idea that some people are allergic to ultra-violet rays," she said.

Finally, a salesmen from Armour Meats told her their company was discontinuing the lights because of the health problems they caused. She turned hers off and Stony recovered with no lasting effects. Jo sighed with relief after experiencing that ordeal.

When Henry got out of the military in 1948, he came back to work at Barjo's. As time went on, Henry and Barbara developed a more intimate relationship and were married on October 4, 1949. Jo and Henry worked side by side in the restaurant kitchen for many years and never had a word of trouble. He continued at the restaurant as a chef until Barbara and he left in 1966 to start their own restaurant, the Country Way, in South Paris.

"Henry deserves a 'Gold Star' for working for over twenty years with his mother-in-law, his wife's aunt and her step-father," Jo commented. "Not many boys have done that and still stayed on good terms with their relatives."

Barjo's was now on solid footing. The renovations had made

the restaurant a modern food service facility.

With a larger family needing to be supported by the restaurant, Jo began to think seriously about what the future would hold. Would Barjo's be able to support three families? What about if Barbara had children, now that she was married? Where would Jo find an additional source of income? She pondered over these questions, and once again she turned to God for the answers.

Barbara and Henry Paradis were married on October 4, 1949.

Father Donald McAllister was ordained in 1971 on his 38th birthday. He said his first Mass at Saint Catherine of Sienna in Norway under the watchful eye of Father Brady.

*Jo, 1955,
behind the Barjo's grill, her home for many years, serving dinner.*

CHAPTER 16

Helping the School Kids

Hi**gh** school students worked their first jobs at Barjo's for over fifty-nine years. It was hard for young people to find employment in the region and Jo was always ready and willing to give a "helping hand."

In the early 1940's, the Kimball family had moved from Waterford to Norway, after their mother died. Leona, Kathy, Alberta, Charlie, Gertrude, Minnie, Frankie and Dickie all worked at the restaurant. These kids were a great help to Jo during the Second World War. Some of the Kimballs worked in the dining room and others in the kitchen. After Jo bought the hotel in 1949, some of them worked there on banquets as well.

Another family was Barbara and Joyce McAllister[45] whose father, Henry, was a relative of Jo's. These two sisters worked at Barjo's for many years. Barbara was the same age as Jo's own daughter, Barbara. Joyce was younger. Jo dressed the girls with the same-style uniforms when they waited on tables. At twelve years old, Joyce was able to run the dining room efficiently, waiting on table and taking cash.

When Walter Bennett became old enough, he worked in the kitchen at Barjo's. He was washing dishes in the kitchen at Barjo's at the same time McAllister girls were waiting on tables there. He and Joyce McAllister were married in 1949.

One day, as Jo was getting ready to take the whole crew to the "World of Mirth" in Lewiston, she said to her daughter, Barbara, "Take Walter over to the apartment and wash his face, hands and legs so he can go with us."

Walter Bennett was a small boy for his age, and Jo thought he was much younger than Barbara. To her surprise, Jo found out, several years later, he was only two years younger. He had kept quiet at the time because he was afraid that Jo might not take him on the outing had she known his age.

One afternoon in the early 1940's, Jo and Stony were going to Paris Hill for a ride. Stony noticed two teenagers walking up the hill, one of whom was Susie Wilson. She had been one of Stony's neighbors when he lived on Paris Hill with his folks. In 1937, Susie and a girlfriend had been the teenagers who had walked by the Dwyer house on Paris Hill on the fateful night that Doctor Littlefield was murdered.

Stony turned to Jo and asked, "Didn't you say that you needed a waitress at Barjo's? I think Susie would make you a good girl. Would you like me to ask her if she would be interested?"

"Sure," Jo replied.

He stopped the pick-up near the girls and asked, "Susie, would you like to come to work at Barjo's?"

She answered, "I'd love to. When can I start?"

"Why don't you come in the morning? I'll get you some uniforms. Marg and I will teach you how to wait on tables," Jo said.

It was a happy decision on both their parts because Susie worked at Barjo's for over thirty years, satisfying the public with her excellent care and attention. She later married Lewis Olmstead and had four children and the Olmstead family were Jo's tenants in a house that she owned on Green Street in Norway.

"Spike" Dillingham and his brothers worked at Barjo's during the 1940's. Spike was so short that he had to stand on a stool to reach the dish window and to wash the dishes.

One day, Spike looked over the dishwashing machine at Jo and said to her, "You know, Jo, Margaret looks so nice, but you look like a Fiji Islander. Your hair is so short and so curly."

Margaret was always dressed in sharp looking white uniforms, but Jo preferred to wear navy blue pedal pushers and a dark blouse while cooking. Because she was working with food, Jo preferred to have a short, curly, hairstyle rather than wear a hairnet to cover longer hair.

Another day, Nolan Jackson, who owned the market next door, was in the restaurant talking to Jo. Spike was a real inquisitive young man. He was standing on the stool, looking over the top of his glasses at Nolan from his spot at the dishwasher machine. He was trying to find out what Jo and Nolan were talking about.

Nolan turned and said to him, "Isn't that right, young man?"

Spike had no idea what had been said, but he snappily replied, "Yes, sir, that's right!"

That was one time that Spike had been caught off guard. Afterwards, the three of them all had a good laugh about it.

Another boy who was a beneficiary of Jo's kindness was Jack

(or Jackie as Jo called him) Smith.[46] He was the youngest of a large family and craved attention, something that was lacking in his home. Jo and Margaret gave him a chance to wait on tables. Having a job in a restaurant was an opportunity he had never anticipated. To be introduced to so many nice people was beyond his wildest dreams.

"Jackie was a good worker. Many times, he and I'd run the dining room alone," Jo said. "He proved to be a very dependable kid and never hesitated to do more than his share of the work."

Jack Smith waited on tables at Barjo's all through his years at Norway High School. During World War II, after graduating from high school, he enlisted in the service.

Another veteran waitress was Veda Millett Taker, one of Barbara's classmates in the class on 1946. She started working at Barjo's shortly after graduation.

For many years, until the breakfast hour was closed down in 1966, Veda served breakfast with Stony doing the cooking. After that, she worked a split shift, 10:30 a.m. to 2:00 p.m. and from 5:00 p.m. to 8:00 p.m. Veda married and had five children. Working these hours, she could get her children off to school in the morning and be home when they returned in the afternoon. She was still working at Barjo's Restaurant when Jo closed in January 1991. By then, she had been serving her clientele for 45 years.

"I was blessed with many faithful employees," Jo commented. "Veda had a following of regular customers who would wait for her tables, even if other booths were available."

Some of the other girls who waited on tables during the 1940's, included Reathyl Bryant, Ivalea and Roberta Hunt, Doris and Beverly Murphy, Frances Mellerup, and Ramona Curr.

Over the years, Jo and Donnie have always had a special relationship, more than just an aunt and her nephew. His personality was much like hers and he shared her interest in helping others. From a very early age, Donnie depended on her for moral support in many of his endeavors.

One day, Donnie wanted to have lunch at Barjo's. Margaret was busy and told him to come back later. Instead, he went around to the back door to see his Aunt Jo.

"Aunt Jo," he asked, " can you get me some lunch? Aunt Marg won't let me stay. She told me to come back later."

"Just a minute," Jo said to him, "I'll write you a note and you take it to Margaret. I'm sure you'll get your dinner."

What Jo had in mind hadn't entered Donnie's head. She wrote a note for him that said, "Give this tramp a lunch for ten cents."[47]

This note was similar to the ones that the tramps were given by the town officers when they were to be fed by the town. Jo never charged the town for their food. Instead, she visited with hobos, enjoyed feeding them and listened to their conversations about their escapades.

When Margaret saw Donnie coming, she knew that Jo had put him up to something. She laughed after reading his "official" town order for food and ordered his lunch for him.

On another day, Donnie came into the restaurant at noontime.

"Aunt Marg," he said. "Would you please put up 40 ice creams so I can take them to school for my class?"

"What are you thinking of, Donnie," she replied. "It's right in the middle of dinner hour, and I don't have the time."

He went into the kitchen and asked, "Aunt Jo will you put up some ice cream for me? Aunt Marg won't, but I thought *you* might be willing to."

"Sure, Donnie," she replied, "just as soon as I finish this."

Home he went and came back with his cart to take the ice cream to school. His class was having a party and Donnie had volunteered to get the ice cream.

While Jo was putting up the ice cream, a customer came to the cash register to pay. Donnie ask her if he could ring the sale into the register and make change for the gentleman.

"O.K., go ahead," she answered.

When Margaret cashed up that afternoon the register was $5 short. Neither Jo nor Donnie was allowed to touch the cash register after that. Margaret made it very plain that the cash register was her responsibility. No one else was to ring in any sales, not even Jo. From that day on, during all her remaining years in the restaurant business, Jo never again touched the cash register.

Knowing Donnie loved people, Jo encouraged him to pursue his wildest dreams. Donnie's young boyhood discussion at the Congregational Church with the minister and Judge A. J. Stearns foreshadowed many future events in his life.

In the fall of 1946, he entered Norway High School, graduating in June 1951. Then, he went to the University of Maine in Orono. During his Junior year, (1953-54), he applied for and received a Norwegian-American Scholarship for foreign study at the University of Oslo, Norway. A student participating in this program was called a "Corin Strong Boy" in honor of our Ambassador to Norway who was a career diplomat. Donnie graduated with a B. A. degree in history in 1955. After college, he enrolled at the Fletcher School of Diplomacy in Massachusetts.

In 1956, while he was taking his final exams at this school, he received his draft induction papers for the United States Army. The same day that he received his draft induction papers, his brother, Freddie, passed away.

"That evening I had a funny feeling come over me," Donnie said. "Freddie and I had been very close. It seemed as though I knew he was gone long before I received the phone call."

Unable to reach Don and Mildred at 11:00 p.m., the hospital had called Barjo's. Jo and Stony had been the ones who told Don and Mildred about Freddie's death.

After completing basic training, the rest of Donnie's division was sent overseas without them. He wondered why he had been detained. After several days, he learned the reason. He was to be assigned to Fort Jackson, North Carolina, and serve as the secretary to the commanding General of that base. This position he held for the remaining 21 months of his tour of duty.

While in the service, he became a Catholic. At first, Jo was the only family member who supported his decision. She felt that it was his decision to make and no matter what he decided, she would always stand by him.

In 1958, Donnie came back to Maine where he taught at Stephens High School in Rumford, in Milo, and in Ellsworth.

Donnie earned a Master's degree in Guidance and Clinical Psychology from Villanova in Pennsylvania and one in American Literature from Columbia College in South Carolina.

Donnie is the only person to ever receive three consecutive Fulbright Scholarships for foreign study. The country he chose to study was Finland. While there, he lived with a Finnish family that included two sons, Markko and Riisto.

In 1964, Donald earned his Doctorate in Historia (Modern European History) from the University of Helsinki, Finland.

When he returned to Maine, he brought a Finnish family, Peter and Paula Pakarinen and their three daughters, with him. They came on teaching visas and lived in Don's family home on Pleasant Street. Don's father, Donald, renovated a small building next door to live in himself. The Pakarinens taught in the Norway school system for two years before returning to Finland. Paula was an art teacher and Peter taught sixth grade.

After returning to the United States, Donnie taught in Amsterdam, New York. There he became acquainted with Margaret C. Keane who had a great impact on his life. Her brother, Father Bill Keane, talked to him about joining the

Augustinians and going into the priesthood. He made the decision to be a priest, receiving his Master's degree in Theology from the Washington Theological Coalition in Washington D.C. Concurrently, he earned his Ph.D. in Clinical Psychology from the University of Chicago.

Donald L. McAllister was ordained to the priesthood in 1971, saying his first Mass at St. Catherine's of Sienna Church in Norway, Maine, under the watchful eye of Father Francis Brady.

His first assignment was at the St. Mary's Hospital and Medical Center in San Francisco, California. Now his title became Father Don and he also helped as the Chaplain of the San Francisco Fire Department where he was known as Lieutenant of the God Squad. He still has "God Squad" on his license plate today. While in San Francisco, he was licensed as a counselor.

In 1974, Donnie was diagnosed with cancer of the liver and sent home to Norway. Shortly after his arrival home, the parish priest for St. Catherine's of Sienna Church, died very suddenly. Father Don, as he was now known, offered his services until the Diocese could find another priest. With the help of God, Donnie was healed of the cancer and able to return to his hospital work.

His new assignment was as hospital chaplain at the Catherine McAuley Health Center in Ann Arbor, Michigan. His peers and other health-care professionals recognized his knowledge in the field of death and dying. While in Michigan, Father Don conducted lecture tours called "The Issues of Death and Dying" at conferences in The United States, Canada and Europe. Doctors and nurses, as well as other medical professionals attended these seminars.

In 1984, he returned Norway to be with his father at the time of his mother's death. Donnie took a two-year sabbatical before taking the position of hospital chaplain at Mercy Hospital in Portland. He has been very involved in genealogy and historical societies in the area, as well as in his hospital work.

During the 1940's, Margaret broke off her relationship with Frank Bjorklund when she found out he had another girlfriend. He had been the attorney who had advised her at the time of the break-up of the partnership called "Marjo's" restaurant. He had given Margaret an engagement ring, which she made him take back. Margaret continued to work at the restaurant and happened to be working on the day that Frank came for his wedding dinner with his new wife, Sigrid.

"Marg stepped right up and waited on them, never blinking an eye," Jo said.

Later, Margaret became interested in Mr. Spencer, one of the partners of Spencer and Damon, dry cleaners of Norway. "Spence", as he preferred to be called, was a regular customer at Barjo's. He and Margaret traveled to many places where she had never been, either for dinner, a movie, the theater, or on day trips.

In 1947, Jo bought a house on Brown Street from a young man who was working for the J. J. Nissen Baking Company. He was promoted and had to sell his home because he was going to be transferred. When Jo went to look the house over, she thought it was a cute little home. With all the furniture still there, it looked much larger that it really was.

"After the fellow moved out, what a change it made in appearance. I had never seen such a bare-looking house with such poorly constructed walls. It was then that I realized what a poor buy I had made. I rented the house to Margaret's boyfriend, Spence," Jo said. "He paid me one month's rent in advance."

Before Spence moved in, Stony's brother, Arnie, had a fire that destroyed his house. Arnie and his family had no place to go, so Jo and Stony fixed them up with furniture in the Brown Street house. Jo had to give Spence back the month's rent that he had paid her. Arnie and his family lived there for several years until they found another place to stay.

After Pa's death in 1935, Frank Lafrance became Norway's police officer and night watchman. This was the same position that Pa had held from the early 1920's until his death. His "beat" began at Snow's Marina at Norway Lake and went all the way to Sanborn's Motor Express, where the Oxford Bank is now located on Route 26. He walked the whole length and back, covering all the back streets as well as the business district in Norway village.

Remembering what a long walk it had been for her father, Jo resolved to help Norway's police officer, Frank Lafrance. In the fall of 1947, she took up a collection and bought him a three-wheeled Scooter with a sidecar, so he would no longer have to walk ten miles every night by foot.

One of the mechanics at the George Hill garage offered to teach Frank how drive the scooter and to do the repair work on it. Frank Lafrance had never even driven a car so this was a whole new experience for him. On Sunday afternoons, Frank Lafrance loaned the scooter to the mechanic so he could take his family for a ride in it.

Norway had its share of unusual events as well. Sam Michaels was great promoter of extraordinary happenings and one of Jo's good friends. One winter, he arranged for "Mush"

Moore and his famous dog sled train to visit Norway. This dog team had just finished the long trek across the Alaska tundra. In 1973, this race became known as the "Iditarod."

"Everybody in town and their brother came to see them. Barjo's was mobbed with people," Jo exclaimed. "What a thrill it was to see those beautiful Alaskan huskies and to know what they had accomplished."

Sam Michaels was also the promoter for the famous Cassius Clay—Sonny Liston boxing match held in Lewiston and many other sporting events in the area. He was a Barjo's regular.

In the late 1940's, Clarence Huff, the local undertaker, was called to go to the Yagger Neighborhood to a pick up a body. At that time, an undertaker's procedure at the time of a death was different than it is now. The medical examiners weren't as thorough before declaring them deceased.

On the way back to the funeral parlor after picking up the body, Clarence Huff and his men stopped at Barjo's for a lunch. One of the waitresses looked out the window and saw an unusual sight. When the undertaker came to the cash register, she told him to take a look outside.

"Please tell me what is going on out there in your hearse!" she exclaimed.

This particular dead man was a little bit eccentric and often had caused a commotion in the village. Much to the undertaker's surprise, the corpse was sitting up straight in the back of the hearse. Somewhere a grave error had been made. Clarence Huff was speechless. This in itself was unusual. The undertaker was noted for his "gift of gab" and was seldom without words.

Hearing shouts and loud laughter from the customers and waitresses, Jo came flying through the swinging kitchen door to find out what had happened.

Looking out the front window to see what everybody was watching, she said, "Well, Clarence, I guess that is one corpse that you will have to take back home. I know him and he's always been a little peculiar. But I didn't think he was smart enough to stage his own funeral. He almost fooled you and made it work."

During the late 1940's, every Friday night for months, an arsonist set one or more fires. At that time, Homer Luck was the Norway Fire Chief and the only elected official in the volunteer fire department. There was no auxiliary, so Barjo Restaurant provided sandwiches, doughnuts and hot coffee for the firemen who were at the scene all night.

One Friday evening, the arsonist burned a house beside the Cummings Grain Mill on Cottage Street, right behind Jo's mother's home. A child was burned to death and the rest of the family barely escaped with their lives.

When the restaurant was closed for the evening, Jo and Stony went to the fire scene to bring a lunch to the firemen.

"I'll have a cup of coffee with cream and sugar with the boys," Jo said. "I'm going to the fire and see what I can do to help out."

She usually drank her coffee black, but it was a special treat for her to be able to join the firemen on their coffee break.

People in town were frightened because they thought they might be the next victims. Many business owners installed security lighting around their buildings. The business community felt this would deter the arsonist from approaching the area.

The fires stopped just as suddenly as they had begun. The arsonist was never found and the cases never solved. After several years without any fires, many businesses discontinued the use of the security lights, but Jo kept Barjo's parking lot well lit from that time on.

In 1948, Father Bowers, an Episcopal priest from Lewiston, became one of Jo's good friends. The Christ Episcopal Church in Norway didn't have a full time priest, so Father Bowers came to help on a part-time basis. All the families of the parish took turns inviting him to dinner. When Winnie Bickford's turn came up, she was scheduled to go on vacation. She asked her cousin, Jo, if Father Bowers could have dinner at Barjo's for that one night.

After that first time, Father Bowers always had dinner at the restaurant because he enjoyed his evenings there. He made himself right at home while waiting for his dinner. He came into the kitchen and made his own *hors d'oeuvres* and played the pinball machine. Everybody was fascinated with him. None of them had ever seen a priest play a pinball machine before. Father Bowers played several games while waiting for his dinner.

The priest entertained them with many cute stories about his own experiences.

One story went like this: several alcoholics came to his home late in the evening and wanted him to *save their souls*. Knowing that they probably had a hangover from an evening of carousing, he made them get down on their hands and knees to *pray*. After he thought they had sufficient time to sober up, sometimes two hours or more, he would let them go home. It didn't take them long before they decided that they had been *saved* and no longer needed his services.

Another day in the 1940's, Father Bowers went to call on one of his parishioners who was considered a pillar of the church. The priest noticed the man acted very nervous as though he was trying to hide something. He asked the man what was bothering him. Finally, the fellow told him that he had a batch of "home-brew" in back of the stove that was ready to be bottled. He was afraid it would foam all over the floor from the yeast.

"That's no big deal," Father Bowers said to him. "Bring it out and I'll helped you bottle it."

He laughed when he told Jo the story, as he already knew how she felt about liquor. But he was sure that she realized just what the fellow was talking about from her experiences with her grandfather and his buddies as a child.

Father Bower's son had to have a "show and tell" project for school. His boy took a bag of "beer bottle" caps to school.

When the teacher asked his son where he got them, the boy said, "Under the kitchen sink at home."

"The teacher was horrified when she found out where the caps had come from," he told Jo. "She told my son that wasn't the kind of hobby that she expected a priest's son to have."

At that time, it was required that Episcopal priests to go to Boston several times a year for seminars. Father Bowers and another priest took turns taking their own cars. One time, the other priest was driving when they had an accident and ran into the back of a tractor-trailer. Father Bowers lost an eye as a result. When Jo learned of the accident, she felt terrible for her friend. When he came to the restaurant the next time, everyone told him how bad they felt about his injury.

But Father Bowers told them, "Something good always comes from something bad. With my accident insurance settlement, I was able to have my daughter's hand operated on. She was born with a serious birth defect. The fingers of one hand all turned backwards. The operation was successful and now my little girl can use her hand and live a normal life."

He had told Jo about his daughter, but until that time, she didn't realize how seriously deformed the child was. He told Jo that God must have had a hand in the accident because it was a miracle how successful the surgery was.

Many of the young people to whom Jo had taught principles of successful work would go on to make their own marks in the world.

Now the time had come for Jo to include a new phase of the food service industry in her own portfolio of accomplishments. The next few years would provide interesting new challenges for her and her entire family.

[45] For more stories about the Kimball family and Joyce and Barbara McAllister, see Appendix I, "Stories of the Barjo's Family."

[46] For more stories about Jack Smith see Appendix I, "Stories of the Barjo's Family."

[47] This was the way the note was usually worded.

PART V

Many New Ventures

Historic Beal's Tavern became Hotel Stone in 1949.

Norway-Paris Senior Class Banquet, 1954
Many credited Jo and Stony with laying the foundation for the combination of the area's
two schools—now Oxford Hills School Administrative District 17—with events like
this at Hotel Stone. Front table (back-to) are Mr. and Mrs. William Wright, Principal
and Mrs. Guy Rowe, Professor Elmer Hussey. Facing the camera are Mrs. Vernbal
Simpson, Fire Chief and Mrs. Homer Luck, Mr. and Mrs. Jerre Hacker. At the other
tables are Norway and South Paris High School students.
The waitress (right center) is Barbara Lawrence.

Barjo's, decorated for the holiday season, 1950.
Note the green glass tile front and the sizeable
fir wreaths at each window, as well as Stony's
"Merry Xmas" sign above the door.

CHAPTER 17

Beal's Tavern Becomes Hotel Stone

In 1949, Barjo's was a fine eighty-seat restaurant with good business and a loyal clientele. With both Stony and Henry back from military duty, Jo reorganized the restaurant hours. She decided that Barjo's would open at 5:00 a.m. and close at 1:00 a.m. six days a week. To accommodate customers from the dances, Jo would stay open until 2:00 a.m. Sunday morning.

With these new hours in place, Stony opened for breakfast and did most of the baking. If he had a busy morning short-order cooking, he finished the baking after Henry arrived at 9:00 a.m. Before finishing his day's work, Stony would freeze Barjo's ice cream in the ice cream room, which had been moved to the basement of the barbershop building across the street.

The rest of the day, Jo and Henry did the short-order cooking. Henry came in at 9:00 a.m., and Jo arrived at 11:00 a.m. After lunch, one of them stayed to serve the public during the afternoon and to get the specials ready for the evening shift. The other returned at 5:00 p.m. to serve the evening meal. After dinner, whoever had worked in the afternoon went home. This left the preparation for the next day and the cleaning to the night shift. Each shift had a kitchen helper, usually one of the school kids.

Margaret managed the dining room and did the banking and the payroll. Jo continued to do the rest of the bookkeeping. Even with the extended hours, Jo was worried about cash flow. Working opposite Henry gave her more free time to look for other projects.

"I couldn't see how the restaurant could support the number of people it would have to: Margaret and Mother, Stony and me, and now Barbara and Henry," she said.

At about that time, Beal's Tavern in Norway came up for sale. Acquiring it seemed a fine solution to financial concerns. Jo felt she could generate additional business income with its purchase.

Beal's Tavern was an important part of Norway's business district, being located in the center of the town. The hotel had been a popular gathering place for traveling salesmen and had a large, steady clientele. The former owners, the Seaveys, had been Jo's friends and were good customers at Barjo's. Jo also knew some of the original owners, the Beals, from her days at Stone's Drug Store. They were an extraordinary family.

Ezra Fluent Beal was born in Norway, June 17, 1797, the year the town was incorporated. He became one of the most successful architects and builders in the state.

In 1823, a new county road[48] was opened between Bethel and Norway. Most of the business between upper Coos County in New Hampshire and Portland was done over this route. Large teams loaded with country produce or goods were constantly on the road. In 1830, sensing the need for food and lodging, Ezra Beal built a public house[49] and stables near the center of Norway village. In 1833, he moved to Portland where he built the U.S. Hotel and the Falmouth House, but he continued to have close ties to Norway and returned in 1839. He was one of the founders of the Norway Savings Bank and its second president. The original Beal's Tavern building burned in 1851. That same year, Ezra Beal built the Oxford Bear Fire Station in Norway. After the Civil War, he was contracted by the Grand Trunk Railroad to build all the stations along the Maine Line, including Union Station in Portland and the station in Bangor. In 1863, he was contracted to raise the Universalist Church on Upper Main Street in Norway and to build the "Concert Hall" underneath the church. The community used the hall for town meetings and other civic affairs.

Beal Street in Norway is named for Ezra Beal. He also built the Beal Block on Main Street near the family home, where his son-in-law, Theodore Webb, had a clothing store, Webb & Wakefield. The second floor of the block was occupied both by Dr. Harry Jones, a dentist, and by other professionals. Dr. Harry Jones sold some land on Deering Street to Ed Cummings where a house, later to become Jo's home, was built.

In 1856, Beal built homes on Cottage Street for his sons, D. Webster and General George Lafayette Beal. George's wife, Belinda, was an expert horticulturist who maintained exotic sunken gardens which Jo had admired on her walk from Deering Street to work at the drug store.

The elder Beal converted his magnificent Main Street house into Beal's Tavern in 1871. Beal thought the hotel would be a good business for his son, George, who had distinguished himself during the Civil War as a regimental commander in the 12th Maine Regiment at Gettysburg under the command of Joshua

Chamberlain. The conversion included two additional stories and a widow's walk on the roof—an unusual sight in the western foothills of Maine as it was more common as a feature of captains' homes on the coast. Beal's Tavern opened as a first-class public house on July 1 that year.

Beal had significant investments in the railroad and encouraged both of his granddaughters, Elizabeth and Agnes, George's daughters, to participate in board meetings of the Grand Trunk Railroad. They were actively involved in the affairs of the local trolley, the Norway and Paris Street Railway, that ran between Norway and South Paris from Advertiser Square in Norway to Market Square in South Paris from 1895 to 1917. The trolley barn was located on Marston Street, Norway.

When General George Beal developed political interests in Augusta, the family hired a series of managers to run the hotel. Around the turn of the century, Beal's Tavern was considered one of the best country hotels in the State of Maine, an honor for Norway village.

In the early 1900's, Beal's Tavern was bought by Robert Seavey and his wife. During their tenure as the proprietors, they catered to the traveling public and to transient salesmen. On October 10, 1944, the Seaveys sold the hotel to William Davis.

Davis was the son-in-law of George Hill, the owner of the local Dodge dealership and Jo's next-door neighbors on Main Street. He had been managing the Eastland Hotel for his aunt in Portland. When they disagreed, he decided to acquire his own business and bought Beal's Tavern from the retiring Seaveys. Before the final papers could be signed, however, Davis and his aunt resolved their conflict and he hired a manager to run the Beal's. He never moved to Norway or took an active role in the daily operations. Soon, the hotel was for sale again.

George Hill agreed to hold the mortgage if Jo bought it. Trying her hand at the hotel business seemed a sound move to Jo. She had successfully paid off all the bills at the restaurant and was ready for a new challenge. Jo and Stony purchased Beal's Tavern on October 8, 1949.

"I knew that George Hill wanted to help his son-in-law, William Davis. But after my experience with him in a land dispute over the lines at Barjo's in 1940, I ought to have realized he could make things hard for me," Jo said. "I made a mistake by agreeing to let him hold the mortgage to the hotel. I knew he was anxious to sell, but I should have given the arrangement much more thought. The $17,000 we paid for it was a fair market price. But as it turned out, I later put much more money than that into renovations the place needed."

On the very day she bought the hotel, Jo was on the fourth floor looking over her purchase when she realized there were only two sound beds in the entire hotel! The rest were tied up with string and wire without proper springs or mattresses.

"The two rooms we were shown before the sale had been renovated and were used by the hotel manager and some of the shoe shop bosses. They were the only rooms in good condition with solid beds."

To make matters worse, state inspectors were downstairs condemning the kitchen and the poolroom located in the basement.

"I had no idea the kitchen was is such poor shape. Meals were being served in the dining room, so I had no reason to think there was any problem.

As she stood on the fourth floor of the hotel, Jo said to herself, "How could I be so *stupid*, to take on this load on my shoulders? I've only just gotten onto my feet at the restaurant!"

Barbara and Henry had been married on October 4, 1949. Jo and Stony moved to Room 25 in the hotel so that the newly-weds could stay in the apartment at 225 Main Street (where Jo had lived with Barbara since 1933). They were still living there when Andrea Lynn, or Andy as Jo called her, was born on July 14, 1950.

When Jo and Stony took over the management of the hotel, they changed the name to "Hotel Stone." The previous owners had catered almost exclusively to transient clientele. For the first time, the Stones opened the dining room to the general public, civic groups and to students from the local high school. Many of local people had never been inside the hotel doors.

"Local people were my customers at Barjo's," Jo said. "I wanted them to feel as welcome at Hotel Stone as they did at the restaurant. We had always catered events using the dining rooms of local churches, the Armory or the local Legion halls. Now banquets could be held in our own hotel dining room."

In April 1950, Jo went to see Dr. Arthur Easton, the president of Norway National Bank, who was also her dentist. She asked him if the bank would consider holding the hotel mortgage.

"I feel very uncomfortable about George Hill holding the mortgage on my property," she told him.

Several days later, Dr. Easton called Jo, telling her the directors of the Norway National Bank had approved the mortgage. On April 8, 1950, Josephine and Ralph Stone signed the papers.

"What a relief it was to be able to pay George Hill in full," Jo said. "All the time he held the mortgage, I felt as if he was looking over my shoulder. He would show up at the hotel nearly every day to check on how we were doing."

Right after they bought the hotel, Jo and Stony started renovating it from top to bottom. The work would take them twelve years to complete. Stony worked hard steaming off all the old wallpaper so they could have the place redone properly. They bought new furniture for all the rooms and had new carpets laid. The renovations were at last completed in 1961.

"Every winter, I borrowed $10,000 from the bank and repaid it the following summer. I used it for the repairs and painting. When the money was gone, I stopped the painters and carpenters, even if they were right in the middle of a project. It took us twelve years to renovate the whole building and have siding put on the outside." Jo said. "We never closed, just worked around the customers as we had at the restaurant. Some days I thought, are we ever going to be able to pay off all this debt?"

In 1956, the hotel lobby was remodeled. Warnings were posted to alert the public to the work being done. The old floor was removed and temporarily replaced with wide boards laid on the stringers.

One evening, Jeannine Austin was waiting on at a banquet in the hotel dining room. She rushed into the lobby and forgot the floor was being replaced. Jeannine completely missed her step and fell through the boards and into the furnace room below.

Stony rushed to her assistance.

"Are you all right?" he hollered. "What happened?'

"It was my own fault," Jeannine said to him. "I don't have any broken bones, just a little shaken up. I knew about the lobby floor and should have been paying more attention."

Luckily, no one was seriously hurt.

The hotel lobby had been drab and dreary. To brighten it up, the walls were covered with knotty pine paneling and carpet was laid to make it more inviting and homey for guests.

To complete the "new look" they wanted for the lobby, Jo and Stony were fortunate to be able to buy two urns on pedestals from the Z. L. Merchant estate. In them, they planted large Boston ferns. Marguerite Merchant, who was an authority on antiques, had obtained these unique urns in Italy.

The Merchants were another business-oriented couple in Norway. Moving to Norway in 1911, Mr. Zeb L. Merchant had bought the Prince Sisters Dry Goods Store on Main Street. He owned the "Z. L. Merchant's Dry Goods Store" on Main Street and operated it for 45 years. The Merchant Block was named for him.

Before coming to Norway, the Merchants had invested in the

stock market. Being a financier, he was able to withstand the stock market crash of 1929 and had watched his holdings grow to their maximum potential. With their vision of the future for a community hospital for Norway, the Merchants were the principal organizers and major benefactors in the construction of the Stephens Memorial Hospital.

While the repairs at Hotel Stone were costly and exhausting, in the end, Jo had an attractive hotel with forty-six modern rooms. Two attractively decorated living rooms were available for public meetings or to serve bridge club luncheons. The spacious dining room, with its Oriental buffets, could serve large groups from the new modern hotel kitchen.

In the 1950's, many fund raising events for the new hospital were held at Hotel Stone in the meeting rooms and dining room.

"I wanted to do my part," said Jo, who now had a large dining hall at her disposal. "We furnished the banquet and donated the proceeds to the fund for the new hospital."

"Maude Kammerling, who had so generously donated the library, helped the hospital cause as well." Jo said.

The first donations to the community's hospital came from Dr. Walter Dixon of Norway, an orthopedic surgeon, who had a private practice and his own hospital on Pleasant Street. His interest in developing a hospital dated back many years.

When he went to serve in the Medical Corps in the European theater and Africa in 1941, Dr. Dixon donated his operating room equipment to Ethel Howe, RN, for use at her privately owned hospital. Ethel Howe and Jo were related through Jo's great-grandmother, Sally Horne.

In 1939, Ethel Howe had opened Norway Hospital at 33 Deering Street. Four nurses were on the staff, Miriam Stetson, Lou Calhoun, Betty Farrar, and Ethel Howe, who was also the hospital administrator. Local doctors Walter Dixon, Chelsey Nelson, Edwin Reeves, Johnson Bean, Roland McCormick, Dr. Paul Villa, and Rosewell Hubbard served as the medical staff.

Ward rates were $4.50 per day; semi-private rooms, $5 per day; and private rooms, $6 per day. The delivery-room rate was $10, and oxygen cost $3. An additional fee of $1 was charged for the babies' board, with over 1000 deliveries in the 1940s. Accident cases and minor surgeries, such as tonsillectomies, were also handled at the Norway Hospital.

In 1951, with new state and federal regulations and the rising costs of medical equipment, Ethel Howe found it impossible to continue. With little or no health insurance, many patients' bills were unpaid. When Ethel Howe was encouraged to raise the fees she charged, her reply was, "But the people don't have the money to pay their bills now."

In 1952, the Hospital Association (later the Stephens Memorial Hospital Corporation) was formed. Ethel Howe sold the Norway Hospital to it, and the hospital's name was changed to the Central Oxford County Hospital and soon the hospital moved to its new location on Lower Main Street in Norway.

After the sale was completed, Ethel Howe bought the Norway Nursing Home on Beal Street, which she operated until 1962. When the hospital was moved to Main Street, the Deering Street building was sold and later become a boarding home for the elderly called "The Home for Creative Living."

By 1953, the donations of Zeb and Marguerite Merchant helped Dr. Dixon see his dream of a modern community hospital become a reality. After the new building was constructed, the hospital's name was changed to Stephens Memorial Hospital in honor of C. A. Stephens, who was a highly respected writer, doctor and research scientist in the area.

By the middle of 1953, the Stephens Memorial Hospital building on Main Street was finished, equipped and ready for use. Thanks to the widespread community efforts, it opened its doors in early 1954 with a staff of six doctors. It has continued to grow and has been a great asset to the whole Oxford Hills area.

Dr. C. A. Stephens was a character. He and his wife, Minnie Plummer Scalar, had been Jo's customers at Stone's Drug Store. Madame Scalar, as she was known, had been an opera singer.

"We waited on them at Stone's Drug Store," Jo said. "Madame Scalar wore large hats and long dresses that swept the ground. Mr. Stephens usually wore white suits and a Panama hat."

He owned a home at Norway Lake called the Laboratory where he conducted much of his research. Built in 1888, it was a mansion with forty rooms connected by winding stairways. The huge dome, weighing three tons, was located seventy-five feet above the ground and served as the observatory. Much of his research involved a disciplined study of the prolongation of life. Through the study of cells, he had hoped to develop research into the "Fountain of Youth".

C. A. Stephens was better known for articles that he wrote for the Youth's Companion, a popular magazine of the era. Many of these articles have been published in book form.

Stephens hoped that, one day, the new hospital could be located on the site of the "Laboratory". Because town water and sewer didn't serve the property, this proved to be impossible. After his death, a court case by relatives ate up all his money. The town's people decided to still use his name, even though many felt this was not the correct decision.

Some of the traveling salesmen who stayed at Hotel Stone over the years represented such companies as John Sexton, Swift, Armour, Squire Meats, Standard Brands, C. H. Robinson Paper Co., C. M. Rice Paper Co., Coffin & Burr Investment Consultants and Millett, Fish & Dresser Accountants.

"Many of the salesmen were my friends. They would plan to meet at Barjo's for dinner," Jo said. "Buster Ives, a salesman for Squire Meats, would come into the kitchen and tell us funny stories about his experiences on the road. After he retired, he brought his wife to eat at Barjo's and he still continued his practice of telling us a joke or story."

Henry Blood, the John Sexton salesman, brought Jo new grocery products his company was introducing. When he stayed at the hotel, he would come to Barjo's during the evening and teach Jo how to make different entrees with these new foods.

Many companies—Central Maine Power, New England Telephone Co., Cornell Construction and the Portland Pipeline—payed for hotel rooms for their crews on the road. All these crews were customers at Barjo's as well as at the hotel.

In the fall of 1950, Jo and Stony held the annual meeting for the members of the Maine Merchants Association at Hotel Stone. At this time, Josephine and Ralph Stone were invited to serve on the board of directors of the organization.

That same year, the Association president, Stanwood Bailey, contacted Jo and told her about a new insurance program that was being initiated for the membership. It was called the Maine Merchants Insurance Trust and included many benefits: health, medical, polio, a life insurance policy, major medical and several others. In 1951, Jo bought the insurance policy for all her employees at Barjo's for a Christmas present instead of holding a party. At the time, some employees were disgruntled, but after several had used some of the health benefits, they realized what a present it really was. Jo paid the entire cost of this insurance package for all her employees until the restaurant closed in 1991.

Even though there was a dining room at the hotel, it was used mainly as a banquet hall. For a short time, Jo served breakfast there, but it proved to be unprofitable.

In 1951, an unusual incident happened at the hotel dining room while Jo was serving breakfast. It involved an overnight guest and one of Jo's best friends, Gladys Greenleaf, who owned the Vanity Beauty Shop on Main Street.

At that time, it was a big treat for the young people of the community to go to Lewiston for Italian food. Some of the local boys got together every Sunday night to go to Steckino's. On the way home, one evening, they saw a man walking toward Norway on Route 26 in Oxford. They stopped to offer him a ride. He accepted. When they got almost to the village, they saw a logging truck tipped over by the side of the road headed toward Lewiston. Wondering if the man had anything to do with it, they asked him. He said nothing. When the boys got to Norway, they stopped at the Hotel Stone and, because it was late, rang the night bell. When Stony answered the door, they asked if Stony would rent the man a room for the night, which he did.

In the morning, the man came into the hotel dining room for breakfast. No one noticed anything unusual about him. It was only when Gladys Greenleaf, a local beautician, came in to have an early breakfast that she noticed a gun on the table beside the man. It made her very nervous because she had no idea who the man was. She told Jo and Stony what she had seen.

"We called the Oxford Sheriff Department, and they came over to investigate," Jo recalls. "By the time the officers arrived the man had checked out of the hotel and was on his way."

Contacting other departments in the area, the police found out the man was an escaped convict. In the morning, before the man had come to the hotel dining room for breakfast, the officers found out that he had been to Woodman's Sporting Store and had bought a gun. They also found out that the previous night, he had stolen the logging truck the boys had seen on Route 26.

With more investigation, the police learned that he had lived in the area for over two years and had worked as a laborer in the woods. Keeping a low profile, he had eluded the authorities. No one had been suspicious. The man thought that by stealing the logging truck, he would be able to leave the area undetected. If it hadn't been for the sharp eyes of Jo's friend, Gladys, who told Jo and Stony what she had seen, he would have been successful.

Even so, the man was able to get out of town and wasn't apprehended until he reached one of the Carolinas. By telephoning his description to other law enforcement agencies, the police were able to identify and apprehended him. Subsequently, he was sentenced to serve time in prison.

One evening in 1952, Jo and Stony were relaxing and enjoying television in their room on the second floor of the hotel. They heard a strange scratching, scraping noise overhead.

"Where's that funny noise coming from?" Jo asked Stony. "I think you better go find out. Is something happening to the building or is somebody in trouble? Hurry up! It's making me nervous. I don't like the sound of it."

"O.K.," he said, putting on his shoes and heading out the door.

Stony went to the third floor and found the noise was coming from Room 35, directly above their room. A customer, who had checked in that afternoon, was digging a hole in the bathroom floor and wall directly above them. The scraping sound was from a knife that he was using to dig the plaster off the bathroom wall.

The police were called. The officers found out the man was a mental patient who had walked away from a mental institution. The police department called the authorities and he was transported back to the Augusta Mental Hospital.

With the climate of growth and reorganization for efficiency in the commercial world, Jo would experience many changes at the hotel. There would be new challenges that would combine the needs of many of the elderly with those of the young people in the area. Jo would soon incorporate her own form of philanthropy into her business at both Barjo's and Hotel Stone.

---

[48] *This road is now known as Route 26.*

[49] *This is a term used in the Lapham history of Norway for hotels of the era.*

CHAPTER 18

Philanthropy Becomes a Way of Life

During the early 50's, changes occurred that dramatically affected Jo's business at Hotel Stone. Many companies stopped paying for rooms for their salesmen and instead provided company automobiles. While this released the companies of additional expenses, it unfortunately meant a diminishing pool of hotel clients for Jo and Stony.

Despite losing an important source of income in this way, Jo continued to help the public. Her generosity came from her genuine love for people and it remained something she never wanted to talk about.

When interviewed in 1955 by a reporter from the local paper about all she did for others, Jo said to him. "Never gave away a meal in my life or furnished a room at no charge. Just cannot afford to in these hard times. Don't have a single penny to spare."

Over and over Jo denied that she had helped people, swearing to him that she didn't have any idea what he was talking about. But the whole village knew better.

"I would rather give to ten people who are putting one over on me than miss one person who really truly needed a lift," Jo has said. "But if I did help them, I wouldn't wanted others to find out about it. That was my secret just between me and those I helped."

In the fifties, Hotel Stone had some interesting regulars. Many of them were in on the secret of Jo's generous nature. High school students from outlying towns stayed at the hotel just as Jo's siblings had lived in town a generation before. These students stayed at the hotel free of charge, thanks to Jo. Many elderly, as well, received special treatment. There were several unique and interesting people who made Hotel Stone their home.

For many years, Elmer Hussey, a former professor and tutor, stayed at the hotel in the winter and at his home at Noble's Corner, Norway, in the summer. One winter, he was having a hard time to raise the money to pay for his room, so Jo accepted an antique grandfather's clock and a unique Chinese lamp from his personal collection in exchange for his winter's stay.

In 1954, after a trip to Spain, Mr. Hussey brought back one of the boys he was tutoring. The boy stayed at the hotel during his visit while he was learning about the way we live in the United States of America. It was a very interesting experience for both the young man and the local high school kids who lived at the hotel.

Another gentleman, Harold Webb, lived at the hotel and tutored some of the local young people. He and Jack Smith, who worked for Jo at the restaurant, became good friends. He taught Jack a lot about God, which, later in life, became Jack's life work.

Roland Beaudoin was another of Mr. Webb's students. Roland learned to love books, helping him greatly to better himself. Later, he would be the one the entire sheriff's department depended on for interpretations of criminal laws and statutes.

Transient paying guests weren't the only regulars at Hotel Stone. There were many elderly people who were Jo's "special" guests. These were elderly people who were trying to live on very small Social Security checks and had no family to help them. At the time, many of the elderly received as little as $35 a month. On this amount, they were barely able to exist. Jo and Stony furnished them a room at the hotel for a very low rate which also included three meals a day at Barjo's.

Shortly after Jo bought the hotel, she had a call from Freeland Howe who had been placed in a nursing home. In the stock market crash of 1929, he had lost all his money and real estate. After returning to Norway from New York State, he had become one of Jo's "special guests" at Barjo's.

"Can't you do something to help me get out of this nursing home?" Freeland asked Jo and Stony. "I know I can't live in my little camp any longer, but I don't want to live here."

Going down to the Tucker Street nursing home, Jo wondered just what she was going to find. Was it really as bad as Freeland had described? When Jo and Stony went in, they walked into a dark, dingy room. It was much worse than they had expected.

"What a pitiful sight that was. Just an old metal bed and a blanket wrapped around his shoulders. All the patients were just sitting there forlornly, just waiting to die," Jo exclaimed. "I told him Stony and I would move him to the hotel where he could have a room. We would bring his meals to him because he was too weak to walk to the restaurant."

They helped him pack what few belongings he had and moved

him to the hotel. In the annex, many of Jo's "special guests" had rooms. Freeland was given Room One because it was conveniently located near the bathroom.

Jo never understood why she was so fond of Freeland Howe. She really disliked *lazy* people, but he fascinated her. He hadn't worked since the early 1930's, but he had studied many different fields and possessed a great knowledge on many subjects.

At the hotel, he entertained many of the guests with his knowledge of the area. Sitting on the hotel porch in the summer, he wore a knitted plaid beret, a trademark of his, and a long coat. With his mustache and long white beard, he was quite an attraction to the summer visitors who often came to talk with him.

Freeland explained to Jo the inner workings and how stocks were traded on the New York Stock Exchange. He taught her how to read the stock quotes and what the many symbols used by the Dow-Jones Industrial Average meant.

During one of their many conversations as they sat in rocking chairs on the hotel porch ,he told Jo, "I think the capitalists are trying to take over the world."

Jo knew that Freeland was bitter because he had lost his money in the crash of 1929. Still, she thought this was a pretty rash remark, since he had been a part of the business community for many years himself.

She said to him, "Freeland, if you think the socialist state is so much better, why don't you move to Russia?"

To this, Freeland made no response.

Freeland was a Christian Scientist. He proved to have accurate foresight when told Jo, "One day, people will live to regret using so many chemicals in food production. It is going to cause sickness and death to many people."

He was Jo's guest at the hotel until he died in the late 1950's.

Another guest, Lillian Powers lived at the hotel from 1955 until 1961, when the hotel was torn down. She was a restaurant guest from 1955 until 1989. She had grown up in the Norway-South Paris area and had been a milliner (designer of hats) at Lord & Taylor's department store in New York City. As demand for her skills declined with changing styles, she tried to continue to live in New York City on her Social Security check of $35 a month, but was unable to do it.

In 1955 when she moved back to Norway, she had a serious case of pernicious anemia. Jo's brother, Donald, was town manager for Norway and was able to get her enrolled in some State of Maine programs for the elderly. With the medical care of Dr.

Nelson, she was able to regain her health.

The local people called Miss Powers "the Lady in Black" because she always dressed in black. This included her coat, dress, shoes and hat. Part of her treatment to get her strength back included walking around town everyday.

"I miss my walks in Central Park," she'd say when she dropped by Barjo's where she ate all her meals. "I still read the New York Times to keep in touch with the business community."

In 1961, when the Hotel Stone was closed, she moved to a rooming house owned by the Sessions on Main Street near the restaurant. Miss Powers had a bad accident with a heater in her room at the Sessions house in 1989.

"I had been to a funeral for one of my friends that afternoon. One of the waitresses, Ruth, came to me and said we haven't seen Miss Powers since yesterday." Jo said. "I immediately told them to go check on her at home."

Ruth and her daughter, Diana, found Miss Powers slumped over an electric heater in her room. One of her legs was burned to the bone. During the previous evening, she had had a stroke. She had been in front of the heater for nearly twenty-four hours when the girls found her.

At mealtime, Miss Powers had always been punctual and arrived at the same time every day for meals. When she didn't come for lunch, Jo felt she should have sent someone to her room to find out what the matter was.

Miss Powers was in a coma for a long time at Stephens Memorial Hospital and was moved directly to Norway Nursing Home from the hospital. She never regained the use of her leg and was never out of bed again. Margie Sessions, the owner of the rooming house, went to see her daily and came to the restaurant to update Jo on Miss Power's condition. She never returned to her room and died in the Norway Nursing Home in 1990.

Jo and Stony donated many sports banquets and Senior Class Suppers to help the high school kids raise money for different events such as the Washington trip, the purchase of uniforms for the sports teams or the band, and other school activities.

The high school kids accepted the idea of the towns and the schools working together before their parents and the rest of the community did.

Jo had graduated from Norway High School and Ralph Stone had graduated from South Paris High School. When they put on school banquets, they always included both schools. Many people felt this was the first step in the joining of the school systems that was later to become School Administrative District 17, which now includes eight surrounding towns.

The hotel was to play an important role in the community, one that Jo had not foreseen. One day in the late 1950's, Jo's neighbor, Nolan Jackson who owned a grocery store, brought in the sports coach to meet her. He told her that the boys were trying to raise some money to buy bats, gloves, uniforms, and other paraphernalia for the coming baseball and football seasons.

After the coach's talk with Jo, the boys decided that a public supper would be a good method whereby to secure funds. The folks would get something for their money and the athletic group would profit. One of the group was delegated to solicit Jo for her assistance in the endeavor.

The young man came to her with a lump in his throat. He wasn't exactly a milk toast but Jo was known in three counties as being a champion heckler. The conversation with the schoolboy went something like this. It isn't reported verbatim because Jo denies any such conversation ever took place and the boy hasn't gotten over what happened even to this day.

"The athletic club is trying to get new equipment like baseball bats, uniforms, and other things. We wondered if you'd be willing to help us in a small way?" he asked.

"Help you? Why you youngsters are sent to school to learn to read and write, not to chase a baseball around! How do you propose to earn money?" Jo demanded.

"We are going to put on a public supper. Our mothers have agreed to cook the food if we can raise the money to buy the supplies. We figure quite a few people will come if we charge a dollar for a banquet supper."

"A *dollar*!" Jo said most disdainfully. "A *dollar* won't even buy the turkey to be cooked! We get at least a dollar and a quarter for a turkey supper."

The lad looked crestfallen. Jo had him hooked good and proper. Not a smile on her face—but inwardly she had ideas of her own, and she was getting keen delight over it! Then she softened a bit and outlined her *own* plans of how to raise the money.

"I tell you what you are to do! First, the tickets will be a dollar and a quarter and there will be turkey and all the fixings. You go out and sell the tickets right and left. You ought to be able to sell 300 tickets at least."

The boy didn't remember half of what Jo told him.

"Now, you sell the tickets and get the cash in advance. Money, you know folding money! We must know exactly how much food to prepare," she told him. "Then you come back and show me how much you have collected in advance."

"We'll prepare turkeys, mashed potatoes, onions, squash and hot rolls. We'll cook the food here at Barjo's and serve it, piping hot, in the Hotel Stone dining room. We'll give 'em a meal they won't forget twixt now and next summer. Now, go out and sell your tickets!"

"But the food," the youngster ventured, "how will we pay for the food you are talking about?"

"Who said anything about paying for anything? I simply said *sell* the tickets! We have a store room filled with just the right kind of food for your banquet."

Jo chuckled. She considered it a favor to her to be asked to do a public service of this sort.

"We are going to furnish everything for free. All you need to do is sell the tickets and bring some around to me. I'll buy some of those pasteboards and I know where to place 'em. But, mind you, don't tell anyone that I bought tickets to my own banquet!"

The boy's eyes brightened. He was beginning to get certain facts of life through his clouded brain!

"And mind you," Jo continued, as the lad raced to tell the others about it, "you tell all the kids that I expect you to go and sell a whale of a lot of tickets!"

They sold tickets, all right—the banquet made just a few dollars shy of $500 to buy their sports equipment.

In early 1955, two local young men, Donnie McGinnis from Bryant Pond and Dolor Lafrance from Norway, both needed help with their medical bills. Donnie had broken his neck in a swimming accident at Norway Lake. As a result, he was a paraplegic. "Dodie" Lafrance had leukemia and required many blood transfusions that were very expensive.

To help the two families, Jo and Stony offered to provide and cook the food, at no charge for the benefit supper. They served a buffet in the hotel Stone dining room from 4:30 p.m. until 8:00 p.m. Everyone from Norway and South Paris and the surrounding communities came to help make it a huge success. The line of people extended from the Hotel Stone dining room out to the lobby and onto Main Street. It was the largest single event ever held at the hotel, raising several thousand dollars that was divided between the two boys.

Many local people used the Hotel Stone for their meetings and annual banquets, as well as for food sales. Some brought their own food, the Stones catered some, but Jo and Stony furnished many banquets at no charge. The Women's Club, Mothers' Club and various Bridge clubs, as well as bowling leagues and many organizations, had luncheons and banquets there. This made the hotel an integral part of the community for the first time. When catering was done, the food was cooked at Barjo's and served in the Hotel Stone dining room.

Many of the high school kids, including Joyce and Barbara McAllister, waited on the Bridge Club luncheons and banquets at the hotel. During fall, winter, and spring banquet seasons, Jo stayed at the restaurant where the preparations were done. She ran the restaurant with Margaret's help. Stony and Henry served the banquets at the hotel with school kids helping in the kitchen.

One of the Kimball boys, Charlie, often helped in the hotel kitchen. One afternoon, he said, "You know, Jo, I've made so many trips from the hotel to the restaurant for Stony that I think I've taken all the bark off the old Elm on the corner."

The Elm was located at the corner of the driveway entering the restaurant parking lot from Main Street.

"Well, Charlie, if Stony could remember what you needed to take from the restaurant, you wouldn't have had to make so many trips up here to fill in for him," Jo said with a grin.

Being a hard worker herself, Jo demanded the same quality of work from those around her. Forgetting to take all the necessary equipment or underestimating the amount of food for a banquet was something she never wanted to have happen. Because all the food was being cooked at the restaurant, all that the hotel kitchen was used for was to keep the food hot.

In 1956, the labor unions were trying to get a foothold in the Norway-Paris area. Union officials held many meetings in the Hotel Stone dining room to urge C. B. Cummings & Sons employees to organize for a vote to accept unionization. The union won the first vote, but they were not so successful when the contract came up for a second vote, C. B. Cummings' employees voted the union out. C. B. Cummings & Sons mill had always provided steady work for its employees. Even though they didn't receive high wages, the people could depend on a paycheck every week. To many in the mill, this was more important than the extra benefits offered by labor unions.

In South Paris, at A. C. Lawrence Leather Co., the union was more successful. One man from the tannery, Suzy Ross, was a real good union organizer and he became the first union-shop steward. Feeling that he would fare better if he represented the company, this same man changed sides, and became a representative for the management of A. C. Lawrence Leather Company. The tannery became a part of a larger company and, in the downsizing process, was closed. The factory continued to be unionized, but when it was shut down, many in the area became unemployed with few benefits. What they received for severance pay, they had to fight for.

During the 1950's, while Jo was establishing the business at the hotel, many things were happening at Barjo's as Jo became more involved in community projects and as her family was increasing with the addition of more grandchildren.

Jo bought the Grand Champion 4-H Lambs every year and put on a special dinner to honor the area's 4-H Clubs. Here she is pictured (standing, left) with granddaughter Darcy and daughter Barbara at the auction with 4-H members and their prize-winning lambs, 1961.

CHAPTER 19

Barjo's in the Early 1950's

In September, 1950, Alpheas Jackson, who was working for the Maine State Department of Agriculture, came to see Jo.

"Jo, would you be willing to work with me to help organize a 4-H Market Lamb Auction at the Oxford County Fair?" he asked.

She replied, "If there is something we can do to help the 4-H kids with their projects, I will be glad to."

They went to see Phil Stone of the Oxford County Fair Association, Razor Crossman, the Auctioneer, and Keith Bates, the Oxford County 4-H Agent. They worked together to organize the 4-H Market Lamb Auction. The event would be held every year, starting that September during Oxford County Fair Week.

The Oxford County Fair was originally held at the corner of Paris and Fair Street between Norway and South Paris, the present site of the Oxford Hills High School. It was held there for many years until the school district won the right, by eminent domain, to build the new high school on the site. At that time, the Oxford County Fair Association moved the fair to Oxford on land off Route 26 donated to Leon Newcomb.

Alpheas Jackson and Jo worked hard to promote the 4-H lamb sale. They contacted many large wholesale meat houses, such as Jordan's, Kirschner Meats, Line Road Auction House, Hannaford Brothers., Shop 'n Save Supermarkets, Chuck Wagon Restaurants, Oxford Foods and Oxford Abattoir. These companies became promoters and buyers for the 4-H club auctions.

Every year from 1950 until 1992 at the 4-H auction, Jo bought the Grand Champion pen of three lambs, no matter how high the price was. Usually, she bought at least ten more lambs as well, so she could serve a special 4-H lamb dinner at Barjo's.

Every October, during National Restaurant Month, Barjo's held Grand Champion 4-H Lamb Sunday, the second Sunday of the month, to honor the 4-H Clubs. That Sunday rivaled Mother's Day as one of her biggest days of the year. Everyone from miles around came to support the children. The Fair Association had pictures taken at the fair of all the 4-H members with their lambs.

Buyers were given a picture of the boy or girl with the lamb when they bought a lamb at the 4-H Lamb Auction. These pictures were always posted on the wall at Barjo's so the customers could see the kids who had raised the lambs. All the suppliers and the restaurant, together, would buy a full-page ad in the local newspapers and sponsor an ad on WKTQ, the local radio station, to promote the 4-H clubs.

Barjo's had special menus printed for 4-H Lamb Sunday using 4-H stationery, furnished by the Oxford County Extension Service. Sometimes a photo of the Grand Champion Lambs was included on the menu which were printed at the Advertiser-Democrat. The menus featured an Irish Stew (lamb stew), Lamb Chops and Roast Leg of Lamb. The community and the restaurant always worked together to help their youngsters.

In 1990, the Oxford County Extension Service presented Jo with a plaque that stated: To Josephine A. Stone in Special Recognition for 40 years of Distinguished Service to the Oxford County Fair and to the 4-H Clubs of the State of Maine.

This award came as a complete surprise to Jo. To her, she had just been helping the 4-H kids with their projects. As was her way, she had stayed in the background never thinking that others even knew what she had been doing.

Recalling a night in 1951, Barbara and Henry tell of an unusual event that occurred on the way home from work at the restaurant. After closing up at 1:00 a.m., they took Jo, carrying the day's receipts in a paper bag under her arm, for a ride so she could relax before going home.

It was a dark night with hardly any traffic. They ran out of gas on the Buckfield Road in South Paris and started to walk when a car came along. Jo figured the stranger might attempt to rob them so on an impulse, she threw the bag of money in the ditch. The stranger turned out to be a Good Samaritan, Maynard Bessey, who owned Bessey Foods. He was returning from a lodge meeting in Rumford to his home in Buckfield. He took them to the South Paris village for gas and then back to retrieve the car. Jo never mentioned what she had done.

"The next day, we returned to search for the paper bag," Barbara said.

"After hunting in the ditch beside the road for a considerable amount of time, we finally found the bag with the money intact. I couldn't believe Mother had thrown the bag of money in the ditch. Thank goodness, no one else had found it first."

It was in 1952 that Jo bought a drive-in restaurant at the foot of Paris Hill on Route 26. Jo and Stony changed its name to "Andy's Drive-in" for her oldest granddaughter, Andrea. They offered curb service with carhops dressed in red and white checkered uniforms and high white boots.

"I sent Stony to run Andy's," Jo said. "After trying it for a couple of seasons, we didn't feel that it was as good a deal as we had thought it would be."

In 1954, she sold it to "Sonny" Norton, who rebuilt it into a private home, which it still is today.

After Joline Leslie, or Jody as the family called her, was born on November 2, 1952, Barbara and Henry moved to their new ranch-style home on 22 Maple Street, Norway. It was an Aladdin Home made of perfect pre-cut lumber that was shipped to the site from Wisconsin. Jo hired local carpenters to build the foundation and do the construction work, paying for all the workmen herself to help Barbara and Henry get started.

Jo still owned the building at 225 Main Street. She rented the apartment to Gladys Greenleaf, the beautician. Scott Kilborn was still operating his barbershop on the first floor, while his wife, Pearl, had her music room in the back of the building.

At this same time, Jo's "Barjo Family" was increasing. She was soon to become the guardian of two children. One of her employees, Winfield Millett, was working part-time at Barjo's and full-time for Welch's Garage in South Paris.

The Millett family came from East Waterford. Winfield's father, Joe Millett, had done odd jobs for Jo over the years. After he was killed in an explosion at Welch's Garage, Winfield's youngest sister, Carla, quit school at sixteen. Although she could have had Social Security benefits, she wanted to be independent and came to work at Barjo's as a waitress.

Winfield and Carla came from a large family of nine children. Five of their brothers were mentally retarded and had been put in the state home[50] in Pownal. They had an older sister, Edith, and another brother who had died in infancy.

Winfield was having problems with his wife, Mabel, so Jo invited him to live at the hotel. They had two little children and Jo always had a soft spot in her heart for kids. The two had been very young and irresponsible when they married. She knew that Winfield had become involved in stock car racing at Oxford Plains Speedway. He was using money that should have been going to support his family to build his stock car. It was too much for Mabel, but she was unstable, too.

"Winfield had no one to take care of the kids. He asked me if I could help him out," Jo said. "I never thought of myself as the mothering type, but it worked out. He came out of a big family and I knew his mother couldn't help him."

When Winfield and his wife divorced in July, 1953, Jo was awarded custody of Alfred and Penny. She had custody of the children until other arrangements for their care could be made.

This wasn't the first time Jo had been involved in a custody case. At the hotel, Stony and Jo were like foster parents to all the kids living there. The Kimball family, in the 1940's, had lost their mother and the only mother the smaller children knew was Jo.

Later, Carla Millett married Bob Witt and moved to Kansas City, Missouri. There she got a job with Hallmark Cards Corporation. With the help of her husband, she was able to go up the corporate ladder and attained a position in the production department. She had her own corporate automobile and toured the United States as a troubleshooter for Hallmark.

At 51 years old, Carla had a major heart attack and stroke. Because of the reputation she had attained with the company for her dedication to her job, Hallmark Corporation paid her full salary and all her medical expenses until her death at 54.

Jo's own family was increasing. Her only grandson, Robert Henry Paradis, "Robbie", was born on March 4, 1954.

"At first, I thought he might have a hard time with two older sisters. But before long, Robbie proved he could hold his own, no matter what happened," his grandmother said. "He became Jody's spokesman, so she didn't think it was necessary to talk. He was a little guy, but he always made his presence known by harassing his sisters."

Many others things were happening at the restaurant with new faces and characters arriving on the scene.

In the early 1950's, one a local character and a regular customer at Barjo's was Billy Bacon. He had a little notebook in which he wrote down the name of everyone he met each day. Billy was at the restaurant for breakfast every morning when Veda unlocked the door for the day. She served him breakfast and was always the first name in his book. He called Veda, "Cinderella", and wrote her name in red ink outlined with blue to show she was very special.

After breakfast, Billy sat by the hour on the steps of the L. M. Longley store near Barjo's. He watched all the people going by and often wrote down their names in his little black book. He had a unique title for a lot of the local folks such as: Little Miss Muffett, Black Widow, Boy in Blue, Howdy-Dowdy, Snow White, and Doctor Doolittle.

Billy Bacon's knowledge of area flora and fauna was amazing. He was an authority on mushrooms. He could take you into the woods and tell you just by looking at them which ones were safe to eat and which ones were poisonous.

In 1953, one of the salesmen for Tidewater Oil came into the restaurant once a week for dinner. His game was to make the waitress who was serving him cry.

He said, "Jo, don't you ever tell the girls what I am up to. I always leave a good tip, but I want them to earn it."

"I thought to myself, what a mean trick he is playing on my waitresses," Jo said. "I decided it was time to give him some of his own medicine. It was time for the hurdy-gurdy man's yearly visit, so I invited him in. I asked him to stand beside the Tidewater salesman's booth while the hurdy-gurdy man sang and played for the restaurant customers."

"All the time the salesman was eating dinner, he sang at the top of his lungs," she said with a hearty laugh.

The salesman was furious with Jo. He was well aware of the reason why he was being serenaded in this manner. He never again harassed a waitress because he knew that he had met his match in *Jo*!

In 1954, Jo hired Geraldine and Arlene Bean[51], identical twins from Milton Plantation, a small-unorganized territory north of Rumford. They were from a large family. Going to Woodstock High School had been a huge challenge for the girls. They had to walk nearly twenty-five miles every day to get their education.

At first, Arlene worked as desk clerk at Hotel Stone and Gerry waited on tables at the restaurant. Later they both worked at Barjo's. The girls were great practical jokers and loved to confuse the customers. They looked so much alike, it was even hard for the other waitresses to tell them apart.

On St. Patrick's Day, the restaurant was well decorated with the green of the Emerald Isle, and the patrons were served by waitresses garbed in fetching Irish colleen costumes. Prizes were awarded to the waitress with the most unique costume. Jack Quinn, the local reporter and photographer for the Portland Press Herald, took the Bean twins' photo. They held a picture frame between them. The AP Wire Service published this picture on St.

Patrick's Day. It looked like one was looking in a mirror when it was really identical twins.

These were years when the Firemen's Carnival, an event the whole area participated in, was in full swing. It was held in July at the Oxford County Fairgrounds at the corner of Fair and Main Street between Norway and South Paris. Every night during carnival week, the firemen sponsored a parade on Main Street with categories for both the children and adults: there were Dolly Carriage, Tricycle, Bicycle, a Horribles parade and a Grand Parade on Saturday. All the business community joined in, vying with each other with elaborate floats and decorated cars. The Norway-Paris Comets Band, the Scarlet Cadets from Lewiston and other groups provided the music. Barjo Restaurant, too, always had an awe-inspiring car in the Grand Parade. Margaret took great pleasure and pride in decorating—just as she had in the Stone Drug Store days. What she and the girls produced was a work of art. As much of the crew as could had a part in the celebration, either riding in the parade or helping to decorate.

In 1956, the Barjo's crew decided to have an entry in the "Horribles" parade. This parade was a real fun thing with everyone trying to see who could be the most ridiculous. The kids borrowed a 1931 Model A Ford from one of the customers. On top of it, they resolved to place a casket built out of a huge packing box. It was lined with pink cloth and the outside was covered with black crepe paper.

Arlene, one of the Bean twins, volunteered to be the corpse. She had her face covered with white face powder. Then she climbed into the casket which was tied to the roof of the car. Two of the boys from the restaurant, dressed in old black suits with tails, rode on the back bumper as if they were the footmen. All of the kids who were off-duty also dressed in black and rode in the car as if they were mourners.

"You'll never be able to drive the whole parade route without losing the casket on top of the car," Jo cautioned. "Where did you ever come up with that idea?!"

Gerry and Arlene looked at each other and began laughing.

"You know how crazy we are, Jo," they said in unison. "What else would you expect?"

"Barbara Lawrence was a good chauffeur and we made it the whole way," Emily remembered. "We won the booby prize, but we had a lot of laughs."

Also in 1956, Kellogg's Foods sponsored a contest to name the best breakfast waitress in the country to be called "Miss Good

Morning". The Kellogg's company asked Barjo's to participate in the contest. The criteria for the contest included: neatness of service, presentation including uniforms, shoes, and personal appearance, quality of service, the use of trays, and personality when waiting on the public. In order for the competition to be fair, the waitresses were not to know who the judges were nor when they were to be observed. The judges came at random times, over a month's time, to make their observations. Some were from grocery houses that covered the area. They submitted their reports to the Kellogg's company for a final decision.

Theresa Lafrance Salacup, who was a niece of Frank Lafrance, won the honor to represent Barjo Restaurant in the state competition and a small monetary reward form Kellogg's. In the state competition, she won the title of "Miss Good Morning" for the state of Maine, which was a nice honor for Barjo's and the town of Norway.

---

[50] *This home was later known as the Pineland Hospital.*

[51] *For more stories about the Bean twins- See Appendix I "The Barjo's Family."*

Oxford County Fair, 1964 Eddie Kilgore, pictured here with Jo, came to Barjo's to ask Jo to buy his lamb at the Fair even though he knew it wasn't a prize-winner. She did, indeed, purchase the lamb, but when she paid him, he was so distressed at parting with his pet, he began to cry. Jo's warm heart won out over 4-H regulations and she gave him back his money— and his lamb!

Jack Quinn took this photo of Barjo's twin waitresses, Gerry and Arlene Bean. It was picked up by the AP wire service and published in newspapers nationwide for Saint Patrick's Day 1957.

Saint Patrick's Day 1957
front row: Joanne Wood, Diane Rolfe, Shirley Rogers, Barbara Blanchard
back row: Emily Foster, Arlene Bean, Gerry Bean

CHAPTER 20

Changing Political Scenery

Jo was about to become "the power behind the throne" in Norway's town affairs. She denies she ever had this role, but many people know she did. Many politic discussions were held and issues settled right in the kitchen at Barjo's.

Even though Jo had voted from the time she was twenty-one years old, she had never been active in local politics. This was about to change, with some surprises for one of her family.

Officials of the town of Norway decided to employ two police officers and Frank Lafrance was afraid he would lose his job. He had been hired as Norway's police officer after Jo's father's death. Several of the people who served on Norway's board of selectmen were harassing him.

The chairman of the board, Henry Packard, told Frank that because he was walking his beat, his services as a night watchman might no longer be needed. Others said that with additional officers on the force and a cruiser to patrol the streets, his foot beat was becoming a thing of the past. Norway's police force needed to be upgraded to keep up with the times.

Over the years, the McAllisters and the Lafrances had been good friends. Frank Lafrance had worked as Norway's police officer and night watchman for over twenty years without a vacation or pay raise. His nephew, Roland Beaudoin, called Jo and asked if her brother, Donald, would be willing to run for selectman. Roland thought Donald might be able to help his uncle Frank keep his job.

Jo thought this was a great idea and called Donald. "Don, Marg and I are taking out nomination papers this afternoon for you to run for selectman here in Norway."

"You don't have to worry, we will get all the needed signatures. All you have to do is serve on the board."

"No way!" Don exclaimed. "Just what do you girls think I know about town business?! I have never run for office—and no one will vote for me."

But Jo and the Norway voters thought different!

An overwhelming majority elected Donald at the town meeting. He served as a selectman of Norway for five years, the last two as Chairman of the Board.

Officer Frank Lafrance was able to keep his job, receive a pay raise and retire with a pension because Donald saw to it that Frank and the rest of the municipal employees would have a benefit package that included health insurance and a retirement plan, something the town had never before provided.

"Many thanks to Jo, Margaret and Don for all the help they have given my uncle," Roland said. "Uncle Frank never had a worry after Don was elected to the board of selectmen! Don made sure he got the benefits he deserved."

In March 1956, the Board of Selectmen selected Donald as Norway's town manager. He served for fifteen years, retiring in July 1971. Continuing to be active, Don then served as Oxford Hills Development Association director for two years. This organization was dedicated to revitalizing the region's business climate by encouraging new enterprises to move into the area.

In 1951, political changes were also being made at the state level. Although Maine had always been a Republican stronghold, the Democratic Party was beginning to make inroads. The Republican Party dominated Maine politics for over a century, from the birth of the GOP in 1854 until the election of Edmund S. Muskie as governor in 1954. Muskie and a small band of young progressives broadened the base of Democratic strength and began to convert Maine into a genuine two-party state.

Jo's entire family were staunch Republicans. Donald's wife, Mildred, was an active member of the Hannibal Hamlin[52] Republican Women's Club.

Norway was such a Republican town that Democrat Franklyn Towne, one of Donald's high school classmates, was having trouble being appointed as Norway's postmaster. At the time, the appointment of a Postmaster was political and was based on which political party had a majority of registered voters there. Towne couldn't find enough registered Democrats to get the job.

"Donald and I went around to all our friends and got them to change parties so he could get the appointment. It was a lot of work because Norway had always been overwhelmingly Republican," Jo said. "Before the next general election, we changed back to the Republican Party. Franklyn stayed at the Norway Post Office, as postmaster, until he retired. He also served on the Norway Board of Selectmen while Don was serving as town manager."

In 1954, Joe Bovine and other Democrats from the Rumford area, as well as Louis Jalbert, called "Mr. Democrat" from the Lewiston area, helped local Democrats organize their own party chapter. Many evenings, the locals gathered at Barjo's to discuss politics over coffee. Ray Arsenault and his wife, Marion, were hard workers for the Democratic Party, signing up many new members. Later, Ray became a deputy for the Oxford County Sheriff Department and the Turnkey (jailer) at the county jail.

During these discussions, some of the young men from the area became interested in moving up the political ladder.

"In the late 1960's, Rodney Scribner, who later become the State Treasurer under Democratic Governor Kenneth Curtis, was one of them," Jo said. "He had just graduated from Maine Maritime Academy at the time. Rodney is now our Maine State Auditor. Even though I was a Republican, I was pleased to see him get a good job in the political arena."

After the elections, Roland Beaudoin went to work at the Oxford Sheriff's Department under Democratic Sheriff Stanley Haskell. He stayed there until his retirement. By then, he had reached the rank of "Captain." He was the administrative officer for the Oxford County Sheriff Department. Studying Maine laws and the judicial system, he was the one the whole department turned to for advice when a question arose about any law or previous case in the Maine court system.

George Cummings was the only Republican in these group gatherings at Barjo's. Roland Beaudoin was one of his best friends and was working with him at C. B.Cummings mill during that time. The others were also his friends and he spent most of his evenings listening to their conversations. Even though he seldom voiced his opinion, George was well read, enjoyed classical music, and loved to listen to the news. He enjoyed the other fellows' company, if not their political views.

That same year, Joe Margolin, a local attorney, was going to run on the Democratic ticket for Oxford County District Attorney. He lived in Lewiston. To qualify for political office in Oxford County, he had to live there.

Joe Margolin asked Jo and Stony if he could rent a room at the Hotel Stone. However, he knew he wouldn't be using it.

"When Joe signed the Hotel Stone register, we assigned him Room 25." Jo said. "This was our own room so it looked as if he was sleeping with me. Anyone opposing him on the Republican ticket could have come in to check the Hotel Register. Everything looked above board, if you didn't know the rest of the story."

None of this helped Joe. He lost the election to the Republican candidate after all. None of his political rivals ever found out about Joe Margolin's seemingly strange arrangement at Hotel Stone.

In October 1955, the A. C. Lawrence Leather Co. opened a new factory in South Paris. Barjo's was selected to cater a buffet for 600 people for their opening with. The whole family worked all night to prepare the food. As it was getting late, Jo felt it was important for the staff to get some rest.

"Stony and Henry," she said, "we all need to get a few hours sleep."

"No, we want to finish up this baking right now," they replied.

She left and went to the hotel for a short nap, but felt they should have listened to her and gone home for some rest, too.

Finally after working all night, Henry decided to go take a shower and change his clothes at 9:30 in the morning. Stony had already been home, had showered and was back at work making some of the final trips to the tannery with the food.

Jo was in the kitchen putting the finishing touches on the Lobster Newburg, one of the last entrees that needed to be ready for the banquet.

At 10:00 a.m., Minnie Stone, Stony's brother's wife, had just arrived to help serve on the buffet line. She was helping Henry load the truck with food for the final trip to the tannery.

It was a dark, rainy day and, with no warning, Henry collapsed in a mud puddle beside the pick-up. Frightened, Minnie ran through the back door into the kitchen.

"Come quick," she hollered. "Something has happened to Henry."

Henry lay face down on the ground, unconscious.

Jo grabbed her raincoat and flung it over him to protect him from the rain. "Get a doctor, quick!" Jo exclaimed. "Let's see what we can do, Minnie."

Barbara was already at the tannery, with Stony, Margaret and the other help, setting up the buffet line.

Henry Blood, the John Sexton salesman, was at the restaurant taking his order. He took off his jacket, rolled up his sleeves and said, "You look after Henry and I'll take his place on the buffet line at the tannery."

"I never can repay you for helping us out like this," Jo said to her salesman.

Jo was apprehensive about what the outcome of this catastrophe might be for Henry and Barbara, who now had three little children to support.

"I blamed myself, for not making him go home and rest when I did," Jo said. "He was so sure he could stay right through the night, but I knew it was too much for him."

Henry was in the Central Maine General Hospital in Lewiston for over a month before he was able to come back to work at the restaurant. The next time any extra work had to be done, Jo insisted that everyone get enough rest so there would be no more episodes like this.

During this time, Jo was helping many young people in the community. At one point, all the rooms on top floor of the Hotel Stone Annex were occupied. Here lived twenty or more students who worked either at the restaurant or at the hotel. These were young people who lived out of town. For many, if it hadn't been for Jo's kindness, they probably would never have had the opportunity to finish high school.

In February 1955, Emily Foster had become one of those high school kids. As time went on, Emily would play an important part in Jo's life. Their relationship would develop into more than that of an employer and employee.

52 *Hannibal Hamlin was vice-president during Abraham Lincoln's first term. His home was located on Paris Hill. Today, Bob Bahre lives in that home.*

Firemen's Parade, 1958
L—R:
Joanne Hawkins,
Helen Bryant,
Margaret Noyes,
Bernice Farrar,
Charlotte Hopkins,
Eleanor Flanders,
Paula Komulanin,
Jackie Jackson,
Harriet Pierce.

— SECTION TWO —

PART VI

Life with Jo the Way I See It!

*Emily Foster
waiting on table
at Barjo's, 1956.
Her customers are
Robert Kingsley and his
wife, owners of the Twin Town Theater and the Norway
Drive-in Theater. Below left: Emily on her way to the
NRA Convention in Chicago.*

1964

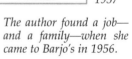

1957

*The author found a job—
and a family—when she
came to Barjo's in 1956.*

1958

1990

1999

CHAPTER 21

Jo's Life from a Different Viewpoint!

From February 1955 to the present, I have a personal perspective on Jo's life and the daily activities at both Barjo's and at the Hotel Stone. So now, I will tell you the rest of Jo's life story from my point of view. Even though Jo never considered herself the motherly type, she included all the employees as part of her extended family. Often she referred to us as her "Barjo family." She has been much more than an employer to me. She has been my mentor and treated me like her own daughter.

From the time of my graduation from the eighth grade at Waterford Memorial School in June 1953, I had been expected to work and to live on my own. My grandmother, Sarah Walker with whom my family lived, had brought me up. After her death in 1951, the relationship at home had become strained because my parents favored my brother who was three years younger.

My parents told me that if I wanted to go to high school, it was all up to me. They couldn't afford to pay for my education, so I had find work doing anything that I could. I was determined to graduate from high school, so I accepted the challenge.

In the summer of 1953, I worked at a summer place, Mt. Tire'm Inn in Waterford. My freshman year of high school, I worked for the Oxford County sheriff as a hired girl with only my room and board for pay. In a tragic turn of events, in June of 1954, both Sheriff Cort Hunt and his wife, Hazel, died nine days apart.

I had just finished my freshman year at Norway High and was helping the Hunts pack to move to their own home in North Norway for the summer. Mrs. Hunt was crippled by arthritis and during the school year it was impossible for her to stay alone while I was in school. Early in the evening of June 10, I was at the farm helping unpack the car with Sheriff Hunt. Suddenly he collapsed beside the car. I ran across the street to his son Elliot's farm for help. Elliot's wife, Dukie, was a trained nurse. Dukie called the ambulance and then came to the house to help. Dukie told me to stay with Mrs. Hunt while she attended to her father-in-law.

When the ambulance came, he was rushed to Stephens Memorial hospital, but he never regained consciousness. He died two days later from a cerebral hemorrhage.

The Hunts' daughter, Doris Jackson, took Mrs. Hunt and me to her house to stay until arrangements could be made. After the sheriff's death, I was helping the family pack their things at the apartment when Mrs. Hunt was suddenly taken ill. Standing in the doorway between the living room and kitchen, her hands froze to the door frame as a blank look came over her face. Dukie rushed to her, but it was all over. She, too, had died of a cerebral hemorrhage.[1]

This was a tragic time in my life. Not only had I lost two wonderful friends, but now I had no place to work. I thought to myself, "What am I going to do now?"

My parents still insisted that I must pay my own way if I wanted to go the high school, so I went looking for work.

That year, I held several jobs. I kept house and babysat for the Bells while Mildred Bell worked at Lambert's Department Store, but after the Christmas season, they no longer needed me. I had to find another job. It was the only way I could pay for my education.

In the 1930's, my mother, Elizabeth Walker Foster, had babysat Donnie and Freddie. Because she knew the McAllister family well, she offered to introduce me to Jo and Margaret, but it was all up to me to apply for a job at the restaurant.

The week before school vacation in February 1955, I went to Barjo's with my mother. I was apprehensive; working in a restaurant would be a whole new experience for me. Though I had waitressed in a summer place, a restaurant was different. I had always loved people, but the idea of being in direct, daily contact with strangers felt overwhelming. Looking around as I walked through the dining room, I couldn't imagine how I could ever learn the menu and respond to customers' needs.

Although I was only 5'2", I was a country kid who had grown up on a farm. At fourteen, I had a sturdy build and strong motivation. I was anxious to show Jo I was worthy of a job.

My mother introduced me to Margaret who met us at the cash register. She told us to go see Jo in the kitchen. Through the swing door we went and found Jo washing the kitchen windows. Her hair was wrapped in a plaid, woolen turban and she was wearing a large, white chef's apron, dark blue pedal pushers and a dark blue blouse.

She looked at me and said, "What do YOU want?"

I was scared half to death by Jo's question and by her brusque tone of voice. Looking at my mother for support, I replied in a shy voice, "I—I've come to apply for a waitress job. Do you have any openings? I am a sophomore in high school, but I can work nights and weekends."

Jo looked at my mother and looked me up and down. Then she said, "If you turn out to be half as good a worker as your mother, you will do all right. Come in Friday night, and Margaret will teach you how to wait on tables. I'll pay you a weekly wage, and you will get tips as well."

This was the first time I would be earning a salary and I hadn't expected that I would also get tips! Every other job had been for only my room and board.

That first week, I rented a room at the Buck Rooming House as traveling back and forth to East Waterford would be impossible. When Jo learned this, she insisted I move to Hotel Stone.

She said, "How do you think you are going to be able to go to school and pay for a room at the same time? All the kids working for me stay the hotel at no charge."

The next weekend, I moved into a room across the hall from Stony's mother. From my very first day of work at the restaurant, Jo treated me like one of her own family, and included me in activities that were not part of my job.

That was forty-five years ago and I still live with Jo today. Looking back, I can never thank God enough for guiding me to her. After my grandmother's death, I had no one to turn to when things seemed to be going from bad to worse. Jo trusted me and taught me to have confidence in myself. She has guided me through many hard times—both in my personal life and through serious illnesses. She became my mentor and is still encouraging me every day.

At Barjo's, I worked both in the dining room as a waitress and in the kitchen if they needed an extra hand. During my high school years, I also worked as desk clerk on the night shift or as a chambermaid at the hotel as well as on banquets. In fact, I worked anywhere they needed me, learning both the restaurant and hotel business at the same time.

Sometimes, I found myself the brunt of a joke, but I was a fast learner and didn't get fooled a second time. A salesman from Freeport who sold eggs at wholesale ate at the restaurant when in town. If he had a new girl waiting on him, he would ask with a straight face, "Would you please go to the kitchen and ask the chef who boned out the liver?"

I was one of the girls he tricked with this joke. I went to the kitchen window and asked, "Jo, who boned out the liver?"

"The same one who boned out the bananas," Jo answered with a hearty laugh. "You come from a farm! Don't you know there are no bones in a liver!"

When I turned back to the table, the salesman was laughing, too. Some of the girls got very upset hat he had tricked them, but not me. I took it with a grain of salt and had a big laugh with him.

As Jo's grandchildren grew up, I was included in many activities that had nothing to do with my job. My youngest brother, Buddy, was included in Jo's family activities as well. He was born in October 1954 after I had been living away from home for over a year. Buddy was more like my own child than my little brother. The same age as Robbie, Jo's grandson, Buddy came along when Jo and Stony took the kids out to supper or to some activity.

When Jo's three oldest grandchildren, Andy, Jody and Robbie, were little, they loved to bring their friends to the Hotel Stone to spend the night. Sometimes there were six or eight kids—often including Buddy—at the hotel for a sleepover.

The first night Buddy was an invited guest, Stony came into the bedroom to help them when it came time for the boys to go to bed, Buddy, who was about two at the time, sat down in the corner and started to cry.

"What's the matter," Stony asked him. "Can I help you undress?"

"Where's my sister?" Buddy asked through his tears. "I don't want to go to bed until she gets home."

Jo and I were serving supper at Barjo's that night and didn't get home until after 8:30 p.m. Buddy was all smiles the minute I came into the room. Though he had told Stony only I could help him undress, he was just homesick. After that first night, he joined right in with the other kids and forgot that I existed.

Many of the kids' friends had never been in a hotel before. They "had a ball" and kept Jo and Stony hopping—and keeping them from doing any crazy things. That was one of my jobs, too, to help keep track of the little kids.

Robbie's pet project was going up to the fourth floor with Buddy and their friends and sliding down the banister in the open stairwell to the lobby.

"You boys are going to break your necks!" Stony said to Robbie. "Don't you ever slide down that banister again!"

The minute his grandfather's back was turned, they went on

the run to the fourth floor to try it all over again.

When I had an afternoon off, I'd take the kids to the Wild Animal Farm in Gray, to the movies, or often to Jo's cottage at the lake for a swim. The animal farm was a favorite. Robbie and Buddy thought fishing in the large pool of huge brown trout would be great fun. Some of the fish must have weighed ten or twelve pounds. The boys thought that they could catch the big fish with their hands. I had to grab them by the overall straps to stop them from falling into the pool. The talking myna bird fascinated them, too. It was a real treat to have the bird talk back when they said "'hello"'. The trainers had taught it quite a vocabulary.

Soon, I was a part of things that made the hotel a fascinating and at times, even a nerve-racking place to live. One such time occurred in 1955, when Stony needed a desk clerk for the day shift (6:00 a.m. to 3:00 p.m.).

Into the hotel came a well-groomed man in tailored Western clothes and a steel gray crew cut. He stood about six feet tall and had a slender build. A stranger to the area, he seemed to have already checked out what jobs were available.

He approached Stony and said, "I understand the hotel is looking for a desk clerk. I would like to apply for the job. I have done the job in other parts of the country and feel I am qualified."

He seemed capable, so Stony hired him on the spot. His name was Gerald "Jerry" Hassan. He was given Room 17, in addition to his salary. His room and mine, Room 18, were in an alcove on the second floor near the dining room area. There was a separate pair of stairs to this area of the hotel, making it easy to come and go without being seen by guests in the hotel lobby.

Had I known what I later found out, I would have been very uncomfortable about this arrangement of our rooms! But at first, the only one who was suspicious of Jerry and his actions was Jo.

"Jerry was a peculiar guy," Jo said. "I never felt comfortable when he was around. Something just didn't seem quite right. One evening when the kids were visiting, he hung around the dining room all the time we were eating supper, eyeing Andy. She was a pretty little girl, just five years old. He seemed to follow every move she made. It was a creepy thing to see."

After that night, Jo and Stony made sure that when the children came to the hotel, Jerry wouldn't be there. Often, I helped entertain the kids.

Jerry went to the restaurant for his lunch every day and picked up the lunches of some of the elderly guests at the hotel who weren't able to walk over to Barjo's.

Not knowing much about Jerry's past, Henry often kidded

him by saying, "Jerry, I think you have been on a chain gang."

Jerry would shrug his shoulders and give Henry a half grin but he made no further comment.

Jerry worked at the hotel for about two years. He was always efficient at the desk and Jo and Stony had no complaints about his work. His one peculiar habit was that when he got off duty at 3:00 p.m., he would change into hiking clothes and boots, put on a knapsack and go out walking until late in the evening.

One evening, Jo and Stony got a call from the Oxford County Sheriff Department requesting one of them come to the jail to identify a man. Stony went. It was Jerry. He'd been picked up in the Alpine Street area of Norway, where there had been several recent calls about a "Peeping Tom." When the Deputy Sheriff arrested him, he was looking in the window at Goodwin's Motel, South Paris. At the time, Norway still had a Municipal Court located on the second floor of the IOOF Block, Main Street. The judge, Neil Dow, ruled that Jerry would have to leave the state.

When the law enforcement officials did a background check to see if he had a federal criminal record, the report they got back on Jerry was staggering.

To begin with, he had assumed the name of his brother who had been murdered in Alaska. No one had proved that Jerry was involved, but it seems suspicious. His real name was Crawford Hassan. And Henry had been right when he teased him about being on a chain gang! He had been on chain gangs while in prison in Colorado and in a southern state. The rest of his record, several pages long, was equally amazing. He had been accused of being a "Peeping Tom" numerous times before the accusation in Norway. Whenever local authorities apprehended him, he moved on to a different part of the country. Evidently, he had served all the jail time imposed, as there were no outstanding warrants for his arrest. How "Jerry" had ended up in Norway, Maine, remained a mystery to everyone.

After he left town, Stony did a little investigating on his own. He discovered that Jerry had bored tiny holes at an angle, so they wouldn't be noticed, in all the doors on the second, third and fourth floors of the hotel. This provided him a way to look into rooms where the washbasins were located, when he made his morning wake up calls to the guests. Apparently no one ever suspected what he was up to, because the hotel staff had never received any complaints.

Jerry's other hobby had been oil painting. After he left, Stony found scenic mountain paintings and some unusual abstract art in his room. Apparently, one of the women he had been spying on was also a subject of a painting. She had long red hair, green eyes and wore very few clothes. The painting was a piece of art in progress, so he must have still been observing her.

Several years after Jerry Hassan left the Hotel, Jo and Stony heard he was working on the Cog Railway, at Mt. Washington, New Hampshire. He even wrote Jo a letter telling her he liked her, but had no use for Stony.

"Perhaps because Stony was his boss and he felt that I just ran the restaurant. It was hard to read between the lines to explain his feelings," Jo said. "One thing for sure, I never let Stony see that letter and I destroyed it after I had read it. I didn't want anything more to do with that guy!"

Other unusual things were about to happen in Jo's life; some would involve the restaurant. Other events would affect her family and some of the employees.

---

[1] *I now know the seriousness of a cerebral hemorrhage after having three brain operations myself. By the Grace of God alone, I survived three brain aneurysms that caused cerebral hemorrhages in 1979 and am here now, twenty-one years later, to tell this story.*

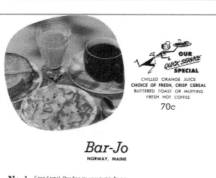

Barjo's Breakfast Menu, 1964

The Easter Bonnet Parade, 1964
Back: Judy Dunn, Mary Dunn, Joanne Elliot, Esther Dunn
Front Sandra Morrissette, Emily Foster, Alice Dunn, Charlotte Crouse.

CHAPTER 22

Always Expect the Unexpected

Police communication in the 1950's was primitive by today's standards. There were no car radios or pagers and no police scanners then. The only way police could communicate was by telephone. If an officer was working in the field, he often had to find a business or a pay station to get in touch with headquarters.

On a Saturday night in the fall of 1955, five prisoners escaped from the Cumberland County Jail. Police all over Maine were alerted. By Sunday morning, the fugitives had headed northwest to the western foothills hoping to cross the border into Canada.

All the local police departments—Norway, South Paris, and Oxford County sheriff—plus the Civil Defense were called out to find them. All day, officers came into Barjo's to use the phone to contact the Oxford County Sheriff Department and the State Police barracks in Scarborough for updates from their superiors. As evening came, the anticipation mounted. The police were certain the men were in the area, but where?

Worried about the escaped criminals, Jo tried to get me to stay until she was through that night and ride home with her. But I wanted to get my homework done and get to bed early. At 11:30 p.m. I insisted I'd be fine and walked home to the hotel after my shift. Suddenly my decision didn't seem so smart! As I walked by, I could hear a disturbance erupt in back of the Opera House on Main Street.

I had no idea what all the commotion was about, but I knew the town was alive with police officers. I realized I should have listened to Jo, but it was too late now. All I thought of was how fast could I run to the safety of the hotel!

That evening, the officers had discovered a stolen car, the Portland police chief's cruiser, in the George Hill Garage, the Dodge dealership in back of Barjo's. No one knew why the escapees had chosen that particular garage or how much they knew the Norway area.

Sometime during the previous night, one of the five, who was known by the police as the "sky-light burglar," had broken into the garage and opened the overhead door from the inside so the car could be driven in. Because it was Sunday, the businesses on Main Street were closed, except Barjo's. All day long, the escapees had broken into stores and loaded groceries and supplies—even ice cream—into a brand new station wagon there.

The robbers needed guns and ammunition for their planned escape to Canada. So, for their last break-in, they entered Woodman's Sporting Goods Store. It was there that Constable Frank Lafrance, making his usual rounds behind the stores in the business district, came upon them. Thinking fast and with considerable bravery, Frank fooled the criminals by using his flashlight like a gun. He brought all five of them up from behind the buildings onto Main Street. This was the commotion I heard on my walk that quickly turned into a headlong race home. But it wasn't until the next morning that I realized how close I came to confronting the escapees face to face!

When the robbers realized that Frank was alone, they ran across Main Street to get back into the garage and escape. But officers from some of the other departments were on the street and captured four of the five. After searching the parking lot, the officers returned to the garage for the fifth man.

Hearing the racket around the garage, Winfield Millett, who worked part-time for Jo and had a full-time job at Welch's Garage in South Paris, ran out of the restaurant and offered to help search. Because he worked in a garage himself, Winfield knew to look in the grease pit, a place the police hadn't thought of. There he found the "sky-light burglar," hanging from the bottom of a car. When Sheriff James Lassiter came in the back door at Barjo's to use the telephone to call Cumberland County authorities, it was 11:45 p.m. Jo, Stony and all the restaurant help went into the garage to see the prisoners.

Jo, being her usual self, gave a hearty laugh.

"I can't believe how much stuff these fellows collected from all those stores! And Frank is braver than the other cops give him credit for. I bet no one else would dare to confront these robbers alone—much less with a *flashlight!*" Jo commented.

Sheriff Lassiter, returning from his phone call, gave her a stern look. He thought she was too boisterous and too critical of the police officers involved in the arrests.

But Jo could see that the police had discounted Frank's ability to assist them because they thought he was just the local night watchman. She was tickled that he had shown them that how much special training you have isn't always as important as just doing your job thoroughly.

When things had calmed down, Frank came into Barjo's as though nothing had happened and had his usual evening lunch—a fried egg sandwich, a dish of vanilla ice cream and a cup of coffee—while the other officers returned the prisoners to the Cumberland County jail.

Still more unusual things were about to happen at Barjo's. This time it was Stony who was involved.

On a cold, dark December morning in 1956, he went to Barjo's to serve breakfast. When he arrived at 4:30 a.m., he entered by the back door of the kitchen and turned on the kitchen lights. The swinging door to the dining room had been propped open. From where he stood, he could see the length of the unlit restaurant.

He thought to himself, "I wonder why that door is open? That isn't the way it's usually left for the night."

He walked through the kitchen and into the dining room, turning on the lights as he went. Looking around, he found the side of the jukebox had been smashed in. The cash box had been taken, leaving a hole. And in the men's room, glass from the window was scattered over the tile floor. Beside the jukebox, on the terrazzo floor of the dining room, he discovered a note which read, *"we are sorry to inconeve you, but we need the money."*

"Before calling the police, I looked around to be sure no one was still lurking in the restaurant watching me," Stony said. "I didn't want to get hit over the head!"

It was a tip off to him that the jukebox people were due the next day to cash-up the machines. Surely it wasn't a coincidence: the thief must have known the schedule. Only two restaurants in the area, one in South Paris and Barjo's were serviced by this particular company so it wasn't common knowledge.

Indeed, when the police arrived, their first question was, "Who knows when the juke-box is cashed up? How would they know that there was enough money in it to take?"

Using some ingenuity of their own, the officers discovered that the note had been written on menu paper with the restaurant typewriter. The paper used for the menus wasn't a standard size and the typewriter was an old 1945 model Royal.

Only two waitresses, Joanne Elliot and I, used the typewriter to type up the restaurant menus. When we arrived for work at 10:00 a.m., the officers questioned us. Without explaining, the officers had us type the message as the officers dictated it to them. Nervous and puzzled though I was, I made no errors.

Joanne was next. Again, the officer dictated the message. Joanne typed the message and handed it to the policeman. He read it silently and then looked up at her from the paper in his hand. She had typed "inconvenience" exactly as it was spelled in the note, "inconeve." The officer placed the two notes next to each other on the counter. They were identical.

Both Joanne and her boyfriend, Freddie, who was a dishwasher, worked at Barjo's. They had broken in during the night to steal the money. They knew when the jukebox men cashed up the machines and when it would be most lucrative for them to rob the machine. They also knew what time the night crew went home and when Stony would come in in the morning.

"Well, Joanne," the policeman said, "I'm sorry but I will have to take you to the Courthouse in South Paris to book you on robbery charges. Do you have any thing to say? Did you do it alone or will you tell us who your companion was?"

"Freddie was with me and he's just as guilty as I am," she replied defiantly.

Going into the kitchen, the officers confronted Freddie.

"Well, young man," they said, "your girlfriend just implicated you in the jukebox robbery last night. Come with us."

Freddie hung his apron up and, showing no emotion, went with Joanne and the officers. When asked why they did it, both Joanne and Freddie shrugged their shoulders but made no reply.

"To me, it seemed as though they were just trying to prove it could be done," Jo said. "They both were working. It wasn't as though they needed the money for any particular reason. I was disappointed they hadn't had more respect for Joe Ferris's equipment. When the boys cashed up the machines, they always left free music for the help to enjoy. Ferris and I had been friends and business associates since 1939 and I was totally ashamed of what my employees had done."

Joe Ferris, of Ferris Music in Madison, pressed charges against the pair, as he owned the jukebox. Joanne and Freddie were given a suspended sentence and had to serve probation.

Jo wanted to help the kids as much as she could to turn their lives around. Freddie's mother was one of the Kimball kids whom Jo had helped raise and Joanne's parents were some of Jo's good friends. Her father furnished the restaurant with summer produce. Jo allowed the two to continue to work at Barjo's, but only under her watchful eye.

In April 1957, the waitresses at Barjo's decided to have their own Easter Bonnet Parade. We challenged each other to fashion our own millinery creations for the Easter Sunday shift.

"The customer who enjoyed the Easter bonnets the most was

probably Miss Powers. Because of her considerable experience in the New York millinery trade, she offered suggestions to the girls on how to construct the hats. The girls could chose anything they wanted for materials," Jo said.

Everything imaginable was used, from Easter baskets, sailors hats, doilies, ribbon, crepe paper, tissue paper and cardboard. The variety was amazing. Some of the hats were quite unique—ranging from works of art to just plain funny. The customers got a big kick out of all of them. The fact that they were the judges made them all the more interested in the contest.

"On Easter morning, Miss Powers was the first one to come to the restaurant and see what kind of creations the girls had designed," Jo commented. "She was just as excited as the girls were about how the customers would react to their Easter hats."

Jack Quinn, the local reporter and photographer for the *Portland Press Herald*, came to the restaurant on Friday, and took pictures of all of us modeling our own creations. At that moment, Jo's oldest granddaughter, Andy, came into Barjo's on her way home from school at the Upper Primary.

"May I try on some of your hats?" she asked.

"Of course you can," we answered.

She was trying on Mary Lou MacDonald's hat when Jack Quinn spotted her. She was standing on a step stool in the bathroom to see how she looked. He snapped her picture.

"She was only six years old!" Jo exclaimed. "But she posed for Jack Quinn as if she had done it many times before. Mary Lou's hat was the winner for 1957."

On Sunday morning, Jo was in for a great surprise when she read her Portland Sunday Telegram. Andy was on the front page! The picture Jack Quinn snapped on Friday had been picked up by the wire service and was published all over the country.

Jack Quinn's photos were numbered and posted by the cash register, so everybody had the same chance at the ballot box. The customers were the judges, with each one receiving a ballot from the cashier, as they paid at the register. Monday morning, when local businessmen came in for their coffee break, they counted the ballots to determine the winner. A prize was awarded and the picture of the winning hat posted for all the customers to admire.

The Easter bonnet contest was held for over ten years. After the first year, we were quick learners. By the time you'd worn your own creation for five hours, you found that while large hats may be pretty, they weigh a ton!

The restaurant had contributed to creating a warm and widespread "family" for Jo in every conceivable way since the 1930's. It continued to do so in the late 1950's.

By now, Jo and I had established a strong working relationship. Living at the hotel, I was involved in many phases of both the restaurant and the hotel operations. I had waited on tables and worked in the kitchen at Barjo's. I had worked on banquets and as desk clerk and chambermaid at the hotel.

We also had a close personal relationship that made a significant difference in my life. Jo included me in many family activities that had nothing to do with my job. Because of the problems with my own family, Jo had become my mentor and the most important person in my life.

In the spring of 1957, I was a senior at Norway High School. I faced a major decision in my life. I had been accepted at two colleges, Maine School of Commerce in Lewiston and Portland School of Fine Arts in Portland. I had also passed Civil Service exams that qualified me along with seven classmates to work at the Pentagon in Washington, D.C. Donald's wife, Mildred, was the head of the Commercial Department at the high school. She encouraged all her students to take the exams and have a chance to go to Washington and better ourselves. Which path should I take? How could I leave Jo and Barjo's and the friends and co-workers who made my life so interesting and meaningful?

"I knew all the opportunities Emily had available to her," Jo commented. "It was hard to think that she would leave us. But it had to be her decision. It wouldn't be right to tell her what she should do just to please me. I didn't want her to have any regrets, whatever she chose."

"In March, she came to me and told me her decision," Jo said. She would stay at Barjo's. It was one of the happiest days of my life! I knew that whatever I asked her to do, she would carry it out to the best of her ability. I had all the faith in the world in her as a person and a worker and I trusted her to help me run the restaurant. She has never let me down."

When I met Jo, she became my guiding light. I searched my heart and realized I could never be happy doing any other kind of work. My love of art and of accounting would still be a part of my work at the restaurant. I had already designed Easter menu covers for the restaurant and Vivian Akers, a local artist, had taken an interest in my artwork. We had a large mirror behind the fountain where the ice cream was listed. He taught me how to use lettering and artwork to promote our many flavors effectively."

In the end, it was the right decision for me. The only decision, really. I have always been grateful that I knew the right path for my life.

After my graduation in June 1957, Jo promoted me to cashier and shift leader in the dining room. I worked in the dining room when Jo cooked on one shift. Henry cooked, and Margaret ran the dining room on the other shift. Stony always cooked for the breakfast hour with Veda waiting on tables.

In the fall of that year, Doris Burns called Jo and asked her if she needed a waitress. Her sister had just returned from California and needed work. Jo told her to bring her to the restaurant to apply. It was a good time, as high school students who had been working at Barjo's during the summer were going back to school. Jo needed a daytime waitress, and Bertha Smith, Doris' sister, came to work that week on my shift.

Bertha had moved many times from Maine to Vermont to California and now back to Maine. Without a permanent home and as a single mother, it was hard for her to make a living. For her son, Maurice, it had been even harder to adjust to different schools and environments.

Maurice, age ten then, did odd jobs at the restaurant and hotel until he was old enough to get a work permit and have a regular job. Born with a bad heart, sports were off limits for him. He was a good worker, never refusing to do what was asked of him. Everyone liked him.

One day, Jo got a call from the court asking if she would take custody of Maurice and she agreed. It came about like this.

Bertha had married Bill Hill. The home they made together wasn't a fit environment for a young boy. One day, Maurice got into trouble at school and had a fight with Si Bean's son. During their argument, Maurice tried to strangle the boy with a coat hanger.

Jo was concerned with the trouble because she knew Maurice was a good kid at heart and needed more support from his mother. On the day the case went to court, Jo was surprised and unsympathetic when Bertha got a ride to court with Si Bean.

Knowing Jo and her reputation well, the court officials were ready to make a deal with her. They suggested that Jo and Stony take custody of Maurice and permitted him to live with them at the hotel. If he was under their supervision, the court was willing to place the boy on probation. Otherwise he would be sent to Reform School.

It wasn't a difficult decision for Jo. "Stony and Henry helped me guide Maurice in the right direction," Jo said. "It was a big thing that had been missing in his short life. No one had ever taken any pains with him."

Shortly after, his mother left her husband and went to work in another state. Maurice stayed with Jo and Stony all through high school and worked at Barjo's. He seemed to enjoy the companionship of the other school kids who also lived at the hotel.

Jo remembers that Maurice and Wade, another of her high school kids, were supposed to help Stony load the trash into the pick-up before they went to school each morning. The boys would often oversleep and be late. Not only did the boys not get their work done but Jo or Stony had to go see the principal, Mr. Pendleton, to get them into school for the day. Jo understood they were trying their best and were probably tired from working the night shift, so she never said a word to them.

When it came time for Maurice's graduation from Norway High School, Henry took him to Block's Store and helped him pick out an outfit. A handsome boy with blond curly hair, he looked as good as any other graduate in his new navy blue suit.

One Saturday night in April 1958, I was cashiering with two inexperienced waitresses scheduled to work with me. At Barjo's, there was a circular booth in the window area, right next to the cash register. It was usually reserved for large parties and take-out customers often sat there while they waited.

That night, Gordon Snow, the owner of Snow's Marina at Norway Lake, came in to place an order for sandwiches and I went to the kitchen to deliver his order to the cook. Two strangers, wearing suits and carrying overcoats over their arms, came in and stood by the cash register.

"What are you fellows doing in town?" Gordon greeted them.

"We've come to sell the restaurant a pie case," they replied.

When I came back, Gordon told me what they had said. It seemed unusual for reputable salesmen to do business on a Saturday night. I asked myself what they were really up to.

While he was waiting for his order, Gordon talked to them about smelting. It was a topic discussed everywhere in the spring of the year. All the fellows asked each other, "Where did you go smelting?" or "How many smelts did you get?"

One of the men decided to have a hamburger to go, so I took his order to the kitchen and brought back Gordon's sandwiches. When I returned to the register, the younger of the two men had gone out. The older one was sitting in the booth directly in back of the cashier's station, waiting for his order.

Because they had told Gordon about a pie case, I thought to

myself, "It seems funny they haven't mentioned it to me." Again, I asked myself, "Is that what they're really up to?" But they were pleasant enough men and the restaurant was busy enough to keep me distracted from my niggling feeling that something about them was amiss.

At Barjo's, we cashed up the register four times a day, after each shift. This made each cashier responsible for her own shift. If there were any problems, this system made it easy to identify when they occurred. The money bags were hidden on the back shelf of the cashier's station until closing, when the police took them to the night deposit for Jo.

At closing that day, I discovered that the noon and afternoon shifts' money bags were missing.

"That money had to have been taken during my shift!" I reported to Jo. "The funny thing about it is that the thief found only two bags. The morning shift's bag was still in its usual place, but the noon and afternoon bags are gone. Why?"

"I couldn't imagine what happened," Jo said. "Why had anybody had gone to all that trouble? They could have held up the cashier and gotten more money from the evening shift than was in those two bags together."

At first, the police and the insurance company contended it was an inside job. They thought it was the new girls working that night or a customer who knew where we kept the bags. Jo wasn't convinced of it, however.

When Henry came to work Sunday afternoon, Jo told him what had happened.

"I've been thinking about this," Jo told him, "and I've decided it had to be those strangers Gordon Snow was talking to."

"Wait a minute, I bet I can tell you what they looked like!" Henry said. "One was a lot older than the other. They had on working clothes, rather than suits."

"How did you know?" Jo asked with a puzzled expression.

"They came in Friday night, too," he said. "They told the waitress they had been smelting."

"So you think they were casing the joint!" Jo exclaimed.

"Yes, they stayed until closing so they must have watched Margaret cash up," he said.

The police caught them after they reached Vermont. They had left a trail of robberies from Bangor to New Hampshire and throughout Vermont.

"Although the police caught them, I never got any money back. We learned a lesson," Jo stated. "No one was allowed to cash up if anyone was in the restaurant. Take-out customers orders were no longer allowed to wait behind the cashier."

I was upset with myself that I hadn't listened to my intuition that night. Maybe Gordon Snow had been trying to alert me that he also thought there was something dubious about them. I wished that I hadn't given them the chance to carry out their plan when I was suspicious of them from the start.

Barjo's insurance company was notified, but they never did pay for the loss. Shortly after that robbery, Jo had the circular booth removed. The cashier's station was turned around so it faced the dining room and no one but the cashier was ever allowed in that area.

In the 1950's, the co-chairmen of the East Stoneham Church Supper Committee were Jo's oldest sister, Helen, and her friend, Sarah Grover. One August afternoon, Helen called to say, "We're having our annual turkey supper, to raise money for the church. Some folks are cooking turkeys, but they need to be picked over and we need to have gravy. Will you help us out?"

"Be glad to," Jo replied. "Bring the turkeys over and we'll have them ready for your supper tomorrow night."

Jo, Margaret and I picked over and prepared her turkeys so that they were ready to serve. Helping Helen out in this pinch was just the beginning. Over the next 25 years, Barjo's donated food, including the buying, roasting, and preparing of eighteen turkeys each year, to the East Stoneham Church. They made ten gallons of gravy—both plain and giblet—extra stuffing, and provided other condiments, including cranberry sauce and pickles. Barjo's also furnished all the paper plates and plastic utensils needed to serve it. Everything was free of charge.

"I grew up in that church," Jo said. "I knew they were having a hard time raising money to keep it open in the winter, providing for heat and other needs. To cook and prepare the food was the least I could do."

All of us at Barjo's pitched in to help. On the day of the supper, the turkey was sliced and arranged on platters, ready to be served. Trout Lake Camp (later called Camp Susan Curtis) brought their campers to the church for the supper each year. Often they were the first to eat. The supper was served buffet-style with a grill to keep the food hot.

About eight o'clock, Helen would call. "She'd tell me how everything had gone during the evening, how much money they'd earned and how many had been served," Jo said. "Often as much as two thousand dollars or more was taken in for the Church fund."

Jo was equally dedicated to helping school kids with jobs, housing, and many kinds of support. The "Barjo family" was about to increase again with the addition of another family.

In the fall of 1958, Rebecca McAllister, one of my childhood neighbors from East Waterford, said, "I wish my grandchildren could have the same opportunity you've had to be able to work in town while going to the high school."

I told Jo about what Rebecca had said. The next day, she had me call Rebecca to invite the girls to come see about jobs.

The oldest granddaughters, Mary and Alice Dunn[2] soon started waiting on tables. Jo had them stay at the Hotel Stone so they wouldn't have to travel back and forth.

As each of the younger Dunn sisters—Esther, Judy, Dorothy and Joyce—graduated from the eighth grade in Waterford, their parents sent them to join the older girls at Barjo's where Jo always found a place for them. At one time, all six Dunn girls worked for her in the dining room.

On her first day waiting on tables, Alice was serving Professor Grover Brown. She knew he was a retired teacher living at the hotel. She was so nervous knowing that he was a schoolteacher that everything seems to go blank.

She asked the Professor, "How do you spell *potato*?"

Neither her sister nor the rest of the family ever let her forget that! Alice took the ribbing with a grain of salt because she had a real good sense of humor. As the younger ones joined the crew, the story of Alice's first day was told over and over again.

Now Jo had many new faces in her "Barjo family." The school kids were all excellent workers and the restaurant was prospering under Jo's direction. She was about to spread her wings and expand into some new endeavors.

In 1957, Jo read a review in the New York Times of the book, *How to Make a Million Dollars in Real Estate*. The next day, she told Henry about how the author had bought, fixed up, and resold real estate at a profit. They talked about some real estate ventures they could embark on. People had doubted the author's methods, so he had written a second book, describing how he had made his second million.

"Stony wasn't interested in real estate projects, but Henry was always ready for a challenge," Jo said. "We had a pretty unusual relationship for a young man and his mother-in-law. I thought of him more like my own son. We talked over what we were going to do, while we worked together in the kitchen."

"What a great way to make money!" Henry remembers thinking. "I was a gambler at heart, and this seemed like something we could do together."

Their first project was to buy the property at 10 Bridge Street, Norway. It was a two apartment house with a large barn. They hired Henry's brother, Lester, who did a lot of the carpenter work. The barn was renovated and made into two additional apartments. The third floor attic area was rebuilt, making two rooms for storage. All four apartments were soon rented. They were started on their real estate venture!

Within a short time, Jo and Henry got the opportunity to buy the Luck house on Green Street. The 10 Bridge Street property came into play in this deal. Mrs. Ethel Luck agreed to sell her home and move into an apartment on Bridge Street with the rent being applied to the sale price of her house.

After the deal was completed, Susie and Nappy Olmstead rented the Green Street house for quite a while. Later, Jo's grandson, Robert, and his family lived in the Green Street house.

"When Mrs. Luck passed away, I paid the remaining balance for the real estate," Jo said. "By contacting the lawyers, I could then rent the Bridge Street apartment to someone else."

They bought a third house on Whitman Street from "Lewey" Cox and for the most part they had reliable tenants. At the Whitman Street house, they remodeled the two apartments and up-graded the grounds. In the front of the house, the retaining wall was falling down and needed to be replaced.

"Henry and I had the retaining wall removed and a new reinforced concrete one built. It was a lot sturdier than the original one," Jo commented.

In 1966, Jo took over all the rental properties herself as Henry and Barbara were working on starting a restaurant of their own. Henry had insured the properties with Frost Insurance Agency, but Eddie Frost was now selling his business, so Jo would have to change the policies. Before Jo was able to switch them to her own company, David A. Klain Agency, she ran into a problem with some tenants.

Jo was sued as a result of one family's New Year's Eve party at their Whitman Street apartment. A guest claimed he had been hurt. A common entrance hall was the only spot in the house where Jo could be held responsible for an injury, so that is where the tenants claimed he had been hurt. Jo learned from some other guests that in the early morning hours of January first, his friends had, in fact, dropped him outdoors as they carried him to his home next door.

When Jo went to court, she had to accept the lawyer sent by the Frost Insurance Agency. A junior attorney from the Portland law firm of Mahoney & Mahoney had been chosen because they were so sure the case had no foundation.

The people suing, however, had hired Jack Simmons of Berman, Berman and Simmons in Lewiston. Martin Berman, the owner of the law firm, called Jo to tell her they would refuse the case if she objected. Martin's father, Ben, had been Jo's lawyer and Martin served as Jo's attorney after he retired. When Jo first met Jack, he was working as an intern for Ben Berman and he had also become a good friend.

"I told him it made no difference to me," Jo explained. "I knew the people suing me would be able to hire a lawyer anyway. I couldn't have Berman because I *had* to be represented by the insurance company's attorney."

I was also subpoenaed as a witness because I had been in the kitchen when Jo's tenants told us about the accident. For three days at the trial in the Oxford County Superior Court in South Paris, the young attorney never challenged the information presented though many details from the defense were contradictory.

The man claimed he could no longer work or have sexual pleasure because of his injuries. Though witnesses all said he been hurt in the hallway, one placed the injured man on the left side; another testified he was lying on the right side, while a third said he was lying at an angle across the hall.

Jack Simmons said in his closing arguments to the jury, "You can see that Mrs. Josephine Stone is guilty as charged. She has been in this court room for three days and her lawyer has never called her to the stand."

Needless to say, they won the case, but Jack Simmons refused to appeal for more money. He advised his clients to take what the insurance company offered, $5000 plus medical expenses.

Shortly after the court proceedings, Jack Simmons came in to have dinner at Barjo's and asked Jo to come into the dining room so he could talk with her.

"Jack, who is considered one of the best criminal lawyers in the state, knew the young lawyer who represented me," Jo said. "He told me that he was the son-in-law of the owner of the firm and had no idea what he was doing. Jack also told me that he knew if the case had gone to the appeals court the judges would have found all the mistakes in the testimony and thrown the case out. That was why he had advised his clients to accept the settlement. They were very upset that they hadn't received a lot more money. They had expected a large settlement."

Ironically, the same man had lived at the Hotel Stone for several years at no charge. Prior to his second marriage, Jo had fed him and his children at Barjo's. He had never done a bit of work and never offered to repay Jo for any meals. The only ones to acknowledge Jo's kindness to the family were his children. As grown-ups, both sons came into the restaurant to thank Jo. Their parents were separated, so they appreciated everything Jo had done to make their childhood memorable. Their father chose a much different way of expressing his feelings.

Soon after the case was settled, these tenants moved out. The next occupants were a retired couple in the downstairs apartment with a single lady, Ethelyn Millett, living upstairs. Several different families rented from Jo until Ethelyn's aunt bought the Whitman Street house for her.

Through her hard work and her strong desire to succeed, Jo was able to make Barjo's an outstanding restaurant and had become a pioneer in the food service industry. She encouraged me to be a leader, too. In the next year, she would show the faith she had in me by asking me to investigate possibilities for a new business.

Now the time had come for others to recognize her for her willingness to help others from all walks of life, while she continued explore other fields of endeavor.

---

[1] *For more stories about the Dunn family- See Appendix 1, "Stories of the Barjo's Family."*

CHAPTER 23

Unusual Name Recognition

From the time Jo joined the National Restaurant Association (NRA) in the early 1940's, she was active in many projects. She worked with her congressmen to help pass laws in Washington related to labor issues, food safety and the FDA. She also worked to help create better working environments for young people in the food service industry.

In April 1957, the NRA recognized Jo for the many ways she had supported the organization. It was the first time she was recognized nationally and it came as a total surprise. She received a plaque from the NRA signed by the President, John Sabotes, the Vice President, Larry Hillaire, the Ex-Vice President, Frank Diffler and the Treasurer, L. C. Langford. It stated the award was in appreciation for all the work that she had done, including contributions of time, thought and effort at the state and local levels, as well as in national industry affairs. Jo was also cited for her cooperation with other NRA members and allied industries, in advancing the food service industry through greater awareness in the public sector.

"When I received the plaque, I was flabbergasted!" Jo exclaimed. "I never thought anyone knew anything I had done. I had no idea the NRA would recognize a small restaurant owner from Maine—least of all, me. I couldn't believe the honor was for the owner of Barjo's."

After closing Andy's Drive-In on Route 26 in 1954, Jo had thought about opening another place, this time nearer to Norway village. Many new things were happening in the food service industry. In one of the magazines she subscribed to, *Restaurant Management*, Jo read about fast food restaurants that used vending machines and Raytheon Radar Ranges and were operated in conjunction with a gas station.This was a new idea that customers could buy prepared food from a vending machine and heat it in a radar oven while their car was being serviced.

Already, Standard Oil and Stouffer Foods had several units in the Midwest and South in operation. Jo was always looking to the future and decided to find a lot in town to try this out. With Barbara's family growing, she felt they were going to need another business venture to support them all.

In the early spring of 1958, Jo's friend, Lucien Frechette Jr., suggested some property on Fair Street in Norway owned by the Hattie Harvey estate as a possible commercial venture. The property was directly across from the new high school under construction for SAD #17. The new school would provide a ready-made clientele, he said. She decided to buy the property.

Jo knew she needed to do more research if her ideas for the property were to become a reality. She read about an upcoming convention in Chicago that would present information and demonstrations of new equipment. Since Jo always felt her first responsibility was at the restaurant, she often delegated other projects to the rest of her family. During the banquet season, for instance, she had always been the one who stayed at Barjo's to look after her regulars. She was indispensable to the day-to-day running of the place. For Jo, herself, to go to Chicago where the headquarters of the Raytheon Corporation were located would be out of the question.

After my high school graduation, Jo had promoted me to cashier and shift leader. I had worked hard to prove I could be depended on to follow through on any project. Even though I was younger than many of my fellow employees, I tried to show Jo that I could meet any challenge presented to me. I wanted to earn her trust and let her know I could carry out her instructions.

I was thrilled when Jo asked me to go to the convention in Chicago. She felt it was time to give me more responsibility and that the trip would give me the chance to meet new people and learn more about the inner workings of the food service industry.

On a Saturday morning in May, 1958, I arrived at the Auburn-Lewiston Airport for my flight to Chicago. Soon, as the plane ascended, I looked down at the coastline of Maine far below. I had never been in an airplane before. As we climbed to 40,000 feet I felt like I was looking down on a bed of fluffy, cotton batting and that the Maine coastline was a picture postcard.

I thought, "I can't believe Jo is trusting me to go to Chicago alone and to meet the people from Raytheon. It must be a dream!" I felt honored that Jo was putting so much faith and trust in my ability to make important contacts regarding how to set up her new restaurant project!

The convention, from Sunday to Friday, was held at McCormick Place on Lake Shore Drive in Chicago with shuttle buses running to the hotels in city every hour. There were over 60,000 people from the food service industry and 10,000 exhibits. People came from all over the world; every major food service supplier and equipment manufacturer was represented. Believe me, it was some experience for a 19-year-old country girl!

Leaving the O'Hare Airport in Chicago, I went by taxi to the Palmer House in the center of city. I contacted the Raytheon sales people in their booth at the NRA convention. When I asked them about radar ranges and vending machines in a fast food restaurant, they arranged a guided tour for me at one of their pilot facilities at the Illinois Bell Telephone Company. There, the dining staff used Radar Ranges and vending machines for two of the shifts in the employee dining room.

I was impressed by the warm reception I received from the Raytheon people. They went out of their way to show me just how this kind of food service facility looked in actual operation. I hadn't expected to be given a guided tour but they seemed proud to teach me how the program was handled.

While in Chicago, I attended seminars from which I gained insight into management, food cost control and employee training. Officials from the FDA and other agencies discussed many laws regarding food and the food service industry.

We saw many demonstrations. The "Omelet King" presented one. The description in our brochure stated that he could make as many as 100 omelets in an hour. I thought to myself, "That's impossible. Jo makes omelets, but they are soufflé omelets and are nearly four inches thick. How in the world can he possibly make that many in such a short time?"

It wasn't long before I found out his secret—he made omelets the same way we made scrambled eggs! When I told Jo back at home, how she laughed! "With all the experience you have had cooking breakfast with Stony you didn't need to go to Chicago for that!" she said. "You learned how to make scrambled eggs the first time you worked the grill. I guess I'll have to call you an 'omelet king,' too!"

I met many interesting people from all over the United States and Canada. Some wanted to learn about new equipment, while others were interested in new food products being offered. One of the pieces of equipment that received a lot of attention was a 'Broaster' for thawing and preparing chicken. With today's microwave ovens, I don't know whether this piece of equipment is even produced now.

On Monday, Hugh Downs entertained us with a food service version of his television show, "Concentration." Members of the audience were chosen at random as the participants of the show. It was a pleasant change of pace from the intense panel discussions and lectures that were a major part of our week's activities.

One of the demonstrations at the convention was conducted by the Southern Maine Vocational School of Portland. The students were under the guidance of their instructor, Professor Brieze. They re-created the entire Andover Space Station in pastry and frosting and won first prize for their creative design.

On Wednesday evening, a couple from Scottsdale, Arizona, invited me to go with them to the "Tip Top Tap Room" at the top of the Allenton Hotel. From the windows that encircled the lounge, I could see the entire city of Chicago in its splendor with its skyline outlined in brilliant neon lights.

On Thursday, the last day of the convention, the annual meeting and banquet was held at the Grand Ballroom of the Palmer House. Henry Montague was elected President of the National Restaurant Association for 1958-59.

After the banquet, I went to the Playboy Club with the Massachusetts Restaurant Association, as a guest of the owner of the Yankee Fisherman in Boston. I was the only representative there from Maine, so at the banquet I was seated with the Massachusetts delegation, the only other New England group.

It was a thrilling experience, one that I had never expected to have. No one could ever have imagined that I would be seeing a live show in the "Playroom" of the Playboy Club in Chicago—least of all me.

When I told Jo where I had been, she had a hard time believing me. "I didn't sent you to Chicago to go to the Playboy Club!" she grinned. "I thought you were going there on *business!*"

Before coming home, I met again with Raytheon executives. They discouraged me about having vending machines and Radar Ranges to heat the food in conjunction with a gas station. A successful operation of this kind would require a high turnover of food products they said. Only in large metropolitan areas would the volume be high enough to keep food fresh—and profitable. They didn't feel the Northeast was ready for this combination. Within a few years, Standard Oil and Stouffer Foods found these units weren't profitable either and closed all their joint units.

Jo had already discussed this idea with her salesman, Bill

Cook, from Jones, McDuffee and Stratton in Boston, but waited for me to get home before making a final decision. When I told Jo what the Raytheon people had advised me, she decided not to pursue the idea any further.

The trip had been a great opportunity to learn about the food service industry and it confirmed my decision to make it my life's work. Jo had pushed me to new heights. She trusted me to investigate the possibilities of a new venture and used the information I brought back to make her business decision.

Because of Jo's faith in me, I was encouraged to grow in responsibility. I knew she trusted my judgment. My own family had cast me aside, but she taught me how to have faith in myself and to have self-esteem. At times, I feared that I wouldn't be able to live up to her expectations, but with God's guidance, I was able to. If she hadn't pushed me and trusted me, I probably never would have had the courage to do as much as I have done.

After Jo decided not to develop the land commercially, she sold the Fair Street property to Nelson Carey. He rebuilt the Harvey house into a store called "Fair Street Variety." It is now D'Amato's Pizza, in reality a fast food enterprise not so different from Jo's original plan for the site.

After managing several pieces of property, Jo found that being a landlord had its drawbacks as well as its more gratifying moments, but she learned a lot in the process. Though she made many business transactions, she never left Barjo's kitchen. In the 1950's, it was less complicated to borrow money from the banks than it is today. With telephone calls, Jo was always able to negotiate with the bank officials. Then she would send me to pick up the paperwork for her to sign or the loan officer would come to the restaurant to complete the transaction.

At 54, Jo was now a mother, an aunt, a grandmother, and a good friend to all who crossed her path. She put in 16 hours a day, seven days a week working in Barjo's kitchen, the headquarters for all her family, business and philanthropic activities as she served hundreds of people three meals a day. She supported individuals and community causes with numerous donations of food, advice and labor.

Now, Jo was about to be surprised with an award that would recognize her as a pioneer not only in the food service industry, but also in the business world.

In 1958, JO—not Josephine —Stone was the first businesswoman in the country to receive the Junior Chamber of Commerce Award. It was presented at Station WKTQ by Gordon Smith, owner of Smith's Shop 'n' Save, and Ben Tucker, Jr., Editor-in-Chief of the Advertiser-Democrat.

Jo's grandchildren
Andrea, Robbie, Jody and Darcy

CHAPTER 24

A Pioneer at the National Level

When Jo was chosen for a national honor in May, 1958. a reporter from one of the local newspapers wrote an article about her.

In Norway, where the town's largest restaurant is owned and managed by a grandmother, the Junior Department of the Chamber of Commerce wanted to give a plaque to, and name, the man who is "the Town's best citizen."

The requirements for the honor were many. The man had to be a public spirited citizen, financially successful in his business, ever alert to any movement for the good of his fellow men, generous and a good neighbor.

The award has just been given to—well, by now you should have guessed it—a woman! They entered her name as "Jo" Stone, so the National Junior Chamber of Commerce would approved the nomination. She is Mrs. Josephine Stone, owner and operator of Barjo Restaurant on Main Street.

Norway's Outstanding Citizen, Mrs. Josephine Stone, better known as "Jo," was so named by the Junior Chamber of Commerce. This grandmother, successful in the restaurant business and hotel management, has unbounded generosity. The full course meals she has given away are uncounted, and she refuses to acknowledge such generosity and helpfulness.

When the reporter approached Jo, her response was, "O.K., but you aren't going to take my picture!"

In her own mind, Jo's still thought of herself as being that little girl in East Stoneham whose mother had made her spend the day in bed because she had refused to have her picture taken. She was camera-shy because she was sure she was too homely and unattractive to be photographed!

Other pictures for the story were easy to obtain—all except Jo's photo.

Jo insisted, "Don't you dare take my picture."

But "all things come to him who waits." Frank Bjorklund, who was also the Finnish Consul for Maine, New Hampshire, and Vermont, happened to be in the kitchen when Jo was approached for her picture. Twenty years before, Frank had been Margaret's boyfriend and also represented her in lawsuit over the break-up of the partnership with Jo. But time had healed the old wounds. Frank was now a Barjo's regular and one of Jo's best friends.

It was Saturday night, and Frank had an understandable failing for Barjo's famous cash-and-carry bucket of baked beans.

Trying to get her off guard while the photographer maneuvered for a flash, he engaged Jo in a heated conversation.

"What gives?" Frank demanded. "When you are at the age when most folks are buying annuities and building up a fund for old age, you just keep on giving to pet and private charities. You assist people whom you do not know, and probably in many cases, will never see again!"

Jo tried to smile. She had a disturbed look as if folks were trying to delve into her private activities. Jo was caught in the mesh of her own game. She was now being heckled.

"Isn't it enough to give to the Heart Fund, the Polio Drives, the Red Cross, Father Flanagan's Boys Town and a lot of other worthy projects?" he demanded.

Nervously, she shifted a curl in her graying hair. Jo spoke in a sincere tone of voice that revealed she fully expected her audience to believe her excuse.

"I would rather give to others and help someone who needs a helping hand, than have all the money in the world."

At that moment when the photographer snapped his picture. The article continued,

> The moral of this story refutes any idea that it is necessary for one to be stingy and over saving to build up a bank account.
>
> The setting for much of Jo Stone's generosity has been right here in Barjo's kitchen. Many a handout has been made in recent years at the restaurant and Hotel Stone. For twenty-five years, she has bought real estate in the town of Norway, while giving freely to feed others who needed her help.

The Junior Chamber of Commerce Distinguished Service Award was presented to Jo by Gordon Smith, the owner of Smith's Shop'n'Save, and Ben Tucker, Jr., the editor of the Advertiser-Democrat at the studios of WKTQ, the local radio station owned by Jud Higgins.

"Before we left for the station, the boys said to me, 'Remember, Jo, that you are going to be live on the radio,'" she said. "I don't know if they were trying to frighten me or if they were worried about what I might say."

I think she was too nervous to do anything else but thank them for all the effort and hard work that they had put into obtaining the honor for her. Jo had avoided being in the public eye all her life. But the young men from the Junior Chamber knew her well and refused to take no for an answer.

Jo was the first woman in the country to receive this award. Though today we may take it for granted that women can be recognized for their achievements, it was only because the local members of the J. C. had submitted her name as "Jo" Stone, and with that ruse, made her a pioneer. They knew the national organization wouldn't accept the nomination if the committee knew she was a woman. Benjamin Tucker, Jr. chairman of the local award committee, and members Gordon Smith, Norway Jaycee president, Dr. Allen Chase and Dr. Robert Easton selected Jo over three male candidates for her outstanding contributions to the community service. She was grateful to them all and keeps the award today, with the picture of the young men presenting it to her, on display in her Deering Street home.

Every year, the Maine Department of Agriculture engaged in promoting locally grown products. Barjo's always participated in these campaigns. June was named Maine Milk Month, and waitresses were asked to mention milk first as a suggestion for something to drink. To make the effort fun and to monitor participation, officials dropped in unannounced at restaurants across the state. If the waitress mentioned milk first, she would be pleasantly surprised with a *silver dollar* under the plate when she cleared the table. But if she didn't, the official left her a *wooden nickel*. These visits really made us stay alert.

I goofed up once. I still have that wooden nickel, but I never got a second one, and I got a dozen silver dollars. A lot of milk was sold though this promotion.

The following year, the National Dairy Council in conjunction with the American Dairy Association & International Association of Ice Cream Manufacturers, awarded Barjo Restaurant the 1959 Appreciation Award for "June is Dairy Month."

"For many years, I had made ice cream and worked with the Dairy Council with all their promotions," Jo said. "I never expected to be recognized. I was very surprised because, to me, I was just doing my part for the food service industry."

On a cold winter day, February 20, 1960, Jo's family increased again, with the birth of her fourth grandchild, Darcy Jean Paradis. Barbara and Henry now had four children, three girls and a boy.

"Andy, Jody and Robbie were all in school," Jo said. "So Darcy was a special treat. Often when Stony and I went for an afternoon ride, we took her with us. Both Barbara and Henry were working, and she loved to go to see the sheep at a farm in Oxford. When she was old enough, we took carrots and lettuce so she could feed the lambs through the fence. The people who owned them were my friends and also customers at Barjo's."

In May 1960, the John Sexton Company, a global wholesale company catering to the food service industry, conducted a contest for the "Most Outstanding Recipes of the Year." The winners were to be published in their Sexton Annual Yearbook, with the winner receiving a leather-bound copy, printed in gold.

"Henry," Jo said, "Why don't you submit a recipe?"

"What about our rice and tomato soup?" he asked.

"Sure, why not," she replied. "Say 'created by Henry Paradis, *chef* of Barjo Restaurant.'"

His recipe was the winning entry. Henry Blood, the Maine salesman, presented Henry a copy of the Yearbook. A photographer from the local paper took a picture of Henry, dressed in a Chef's hat, receiving his award in the Barjo Restaurant kitchen.

The following article composed by Margaret, appeared in the local papers with the picture:

> Practicing philanthropy, in any business, is the greatest boon to success. The owner of Barjo Restaurant has, for many years, sponsored different school activities such as donating food for dinners and giving a scholarship for a deserving student. Last fall two "Future Farmers of America" raised lambs to be auctioned at the Oxford County Fair.
>
> The proprietor personally bid a fantastic price on the lambs knowing she would never realize a profit on the meat but, through radio and several newspapers, the acclaim she received was worth much more than the purchase price.
>
> Every year she gives several students an opportunity to work, consequently, one girl has been in her service five years and is now manager of one shift. A young man, now thirty-two, has been in her employment since he was sixteen years of age and has made himself invaluable to the business.
>
> John Sexton Company awarded him the honor of printing, in gold, an original recipe, "Rice and Tomato Soup," in their Annual Yearbook which has a nation wide circulation.

Any work-saving device or gadget is always inspected by the proprietor, and put into use if practical. One of the boys in the kitchen invented a go-cart with four wheels and a foam rubber mat so the floor washer could glide around the floor to reach cracks and crevices that a mop would miss.

Last, but the most important, is the knowledge that without the help and guidance of the Great Creator, her business or any business would cease to exist."

By Margaret McAllister, 1960

Barjo's sponsored many local sports activities during this era. The Little League baseball teams were one of them.

In the spring of 1960, Jo told the Norway Little League team, "Every time you win a game, I'll treat you to hamburgers, french fries and cokes after the game. If you win every game this season, I'll put on a banquet for you at the Hotel Stone."

They took her challenge to heart and won every single game—and the championship. True to her word, Jo treated them every game night.

"What do you kids want for dessert at your banquet?" she asked.

"Chocolate Cream Pie!" they hollered in unison.

"That's what we'll serve," Jo said. "We're going to make this a humdinger of a banquet for you. You earned it!"

Some of the boys on the team were: Billy Cordwell, Frances Keisman, Rawn Phinney, Barry Cordwell, Chris Weston, Peanut Guilford, Tommy Guilford, Wayne Chandler, Tommy Noyes, John Butters, Eddie Butters, Randy Butters, Donnie Butters, Dennis Arsenault, Rusty Frothingham, Doug Mawhinney, Bucky Getchell and many others. Their coach was Donald Guilford and one of his younger sons, Richy, served as the batboy.

Several weeks later, Jo was serving supper when we heard someone holler, "Surprise, Jo, surprise!"

When Jo opened the back door, there were the Little League boys with a beautiful red leather hassock. They had bought it for her to show how much they appreciated her kindness to them. They had all saved their money to buy it, really something for kids eight to 12 years old to do. She still has the hassock in her living room. It is one of her special treasures because the Little League kids gave it to her.

Little did Jo know that her future was about to change dramatically. She was about to be called to serve the National Restaurant Association in a unique role. A dream was about to become a reality.

And, once again, she was about to face challenges at the restaurant. Only this time, she would be able to make the decisions and plan some of the strategies that would transform her life and her business.

25 Deering Street, Norway

CHAPTER 25

New Plans in 1961

Because of changes in the business world, old hotels which had been a mainstay for travelers were being torn down all over the Northeast to make way for the new, more popular motels. Salesmen who had been Jo's major clientele were now traveling in company cars and going home at night. Two new motels had already been built in the area, Ledgeview on lower Main Street, Norway and Goodwin's on Route 26, South Paris.

The final mortgage payment had been made on the Hotel Stone. With characteristic foresight, Jo saw that it was time to broaden her vision. She had been thinking about expanding her restaurant business. But the buildings on Main Street were close together. There was no room for an addition to Barjo's.

"Stony and I began talking about tearing down Hotel Stone to make way for something new," Jo said. "In new ventures when I furnished the financial backing, Henry was always ready to take a gamble. He and I began to discuss the possibility of a new venture on the hotel lot."

Perhaps, she thought, the site could have a modern building that would include all the features of a family restaurant like Barjo's, banquet facilities, cocktail lounge and also motel units on the second floor. Parking would be no problem because of the large lot behind the hotel.

In September 1961, Hotel Stone was, indeed, torn down. For three days, an auction was held. All furniture, fixtures, carpeting, and even much of the wood in the building were sold. This made the site available for the new restaurant with motel units on the second floor, if that was what they decided to do. Jo paid a local contractor $17,000 to clear the site where the hotel had stood for nearly a hundred years. Interestingly, this was same amount she had paid for the original building.

Before proceeding with her plans, Jo had soundings done to establish that the lot could be used for a new building and that all the water and sewer lines were intact and solid.

Architects from Portland, Galland Associates, were hired. They drew blueprints for a new building that included a family-style restaurant, a cocktail lounge and a banquet hall on the first floor with motel units on the second floor. The plans included a swimming pool in front with a well-landscaped patio around the pool that could also be used for outdoor dining in the summer. All the paperwork required by State of Maine was done, but approval of the plans proved to be a very slow process.

True to form, Jo explained, "Tearing down the hotel was the end of an era. But with the changes in the food and lodging industries, I felt that it was time to reorganize and look to the future. Soon my grandchildren would be of age to participate in the business, and I wanted to be able to help provide for them."

In 1962, while having the legal papers examined, Jo found that the Rex Theater, owned by Victory Amusement Company, had used a footpath for many years between the hotel and the back parking lot (originally the Starbird Stables lot). According to state law, if such a path isn't posted as private every seven years, it becomes "a common way."

The fact that former owner William Davis had given Victory Amusement Company a quit claim deed in 1948 granting a right-of-way or easement was not noted in her original deed. The theater's deed gave them the legal right to go on foot or by vehicle between the two parcels owned by Beal's Tavern, and prohibited anyone from blocking the path as Jo must if she carried out her building plans.

Victory Amusement was a stock company. For Jo to get a clear title, all stockholders had to be notified. It took several years. In order to use the full lot, she decided to buy the Rex Theater in 1964. Now she owned three properties that formed an L-shaped piece of land with no encumbrances.

When final papers were signed on the theater property, Jo had been in consultation with the architects and business consultants for some time. No plans had been finalized, but the building project was still on the drawing board.

After the Hotel Stone was torn down in September 1961, Jo and Stony moved to the Pendexter house beside the Second Congregational Church on lower Main Street. It was a large building with three floors. Jo and Stony invited some of us— myself and the five Dunn sisters, and Maurice Smith and Wade Herrick , high school students working at Barjo's, and Hayward Lord who did odd jobs for the Stones—to go with them. We all had bedrooms on the third floor. Doris Cummings Henry, Jo's high school classmate, had been working at the hotel as a chambermaid. She took the middle bedroom on the second floor.

Jo and Stony had the large bedroom in the front. From there, Jo could see the whole length of Main Street. It reminded her of her first view of Norway village in 1918.

The house had many unique features. My bedroom had been Mr. Pendexter's study. It had a distinctive alcove with a built-in semi-circular writing desk where he had done much of his creative writing. There was a dumbwaiter,[3] with a latticework, that opened into my room, so books and writing materials could be transported from floor to floor.

The Pendexter house was owned by Dr. Miller, who had been a surgeon at Stephens Memorial. Moving to another hospital, he wanted to sell the house. After renting for a year, Jo felt the building needed too many improvements and decided not to buy it.

Instead, in 1962, Jo and Stony bought the Ed Cummings property at 25 Deering Street, in Norway. Ed had passed away and his son, Elliot, was handling the estate. Elliot's wife was Grace, Jo's sister. This house was especially well built, had beautiful grounds and had a special meaning to Jo.

"I had never owned a home of my own," Jo said. "All my other ventures had been for commercial purposes. To own this particular house, which held so many memories for me, was beyond my wildest dreams."

Jo had admired the house from the time it was built in 1925. The lot had been an apple orchard. When she was walking to work at the drug store, Jo had watched the house go up.

Ed Cummings had been one of the owners of the C. B. Cummings & Sons dowel mill. The mechanical mastermind who designed most of the machinery for the factory, he used the garage of the house as a workshop.

The two-story Colonial with its beautiful lawns was prime real estate in the center of the village. Western red cedar had been imported as logs from Washington State and all the lumber, including shingles, was milled at C. B. Cummings. Ed had used copper nails, also an unusual feature. No outside wiring showed. Electrical wires and telephone cables ran through underground conduit pipes. The heat for the garage also ran through a pipe under the lawn.

Being an engineer, Cummings had incorporated many unique features: interlocking metal casings on all the doors and window frames to protect the wood and to provide security, double-pane glass in the windows, so no storm windows were required, removable panels in the closets to access plumbing. There were hard wood floors throughout the house and French doors on the first floor. The attic and cellar ceilings were made of match board with the beams at one-foot intervals.

Jo and Stony moved to their new home in October. Because there were only four bedrooms, it was no longer possible for all of us to stay with them. I was the only one who moved to Deering Street with Jo and Stony. I still live with Jo today.

The six Dunn sisters moved to a five-room apartment in the George Hill building next door to Barjo's. Stony got Wade Herrick and Maurice Smith a room at the Bishop house on Whitman Street. Doris Henry married Durwood Bean and left during the year, while Hayward Lord moved to the Norway Inn.

After we moved to the new house, Jo's grandchildren often came for a visit or to spend the night. One day, right after Darcy started school, she came to visit "Nana Jo." Darcy had just learned how to print. After a bit, Jo realized Darcy had gone off by herself, so she and I went looking for her.

We found the little girl downstairs at a desk in the basement, laboring away at writing a story about the Hotel Stone based on tales the older children told about all the fun they used to have there. The last sentence of her story was, "And when Nana got it paid for, she tore it down."

"That part was something I had told her," Jo said. "Because she was so little, I didn't think she would remember what I had said."

"I was born too late because I can't remember Hotel Stone," Darcy said. "I feel sad 'cause I missed all the fun there."

The hotel was gone, but the sleepovers and other fun didn't stop. I remember one night shortly after we moved to Deering Street when all four kids came to spend the night. Darcy was about 18 months old. That night I rocked her and my huge, pink stuffed dog nearly all night in my rocking chair. She wanted to be a part of what the other kids were doing, and every time I tried to put her down on to sleep she cried. Because I lived with Jo when she was born, Darcy thought of me as a big sister and wanted me to take care of her that night.

As a well-respected member of the community, Jo continued to make helping people, especially high school kids who needed work, a cornerstone of her business practice. In most cases, the risks she took by being trusting and generous paid her back with a loyal and appreciative crew who acted and felt like a part of Jo's

"Barjo family." But occasionally, Jo was sadly disappointed.

One spring evening in 1962, after finishing the cleaning at the restaurant, we took the Barjo's crew for a ride to Norway Lake. When we returned, Jo and I stopped to let Wade out at his room on Whitman Street.

Suddenly, we heard people running at break-neck speed up to the truck. It was three of the Dunn sisters, whose second-floor apartment was next door to the restaurant.

"What is all this commotion about?" Jo asked them.

Panting, they said, "We just heard somebody breaking into Barjo's! We heard glass shattering by the back door."

"Hurry up! Get in the back of the truck," Jo said. "We'd better go find the police officer before we go there."

In they climbed and the six of us went down Main Street to look for the police officer on patrol.

"This was Raymond Judkins' first night as an officer on the Norway Police force," Jo said. "The last thing he expected was to investigate a burglary at Barjo's."

Officer Judkins, the Dunn sisters, Wade and I went to the front door of the restaurant. Jo stayed by the back door.

When the police officer shone his light into the dining room, we could see a dark, shadowy shape sitting in the back booth. When the bright beam shone on him, he jumped up, ran through the kitchen, and out the back door, right into Jo's arms.

It was no stranger!

It was Maurice Smith, Wade's roommate and fellow employee, the boy Jo had been helping for years.

"What are you doing here?" Jo exclaimed.

She could smell the aroma of sizzling steak in the night air. Looking through the kitchen window at the electric range, we could see the imprint of the meat on the grill top where Maurice had cooked his steak.

After we had left the restaurant for our ride, Maurice had broken into the restaurant by smashing the glass in the window by the back door. He reached through the broken window to release the night lock on the door. Then he turned on the grill and cooked himself a steak. When he got a steak knife in the dining room, he left the drawer by the fountain open; getting himself a hot fudge sundae, he dropped some sticky topping on the fountain. When the Dunn girls had left, the fountain had been spotless.

With a puzzled expression, again Jo asked him, "Why did you break into the restaurant, Maurice? I got you a big supper earlier tonight. You couldn't have been that hungry."

He was still standing in the backyard behind Barjo's when the officer asked him, "What you were doing in the restaurant?"

Maurice went over and sat down on the cement curbing in back of Barjo's to ponder what his next move would be.

Maurice told Raymond Judkins, "Well, Officer, I lost my fishing license and just went in there looking for it."

"I can't believe you would do this to me," Jo said in a sad voice. "I've always stood up for you through thick and thin. When no one else was there to help you, all of us at Barjo's did everything we could to stand by you."

Maurice made no reply.

His explanation to the police didn't reveal anything more. We never understood why he got himself a second meal nor any real reason why he had broken into Barjo's. He knew there was no money in the restaurant. The deposit had already been made.

Jo didn't press any charges, but it remained a conundrum to her why he didn't tell her the truth about his night's activities.

Many changes had happened in Jo life during the last several years. She had torn down the hotel in anticipation of a new venture in the food and lodging industry. For the first time in her life, she now owned a home, located on Deering Street next to where she had grown up.

Helping young people around her produced many happy moments, but there had been sad days as well. Now, she was about to embark on a new phrase of her life in the food service industry that would include a new venture at the national level.

---

[3] *It was similar to an elevator, but run by a pulley from the attic to the basement. His dumbwaiter had shelves that were only wide enough to carry his books.*

Holiday Coffee Break, 1965

*Barbara,
Chief Guilford,
Susie Olmstead.*

NRA promotions like ROSCO gave Jo and Barjo's an opportunity to meet and compete with her small business peers regionally and nationally.

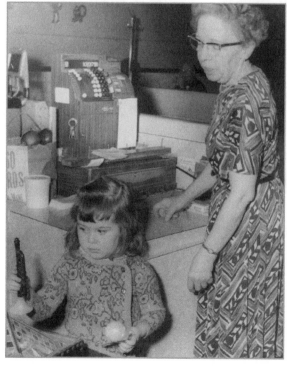

Margaret looks on while working the cash register as little Darcy chooses a toy from the toybox kept at the front of Barjo's for young patrons.

Senior Class Supper Award, 1966
Jo was particularly fond of these young men who took delight in surprising her with
their appreciation. L—R: Bob Dixon, Jo, Knox Bickford, class president, and Peter
Towne. (Bob Gardner photo)

CHAPTER 26

NRA and Carl Broome

One evening in the fall of 1962, after closing time at Barjo's, while the Dunn girls were finishing up their cleaning and I was cashing up, Jo came into the dining room. Every night, she washed the floor herself, pushing herself up and down the aisles on a go-cart as she washed under the tables and booths.

Jo was thinking out loud when she said, "I would really like to be one of the National Restaurant Association 400."[4]

Alice responded, "Jo, you're always telling *us* to try new things! Why don't you drive *yourself* to try something different?"

"I got to thinking about what Alice had said. Maybe this is the kind of project I could do without leaving Barjo's," Jo said to herself. "I always put the restaurant first because I felt my responsibility was to my customers."

By coincidence, the next day there was a call from Donald Grant, Secretary of the NRA. He asked for Josephine Stone. I called her to the phone with some excitement! Grant was calling to ask her to accept an appointment to the NRA 400.

"Of course, I agreed. It was like a dream come true. I couldn't believe it!" she exclaimed with awe.

One of the many projects Jo participated in for the NRA 400 was helping to get a commemorative Stamp issued for the 50th Anniversary of the NRA. From Barjo's, she called Bill Hathaway, Maine Senator and Democrat from Lewiston. Even though Jo was a staunch Republican, he had been her friend for many years. He agreed to help and together they accomplished a lot, including the 50th Anniversary Stamp.

There were many projects organized around issues of concern for the food service industry. The FDA was issuing many strict new regulations. Some were opposed by the NRA. Also at that time, the IRS was trying to tax waitresses' tips. The NRA attorney, Sam Nunn, was working hard to oppose this infringement on restaurant personnel. Hathaway worked to get a minimum wage increase through Congress. Jo helped in projects like national letter-writing campaigns by restaurant owners to Congressmen.

"I could never thank Bill enough for all the help he gave me,"

Jo said. "He came to Barjo's many times, to talk with me and guide me with legislative issues being presented in Congress."

The same year, the NRA 400 started working on a membership drive called "Operation ROSCO."[5] Barjo's was one of only seven restaurants in the State of Maine that belonged to the NRA. Over the next four years, Josephine Stone got many awards for outstanding achievement for work on "Operation ROSCO" and changed that statistic significantly.

Jo developed quite a system to sell memberships. It used the whole Barjo family working together. And it was successful because of Jo's often behind-the-scenes perseverance. Because Barjo's was small, she felt she couldn't leave to go out on the road herself. Cooking for her clientele was always her priority.

"Margaret was fluent with words," Jo said. "She wrote a letter about the purpose of the NRA and outlining member services."

The next step was to make out a list of New England restaurants to be contacted. I took the form letter and the list to George Thayer, a professional typist from South Paris. We mailed hundreds of letters to prospective members.

Within a week, when Jo thought the restauranteurs had had enough time, she had me call them. If anyone showed interest in joining, I set appointments to meet them at their businesses.

"Emily was young and enjoyed meeting other restaurateurs," Jo said. "So, I thought it was good experience for her to be involved in the project."

I packed my briefcase with all the material available though the NRA: letters, food service and sanitation reports, educational materials, seminars information, and membership applications.

My part of the project was to convince restaurant owners that NRA membership was an important component for their business by explaining, in detail, all the benefits. These included the political clout in Washington of a strong national organization as well as local and even day-to-day benefits like being kept up-to-date with the latest information about industry standards and innovations, and participation in effective marketing and promotional campaigns. Before leaving, if I had them convinced to join, I always asked the owner to sign a contract and to give me a check for the first year's dues in advance right on the spot.

Many owners gave me guided tours to let me to see how they handled the different phrases of their business. This was a learning experience in itself and increased my sense of myself as an active food service professional.

Once, when I was selling memberships in Brunswick, I was

almost arrested. I had an appointment with Mr. and Mrs. Bill Bourassa at Bill's Restaurant. When I introduced myself, Mrs. Bourassa told me to sit down while she made a telephone call.

She called the Better Business Bureau to see if Emily Foster was a legitimate salesman for the NRA—or a fraud. There had been a lot of warnings to restaurant people to be on the alert for people selling memberships to bogus organizations.

I was beginning to wonder if Jo was going to have to bail me out of jail or what was happening when Mrs. Bourassa came back to the table, explaining her call. After it was established that I was legitimate, I had a productive discussion with the Bourassas and sold them a membership!

In April 1963, we were working on Operation ROSCO when Jo got a telephone call from the Membership Director of the NRA in Chicago. Carl Broome wanted to come to Maine to visit Barjo's and study our methods for selling memberships, he told her. The success of our system fascinated him. In Chicago, they were impressed with our results.

That we collected dues in advance surprised him and his membership team. Few others had ever done this. Jo's system, of course, assured that the restauranteurs who said they'd join really did become NRA members because of those payments. Sometimes getting people to pay when they signed up had been hard. But I knew that was what Jo expected me to do and I never disappointed her.

The Chicago team also couldn't believe how many miles we traveled from restaurant to restaurant in the Northern New England region.

"We made a map using Norway as the hub, drawing lines in all the directions we had to go. We included the mileage to each place we visited," Jo said, "and when we sent the chart to him, he was amazed! In the city, multiple memberships could be sold within a few city blocks. The city folks in the home office were pretty surprised how far Northern Maine, New Hampshire and Vermont were from Barjo's."

"I invited Carl Broome to be a guest of the restaurant," Jo said, "and asked what kind of a schedule would he like to have us set up for him?"

"Whatever Jo Stone can do, I can do!" was his reply.

But Carl Broome didn't know Jo. What a surprise he was in for! Her stamina and determination to get the job done and done right was beyond his experience. But as we prepared for his visit, I knew what a challenge this was going to be.

It was a sunny, spring morning when Mr. Broome arrived in Portland. Renting a car at the airport, he met Jo and me at Southern Maine Vocational Technical School in South Portland where we had arranged a meeting with students of the Culinary Arts Department and their instructor, Mr. Breize. Broome was "red hot" as he delivered his speech about the National Restaurant Association. He and Jo and I then participated in a discussion of the merits of membership with the students. Afterwards, many of them signed up as Special Associate Members through the school.

Broome, Jo and I went to the Spurwink Country Kitchen restaurant in Scarborough for lunch. There we met Hope Sargeant, the owner, and signed her up for the NRA. Then, it was on to the Portland Chamber of Commerce where we kept an appointment arranged with restaurant people from the Greater Portland Area at 2:00 p. m.

By this time, Mr. Broome's stamina was lagging behind Jo's. The bounce was missing from his step and he was much more subdued than at our morning meeting with the VocTech students.

"He wasn't as fluent here as he had been, but things went well," Jo added. "Some of the Portland restaurateurs joined the NRA at the afternoon meeting."

Jo had scheduled another meeting at the Stowe House in Brunswick to meet with Bath-Brunswick area restaurant owners at 7:00 p. m. Stony, who had been working at Barjo's all day, met us there to participate.

"Mr. Broome told us he was going to leave his things at the motel on the way to Brunswick," Jo said. "He said he'd meet us at the Stowe House at 7:00 p. m."

When Jo and I got to Brunswick, Stony was there as agreed, but *no Carl Broome*. The restaurateurs from Bath and Brunswick began arriving, and were waiting for us to start the meeting.

"Where do you suppose he is?" Jo asked me. "Suppose he took the wrong road, and got lost. He doesn't know much about the state of Maine."

7:00 p. m. crept to 7:30. Still no Carl Broome.

We had almost decided to start without him when in walked a very tired Carl Broome. He sat down, looking bushed. He was a shadow of the energetic man we had met that morning. Jo and I exchanged looks. Perhaps we might still have to conduct the meeting ourselves.

Finally, he got up and gave a good speech. The energy he had shown that morning with the students was gone, however.

"I was completely amazed by Jo's stamina. She was still as

enthusiastic as if it were 6:00 *a.m.* instead of *11:00 p.m.!*" Carl said. "I couldn't believe a woman could do me in."

The next morning, Barbara and Henry caught up with Broome at his motel, and traveled with him to the Pilot's Grill in Bangor for a meeting with the restaurant owners of the Bangor-Brewer area.

We returned to Barjo's, promising to meet him in the Club House at the Lewiston Raceway in Lewiston, at 7:00 that evening for a meeting. Jo and I arrived at on time and waited for Mr. Broome. Jo was always on time and didn't like to wait for anyone. Again we waited and waited.

In all, about 30 restaurateurs from the Lewiston-Auburn area had come for the meeting. Two of them , Jim Cooper of Cooper's Restaurant and Bert Poulin of Bert's Restaurant, were at the bar drinking beer. By the time Carl Broome arrived at last, the two men were feeling no pain. Mr. Broome launched his sales pitch, delivering his talk on the merits of membership in the NRA.

From across the table, Bert said to Jim, "Don't do it, Coop, too much mail." He had been a member in the past, but had canceled his membership.

From the other end of the table, Lucien Levesque of Sim's Restaurant and Bill Dumais of the Chuck Wagon yelled in unison,"Shut up, Bert, and listen!"

It was a riot to hear Lucien and Bill trying to keep order.

Carl Broome signed up several members, but not Bert Poulin or Jim Cooper.

After the meeting had adjourned, Jo and I sat down with Bert and Coop at a table in the corner of the room. During a previous restaurant visit to Lewiston, I had met both these fellows.

"Listen, guys," Jo said to them. "I've been a member a long time. Bert, I think you'd better give the NRA another try. Coop, you don't know what you are missing. Don't listen to Bert, he's just trying to discourage you from joining."

Jo kept telling them how useful it was to be an NRA member and, in the end, not only got their signatures on applications, but their checks for a year's dues. Broome was amazed with Jo.

"This must be the Maine way," he said. "I've never seen anybody sign up members like this. These two guys totally ignored *my* sales pitch, and refused to listen to anything about the NRA."

On Wednesday, we had arranged for Mr. Broome to go to Presque Isle, to meet Northern Maine restaurant owners. But he begged us to call the meetings off, so he could rest up before going back to Chicago.

"I'll visit you at Barjo's, but I'm too tired to hold any more meetings," he said to Jo regretfully. Jo and I smiled as we remembered his claim that he could do "whatever Jo Stone could do!"

Over the years, Jo had worked long hours and required little sleep. Always a hard worker, the restaurant meetings were like child's play to her. To Carl, it was a different story. He worked in an office all day, and had never had to do the kind of physical labor Jo was used to. The difference in their lifestyles showed.

Broome came to Barjo's and liked what he saw there. During that week, the Easter Bonnet Contest was being conducted. When he got back to Chicago, he sent a broom-shaped trophy with a nameplate to be engraved with the winner's name. The next year, too, he sent a one.

"When that first trophy arrived in the mail," Jo said. "I was quite surprised. The girls told him about the contest, but I didn't think they'd made an impression. But he had taken it all in, and when he got home, had gone to the trouble of having something special made for our winner."

In 1963, Jo and I signed up a total of 68 new NRA members in the Northern New England area. In May, Jo was awarded a trophy for her efforts, declaring her the 1963 ROSCO winner.

Also, in 1963, *Restaurant Management*, the premier magazine for the food service industry, awarded Jo the Golden Host Award of Merit. It recognized her for "outstanding devotion and achievement in the field of civic welfare" and for her contributions to the food service industry.

"Stony first bought the *Restaurant Management Magazine* for me back in the 1940's," Jo said. "It guided me through many changes in the industry and offered useful organizational tips. For instance, there was a section laying out menus for each month. It never occurred to me that the editors of this informative national magazine knew who I was. I never did find out who had entered my name for the award but it must have been someone who knew me when we first went into business, because the award came in the name of 'Josephine McAllister Stone' as I used to be known, not 'Josephine A. Stone' as I signed my name now."

The next year the board of directors of the NRA asked Jo if she would forfeit the ROSCO trophy she again earned by signing up the most new members so that they could give it to Colonel Sanders of Kentucky Fried Chicken. They wanted to recognize his growing business success connect the organization with him.

"I told them I didn't care," she said. "But I really felt if they were going to give him the award, he should have earned it. They sent me a silver clock engraved with 'Special Achievement Award—Winner of Operation ROSCO, 1964,' and a trophy for being a two-time winner of the membership drive. It was political—he was Colonel Sanders and his success was huge. I still felt it was an unfair decision, though."

The NRA had other honors and more projects for Jo, however. From the membership of the NRA 400, forty members were chosen by invitation to form the "Silver Spoon Society." This elite group participated in numerous special national projects. Jo was one of the charter members of this society during the year 1964-1965. She received a silver medallion on a blue grosgrain ribbon to be worn at all their meetings, as well as a lapel button. Her membership plaque is on display in her home now.

In the spring of 1965, Jo sent Margaret to an educational seminar conducted by Kathyrn Bruce, Education Director of the NRA, held at Cornell University in Ithaca, New York.

"Margaret needed the opportunity more than I did," Jo said. "This was something she had always wanted to do. I was responsible for the daily operation of Barjo's, so I encouraged her to go."

At the seminars, Margaret learned a great deal about cost control, restaurant accounting and other related subjects. She and Kathryn Bruce became good friends as well, keeping in touch for many years.

In May 1965, Barbara and Henry made a business trip, too. Jo hadn't let the Colonel Sanders incident slow down her enthusiasm for the NRA. Barbara and Henry went to the NRA Convention in Chicago to accept the ROSCO 1965 Three-Time Winner award for her. Again, Jo stayed where she was most comfortable, in the kitchen at Barjo's and sent one of the family to receive the honors. For overall achievement in the NRA, a Silver Bowl engraved with Jo's name was presented as an "Award for Outstanding Achievement" in the NRA 400.

That spring, Jo received a note from Molly May, owner of May's Drug Store in South Paris. This local acknowledgment of Jo's success from an old friend perhaps meant even more to her than all the honors from the national professional organization. Molly wrote,

There are many in our community, including myself, who can still remember the first year you started your restaurant career. It wasn't easy. You certainly had your share of grief, heartaches, and many disappointments, which you were forced to endure. But you managed to rise above it all because you had the ambition and, above all, the will and determination to succeed.

"I think you should look upon this moment as the most gratifying experience of your life. For all the years of hard work, you finally have reached the 'Peak of Success' when the National Restaurant Association presented you with the "Award for Outstanding Achievement in the Food Service Industry". This honor is one you have earned by hard work and rightfully deserve."

After reading Molly's letter, Jo thought to herself, "And she knows only half the story. Many days, if I hadn't had a strong faith in God and asked Him to guide me, it would have been almost impossible to keep striving for my goals."

The Director of the NRA for Northern New England was Anthony Anthanus of Anthony's Pier 4 Restaurant in Boston. He owned several others restaurants in Massachusetts as well. He asked Jo to sit on the Board of Directors to represent Maine.

"It was a great honor to be chosen, but I declined because I felt my customers were my priority," Jo said. "Barjo's was a small restaurant with twelve employees, not one where the work was delegated to others. I had my shift in the kitchen and needed to be there every day. Many on the Board were from large corporations, not part of the daily operation of a small restaurant."

Pilot's Grill, in Bangor, was one of the original seven NRA members from Maine. The Zoidis family had started their business at about the same time as Jo. Bill Zoidis, the son of the owner, was chosen to be the NRA Director for Maine when Jo declined. Interestingly, he had many connections in the Norway area. One of his aunts and her husband owned the Ledgewood Motel in Norway. His uncle, Mike Hassas, ran the lunchroom for the shoe shop. Later, Mike was a car salesman for a local General Motors dealership. They were Jo's friends and good customers.

"I was pleased Bill was chosen. He was young and had a lot of pep," Jo said. "His participation at the national level was a big stepping stone for Maine. He had already served as president of the Maine Restaurant Association. Coming from a hard-working family, he worked diligently with the food industry leaders for the good of his home state."

During the summer, Barjo Restaurant was invited to join the International HO-RE-CA.[6] The President was from Paris, France and the organization's Headquarters were in Zurich. Because of Jo's work with the NRA 400, Barjo's was one of a few restaurants from the US to be given this honor.

By this time, Barjo's was well-loved by people from many countries and regions of North America who came to Maine as visitors. Barjo's was a favorite dining spot for most everyone who passed through the western foothills to the lakes region or explored the northern wilderness.

During this same time, many more customers became Jo's close friends and joined the "Barjo's family," and Jo continued to help young people, but in different ways. More surprises were in Jo's future, both locally and internationally. Through her participation with others at Barjo's and within the community, many local, national and international organizations recognized her accomplishments in her profession.

In the spring, the Senior Class of Norway High School asked Jo, "Would you be willing to help us raised enough money so we can go on a trip to Washington, D.C.?"

"Sure," she replied, "we'll ask the Second Congregational Church if we can used their dining room. I'll furnish the food and prepare it for you at Barjo's. The Dunn girls and the rest of us at Barjo's will serve at no charge. But, all this on one condition—I expect your class to sell the tickets."

This was a determined group of kids. With the help of Harold Wiley, the owner of the local GMAC dealership, they organized the town into sections. Each student was assigned a territory.

"Rusty Frothingham, the Class President, with the help of Peter Wiley and his father, showed me just how much they wanted the banquet to be a success," Jo said.

The banquet was a huge success because the kids and their supporters matched Jo's enthusiasm. Afterwards, Rusty and the class advisor, Ronald Kugall, came see Jo. "We appreciate everything you have done for us," Rusty told her. "We raised more than enough to go to Washington. We'll be gone for a week and see New York City, the Amish County, the Endless Caverns in West Virginia, and and the Naval Academy in Baltimore." The pair then presented her with a trophy.

"What a surprise!" Jo exclaimed. "I didn't want you to spend your money on me. All I wanted was help you reach your goal."

At the Alumni banquet in June, Jo was named the "Norway High School Alumnus of the Year." Over the years, she had dedicated many hours to teaching school kids how to work. For many, working for Barjo's was their first job. Through the work ethics she instilled in them, they were able to be a productive part of the labor force in the community.

Jo donated school function banquets at no cost to the students to raise money for numerous school projects. She also set up a fund to present a $400 scholarship to a Norway High School senior each year.

Through Barjo's, she held various benefits for the local Boy Scouts, 4-H clubs, schools, and local Drum and Bugle Corp. All of these promotions to the assist local clubs and organizations resulted in local and regional press coverage.

In the summer of 1965, the country celebrated the Civil War centennial. At Barjo's and in the town of Norway, the merchants all participated in their own ways.

Donnie had a connection with a costume house in Boston. At the time, he was a teacher and drama coach for Stephens High School in Rumford. All of us at Barjo's were measured and fitted for period costumes. During work hours, each waitress wore a full-length gingham dress and a hat with a large bow, for the week of the Civil War celebrations.

On Friday, all the businesses turned back the clock and sold their goods at prices that were in effect at the turn of the century. Barjo's sold a roast turkey dinner with all the fixings for 35 cents. What a night that was! Though our seating capacity was 80, Barjo's served over 300 people in three hours. We were packed solid from 5:00 p.m. to 8:00 p.m. With those long dresses on, it was some challenge just to move around the restaurant, to say nothing about getting everyone served!

A soldier on leave, Sgt. Rodney Rolfe, who worked in food service facilities in the Army, pitched in to help Jo in the kitchen.

"Without Rodney's help, I would have been swamped with orders!" Jo exclaimed. "I don't know where all the people came from, but we certainly served a lot of turkey in three hours!"

In October, Barjo Restaurant was awarded an "Award of Appreciation" from the Maine Department of Agriculture "For the Promotion of Maine Products in Menu Planning." Maynard Dolloff, at the Sheraton-Eastland Hotel in Portland, presented the award to Jo and Stony.

Jo understood that promoting Maine products and Maine's seasonal atmosphere was good for business. Our clientele always responded positively to our menu promotions that praised the food, atmosphere, service and hospitality of the restaurant. We were proud to participate in state promotions like Maine Apple Month, when we had a large display of locally-grown rosy-cheeked apples near the cashier's station where patrons could purchase them. And we used menu clip-ons and table tents to promote Maine Potato Week with eye-catching displays that featuring the Pine Tree State's well-known product. Jo also promoted Maine as the recreational state through the Vacationland Show on WKTQ, the local radio station, and the Fish N' Seafood promotion of Maine lobster and fish.

Throughout October, Jo featured her connection with the NRA with posters, place mats, and waitress aprons, all bearing the NRA slogan.

Barjo's participated in the local Chamber of Commerce Dollar Days twice yearly, in "Turkey Trot," a Thanksgiving radio feature to award turkeys, and in "Mystery Record" naming contests with Barjo's sandwiches as prizes.

Through this varied advertising, Barjo's Maine Downeast menu attracted diners from all over Maine, as well as tourists from every state of the nation and many foreign countries. Meals were served with vegetables from local farms with the names of the farmers listed on the menu. Jo is still known far and wide for Barjo's home-cooked pies and other delectable desserts many of which featured fresh, locally grown ingredients.

"Whenever one of my friends sold me produce for the restaurant," Jo said, "I liked to have the customers know who had contributed to their dinner. Jim Cleveland and Harry Walker brought in shelled beans. 'Doc' Wyman brought us many different kinds of greens. Lucy Richardson and Fred Foster brought in beautiful fresh raspberries in season. Raspberry and custard pies were the two most popular. I wanted to give my friends and neighbors recognition for their efforts since they collaborated with us in creating such a popular menu."

One day in 1965, Rev. Jay Lello, the pastor of the Second Congregational Church, called Jo. Jud Higgins who owned the radio station WKTQ, and he had been broadcasting inspirational programs, "Imprints" and "Reflections," for over 30 years. These programs were especially for shut-ins and people who were unable to attend regular church services. He asked her if she would be willing to help him get 10 sponsors for these programs. Both Jud and Rev. Lello had donated their time, and thought they should have some support.

"Sure, I'll be glad to," she answered.

Jo called several business people who agreed to be sponsors. Then she called Charlie Goodspeed, the owner of Goodspeed Oil Company at the head of Main Street.

After she explained the purpose of her call, Charlie's first question was, "Have you called Elliot Cummings?" Grace and Elliot's daughter, Margie, had married Charlie's son. Elliot was the treasurer at C. B. Cummings & Sons and that firm seldom supported any local charities or school activities. Being involved in the Kiwanis, Charlie could guess the answer before he asked.

"I didn't call Elliot. But what I want to know Charlie is, are *you* going to help us or not?" Jo asked.

"O.K., but don't use my name!" He said.

Charlie was much like Jo, herself, and liked to do for others, but "on the QT." He was a hard worker in many community projects and, like Jo, was self-made business person.

"Are you afraid to let people know that you believe in *God*?" she challenged him.

He quickly responded, "Use my name!"

Jo was able to get all the sponsors in less than half an hour. Rev. Jay Lello and Jud Higgins were amazed at her ability to persuade her friends on their behalf.

Shortly after, Rev. Lello retired and Rev. John Ellis replaced him. His wife, Karen, taught third grade in the Guy Rowe Elementary School.

One afternoon, Karen came into Barjo's kitchen with a request for Jo. That weekend the church was holding a youth retreat and she needed help to feed the young people expected to attend.

From the time Jo was a child in East Stoneham, one word that never entered her vocabulary was "tired;" all her friends and family knew it. Karen's started off on the wrong foot when she said, "Gee, Jo, you can't believe how tired I am!"

I looked at Jo with a smile and thought to myself, "Karen that's your first mistake if you want any assistance from Jo."

"If you want me to help you, never tell me you are tired," Jo replied strongly.

Karen, a quick learner, replied, "I'll never say it again, Jo!"

Jo turned from the grill and said to the minister's wife, "I'll be glad to do the cooking for the kids. What do you need?"

"We're holding a youth retreat at the church and I have no idea how to feed that many people at once! I'd really like to have you make a chicken pie to feed 25 kids and several pies for dessert," Karen answered.

"Anything to help the kids," Jo replied.

She had always done a lot of cooking for church activities. She knew that cooking for a large group was a challenge to the new minister's wife and was glad to help out. This would be just the beginning of a long relationship between them and Jo would later help her out in other ways over the years.

All the awards and public recognition during this era puzzled Jo. She had just been doing what came naturally, working for the good of her town, state and country while promoting her business as a meeting place and home away from home for her growing "Barjo's family." When she helped young people, her goal was to give them a start for their future. Buying from local farmers, she was glad to have access to high quality goods while helping out her neighbors and friends.

The next phase of her life was about to begin and tragedy was also about to strike.

4 *This was a select group of 400 of the 10,000 members of the National Restaurant Association who worked together on special projects.*

5 *ROSCO stands for "Recognition of Outstanding Service Commitment Operation."*

6 *The international organization of Hotels, Restaurants, and Caterers*

Nana's Helpers
Barbara's daughters, Andy, here age 12, and Jody, age 10, enjoyed helping Nana Jo at the restaurant. They both worked at Barjo's as waitresses when they got older.

Barbara and Henry opened Country Way Restaurant in 1966. Its capacity to host large functions made for a natural partnership with Barjo's established clientele and banquet schedule. It was a challenge for Jo to reorganize her staff in 1966 after having Henry and Stony in the Barjo's kitchen with her for 20 years. Some of her waitresses went to Country Way with Barbara and Henry, too.

Barjo's staff dressed to celebrate the Civil War Centennial in 1965 included (above), Jo's granddaughters and four of the Dunn sisters. L—R: Andy Paradis, Alice Dunn, Esther Dunn, Emily Foster, Veda Taker, Jody Paradis, Dot Dunn, Judy Dunn, and Susie Olmstead.

CHAPTER 27

Country Way is Born!

The plans for the new restaurant were moving very slowly. Many things delayed the project. By 1965, Jo had spent $80,000 for the architects and consultants to get the new undertaking going but had little show for it.

At this time, Jo planned to close Barjo's once a new restaurant complex was built. The possibility of the current restaurant building being used for the Norway town office was being discussed. The delays meant that Jo held off on any renovations at Barjo's, but she was always concerned with efficiency and cost controls.

Jo hired Donahue, Groover Associates from Florida as restaurant management consultants. The firm studied Barjo's operations in detail to determine the next steps to take in the new venture. The consultants also studied how Barjo's could be operated more efficiently.

Palmer Bessey was assigned to work with Jo. After studying the restaurant books, he told Jo the breakfast hour wasn't showing a profit and should be closed down.

"To close the breakfast hour was a big change for Barjo's, but I took his advice. Since the early days, we had been serving breakfast and Stony had been doing the cooking," Jo stated. "The change would mean that Veda would now be working a split shift, 10:30 a.m. to 2:00 p.m. and then come back at 5:00 p.m. and work until 8:00 p.m. Stony would still be doing the baking, but he could help out in other ways as well."

For the first time, Norway had passed a law allowing liquor to be served in a Class A Restaurant. Previously, the town had a State Liquor store, but no place where liquor could be served to the public.

When Jo closed the morning shift, Mr. Bessey told her to consider serving liquor. It would be a service to the public and generate additional income for Barjo's.

"Serving liquor was the furthest thing from my mind," Jo said. "After Mr. Bessey showed me the difference it could make on the profit and loss statement, however, I agreed to try it."

Palmer Bessey taught us how to run a bar efficiently. He scheduled a bartender's training program at the Holiday Inn in Auburn where Henry learned how to mix cocktails and then taught us what he had learned about mixing and serving liquor.

"The Maine State Liquor Commission sent the chief liquor inspector to explain the laws and requirements for a Class A liquor license to us," Jo said.

One of the first things he did was measure the distance from the Universalist Church and the Upper Primary school to Barjo's. The state law in 1965 required the front door of a liquor-serving restaurant to be at least five hundred feet from a church or school.

"Barjo's had no problems there, but he recommended I serve the liquor from the kitchen," Jo said. "This made a lot of sense for a family restaurant. Many of my older customers weren't pleased with our change."

With Margaret running the dining room, there was no danger of anyone having too much to drink. If anyone had two cocktails, she thought that was plenty.

Mr. Bessey taught Margaret a detailed new accounting program, too. This new method gave her a daily inventory of food stock and food cost percentages. The liquor was inventoried every night.

"I had all the faith in the world in Margaret," Jo said. "She would hunt for a penny for hours. Having a perfect set of books was always her goal. Margaret received many compliments from state and federal inspectors for her neatness and accuracy in all her payroll records, cash book and general ledger for Barjo's."

Marion Martin from the Maine Department of Labor and Margaret became very good friends. Margaret called her whenever new labor laws went into effect. She wanted to be sure she fully understood their meaning and effect at Barjo's.

In the summer of 1965, Jo and her family were still working on plans for a new restaurant on the hotel lot, but things were moving at a snail's pace. A new shopping mall had just opened on Route 26 at the corner of Alpine and Main Street in South Paris. This area was expanding rapidly with the new Oxford Hills High School being built on the other side of the street.

On a Thursday afternoon in the fall, an accountant who had worked for Millett, Fish and Dresser on the Hotel Stone books approached Jo. This meeting gave Jo some fresh ideas to think about. She knew that Henry and Barbara would also be interested in this new development.

"I am working for Sampson Super Markets chain," the

accountant told her. "Mr. Sampson has just built the Twin Town Shopping Center in South Paris. The two spaces are occupied, his grocery store on one end and a beauty parlor on the other end. Why don't you come over to look at the middle section and see if it holds any possibilities for a restaurant?" he asked her.

The next day, they went to South Paris to see the space.

When Lester Soule, who owned Twin Town Hardware directly in front of the new mall, saw Stony on Saturday, he suggested, "Why don't you buy my store instead of moving into the Mall?"

"I'm not interested, but Jo and Henry may be," Stony said.

Monday morning, Stony went with Henry to see Lester. After some discussion, they closed the deal on the hardware store. After they had agreed to buy the property, Jo and Stony had a talk with Barbara and Henry.

"We asked them if they wanted to go it alone or have us join them," Jo said. "If we opened a new restaurant together, I would close Barjo's and sell the real estate. If not, Barjo's would need to have some renovations."

"We thought about it for several days," Henry said. "We had a talk with Jo and Stony. Barbara and I decided to try operating our own restaurant. We both had grown up in the business. We felt it was time to take the step to go it alone."

Because of this decision, Jo and Stony stayed at Barjo's. "The Country Way Restaurant" in South Paris was about to be born.

Barbara and Henry had many renovations to do to turn the Twin Town Hardware store into a restaurant. Bill Cook was one of their salesmen. He told them if they bought the material and equipment through his firm, Jones, McDuffee & Stratton, they would furnish all the engineers and interior decorators, at no charge. This meant that none of the Jo's original architects' plans could be used at the new location.

"All the money spent for blueprints and plans was wasted," Jo said. "But Palmer Bessey's advice had increased our profit and the new accounting procedures he taught Margaret meant that the $80,000 wasn't a total loss."

Having Barbara and Henry leave Barjo's wasn't the only challenge that Jo was faced. Jo offered her waitresses a choice to stay at Barjo's or to go with Barbara and Henry to the Country Way. Only Susie, Veda and two Dunn sisters stayed; the others decided to go to the new restaurant. With Henry gone from the kitchen, Jo was about to teach me a new vocation at the restaurant.

When Jo and Stony decided they weren't going to build on the hotel lot, they turned it into a parking lot. They had the lot paved and added parking meters. It was called "J & S Parking."

"Walking home today," I told Jo one day, "I met people talking about the parking lot. They thought it was ridiculous to put meters on it. They said, 'No way will we ever pay to park there!'"

I was thoroughly disgusted with some of the town's people. But it was true, hardly anyone ever did put money in the meters.

But, reorganizing her staff and dealing with parking issues weren't the only problems Jo was about to face.

On Memorial Day in 1966, Henry said to Jo, "Why don't you go for a ride today for a change and I'll get the boys to help me serve dinner? You deserve some time off!"

Stony got out their new Dodge from the garage behind the restaurant. Normally, Jo and Stony rode in the restaurant pick-up truck, using their car only on special occasions.

"I would like to ride over to East Stoneham," Jo said to him.

"Wherever you'd like to go," he replied.

"We went through the village and up into Bartlett Borough, the section of Stoneham where I had gone berrying as a kid, said Jo. "It was a lovely ride. I noticed that Stony was driving much slower that he usually did, but I didn't think much about it."

When they got back home, Jo told him, "I am going to rest for a little while before I go back to work."

At 5:00 p. m., Jo and I rode to work in the pick-up for the night shift. After helping Jo for a while, Henry went home. About 7:00 p. m., Stony came into the back room of the restaurant. He was so weak he was practically crawling. He was pale and numb.

The neighbors later told Jo that it must have taken him over an hour to get from the house to the restaurant—normally a five-minute walk.

"He wasn't the kind of a guy you offered to help," one of them told her. "I would have offered him a ride, but I know how independent he likes to be so I thought he'd refuse me."

Once in the restaurant kitchen, Stony sat down on a stool, but he couldn't move his right side or speak. Immediately, Jo had me call the ambulance.

He was rushed to Stephens Memorial Hospital. Jo went with him, leaving me in charge.

"I said to Dr. Bean, the emergency room physician, I think he's had a stroke," Jo said.

"It looks like you are right," he commented.

"Stony's own doctor, Dr. Dixon, had left for a medical cruise on the hospital ship, Hope," Jo said. "He thought Stony's sugar diabetes was under control and would be O.K. until he got back."

The physician determined that he had, indeed, had a massive stroke. He was already on medication for a serious case of diabetes. Though Stony improved from that night, he never regained the use of his right arm, and walked with a shuffle. He also had a hard time talking. His days of cooking at Barjo's were over.

As a World War II veteran, Stony felt he should be able to go to Togus Veterans Hospital in Augusta for physical therapy on his arm and leg. But, it was not to be. Though he felt the doctors there would be better trained to help him, he had to be referred by his local physician to receive treatment there. Stony decided to take the first step of going there for a physical.

At Stephens Memorial, Jo went to to see him and to bring the papers came from the VA Hospital for signatures. But when Dr. Bean learned Jo was with Stony, he was so upset he closed his office right in the middle of visiting hours. It was very apparent to Jo that this doctor felt he would be losing a private patient and had no intention of letting that happen. If Stony entered Togus, he would be eligible for government benefits and would no longer need the doctor's services.

Sure enough, Dr. Bean refused to sign the Togus admission papers for Stony.

"The doctor made it very plain that he had no intention of signing anything," Jo commented. "I really didn't understand why he was so upset."

"Stony is staying right here in Norway," the doctor told her with sarcasm. "I don't want you to interfere with my patient."

"What a disappointment that was to Stony. The doctor also told me that he didn't want me to try to go over his head," Jo said. "Neither Stony or I ever did."

For Jo, without Barbara and Henry to help her at the restaurant and with Stony's illness, she once again had to reorganize her restaurant strategy. Having faced many difficult moments in the past, she turned once again to God to help her through this latest crisis.

To compound the situation, another concern arose. Mother's health was failing and Margaret began to stay at home with her. Marg could still do all the bookkeeping and banking, but not work in the dining room, so Barbara had taken her place as hostess. Now she would leave for her own restaurant.

Jo gave the situation much thought. Jo told Barbara and Henry ,"Stony won't be able to help us much now. So I'll have Emily help me in the kitchen. Susie and Dorothy can run the dining room. Veda will work her split shift. Jody can train some kids to wash dishes.I don't want this to stop you from going ahead with your plans for the new restaurant. We'll be able to manage."

The Country Way restaurant was opened on July 13, 1966. It was a difficult year for everybody. Barbara and Henry were starting out on a new venture and we had only a skeleton crew of old help back at Barjo's.

"Every year, the first week of July was one of the busiest weeks for the summer," Jo said. "In 1966, it was the slowest week of the summer season. All of our customers went to Country Way to try out the food. I never said a word, because I knew what had happened. After that first week, our regulars came back and business was just as good as ever."

Only Veda, Susie, Dorothy and Joyce had stayed in the dining room. Jo took me out in the kitchen to help as her assistant cook. With Stony on the disabled list, she also taught me how to do the buying. Jody, her granddaughter, was thirteen. She helped train the kids in the kitchen and ended up doing most of their work. The group of school kids at that time weren't very ambitious, either in the kitchen or the dining room.

"The Dunn sisters were such good workers," Jo said. "They had spoiled us. None of the kids we hired had a fraction of their get up and go. What a change that was in my life! Having worked with Henry for twenty years and Stony since the 1930's, I had to reorganize my whole method of operation."

One afternoon during that summer, Mr. McManus, the state food inspector at Barjo's, came to the restaurant on an unusual mission. He had been one of Jo's friends for many years.

"Would like to buy a Saladmaster?" he said. "My wife is selling them to earn some extra money."

"Why?" Jo asked. "Are you calling on all your clients for her?"

"No one in the Department of Health and Human Services has ever gotten a raise. All the other departments of state government have received raises at one time or other, but not mine," he told her. "My wife felt we will need some extra income to supplement my retirement."

"I'll get Donald, and my friend, Frank Bjorklund, to help me get a petition signed for you to have a raise," she said. "Through his work as town manager, Don knows the head of the Department of Health and Human Services, Dr. Dean Fisher, well."

"I don't want a raise just for myself, but for the whole department," he said.

Within a week they had several pages of names on their petition for Mr. McManus. Donald, Norway's town manager, and

Frank, a local attorney and the Finnish consul for the area, took the signed petition to Dr. Dean Fisher.

When they returned from Augusta, Donald told Jo, "We were able to obtain a new pay scale for the employees of the Department of Health and Human Services. We were also able get a new three step program put in place, so the length of service would be considered as well."

Mr. McManus thanked Jo over and over for helping his whole department, as well as himself personally. He was able to retire at sixty-five with a good pension. Now able to enjoy their home in Minot, the McManus family came to Barjo's often for lunch or dinner.

In the midst of her own crises during the mid-1960's, Jo wondered how she could continue to help Maurice Smith. He was 18 and graduated from high school. Jo wanted to help him further his education. She asked Henry to help her get Maurice registered in the Manpower Training Program in Lewiston. Maurice did enroll in the culinary arts program and earned his certification as a cook. Then he could work in any food service facility.

When Maurice graduated, he worked for a short time at the training facility at Poland Springs. This was where he met Charlotte, who became his wife. They had three children, two boys and a girl.

His mother, Bertha, had moved back ito the area, but he still looked to Jo and Henry for guidance. When Maurice moved back to Norway from school, he worked for quite a while at Country Way. He was a very good worker and everyone liked him.

From the time he was small, he had a heart problem. In 1988 he had open-heart surgery and died on the operating table. It was a tragedy. Everyone at the Barjo's felt very sad about his death.

1966 was quite a year for Jo. In January, she could never have imagined all the roadblocks that would occur along her way. From this point on, the challenges at the restaurant were a motivation for both Jo and me, her helper. The bond between us would grow even stronger as we looked to God to guide us through these hard times. Working long hours together with minimum help, we would continue to provide our clientele with the service they had come to expect. There would be satisfactions and also puzzling moments at Barjo's.

PART VII

Public Service to the Community

Maine State Police Honorary Captain Josephine Stone displays her Captain's bars and commission, 1980.

CHAPTER 28

Looking Forward with a New Perspective

When Barbara and Henry opened their own restaurant in South Paris, Jo was already 62. Though Stony had suffered a stroke, he still was able to able to attend to his own needs, but he was unable to work at the restaurant. He never complained about his condition and didn't want Jo to fret about him.

The idea of retiring never entered Jo's mind. Instead she did some reorganizing at Barjo's. In July 1966, she adjusted the restaurant hours so that, with my help, she could always be there while the restaurant was open. Barjo's now opened at 10:30 a.m. and closed at 9:30 p.m. The late evening shifts were eliminated.

With Henry gone and Stony ill, Jo did all the baking. She taught me how to prepare soups and dinner specials. After supper hour, I did the short order cooking while Jo made the pies for the next day.

I really didn't know all that much about short order cooking. During high school, I had helped Stony some on the morning shift, but since then I had always worked in the dining room. If Jo needed an extra hand to make salads or mix a cocktail, I had done that. But this was a whole new experience for both of us.

"I knew Emily was a little apprehensive about working full-time in the kitchen, but she never said so," Jo explained. "Knowing how quickly she had learned the routine in the dining room and at the hotel, I never doubted for a minute that we would be able to meet this new challenge. I gave her a raise and made her my assistant. I also taught her how to do the buying for the restaurant."

Jo and I did all the cooking and ran the restaurant kitchen with the help of several high school kids. We worked long hours. Jo never allowed any cleaning to be done when the restaurant was open. After closing at night, the waitresses dusted the booths, filled the sugars and salt and pepper shakers, and polished the fountain. Jo did the rest herself. As she had done for years, she continued to wash the dining room floor on her hands and knees. Before leaving, Jo cleaned the fry pots and the grill and washed all the tin dishes. I cleaned the dishwashers and helped her finish up.

Depending on how much food preparation Jo had to do in an evening, many times she would finish the cleaning in the early morning hours before the next day's opening. Our nights were very short! At 4:00 a.m., we were back at Barjo's to finish the cleaning and to complete the prep-work for the next day.

Jo always scrubbed the kitchen floor with a GI brush and rinsed it with a hose. By pushing the water down through the floor drains with a squeegee, I helped her finish drying the floor.

"We wore high rubber boots when we were washing the kitchen floor," Jo said with a laugh. "We got a lot of comments about how funny we looked, but how else are you going to wade around in six inches of water!"

This practice lead to a funny incident. One morning about 6:00 a.m., Ray Bizier, the supervisor for J. J. Nissen, came to the back door just as Jo was getting ready to scrub the floor.

"Wait a minute," he said to her. "I've got a new driver on the route today. I've been trying to tell him he should wear work boots on the job, not sneakers. Put the water on the floor after he goes down cellar with the bread. When he comes back up he'll have to wade through. Maybe he'll finally get the message."

"O.K.," Jo said. "Let's try it."

Their prank did the trick. That same driver came for many years—but he never wore sneakers again!

"I don't know if Ray ever told him about our deal," Jo said with a twinkle in her eye. "But we became good friends. He never mentioned that first morning, though."

In the late 1960's, crime had begun to filter back into the rural areas of Maine. Norway was no exception.

Many nights, it was after 1:00 a.m. when we were ready to leave the restaurant. After finishing our work in the kitchen, we quite often went out and swept off the front sidewalk. One summer evening, two strangers drove by with a buxom woman at the wheel of a Thunderbird convertible. They stared right at us, turning their heads to look back as they drove down Main Street. Norway still had parking meters on the street. Thank goodness they did! That night those meters proved to be a lifesaver for Jo.

Making a U-turn in the middle of the street, the car came roaring back up Main Street to make a second trip around the block. As I watched in growing alarm, I saw the driver head right for where Jo was sweeping.

"Jo, run for your life!" I screamed. The spiteful look on the woman's face and her partner's obscene gestures made me think that they were trying to kill her. If the meter hadn't been between Jo and the car, she would have been run over.

"I was scared to death as we made tracks for the restaurant," Jo exclaimed. "That was the last time we swept off in front of the restaurant at that time of night."

Changes had to be made in running the dining room as we reorganized that year. Margaret was staying at home to nurse Mother and Jo missed her expertise as hostess and cashier. Jo chose two girls, Susie Olmstead and Dorothy Dunn, to become shift leaders. Veda Taker worked a split shift. She opened the restaurant and worked through lunch. Then she came back and worked through dinner. This assured Jo of having two good waitresses during the rush hours each day, but the rest of the help was a disaster at that time. One girl couldn't even remember to bring all her clothes with her and had to go downstreet every day to buy a pair of stockings or a slip to wear under her uniform.

"Thank goodness, I furnished all the girls' uniforms and had them laundered for them," Jo said. "If I hadn't, I don't have any idea what some of my waitresses would have worn in the dining room that summer."

So as never to embarrass any of the people Jo treated as special customers, the waitresses took the orders of Jo's friends in the same manner as they did the regular customers. The only difference was that the girls used checks from "the food book." These checks were put on a spindle in the kitchen and never returned to the dining room.

One girl couldn't recognize the difference between the people Jo treated and the regular customers. That waitress the girls nicknamed "Vera Vague." One day, a regular came to the serving window and said to Jo, "Thanks for my dinner—I didn't know I was going to be treated!"

"'You're very welcome,' I told her," said Jo. "But I knew immediately what had happened. That particular customer looked something like Helen Borneman, one of my friends who ate with us regularly." With typical patience, Jo took the shortcomings of her staff in stride.

When the accounting firm, Millett, Fish and Dresser, was sold, Jo hired another firm to do her year-end financial statements. These accountants noted that Barjo's had an unusually high food cost. When it was explained to them why, they asked if I would keep Barjo's "food checks" for a month so they could add them up. That way they could determine what the true food cost was. By doing this, they showed that Barjo's actual food cost was around 20% not over 40% as the records had previously shown.

The figures demonstrated that Jo was giving away around $1000 a week or in the vicinity of $50,000 a year. Over the years, she had enjoyed doing for others and felt this amount was similar to what other people spent on trips, vacations, or just having a good time.

The accountants asked her if they could add this amount on to her books and then deduct the sum as a donation. Jo thought this was foolish and couldn't understand why they questioned her. In her mind, what she gave away was not to be discussed. Over the years, many had received a helping hand, but she never wanted anyone to know.

"I told the accountants 'no way!' I never had kept track of anything I gave and I didn't intend to now," Jo explained. "I felt that what I did for others was my private concern."

One of them said, "It's your choice. If you have never included these donations in your accounts, we can skip it now."

"Case closed!" she said emphatically.

Many of the summer customers entered Barjo's through the back door on the parking lot side. As they passed through the kitchen, Jo became acquainted with many of them.

One Sunday, in August, a stately, elderly gentleman and his wife, who had a summer home on Lake Kezar in Lovell, asked an unusual question. He was a very observant retired professor who lived in New Jersey during the winter. They had been in for dinner every Sunday night during summer and he had been keeping an eye on the other customers.

"How come so many people come in to eat and then leave without paying?" he asked.

Jo laughed and said, "Oh, they are all my friends who eat with us every day."

What she didn't say was that they never paid, because they were people she felt needed an extra bit of help or were lonesome. Many of these elderly people lived alone in a single room. Giving them the chance to socialize with others and serving them a hot meal was her way of assisting them.

The next week, when the professor came in for Sunday night dinner, his check, somehow, never made it back to his table. When he went to pay, the cashier told him it was already paid. He said nothing that week, but when he came through the kitchen the following week, he passed Jo an envelope that contained a check for $25.

"Please give this to St. Catherine's Catholic Church," he said with a smile. He fully comprehended what she was doing, but neither one them said a word. Jo understood his gesture, too, because she operated in the same manner herself.

During this same time, Barbara and Henry were having their own problems. Because the Country Way had a distinctive style that was different from what local people were accustomed to, the restaurant got some initial bad publicity. People didn't seem to understand that Barbara and Henry were more than willing to bend over backwards to obtain the local business.

"A story was circulated around the community that there was a $25 cover charge at the Country Way," Jo said. "These reports were totally untrue."

When school opened in September, there were teacher workshops at Oxford Hills High School on opening day. For years, the teachers had been coming to Barjo's for lunch. The new school was directly across the street from the Country Way. So Jo made arrangements for the teachers to have their luncheon at Country Way instead. By promoting this project, Jo was able to encourage people to find out for themselves what the service was like at the new restaurant. They found that no cover charge existed. Many of the teachers were local residents, and they spread the word, as Jo had hoped they would. Jo also promoted the success of the Country Way in another way.

One afternoon a grocery salesman said to Jo, "Why don't you build a central warehouse, Jo, then the boys at Country Way won't have to go so far to replenish their inventory?"

She looked at him with a knowing grin. "Whatever do you mean?" she asked.

But, she knew exactly what he meant. Whenever Country Way ran out of something, the cook called Barjo's and Jo willingly supplied him with the needed groceries. Whether it was a gallon of clams, a case of Alaska King crabmeat, jumbo shrimp, french fries, or ice for the bar, she would go without at Barjo's rather than refuse to help Barbara and Henry. During the many years that Country Way was open, she continued this practice of supplying stock they needed from her own inventory.

As the fall of 1966 arrived and high school kids went back to school, Jo was able to hire some older girls who were more efficient. One was Roberta (Hunt) Doughty, who, with her sister Ivalea, had worked at Barjo's during World War II. For several years, Roberta and her husband had owned the Wilderness Campgrounds in the Yagger neighborhood of Norway. She sent many of her campers to Barjo's to have dinner. Roberta was looking for work during the winter months, so Jo hired her. Another Dunn sister, Joyce, had joined the crew during the summer. With these changes in the dining room crew, the restaurant could now be managed much more efficiently.

When Roberta Doughty left to open her camping area in the spring of 1967, she brought Gloria (Bonney) Day[7] to replace her. She was one of Gloria's neighbors in the Yagger neighborhood. Trusting Roberta's judgment, Jo hired her. Gloria became a waitress at Barjo's in 1967 and stayed there until the restaurant closed in 1991. She was a dark-haired, petite girl and proved to be an energetic worker. Many customers asked for her by name or asked which section of booths was hers so they could sit there.

"Gloria's customers loved her," Jo said. "And she was so reliable! If someone called in sick or didn't show up for work, all I had to do was go to the phone and call her. In five minutes she would be there, even if it meant she'd have to work a double shift. She never refused to do a favor for anyone."

In the winter of 1967, the Dunns' cousin, Pamela Dingley[8], applied for a job. She was in high school and looking for weekend work. She was in the same Oxford Hills High School class as Jo's granddaughter, Andy. She, too, was a good worker but at times, she did some reckless things.

"One thing in particular that I remember about Pam," Jo said. "After her dinner shift, often I would find her a ride home to Oxford with one of our friends. Half the time she would be back upstreet before they got back to Barjo's! She was always looking for excitement—and she didn't think Oxford was very exciting."

For several years, Margaret had nursed Mother at home. Finally, she was moved to a nursing home, so sick she didn't even realize she had left her own home. Her sister Nettie, had died that summer at age 95. On September 19, 1967, Mother passed away. She was 91 years old. Though her passing was not unexpected, it was a time of sorrow for the family.

With their mother's death, Margaret resumed her duties as hostess and cashier at Barjo's. Though Margaret had done the bookkeeping during this period of time, Jo missed her sister's daily presence. With Margaret back on her Barjo's team, she felt a big burden was being removed from her shoulders.

"With Marg in the dining room, I knew our customers were

going to be greeted with a kind word and given the best of service," Jo said with relief. "I had always worried about how the waitresses approached people, but Margaret had a wonderful knack for making everyone feel welcome."

After the rest of the family had grown up and moved to homes of their own, Mother and Margaret had made the second floor of their house into a separate apartment. After Mother passed away, Margaret lived alone downstairs and rented the upstairs to a retired lady who enjoyed the peace and quiet of this residential section of Norway.

Margaret's downstairs apartment had polished hardwood floors and attractive carpeting. The walls were elegantly papered with ivory brocade and had crystal and brass wall sconces. She had installed a new rosy-tiled bathroom in the apartment. In one corner of the dining room, stood Margaret's desk where she did the bookkeeping for Barjo's. Her home was always immaculate. Never could a speck of dust be found anywhere.

During the '60's and 70's, local teenagers spent a lot of time at Barjo's. It was the local meeting place for the kids after school and on weekends. On Friday nights, there was a dance with Scrapper Pratt's Band at the Opera House, across the street from Barjo's. Afterwards, the kids came in for a lunch before going home. After Jo had served them, she often came into the dining room, put quarters in the jukebox and turned it up. She let the kids pick out their own music and push the booths to one side so they could dance. If their parents didn't know where their children were, the first place they called was Barjo's. Nine times out ten they were there having a good time with their friends. Jo had just as much fun as they did.

One Friday, Jo noticed that Wally Jones, who was supposed to be washing dishes, was missing. She had a suspicion where he might be. Across the street she ran and up the stairs to the Opera House. Sure enough, there was Wally dancing with a girl friend.

It didn't take long for him to figure out that Jo had caught him red-handed. But Wally was quick thinker. He turned to her and said, "How about a polka, Jo? My dad says you are an expert!"

She ignored his invitation and marched him right back across the street to the restaurant. He spent the rest of the evening in the dishpan with no more visits to the dance.

While I was in the Maine Medical Center in Portland in 1979,[9] Jo had several high school girls help her with the cooking. Two of them were Tanya "Meme" Goddard, whose grandfather, Bob Curtis, had been a chef at Barjo's during World War II, and her cousin, Susie Blais. Jo had a habit of humming parts of songs while she was cooking, but she never finished the whole song. The kids thought she was making up these tunes.

One day, Meme, (whom Jo always called "Bob" because she never remembered her nick-name), went home and sang Jo's song to her father, a retired army officer.

He laughed and said, "Listen, and I will sing you the rest of the song. It's an army song."

All Jo ever sang of that one was, "over here, over there" again and again. Some of her other tunes were "Smoke, smoke, smoke that cigarette," a song from the 1920's, and "I've got the blues!" This song she sang as fast as she could whenever she was busy. She would whistle many, many more old songs.

If Jo's nephew, Edwin Cummings, happened to come into the restaurant, he always joined in, either singing or whistling along with her.

Shortly after I went into the hospital, one of the kitchen boys, Stephen Douglass, got through. The next morning, Meme brought in two friends as replacements. These high school girls were all four helping Jo when I was able to go back to work many weeks later. One was Kimberley O'Connor. Her father was the guidance counselor for Oxford Hills High School. Jo had a nick-name for her, "Pissamire," because she was so small. Kim has never forgotten those days and still reminisces with the others about their fun during high school.

Jo had made it her generous habit to share more than just her time and food for local causes.[10] She regularly used her business experience to help groups and organizations in the community. The community recognized Jo for her kindness to others.

In 1971, she discouraged Donald and Franklyn Towne, who were working with the Kiwanis, from selling hot-dogs on Main Street as a fundraiser. When the Kiwanis suggested this project that she thought would hurt the other business people, she had been quick to come to their defense.

With all the reorganization at Barjo's and having many new faces, this had been a tumultuous time for Jo. Over the next few years, it would look as though she might even leave the restaurant industry and turn her interests elsewhere.

But circumstances beyond her control would come into play, while many more changes were about to happen in her personal life as well.

[7] *For more information about Gloria, see Appendix 1, "Stories of the Barjo's Family."*

[8] *For more stories about Pamela, see Appendix 1, "Stories of the Barjo's Family."*

[9] *Details about my illness and recovery appear in Chapter 32.*

[10] *See Appendix 3, "Jo's Honors and Awards," for a lengthy list of Jo's community involvement.*

The familiar landmark as it looked after the 1972 renovations.

Barjo's interior after the 1972 renovations.

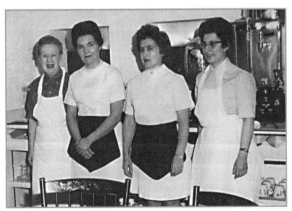

Jo, Susie Olmstead, Veda Taker and Emily

CHAPTER 29

Possibilities of a Sale

After Barbara and Henry left in 1966 and started their own restaurant, people in town thought that Jo would retire. Since Stony was sick and Barbara and Henry were gone from Barjo's, they presumed she would no longer be able to operate the restaurant. What they seemed to forget was that she was a positive thinker and trusted God to guide her.

Over a period of several years, Jo considered offers from many different people, but none were successful in raising the money to actually make the purchase. Jo began to feel it was time to move on.

In the meantime, I had ideas of my own. If Jo was serious about selling Barjo's, my dream was to be the new owner. She had instilled in me the concept that anything is possible if you are willing to put your trust in God and then work hard to accomplish your goal. Jo had taught me the mechanics of operating the restaurant. As her protegee, I had learned how to work with the public, how to do the buying and how to manage the restaurant. Now, I felt ready to become Jo's colleague.

In 1968, my plan was in place and I was sure that I could raise the money for the mortgage at the Norway National Bank. Jo had given me all the financial statements the bank asked for. I had even gone to the home of one of the directors for a consultation about the sale.

On a Wednesday afternoon, the bank scheduled a meeting with my accountant, Donald Preble, and me. I had the cash for my down payment already in my savings account. At 3:00 p.m. that afternoon, the bank officials told me that the loan had been approved. I was jubilant.

However, at 7:30 p.m. that same evening, the directors changed their minds and called Donald Preble. They told him they had changed their minds and the loan would not going be approved. The reason they gave was that I was a single woman. Today, of course, this would be recognized as discrimination—and illegal.

Calling my accountant instead of me seemed a strange thing to do. I had established good credit at the bank. But, if I had been married, they told me, the loan would have been approved. They needed to have more than my signature alone, even though they would hold a mortgage on the restaurant. I never did understand the bankers' logic. All the directors knew that I had worked at the restaurant for almost 14 years and that I was reliable. I was surprised that they didn't have faith in my word or in me. It was a blow to my confidence and a great disappointment in my life.

The bankers didn't even give me the option of asking Jo to sign the legal papers with me. But even if they had, that was the one thing that I would never have done. To this day, I've never asked Jo to co-sign with me for anything, no matter what the circumstances. I have felt it was important to be scrupulous in not taking advantage of our relationship in such matters.

Three years later, in December 1971, I bought the "Barbershop Building," at 225-227 Main Street from Jo. I thought if some changes were made at the restaurant, I would be able to live in the upstairs apartment and have my own business on the main floor. I financed my purchase at the same bank and the loan went through with no problem. Ironically, I now owed the bank more than I had asked to borrow in 1968!

During his administration, President Lyndon Johnson had initiated a program called the "War on Poverty." After the Cook Barbershop closed, Jo had rented the office space at 225 Main Street to the Oxford County Economic Opportunity Council, which was a part of that program. This organization was renting the office space when I bought the building, but I had other plans for the building.

I had been to Boston to visit my uncle and had been fascinated by the "Olde Salem House" on Route 128. They served an ice cream Smorgasbord and made all the ice cream on the premises. So I decided that when the time was right, I was going to have an ice cream parlor of my own.

Having done no remodeling at Barjo's since 1946, Jo felt that she needed to do some major renovations. After tearing down the hotel, she had devoted her time and efforts to planning for a new restaurant. When that undertaking hadn't come to pass, she had helped Barbara and Henry with the opening of the Country Way.

"Now, I needed to spruce up Barjo's," Jo commented. " It was beginning to look shabby. I wanted to make it attractive, a place my customers would enjoy bringing their friends."

In March 1972, many changes were made at Barjo's. After Jo discussed her ideas with Bill Cook from Jones, McDuffee and Stratton of Boston, the company sent engineers and interior decorators to lay out a blueprint for the renovations. This would mean that the restaurant would be closed for the first time since Jo had become the owner. The engineers estimated it would take three weeks to complete the renovations. Jo agreed to their schedule and hired Gordon Snow to do work required, with all the materials being supplied by Jones, McDuffee and Stratton.

After Stony was taken ill, it had become increasingly difficult for Jo to make the ice cream and do all the cooking at the restaurant. Jo decided now was the right time to make a change. For the first time, there would no longer be a fountain in the dining room. She decided to buy her ice cream from H. P. Hood instead of freezing it herself.

The interior decorators decided on a "Colonial Americana" theme that would create a homespun atmosphere at Barjo's. The ceiling was decorated with beams, one wall had mirrors and the other wall had striped wallpaper with every other section decorated with yellow paneling and wooden animals. Some of the center booths were removed and replaced with "Hitchcock" tables and chairs—some to seat six and some to seat two. In the fountain area, more booths were added to increase the seating capacity. The venetian blinds were removed from the windows and replaced with hourglass curtains—two different sets were provided for the different seasons, one set was a deep, golden material with red fringe and the second set was bright red with white fringe.

Every morning as I was leaving the house to go to work at Barjo's, Stony asked me to wait for him so he could ride with me. By this time, the kitchen counter looked like a drug store as he got his medicine ready for the day. He was taking two kinds of insulin twice a day plus numerous other drugs for his condition. He had a hard time walking because of the weakness in his right leg. His right arm was practically useless and he had a hard time talking. He tried to do everything that he could for himself. He didn't like to be fussed over, though, and never asked for any help.

During the renovations, Stony came to the restaurant everyday and watched the workmen as they transformed the restaurant to a rustic look. Even though he wasn't able to help, the carpenters called him their "sidewalk superintendent."

When the carpenters were almost finished and the restaurant was to reopen in two days, it was discovered that the interior decorator had measured the bright red Naughyde material for the booths wrong. A man from Auburn who was doing the upholstering needed to have one more roll of the red leather-like material for the booths. He promised Jo that he would work all night to finish that section of booths if she could get him the material. This would make it possible for Barjo's to open as scheduled.

The next day, I volunteered to go to Boston in a Northeaster with freezing rain, sleet and snow, to pick up the material. In that terrible storm, God was with me all the way. From Scarborough south, the road was just a sheet of glare ice. I had no idea where the warehouse was in Boston. I had never driven in a city before and all I had was a map given me by Bill Cook, our salesman. I was able to drive right to the door where the factory-men were waiting. It took me from 9:00 a.m. to 10:00 p.m. to get from Norway to Boston and back. Tractor-trailer rigs were off the road everywhere with the bridge going into Boston closed because of the severe weather conditions. Everyone had to use the Tunnel to get to the city. It was one of the worst Northeasters of the winter.

Driving twenty-five miles per hour seemed like speeding because of the high winds and ice. I asked God to guide me and He did. Those were the worst driving conditions I had ever encountered in my life. If I had been a little older and a little wiser, I probably would have realized how dangerous it was. But at that point, all I could think of was how badly we needed that material so the restaurant could reopen. I didn't want to let Jo down.

When I got back to Auburn, the man was waiting for me. He kept his word and worked all night. The restaurant was able to reopen as planned.

The interior decorators coordinated the golden placemats with the word Barjo's in white letters with embossed red napkins to match the color scheme. The red leatherette menus embossed with gold letters had golden cords to complete the "Colonial Americana" theme.

Jo dressed up her waitresses to complete the new look at Barjo's. For Sundays, she bought them white satin blouses with black bow ties, black satin skirts, and gold brocade vests. This outfit was chosen as the "Uniform of the Year" for food service industry in 1972. During the week they wore white uniforms with black aprons, which the restaurant provided and had laundered for them.

When Barjo's was remodeled in the spring of 1972, Jo knew that I had been thinking about opening an ice cream parlor. Jo was no longer making ice cream for the restaurant.

Aware of the fact that I had the desire to have my own business, Jo wanted to give me some assistance. When the fountain was removed from the dining room, she gave it to me. She included all the ice cream supplies and the fountain dishes as well. The room where the ice cream for Barjo's was made was already in the basement of the Barbershop building that I now owned.

Jo's gift was totally unexpected. It was a big boost in my quest to own my own business.

But as it turned out, God had different plans for us. Other things were about to happen that would change our future. For a third time, tragedy was about the strike in Jo's personal life.

On the afternoon of Tuesday, August 8, 1972, I had gone home for an hour's rest. At Barjo's, Jo was cutting tomatoes on the table by the kitchen door to get ready for the supper hour. About 3:30 p.m., Ed Petipas, one of Jo's tenants on Whitman Street, came rushing through the back door. His face was as white as a sheet.

"Something is terribly wrong! Something bad has just happened to Stony! I was down to the dump and I saw him just barely rolling down the hill in the pick-up," he told Jo in a frightened voice. "When I went over to see what the matter was, he fell out of the truck door into my arms and onto the ground."

About that time the telephone rang in the dining room. It was for Jo. When she answered the phone, it was Dr. Bean, Stony's doctor, who was also the Norway medical examiner.

"Jo," he said, "I was just called to the Norway dump by Mr. Cushman who is in charge there. He told me Stony stopped at the top of the hill and then his truck rolled down to the dumping area. He was on the ground beside the truck when I got there."

"I just examined him, Jo. Stony's gone. It was a massive heart attack."

Just then, I walked in the back door and was ready to take Jo home so she could rest. The minute I saw her face, I knew that something was terribly wrong.

"What's happened? What can I do to help you?" I asked her.

"Well," Jo said in a dazed voice, "I'm not sure. It is Stony. He's—he's dead, Emily. He is gone." Suddenly she sat down.

"Probably you'd better call Barbara and Margaret," she said looking up at me with a stunned look on her face.

Barbara and Henry arrived at the restaurant in a few minutes.

It was hard for us all to comprehend that Stony was dead at 59 years old. They offered to take her to the funeral home to make arrangements and Jo went with them, leaving me in charge at Barjo's. Shortly after, Margaret arrived to run the dining room during supper hour.

As Margaret came into the kitchen, she turned to me and said, "You know Jo needs you more than ever now. We both need to help her in every way that we can."

I never forgot Margaret's advice. No matter what has happened over the years, I have stood resolutely by Jo's side. Jo, Margaret and Donald had become family to me. I felt my loyalty and my ability to help them in any way I could would always be focused on that.

That evening, Jo's grandchildren pitched in. Robbie came to help me with the cooking. For several days, Jody helped me serve dinner. This gave Jo more time to deal with Stony's death and to straighten out and settle Stony's estate.

"After Stony's death, there was one thing that puzzled me completely," Jo commented. "When I went to get his papers out of our safe, they weren't there. He had taken his birth certificate, life insurance policy, military discharge papers and his will and fastened them together. They were in the kitchen cupboard where he kept all his medicines. Did he have a premonition of what was going to happen that day or had he been looking the papers over for some other reason?"

On Thursday, August 10, Father Donald McAllister and Rev. Jay Lello officiated in the 2:00 p.m. service for Stony at the Second Congregational Church. Donnie did the eulogy. Jo insisted that he participate in the service, making it the first time that Norway had seen a Catholic priest and a Protestant minister do a funeral service together. The church was packed with friends, relatives and business associates. Enormous bouquets of flowers filled the sanctuary of the church.

Stony was buried in the Pine Grove Cemetery beside Jo's other two husbands, Robert Meserve and P.Y. Fogg. Only one spot was left for Jo, a thing her nephew pointed out with a gentle teasing tone.

"You can't marry again, Aunt Jo," Donnie said, "or you'll have to have your ashes scattered over all your husbands."

Barjo's was closed for the day of the funeral, but Jo felt it was better for her to continue working as she had in the past. She knew praying to God for guidance would help her to overcome her grief and she would be able to move on.

Shortly after Stony's funeral, one of the waitresses came into the kitchen and said to Jo, "I have something to tell you that I think you should know. Do you know that Stony has been going with one of my friends for years? She used to work for you."

"Well," Jo replied, "you aren't telling me anything that I didn't already know. I happened to also know that I roasted the Thanksgiving turkey for that family and that he spent the day with them while I was serving dinner at Barjo's."

Taken completely by surprise, the girl retreated to the dining room. She couldn't believe how calmly Jo had stated the facts and how she had known more about the situation that she did.

There were many more unhappy questions than answers about Stony as Jo was soon to find out. His lifestyle was proving to have been a real conundrum.

Shortly after Barbara and Henry left Barjo's in 1966, Jo learned that Margaret had also helped them financially to get their restaurant started. She knew that Margaret had saved $10,000 for her own funeral and their mother's. Jo had continued her practice of sending money to her mother as she had done for years, but she also knew the family had no money to spare.

Jo had had a talk with Stony. Because the Hotel Stone had been a partnership, she asked him if he would be willing for her to take his name off the parking lot deed. She wanted to be sure that she could protect Margaret financially if anything should happened. In exchange, Jo offered to have her name removed from the deed to their house, making Stony the sole owner. He agreed.

It was Frank Bjorklund who had handled these legal transactions. After he passed away, his wife dismantled his office and brought Jo a large box containing all of her files and Stony's.

When we were going through these files, Jo found papers about another transaction that was news to her. Stony had had Frank contact the Veterans Administration for a VA loan in 1967. Oddly, the loan was written by a bank in Farmington, not one of the local ones. And the purpose of the loan was to buy a building on Main Street. The transaction was to be completed in 1968 and would have included a mortgage on Jo's Deering Street home.

The building and business at 197 Main Street involved had nothing to do with Jo, but with another woman who was working at that hardware store. And it was a different woman from the one the waitress had been talking about.

We also found application papers to the VA to have his

$10,000 military life insurance, of which Jo was the beneficiary, canceled. She had found that policy in the kitchen on the day of his death, along with his discharge papers.

Jo was more puzzled than ever. Was this was an explanation for Stony's legal papers being in the kitchen not in their safe? She will never know.

"Whatever he was planning to do, he apparently had cold feet," Jo rationalized. "I had known for some time about his many escapades, but I never thought he would go so far as to tie up our home. When he came out of the service back in 1946, he was a changed man. I knew then we shouldn't stay married, but I just don't believe in divorce and he never asked for one."

Because all the offers to buy the restaurant had fallen through, I laid my own plans aside and continued to help Jo at Barjo's. I prayed for guidance and realized that God's plan was that my place was to stay with Jo. My loyalty was to her, as hers had been to me since my teen years when I so needed her kindness and trust.

With Stony's death, it became evident that I would always stay at Jo's side and continue to live with her. Our friendship was more than one of mutual respect and it grew stronger with every passing day. Jo treated me like a daughter, giving me more responsibilities as different situations warranted. My devotion and admiration for Jo was limitless. When I had desperately needed a helping hand, Jo had stood by me and encouraged me. Now, I wanted to be there to help Jo in every way that I could.

The restaurant had been the main focus of Jo's life for so many years. In the past when tragedy had struck, Barjo's had been her stabilizing force. She would be lost without her work and her regular schedule to keep her going through this transition period.

Looking back at the events of that year, Jo pondered, "What could I have been thinking? What did I think I was going to live on if I sold Barjo's? It was my only source of income. Thank goodness, I could still work and run the restaurant."

One day, the salesman for Schlotterbeck & Foss asked me what I planned to do with the fountain and other ice cream equipment I had once hoped to make the foundation of my own business venture. He knew the freezer and the holding units were still in the basement at 225 Main Street. He also knew that Jo had given me the fountain dishes and the ice cream supplies and that these were not in use. He offered to sell them for me in

Boothbay Harbor, and I agreed. After having some renovations done to the building, I rented the first floor to the Family Fabric Shop. Because I was living with Jo, I rented the upstairs apartment to different tenants. Later, the Lewiston Daily Sun rented the office space. When the newspaper moved in 1989, an artist, Duncan Slade, had his studio there. After owning the building for 26 years, I sold the Barbershop building in January 1997.

It had been a tumultuous time of change for Jo. The loss of her third husband was a shock, and the unpleasant circumstances of his having kept relationships secret from her was a puzzle and a trial. But better days were coming. She would soon see her first great grandchildren arrive on the scene, and this would be a great joy to her. In fact, the seventies were years of expansion for Jo's family. In 1973, Jo's first great-grandchild, John Peter, was born on September 4. Jody, his mother, worked in the kitchen with us that summer, so Jo has often told John that he had an early start in the restaurant business.

Shortly after John, Robbie's son, Nick Alan, followed on December 28. In 1974, Andy's son, Ben Tucker IV, was born on February 23. These boys were the first of Jo's five great grandchildren. Robbie's second son, Scott Robert was born on February 16, 1977. Jo's only great granddaughter, Katherine Lynn Tucker, joined the family in the next decade, September 27, 1984.

Once again, new ventures were on the horizon for Jo. The town of Norway and her fellow merchants would be involved in one, the hospital in another. And Jo was about to face what would prove to be one of the greatest challenges in her life.

In their new "Uniform of the Year," the Barjo's waitresses in this 1972 photo included—
back: Roberta Doughty, Susie Olmstead, Dorothy Dunn and
front: Pamela Dingley, Veda Taker, Gloria Bonney Day, and Emily Foster.

*Jo was declared an Honorary Captain in the Maine State Police in December, 1980.
Presenting the award are Lt. Col. Albert Jamison and Col. Alan Weeks.*

*In attendance at the surprise banquet in her honor were Jo's sisters, Margaret and
Helen, Col. Jamison, Jo, and Emily Foster.*

CHAPTER 30

Involved in Community Affairs

In 1975, the Main Street Merchants Association began talking about the parking situation on Main Street in Norway and the competition of the shopping malls being opened in the area. Jo's brother Donald had retired as town manager in July 1973. Several other town mangers had been hired but had not stayed. Now, Norway's town manager was Larry Todd.

After purchasing the Rex Theater building (which cleared up the right-of-way entanglements she had encountered in her plans to develop the former Hotel Stone property), Jo donated the movie screen and projector to the Norway Recreation Department, whose director had organized a program of entertainment and sports for the young people at the Opera House.

Now Jo owned the whole L-shaped piece of property bordered by Temple Street in the back and Cottage Street on the side which included the Hotel Stone lot on Main Street. She listed this property with a broker and had the hotel site graded and paved. Its use as a parking lot was popular.

At the same time, the Masons put their lodge on Cottage Street on the market as they made plans for a new building. Both Jo and the Masons were hopeful that the two pieces might go to the same buyer to make a new downtown shopping area.

The Androscoggin Valley Council of Governments did some research into this proposal. They thought a 10,000 square-foot grocery store on one end, with a department store, possibly J. J. Newberry's, on the other end and smaller stores in the center section with parking in front would be good for the town. Any existing stores at the front of the lot would be moved into the new shopping area. There was much talk but, in the end, nothing came of it.

Main Street merchants began thinking about sprucing up the town's major commercial artery. A downtown revitalization effort was planned. Aware that Main Street commerce had been strangled in other communities by lack of parking, the merchants knew this feature would be essential to their plan if they were to compete with the new shopping malls on the outskirts of town.

Four potential long-term parking areas existed in the early 1970's. In addition to Jo's lot, there was the Gayton lot next to L. M. Longley, a lot across Main Street from the Advertiser-Democrat, and the George F. Hill property on the west side of the street next to Barjo's.

One by one these properties changed hands and/or use until only the Jo's lot remained available for public parking. By this time area shopkeepers knew something had to be done and quickly. Malls in South Paris and Oxford which featured plenty of parking were thriving. Norway's Main Street had to provide accessibility to parking if it was to survive.

Until 1975, Jo had maintained the lot and paid all taxes and insurance on it. Parking meters had been installed in an attempt to recoup her investment, but that effort generally was unsuccessful. The lot was used every day, but people were unwilling to pay.

One day when I was coming out of the bank, someone said to me, "Why did Jo bother to put meters on that lot, nobody will ever pay to park there!"

"Even our little tickets that read 'Please Feed the Meters' didn't work," Jo commented. "Finally, I told the town that if they policed the lot, they could have all the money collected."

But that idea didn't work because the new town manager and the downtown merchants, including Jo, were at odds on how the parking problem should be handled.

Jo increasingly felt some compensation was in order since she was providing a public service at her expense. To press her case with the town, she blocked the entrance with her old pickup truck. After several weeks of negotiations, the town agreed to reduce her taxes and to pick up the insurance and lighting costs. Jo rolled the truck away and again the lot teemed with activity.

But the merchants were nervous. The need for additional parking was increasing all the time. There was more and more competition from new out-of-town shopping centers. A Main Street Parking Committee with the principal goal of checking into the loss of Main Street parking opportunities was formed.

They approached Jo about purchasing her lot. A professional appraisal determined a fair price of $90,000. That was a lot of money for a small town to raise, regardless of the value and the wisdom of the purchase. In 1976, the Main Street Merchants Association made plans for a pledge drive to raise $40,000 towards the cost but it was several years before they reached their goal.

In 1978, Jo and Donald got involved. This was just the beginning of a long battle between the merchants and Jo versus Town Manager Larry Todd and the town of Norway. In the next few years, various solutions were proposed and then more questions would arise over legal rights. The central hang-up was whether or not a legal contract existed between Jo and the town for the ownership of the lot.

Jo hired Gary Goldberg of Berman, Berman & Simmons to represent her. The merchants came to Jo to see what either she or her attorney could give them for advice, as they were caught in the middle. Finally, the issues became so entangled that Jo's attorney told the merchants it was time for them to have their own legal counsel.

A 1978 agreement between the town and the merchants set the 1979 town meeting as a deadline for their matching funds to be raised. In order to guarantee their pledge of $40,000, a master note had to be signed with the Norway National Bank. The merchants were unable, however, to find anyone to sign that note.

When Jo found this out, she called Donald and asked if he would be willing to sign the master note at the bank for $20,000 and she would sign the note for the remaining $20,000. Actually, she was agreeing to help finance part of the sale to herself, in order to resolve the problem and see the merchants have their parking lot.

Then, Jo received another offer for the hotel lot. I returned a call from a real estate agent in Massachusetts. Purely by accident, the agent told me his client was Cumberland Farms. Though an offer was made, that deal fell through because of the continuing legal entanglements with the town.

Jo decided the court case had dragged on long enough. She told Gary Goldberg to settle with the town attorneys. Maine Municipal Association, Norway's insurer, was also involved.

Finally, the case was settled. But still the original issue of whether or not a legal contract existed was not decided and never will be.

In January 1981, Jo received $7,500 for court costs from the town's insurance. It didn't begin to cover her expenses.

"What's important," Jo said, "is that the case was out of the courts and the land untangled from its legal web."

When asked by a reporter, "Are you glad this case is behind you?"

"Yes, I am!" Jo answered with quick, warm smile. "I'm happy. But a lot of people have come into the restaurant and told me they're not pleased. They think the town officials acted unjustly. But," she added philosophically, "I suppose others are happy."

Some merchants had been hurt, she conceded, and for that she was sorry.

"Would you do it again?" asked the reporter.

"No—well, I guess I would if I thought it would do some good for the town and for Main Street. It's always been the best place to shop. We have good merchandise, and people are friendly. The original parking lot plan would have provided benches and places for people to sit, and public restrooms. That would have been good," she replied.

"Any hard feelings?" he asked.

"No. I think if I'd been home, living the life I should be for my age, maybe I would have. But I've been too busy here at Barjo's to worry about it," she answered.

Then, with her hand thrust deep in pie dough, she tossed off a quick, almost naughty laugh and said, "Really, it's caused a lot of excitement. This is the only major trouble we've ever had with the town."

"Look," she went on, "I've been in business on Main Street since I was 27 and I'm 78 now. I've been blessed with good business, good friends, good health and great help. What more could anyone ask for?"

"How about justice?" he asked.

Jo answered quickly and with conviction, "We'd have won if it had gone to trial—I know it and everyone involved does, too."

The words of Supreme Court Justice Oliver Wendell Holmes seem offered precisely for this situation:

> My job is not to dispense justice,
> But to see that justice is obeyed!

But as he had noted so many years earlier, "Justice is not always the goal."

That same year, the hotel lot and adjoining back parking lot were sold to Frank Shorey of the Western Auto Stores, Inc. for $60,000. Because Western Auto was located on Main Street in front of the Temple Street lot, they built a new building on the back lot (also known as the Starbird Livery Stable lot).

After Western Auto built their new building, the town of Norway then bought the Hotel Stone lot from Shorey for $50,000 to be used for a municipal parking lot.

The irony is that the town purchased that one lot when they could have had all three pieces of property for exactly the same amount. Jo, in the end, was paid more from the transactions on the property than she would have, had the original sale to the Town and the Norway Merchants Association gone through.

The other good thing that came out of these transactions was that Jo and Donald were no longer committed to pay back $20,000 each on the master note at Norway National Bank since the merchants had failed to pay their pledges as agreed.

Now, Jo was able to give Margaret $40,000 from the sale to repay her for all she had done for Barbara and Henry and for her loyal support at Barjo's. Jo paid the commission to the business brokers and also all the legal fees. Margaret invested her money in CD's. This money would help her maintain her independence in later years.

Jo was relieved and happy with the outcome. She never called names or pointed fingers about the court case. But she does have strong feelings about virtually everything else.

"I think the selectmen should come under the same rules as the police department and be required to take a course in municipal law before they assume office," she said. "If the selectmen had known more, this would never have happened."

Back in the 1940's, an arsonist who was never apprehended had burned many buildings and caused the death of two children. Jo had installed an area light behind Barjo's at that time as a deterrent. Now, once again, an arsonist was thought to be on the loose. During late summer and fall of 1975, churches in Portland and Westbrook had been burned to the ground and no one knew where the arsonist might strike next.

In November that year, Ned Truman, a local boy who had moved to Connecticut, was home for hunting season . At about 8:30 p.m. one gloomy fall evening, Ned came into Barjo's and mentioned to Jo that he'd seen a man walking up the street acting very strangely. Ned had just come from Verenis' Market, about two blocks away, and had seen this man walking slowly along and looking up at all the buildings.

"Don't you think that's a funny thing to be doing at this time of night? Do you think he's planning to break in somewhere?" Ned asked Jo. "What do you suppose he's up to?"

Within a half-hour, a teenager, Clifton Hill, came running to the back door of Barjo's shouting, "Come quick and help me! A man just dumped something from a can on the bushes in back of Jackson's Market and he's lit it with a match!"

Grabbing the fire extinguisher from the kitchen wall, I ran out behind him. One of the waitresses called the fire department.

When they arrived, Clifton and I had gotten the fire almost out. They doused the side of the Jackson building and surrounding bushes to be sure no sparks could cause another crisis.

"What a close call that was," I told Jo. "Clifton saved the day!" Clifton had been in a car in the parking lot waiting for his friend when he saw the man. If he hadn't been there, the fire might easily have burned that whole end of Main Street, where all the buildings were made of wood and some were over a hundred years old. They had survived the Great Fire of 1894.

Late that same night on Route 26 in West Paris, a passing motorist noticed a shadowy figure in a local lumberyard and reported it to the Oxford County Sheriff's Department. The arsonist had also started a fire at Emery Building Supply. Because the police were on the lookout for him, he was caught before much damage was done. When questioned, the man admitted to setting the church fires in the southern part of the state during the previous months. This solved those cases as well.

In 1975, another development in the area involved the hospital. Stephens Memorial had outgrown its building and plans were being made for a major expansion project. A team was organized to raise funds for the $1.9 million expansion of the facilities to meet the growing healthcare needs and to better serve the area's growing population. There were also many new federal and state health codes to be addressed as well.

In 1976, Mrs. Hamilton O. Cornwall, who was the president of the hospital Board of Trustees, named Jo an honorary chairman of the Stephens Memorial Development Fund. Robert Goodwin from Goodwin's Insurance came to Barjo's with her when she presented Jo with a certificate naming her to this post.

"We're extremely pleased that Josephine Stone has accepted this position," Mrs. Cornwall told reporters. "She's a woman of great integrity and compassion and is deeply interested in seeing that our hospital will continue to provide high-quality medical care to all who need it."

Commenting on the appointment, Jo said, "There is no institution more worthy of our support than Stephens Memorial Hospital because in its hands lies the overall safety and health of our community."

Privately, Mrs. Cornwall told Jo, "We just want you to be the honorary chairman. That doesn't mean you have to give us money."

One morning, however, Jo had a call from Jim Phillips, President of Norway National Bank. He told her that Mrs.

Cornwall and he were planning to meet with her at Barjo's at 2:00 p.m. that afternoon. Jo had a pretty good idea why. She had surmised from the beginning that this day would come. She sent me down to the hospital fund-raising office to get a pledge card from Denise Whitley, a local girl Jo had always taken an interest in, who was office manager for the campaign.

"I wanted to have my pledge all in place before they arrived," Jo said with a laugh. "I knew that if I didn't, Mrs. Cornwall would expect to tell me just how much my donation should be."

Sure enough as they entered the restaurant, Jo saw the pledge cards in Mrs. Cornwall's hand.

"Well, Jo," she said, "how much you think you can give to the hospital fund drive?"

"Why, I have already made my pledge," Jo told her. "Emily just went down to the office to see Denise. Barjo's pledges $10,000 to be paid in $2000 installments over the next five years."

Jim Phillips laughed and winked at Jo. He knew his telephone call had alerted her. Mrs. Cornwall wasn't pleased that Denise would get the credit for Jo's pledge instead of her.

As in the 1950's, when she had contributed several banquets to the original fundraising projects when the hospital was first built, Jo worked hard to encourage widespread support of this important community effort. Through Barjo's, she furnished many hours of hard work.

The funds were raised and the new wing was built. At the groundbreaking ceremony, Jo was presented with a "Silver Shovel" by the chairman to honor her for her work during the hospital's many fundraising campaigns. On it was inscribed, "Josephine A. Stone, Honorary Chairman of the Stephens Memorial Hospital Development Fund, 1976."

Christmas lights brighten the winter sky around Jo's Deering Street home, a tradition carried on thanks to generous friends.

SEASON'S GREETINGS

Dinner Menu

Tomato Juice   *Chilled Fruit Cocktail*

Nuts   Mints   Relish Tray

ROAST TURKEY or ROAST CHICKEN
Giblet Gravy—Stuffing
Mashed Potato—Squash—Onions
Cranberry Sauce—Fruit Salad
Rolls
Coffee—Tea—Milk
Pudding or Ice Cream

$4.50

Tomato Juice   *Chilled Fruit Cocktail*

BAKED HAM or ROAST PORK
Potato—Spiced Apple Rings
Squash—Onions—Rolls
Coffee—Tea—Milk
Pudding or Ice Cream

$4.50

1975

CHAPTER 31

Holidays and Special Events at Barjo's

Over the years, Jo had served the public in many ways. Helping anyone she felt needed a hot meal or offering encouragement when times were hard became her way of life. Although she often denied her role or failed to acknowledge her generosity, many in the community either knew about her kindness or had been recipients of it. For Jo, Christmas always provided a special time of year for giving.

After Stony's death, Jo wondered how she could continue their Christmas tradition at 25 Deering Street. Every year, Stony's friends had helped him decorate with Christmas lights the majestic cedar trees that stand as high as the roof on three sides of the house. Inside, he placed a candle in each window.

Archie McAlister's daughter, Barbara, had worked for Jo at Barjo's. While there, she met and married Raymond Farr from West Paris. They had five children and always kept in touch with Jo. To this day, Barbara Farr never forgets to send a card on Jo's birthday and on other special occasions.

In 1973, Barbara's son, Donald, who had just returned from a tour of duty in the Navy, was doing odd jobs for Jo, so she asked him to do the decorating. He and his brothers, Kevin and John, continued to take care of the lights for over twenty-five years. Some of the wires on Stony's lights had become badly frayed. Kevin, with Donald's help, rewired all the Christmas lights as a project for CMVTI, where he was training to be an electrician.

Over the years, the boys added personal touches of their own. Over the front entrance, they made a unique five-pointed Bethlehem star to go over the manger scene. On the huge cedar by the sun-porch, they created a six-pointed Jewish star, so both major religions would be represented. The house was a real holiday showcase and many people in Norway made it a point to drive by during the season.

After Donald's son, Troy, became old enough, he helped his father and uncles. Now Troy, his wife and two children decorate Jo's home with lights at Christmas time. He has added strings of tiny bright twinkling lights supported by four-foot candy-striped candles. These were placed in a row from the front entrance down the brick walkway to the street. Continuing the holiday lights tradition has given Jo a lot of pleasure over the years.

Jo had always thrown a Christmas party for the Barjo's family of staff and regular customers at the Hotel Stone.[11] In 1950, there were problems when some employees brought outsiders to the celebration. As a result, Jo discontinued the employee parties for a short while.

Instead, in 1951, she bought the entire crew an insurance plan through Maine Merchants Insurance Trust. She continued to buy all of us an extensive employee's insurance package including life insurance until the restaurant was closed in 1991. In later years, Congress passed a law requiring all employers to furnish basic health insurance coverage for all full-time employees, but when she began this practice at Barjo's, it was not yet mandated.

In 1973, after Stony's death and with Country Way open, Jo decided it was time to start having Christmas parties again. Many of the employees were now young people and many of the older folks who ate at the restaurant had no families to celebrate the holidays with.

For several years in the 1960's, the Christmas parties were held at Barjo's. In 1973, after Stony's death and with Country Way open, Jo decided to start having the Christmas parties there as there were over 100 regular customers, police officers and friends whom Jo wanted to include.

Because Barjo's was open on Christmas Day and Country Way had many banquets during the weeks before Christmas, December 26 was usually set as the date for the party. This also happened to be Jo's birthday—although she told the help not to mention that fact to anyone or make any fuss. Each year, a birthday cake made by Gloria Day's mother mysteriously appeared at Jo's table as dessert was being served. Sometimes, Barbara was responsible, sometimes a few of the rest of us were the "guilty" parties. We all enjoyed getting the best of Jo at this celebration.

Cliff and Louise Provencal from Lewiston dined at Barjo's often and enjoyed all of the other Barjo family members. Cliff was a retired Metropolitan Opera singer and after they had eaten dinner, he often went into the kitchen to serenade Jo. Everyone in the restaurant could hear his rich tenor voice singing "Amazing Grace" or some popular old-time song.

"Sometimes I was a little embarrassed," Jo said. "All the customers would come down to the kitchen door to listen to Cliff."

The Provencals came to our Christmas parties and Cliff made

it a to point to sing "Happy Birthday" to Jo in his own elegant presentation as the birthday cake was being served.

Every year Jo had some form of entertainment or musical treat for her guests. Sometimes it was a dance band, or it might be dinner music provided by a local group or musician. Other festivities included visits by the Celebration Barn Mime Theater and dialogues by local humorist, Joe Perham.

In the fall of 1980, the State Police decided they would like to do something special for Jo to show their appreciation for all she had done for them over the years. Percy Turner, one of the local officers, talked secretly with Barbara and me to make the arrangements. They put together plans to surprise her with a special award at the Barjo's annual Christmas party held at the Country Way Restaurant.

Because Jo invited the officers each year, they didn't think she'd be suspicious when she saw their cruisers at the restaurant. All the boys who were off duty from the Norway and Paris departments, the State Police and the Sheriff's Department came.

When Jo arrived at the party this time, she noticed there were many more police cars outside than usual and she asked me why. I played dumb as I walked her into the banquet hall. Then Col. Allan Weeks, Lt. Col. Albert Jamison and a large group of officers from all the local departments as well as the State Police greeted us. Everybody stood. The officers saluted her at attention as Col. Weeks and Lt. Col. Jamison presented her with a Commission as Honorary Captain of the Maine State Police. This appointment to the rank of Captain was made on December 29, 1980. Governor Joseph Brennan and Col. Weeks both signed her commission and she was presented with shoulder patches and Captain's Silver Bars.

"To see all my friends from the State Police standing at attention for *me* was beyond my comprehension!" exclaimed Jo with awe. "I couldn't believe they were giving me this honor. I don't know what I said when I thanked them. It was all like a dream."

At the time, Jo was one of only five people ever to be given this honor in the State of Maine. She was, and is, the only woman ever appointed an Honorary Captain in the State Police.

After dinner, Col. Weeks went around to the tables and visited with many of the senior citizens who were guests. All the elderly ladies were thrilled to have him notice them. It was a high point of their evening.

I said to Jo, "Did you notice how Col. Weeks got right down on his knee to talk with all our friends? What a nice gesture for him to make."

Later, one of Jo's friends, Donald Roy, had the photo taken by a local reporter enlarged to 2' by 3' and framed. It hung on the wall at Barjo's until she sold the restaurant. It is one of her prized possessions and now hangs in the front hall of her home beside her framed commission.

As festive as the Christmas party was, it wasn't the end of the holiday celebrations. After 1966, we closed on New Year's Eve, at 9:30 p.m., so we gave out hats and noisemakers during dinner hour. Many folks brought the whole family to take part in the fun. The kids had a ball tooting horns and noisemakers and blowing up balloons that were then batted from booth to booth.

On New Year's Eve in 1977, Jo asked Molly May[11] if she would like to give out party hats and favors. Molly was one of Jo and Margaret's old friends from their Stone's Drug Store Days.

"You would have thought I'd given her a million dollars," Jo commented. "Molly got right into the swing of things and had a great time, right along with the customers! Larry Fournier and his family and with my nephew, Edwin, led the singing and merry-making. All the other customers began tooting party horns and blowing noisemakers."

Another holiday celebration in Norway, as around the nation, centered on the Fourth of July. In 1976, for the Bicentennial of the United States, we decorated Barjo's with bunting around the front door and made a flag display on the marquee. It included a copy of the original Betsy Ross flag, a white Bicentennial flag, and one with red and white stripes and "76" surrounded by stars on a blue field in the upper left corner. The waitresses wore white pants suits, white straw sailor hats with hatbands of red and blue ribbons. During the week's festivities, all of us wore red and blue medallions to signify that the restaurant was participating in the Bicentennial celebrations.

A local man and Vietnam veteran, Dean Bartlett, came into the restaurant and asked Jo if she wanted him to guard the flags during the night.

"You know the United States flag must always be guarded! Don't you want me to guard them for you?" he asked.

"Why, of course you can," Jo replied." I hadn't thought about that. Thanks for reminding me."

He went home and put on his full military regalia complete with weapons. I got him a chair to sit in on the sidewalk while he guarded the flags. Later, Jo rewarded Dean for being interested in the welfare of his country's flags.

Our home was also decorated with patriotic bunting and three flags to match the ones at Barjo's. Experts from their Christmas decorating, Donald Farr and his brothers did the festive Bicentennial decorating for us.

Through the years, Jo had been an active supporter of the Norway Chamber of Commerce. Because the area had grown, the organization included eight surrounding towns and its name had been changed to the Oxford Hills Chamber of Commerce.

In 1975, Barjo Restaurant had been initiated—a "by invitation only" honor—into the national Chamber of Commerce as a Business Member in October, 1975. Jo proudly displayed the plaque she was presented at the cash register in the restaurant.

"It came as a total surprise to me," Jo said. "I couldn't believe that a small restaurant from the state of Maine had been chosen to receive this honor from the national board of directors."

In 1977, the Oxford Hills Chamber chose Jo to receive its first Annual Outstanding Community Service Award. Again, the president, Tom Kenison, caught Jo completely by surprise when he came to Barjo's to present the award to her.

"Jo," Tom said, "you're so well-known for all you do in the community that there are too many things to name."

"I was flabbergasted," Jo exclaimed. "I had no idea what Tom wanted when he called me into the dining room. I thanked him and then told him that I would treasure it for the rest of my life."

That same year, the Maine Restaurant Association singled her out for a "Special Achievement Award" for work in Maine to promote the food service industry. Carl Sanford, the Executive Secretary of the organization presented this honor.

In 1977, Jo was in for another surprise from an entirely different group. One of her friend's, Ollie Dore of the Maine State Police was also the president of the Mid-Maine Motorcycle Club of Lewiston-Auburn. This club was limited to 50 members who were business and professional people. They owned beautiful machines, every one polished to perfection. One member, a retired lawyer, had paid over $20,000 for his motorcycle.

Each Wednesday, the club rode to Norway for an evening treat at Barjo's. Several times during the year, they also made trips to scenic spots such as Nova Scotia, Niagara Falls or the home of the Von Trapps (the *Sound of Music* family) in Vermont.

Many of the club members were good customers at Barjo's. Some were salesmen with whom she did business. Many of them came to Norway to shop and brought their families to eat at the restaurant.

"When my friends came to the restaurant," Jo said, "we always went out on the front steps to watch them leave. The whole club, riding two by two, would go to the head of Main Street and circle back to head to Lewiston. What a beautiful spectacle that was! Often, one of them would offer me a ride and, a few times, I took them up on it!"

One Wednesday night, the club president surprised Jo when he called her to the dining room. Thinking he was inviting her out just to visit with them, she came through the swinging doors wiping her hands and said, "How was your ride tonight, folks?"

"Well, Jo," Ollie said to he, "we've taken a vote and we have decided to make you an honorary member of the club. I want to present you with this Certificate of Membership in the Mid-Maine Motorcycle Club. We know you don't own a motorcycle yet, so we want to give you this one for your very own."

"My goodness. What a surprise this is!" said Jo as Ollie handed her a ceramic motorcycle with a gray-haired lady seated on it. She was dressed in full motorcycle attire from the helmet, leather jacket down to the leather boots.

The surprise honors acknowledging Jo's widespread popularity kept coming. In the spring of 1978, Hattie Harman the Lecturer of the Norway Grange called the restaurant and asked if Jo could attend an open meeting at the Grange Hall on Whitman Street in back of Barjo's in April.

"But why?" Jo asked, puzzled. She had never been a grange member.

"I just want you to be my guest for the evening," was all Hattie Harman would tell her. Finally, Jo agreed.

Unbeknownst to her, the Norway Grange had selected Jo for its National Community Citizen Award. When she went to the meeting, the Grange members presented her with a bouquet of red roses. The Master of the Grange, Al Harmon, commended her for her work in feeding everyone—rich and poor alike—at Barjo's, and for giving free meals to senior citizens and to members of various organizations. He also noted that for many years she had bought 4-H market lambs at the Oxford County Fair to help area youth. Jo also promoted local agriculture, a cornerstone of the Grange ideology, by buying milk and produce from area farmers. Hattie Harmon made the presentation of the National Grange Award Certificate, which was signed by the Master of the National Grange in Washington, D.C. and of the accompanying marble paperweight with the Grange Seal.

"It was quite an honor," Jo commented, "to have all my neighbors and friends choose me for this award. Buying from the farmers and helping others was something I enjoyed. I didn't even know that they knew what I had been doing. I certainly never expected any recognition for it."

In early 1979, Bob Gardner came to the restaurant to see Jo. As a young reporter for the *Portland Press Herald*, he had lived in Norway where several of his children had been born. Jo and Donald had helped him get started in his career. Now he was president of the public television station in Lewiston, WCBB. The station was trying to raise enough money to buy equipment to broadcast in color.

"Jo," Bob said to her, "I know how much you have helped me over the years, but would you be willing to donate to WCBB?"

"What do you have in mind?" she asked.

"A donation of $2000 to help us in our fundraising drive so we can buy color equipment for the station," he asked.

"Sure!" was her answer.

In 1979, Bob Gardner presented Jo with a plaque of acknowledgment:

> For the interest and support given in Advancing the
> Goals of Public Television in the State of Maine,
> for Capital for Color Equipment at WCBB-TV Channel 10.

This plaque was on display at Barjo's for many years. Jo has continued to be a loyal supporter of public television at all levels.

One day recently, I was talking with Bob about writing a book of Jo's life. He was thrilled by the idea and offered to help out in anyway he could, either with some of his pictures or stories he had written about her in the past. He has remained a good friend.

In another kind of community service, Jo was recognized in 1980 for all the compassion she had shown area senior citizens when she received an award from the Norway-Paris Senior Citizens Club.

During the 1970's and early 80's, the Senior Citizens Band, a group organized by Evelyn Bonney and directed by Sarah MacIntosh, came several times a year to have dinner at Barjo's as guests of the restaurant. After they finished their dinner, they entertained. Once she knew when they were coming, Jo made it a point to invite many local patrons to enjoy the old-time songs and hymns. Many in the band played instruments, while the rest formed the chorus.

In 1976, the president of the Senior Citizens Band, Evelyn Bonney, presented Jo with a plaque commending her for her help in making the band a success.

In 1980, the Western Maine Senior Citizens Volunteers were planning an awards dinner. They came to Jo for help in organizing the affair, as it was to include people from Oxford, Franklin and Androscoggin counties. They anticipated that more than 600 would attend.

Jo had a talk with Henry and told him she would donate the food if he would serve the banquet at the Country Way Restaurant. Even at the larger restaurant, there would have to be two seatings. Because the dinner could be served smorgasbord style there, she thought it would be much easier than hiring a hall. He agreed to make it a joint venture and not to charge the members of the organization. The seating capacity when using both the main dining room and the banquet room was over 300.

On the day of the dinner, sure enough, over 600 people were served as guests of Barjo's and Country Way. When the awards ceremony began, Jo, who was, as usual, in Barjo's kitchen, got a call from Larry Tidswell, president of the Senior Citizens.

"Jo," he said, "would you please come to Country Way. We'll send someone to pick you up in a few minutes."

Not knowing what to expect and puzzled by the call (Had something gone wrong? Was Henry having some difficulty with the banquet?), Jo put on her coat and left me in charge at Barjo's. But when she arrived at Country Way, she was escorted to the head table. There Larry Tidswell and his friend, Charlie Poole, presented her with a beautiful wall plaque with a bronze scroll in the center. On it was inscribed the following:

To Josephine Stone,
in recognition of her faithful service and dedication
to the Norway-Paris Senior Citizens
from the club's inception in 1967 to 1980.

"This honor comes as a complete surprise to me," Jo exclaimed. "I thank you with all my heart, but I don't deserve this kind of testimonial."

"We think you do," Larry told her. "This is just a small token for all you have done for others."

The bronze plaque is on display in our home now.

Because Jo and Henry had not charged them for their awards banquet, the Western Maine Senior Volunteers were able to have an additional outing that summer. With the money the members had collected for the banquet, they hired a riverboat, the Songo River Queen in Naples, for a day trip. The members were treated to a scenic tour around Sebago Lake with a side trip through the Songo Locks. Dinner was served on the boat with entertainment in the afternoon.

After they returned from their trip, Jo received a huge card, signed by all the members, thanking her for making their special excursion possible.

Although Jo had been recognized in many different fields as a leader and a benefactor, legal problems with the town were on the horizon. This controversy would become more and more involved with each passing day. The town manager and the merchants, including Jo, were about to become entangled in a hot and heavy legal battle over the parking issue.[12]

Besides the parking lot controversy, other things were happening at Barjo's in April 1979. One particular situation would prove to be the worst time in Jo's life. It would be a peril that only God could have predicted and would almost cost me, my life. At seventy-five, Jo was going to have to face some major decisions about the future. Little did I know that I was about to meet *Jesus* face to face.

---

[11] *For more about all Jo's friends see Appendix 2, "Customers Fondly Remembered."*

[12] *The story of this controversy is told in Chapter 33.*

Jo was called out of the kitchen to be presented with honorary membership in the Mid-Maine Motorcycle Club in 1975 by the club's president, Ollie Dore.

Jo celebrated her 71st birthday in 1974 with her brothers and sisters. standing: Margaret, Donald, Grace; sitting: Helen, Gerald (Jim) and Jo.

CHAPTER 32

My Life On the Line!

Over the next several months, there would be moments when Jo and I both thought her relationship with me was to be ended—not by any difficulties between us, but by a life-threatening health problem. At thirty-nine, I had never had a sick day in my life, but that was about to change dramatically. I would never choose to relive those days and weeks, for they were dark times, indeed. But something so very special saw us through that crisis that I feel compelled to include it here in the story of Jo's life. My life now was so entwined with hers at Barjo's, at home, amongst our many friends and all the Barjo's family, that the story of my illness—and remarkable healing—are part of the story of her life, as well.

On April 4, 1979, the same day the deed for the parking lot was to be signed, I came down with what I thought at first was a severe case of flu. I had horrendous headaches and terrible bouts of vomiting.

I was so sick I went to the hospital emergency room. I didn't want Jo to know how sick I really was, so I tried my best to recover and to hide it. But I can't even remember my fortieth birthday on April 13th of that year.

"Of course, I noticed Emily wasn't her usual self," Jo said, "but I wasn't sure why. I didn't know if she was dissatisfied with her job. I thought maybe I had done something she didn't approve of or maybe there was some unexplained reason. We were as busy as usual and I put it out of my mind, hoping whatever it was would take care of itself."

Every afternoon during April and early May I would leave the restaurant for an hour's rest and go to the emergency room instead of home. The doctors there tried to help me, but to no avail. No medicine they gave me did any good. None of their exams or tests revealed what was causing my problems. I became so sick that nothing, not even water, would stay down. Finally, they told me to have my medical doctor order additional tests.

The headaches intensified and it felt like someone was holding a hot, searing iron to the top of my head every second. When they were the worst, I thought I was going out of my mind. The only relief I could find was lying on the cold tile floor of the bathroom at the restaurant. Still anxious not to worry Jo, I knew that if I were gone for long, she would come looking for me, so I only stayed there a few minutes at a time.

Trying to find a primary-care doctor to order additional tests was a real problem. The doctor that I had seen over the years had retired and all the local physicians were either booking far ahead or weren't taking on new patients.

Finally, on May 8, I got an appointment with Dr. Richard Bean, who had been Stony's doctor. He gave me a complete physical and ordered a battery of tests to be done at Stephens Memorial Hospital on May 15. Still, the horrible headaches continued along with the dreadful projectile vomiting. Nothing helped.

Still, I didn't tell Jo how sick I really was and continued to do my work to the very best of my ability. It was a real struggle for me. By this time, my head was so bad it was impossible to lay it on a pillow at night. I had to sit up because of the awful pressure and piercing pain. My left eye began to give me trouble. Sometimes, it was almost impossible to open my left eyelid because of the intense pain around my eye.

"I thought Emily was mad at me or wanted to quit her job," Jo said. "I never thought that she was awfully sick. She didn't confided in me or tell me about her many hospital visits. She'd be serving dinner with me and the next minute she'd be gone. When she came back, she never told me she was fighting a losing battle for her life. At that time, I don't think she had any idea what was happening herself."

When Dr. Bean got the test results, he still had no answers. He told me that maybe my eyes were really the problem. He made an appointment for me with Dr. Tchao in Lewiston. But I canceled it and told him I would prefer to see an eye specialist in Portland.

"It had to have been God that interceded in that decision," I told Jo later. "I don't know why I canceled that appointment, it just seemed the right thing to do."

Dr. Bean made me an appointment with Dr. Richard Goduti at the Maine Eye Center for May 24.

That morning, I prepared vegetables for boiled dinner at the restaurant the same as I always had. Then I drove Jo home from Barjo's. I had no idea when Donald and Mildred picked me up at 9:00 a.m. to drive me to Portland that I would be gone for over a month. I thought I'd be returning with them that afternoon.

In the seven weeks before I went to Portland, I had lost thirty-five pounds and my kidneys had stopped functioning. I hadn't told Jo about any of these developments.

Dr. Goduti examined me and gave me a visual field test, then he said, "You stay seated while I make a few phone calls."

When he was finished talking on the telephone, he turned to me and told me that I was to go directly to Dr. Leschey's office on Park Avenue. He was a neurologist who would perform an EEG on my brain. Now, I was really scared. Dr. Goduti passed me a card with the directions of how to get there. He told me that he had seen a problem inside my head when he looked into my eyes.

He said, "Your eyes are a mirror to your brain. I found some damage that Dr. Leschey will be able to document."

In the meantime, Don and Mildred had been waiting for me in the parking lot. I remember getting into the car and giving Donald the directions to the neurologist's office. I remember Donald and Mildred driving me to the office and going up the steps of Dr. Leschey's.

But from that moment on, everything was a blur. I don't remember leaving that office. Two hours later, I recall being put in a wheelchair at Maine Medical Center's emergency entrance. I remember nothing else that happened during the next week, only the terrible angiograms when I thought I was dying for sure.

After extensive testing which included CAT-scans, too many spinal taps to count and a series of angiograms, Dr. Carl Brinkman, a neurosurgeon, was called in on the case. By this time I had been admitted to a private room on the floor devoted exclusively to neurosurgical patients.

In the meantime, Jo was looking for me to return home. She was beside herself worrying about what might have happened.

"Where are they? What is taking them so long?" she wondered to herself. "I thought for sure that they'd be back by the middle of the afternoon."

It was evening when Donald and Mildred returned home, but without me. Jo could hardly believe what had transpired when they told her about the day's events. Now, she understood why I had acted so strangely and disappeared mysteriously at times.

"Still, I couldn't understand why she hadn't told me that she was sick," Jo said with deep sadness in her voice. "I know she didn't want to upset me. But if she was that sick, why did she even try to continue working? I certainly needed her help, but that was nothing compared to realizing I might lose her forever."

Though Jo knew about the problems between my family and me, she called my mother and told her I was in the hospital. She wanted to be sure my family knew exactly what had happened and where I was. She knew they probably would not keep her informed about my progress. Afterwards, this disturbed me greatly. Any problems between us should not have been used as an excuse to keep her in the dark about my condition. It was impossible for her not to be all the more anxious.

"I wonder if Emily has the same thing that caused her father's death," Jo worried. "Maybe this aneurysm thing is hereditary—his three brothers had died of the same condition."

My father had passed away very suddenly in 1968. It happened like this. On the afternoon of July 3, my folks had come into Barjo's kitchen around 5:00 p.m. My father had been brook fishing with Buddy. My father told me he didn't feel quite right and was going to the hospital to find out why. At 7:00 p.m., the family doctor, Dr. Beryl Moore called to say that if I wanted to see my father, I must come to the hospital immediately. He had an aneurysm on the aorta and she had predicted that he had less than four hours to live. I went in to say goodbye to him and then returned to Barjo's, full of dread. At 11:00 p.m., the hospital called to tell me that my father had just passed away and that my mother had just left the hospital.

"Now, I was afraid this was happening to Emily. One of Barbara Farr's daughters, Nancy, worked in the X-ray department at Maine Medical Center," Jo said. "She called every day to tell me Emily's condition. For that, I can never thank her enough."

Though I couldn't watch television or read because of the damage to my brain, there was a telephone and a radio in my room. Every night at 10:30 p.m. when I was able, I called Jo at home to tell her how I had gotten through the day and, early each morning, I called her at Barjo's to tell her how I had gotten through the night. By watching the sunrise over Portland harbor, I was able to come pretty close to the right time. I could also tell the time by an ad on the radio station, WPOR, for the "Cod-Fish Emporium." It was through these calls to Jo that I was able to keep my sanity. Her love and concern were the foundation of my hope.

The other person who provided important support was Barbara Ethridge Thomas, a high school classmate of mine. She came to see me every day and helped me understand what was happening to me. Over a two-year period, her husband, Ralph, had been operated on several times for a brain tumor. He was a patient on the same floor and was recovering from his third brain surgery at that time. Barbara told me what to anticipate day to day and about all I could expect to experience.

Meanwhile at Barjo's, Jo was working day and night with extra help from Margaret who worked with her until closing when the Norway police officers on duty took them home. Jo tried to do her work and mine, too. At 4:00 a.m., one of the officers, often Donald Guilford, would pick her up and take her to Barjo's to finish her cooking and cleaning. After a week of this all-out schedule, she hired a woman to help with the cleaning and vacuuming. The schoolgirls who were working for her took turns helping serve dinner and supper.

In the midst of this crisis, Jo experienced an additional incident I didn't find out about until I got home. She swore everyone to secrecy because she didn't want to upset me.

Several days after I went into the hospital, as Jo was getting ready to go to work at 4:00 a.m., she smelled smoke. She has always disliked using the telephone, and the only phone numbers she could remember were Margaret's and the number at the restaurant. So instead of calling the fire department, she called Margaret and asked her to call them.

As she was coming downstairs, Donald Guilford drove up to take her to work. She said to him, "I think something is burning, but I don't know where."

"Aren't you going to stay until the fire department gets here?" he asked with some surprise.

"Oh, no," she replied. "I've got to get dinner, but perhaps you could come back and see what they find."

What the firemen found was a kitchen light that had burned out and started a fire that followed the wiring all across the ceiling and down inside the wall to a light switch before it petered out. Jo's guardian angel had certainly been with her—her bedroom was directly above the kitchen, but the damage hadn't reached the second floor.

Ever since her childhood, Jo hated to stay alone at night and until my illness, she had never had to. The fact that she was working so much and only home for several hours during the night helped some. Now, following the fire, she had no electricity on the first floor. It would be three weeks before she could get the electrical work done and have the ceiling replaced. Meanwhile, she entered a dark, empty house and stayed alone each night. The darkness and loneliness at home corresponded to her worry and dread about what was happening to me.

"Over the years, we had been employer and employee, mother and adopted daughter, business associates, co-workers, dear friends and just plain family. A future without the comfort and companionship of my relationship with Emily looked pretty bleak to me," Jo said sadly.

Meanwhile, she told everyone to keep quiet about the fire, and I had no idea what had happened at home. I was fighting as hard as I could for my life and just to maintain my sanity.

A week after entering the hospital, on Friday, May 31, my first brain operation was performed by Dr. Carl Brinkman of Southern Maine Neurosurgical. He found that my problems were the result of sub-dural hematomas (blood clots in the brain) including cerebral hemorrhaging. A ruptured brain aneurysm was the root cause. He performed a Burr-hole operation.[13]

On the following Sunday night when the nurse took my temperature at 10 p.m., it was hovering at 101 degrees. But within a half-hour, I began to have chills and my temperature rose to a dangerously high 107 degrees. The head nurse called Dr. Brinkman's assistant, Dr. Wilson who was covering for the Southern Maine Neurosurgical team.

Dr. Wilson entered my room carrying one of the very long needles similar to the ones they used for spinal taps. Because time was crucial, he didn't dare wait for an anesthetic. He inserted that needle directly into my brain to stop the infection that had caused the sudden rise in my temperature. The nurse stood by my bed and held me while he did it, but I am sure my fingerprints must still be imprinted in those bed rails!

Dr. Brinkman told me if my temperature went back to normal and stayed there, I could go home by the end of the week. This was good news! Now I could concentrate on recovery and getting back to normal, I thought.

By Wednesday, however, I started to have a prickly feeling in my right leg. At first, I thought the surgical stockings were too tight. But, that wasn't it; it was the beginning of paralysis.

When I asked for water late Wednesday night, the nurse told me I couldn't have any. She said I was going to have another series of those miserable angiograms the next morning. I dreaded the prospect. I thought then, and still think, that they are the worst test on the planet. They made me think I was burning up inside and had chain lightning exploding in my head.

With my leg nearly paralyzed and knowing that I had to go through those awful tests again, I thought to myself, "Well, I'll make one last call to Jo. If God takes me home at least I've had a chance to talk to her one last time to say good-bye."

"I got a call from Emily at 3:00 a.m. Thursday morning," Jo

said. "I knew she was awfully upset just by her voice. It wasn't like her to call me at that time of night because she knew I would be asleep. Earlier, she had told she would be home sometime that week. Now, her news was different. She was afraid that she would never see me again. It was one of the worst moments of her life and mine, too."

The new tests showed the hemorrhaging had returned with a vengeance. I was operated on again on Saturday, June 9, and still the bleeding in my head persisted. This second operation involved sawing out a piece of skull in order to repair the blood vessel system. It took over five hours. Dr. Brinkman told my family he removed blood clots as large as silver dollars that were pressing on my brain.

When I got back to my room at 8:30 that evening, I was able to call Jo to tell her that I was, after all, alive. But that was the beginning of a horrible night. The nurse tried to feed me some tomato soup with a straw. I nearly choked to death because I couldn't swallow and the soup went down my windpipe.

When the nurses lifted my right arm and leg, I could see that they were both white as snow and limp like a rag doll. I couldn't believe they even belonged to me because I had no feeling in either of them. I couldn't tell the nurses what was happening or how I felt because I was losing my ability to speak.

My throat was gradually paralyzing. No one realized this was happening. By 10:00 that night, my whole right side was paralyzed, and I had totally lost my speech.

At home, Jo was beside herself with concern and began to marshal the kind of support she knew was the only kind of help she could offer.

"Emily had made hundreds of friends at Barjo's. She was a special person—so warm and friendly. She always had a kind word for each of our customers," Jo said. "When they heard she was so ill, they put her on prayer chains in their churches and many organized groups especially to say pray for her recovery."

On the Sunday morning of June 10, Dr. Brinkman called in my family and told them that if he operated for a third time, the odds of my survival would be 1 in 300,000. He had never operated on a patient three times in such a short period of time, he told them, and he couldn't be sure of the results. If I survived, he went on, it was likely I would be in a vegetative state—so much damage had already been done! A complete blood exchange would have to be done because my own blood would not heal.

This time my mother did call Jo.

"I can't tell you what I served that Sunday or how many customers came into Barjo's," Jo said. "My heart and soul were focused on only one thing, to pray to God to save Emily's life. No one knew how much that kid meant to me. What a tragedy it would have been if she had lost her life at forty years old! With all the other things that had happened in my life, this was the very worst moment. I was 75 years old. How could I possibly go on without her?"

Full of trepidation, I was taken into the operating room for the third operation at 1:00 p.m. The procedure would last over seven hours. It was during this operation that I underwent a life-changing out of body experience.

As I came aware, I felt as though I were floating in the air above my own body. I heard Dr. Brinkman saying, "We've gone this far—we can't lose her now!"

My attention was drawn away from this scene, and looking up with growing awe, I saw a magnificent tunnel filled with a brilliant, angelic-like white light. I was overwhelmed by a flooding sense of peace and my anxiety melted away. It was the most beautiful thing I had ever seen. At the end of this tunnel I watched as a figure came into focus. There stood Jesus in a shining, impeccable white robe. His hair glowed like spun gold.

He said to me kindly but with certainty, "Go back. Your work is not finished. You will be healed!"

My vision of light faded as He moved away.

The next thing I remember is being in the ICU unit the next morning. As Dr. Brinkman came into the room, he looked at me searchingly and said, "Emily, if you can speak, tell me what I have on my head."

"Hat," I replied.

A huge smile lit up the surgeon's face. He could hardly believe his ears. He hadn't truly expected me to live and he certainly hadn't thought I'd be able to speak. But I knew the answer. Jesus kept his word. Now it was up to me to do my part and follow His instructions for the rest of my life.

It would be three more weeks before I was able to go home. At first, I had four drains in my head and my arms were strapped to the bed rails so I couldn't move.

The left temporal lobe of the brain is where the body's motion controls are located. This was where all the damage had been done to my brain. Before Dr. Brinkman let me go home, I had to relearn all normal body functions just as a baby does. The left side of my head still has a section 3 inches wide by 8 inches long, which has indentations that are anywhere from 1/2 inch to a 1 inch deep. The pressure of the blood clots in my brain caused these depressions. The left temporal area of my brain had been almost completely destroyed.

Because my kidneys had stopped functioning and I had been paralyzed, I had to learn to concentrate on how to do every little thing that was normally an automatic function for my body. Learning how to walk, how to talk and how to make my body respond to simple commands was a real challenge.

The doctor told me clearly that, if I had lost my will to live or my strong faith in God, I wouldn't have survived for even a second. Without my determination and my faith, I wouldn't have made it through that third operation. I knew why I had survived, but I never discussed it with him. I just kept working at my recovery and thanked God for His intervention in my life.

As I got better, it bothered me to know that Jo was doing her work and mine, too. Repeatedly, I asked the nurses, "What if I forget how to cook a hamburger? What if I forget how to help Jo prepare dinner? When can I go back to work? Will I be able to still work at the restaurant?"

By the grace of God, I was able to come home on June 24. Donald and Mildred brought me home in the middle of the afternoon while Jo was home having a nap, so she didn't hear me come into the house.

"When I got up, I looked in Emily's room," Jo explained. "I knew that Don was going after her, but when I saw her, I wondered to myself, who is that in there?! That doesn't look like my girl!"

I knew that Jo didn't recognize me. My head had been shaved and on the left side it looked as if someone had embroidered a huge letter M. This was where the two sections of skull had been removed. After her initial shock, Jo embraced me with open arms. We had a good laugh about how funny she thought I looked. The hospital had given me a foolish-looking little skullcap made of a jersey-like material but I seldom wore it after I got home.

For the first several months, my speech was limited, but I tried harder than ever to overcome my difficulties. I knew what I wanted to say, but the words just wouldn't come out. It was very frustrating! To this day, sometimes it is hard to remember different events or names. Jo will ask me about something we said or did and it might be hours or days before I can remember.

After having physical therapy on my right arm and leg, I was able to go back to work at Barjo's. The paralysis had destroyed my right kneecap, but I managed until February 1993 when I started having to wear a brace on my right leg.

At first, I was only able to help Jo prepare for the next day for only four hours. Many nights we would rest for several hours before finishing our work and starting the cleaning. The doctors felt I wasn't strong enough to deal with the pressure of working during rush hours or of doing short order cooking.

Gradually, my strength and coordination returned. My stamina increased and, thanks be to God alone, I was finally able to go back at Jo's side to work the same hours I had always worked.

My healing was a miracle. Against odds—because of God's love—I overcame the illness that had killed my father and brothers. My near-death experience strengthened my determination to make Jesus and his teachings the center of my life. My faith and Jo's have given us a sense of purpose and a positive outlook on life which we draw on everyday, in every way. Because we shared the experience of this crisis, our relationship grew deeper than ever. I can never be grateful enough for the day I met Jo. She has always treated me as a daughter rather than as an employee.

The amazing story of my recovery continues to this day. After three years, I was able to stop taking Dilatin. For ten years after that, I took no medicine at all.

Then in December 1992, I developed partial-complex seizures caused by scar tissue on the left side of my brain. Many nights, as my seizures continued, Jo sat by my bed for hours at a time to be sure I didn't suffocate or hurt myself during a seizure. Once again, God's hand was on my shoulder and He guided me though those terrible reactions as my body rejected both Dilatin and Tegretol, the usual drugs used to treat seizures.

In October 1993, Dr. Leschey was part of a team working on clinical trials for a new drug called Felbatol. I was one of the patients in these studies. Even though Felbatol is used as a last resort when all other avenues of treatment have failed, I have had no side effects from it and no seizures since July 1995.

Finally, as I grew stronger and our lives returned to normal, Jo was able to breathe a sigh of relief. My life had been saved by the grace of God. I was able to come back to work and help her at Barjo's. Now, it seemed like that nightmare had never happened.

---

13 *The Burr-hole operation is done by boring a hole in the skull to release pressure on the brain.*

CHAPTER 33

Custard Pie and Politicians

Looking forward, there were many more undertakings in store for Jo. Some of these would be exceptional in nature, while others would take her in an entirely new direction.

Friendly relations with the police department had always played a big part in Jo's business life. She had treated the officers to their meals and in return, they had nightly taken her day's deposit to the bank. Jo felt it was good for her business for people to know that officers often came in.

One day, a reporter asked Jo and Margaret if they knew everyone in Norway.

"Just about! You know we're older than dirt," Jo quickly replied. "We should both be at home. But I'm having the time of my life. I love seeing my friends and neighbors every day. And over the years, we've also catered to quite a few celebrities, not to mention, politicians."

Jo's expression, "older than dirt," came from a conversation with the local police officers. Every evening they came in around 9:00 p.m. for their coffee break and to discuss sports with her.

One particular night, the conversation turned to politics. One of the boys asked her, "Jo, do you remember who was running for president the first time that you voted?"

"Well, let me think a minute," she replied. "I think it was Calvin Coolidge."

"Gee, Jo, you must be older than dirt to have voted for Coolidge!" he told her. "That was way back in the Dark Ages!"

This caused quite a few laughs and many more wise comments. Now, Jo uses the expression to make a joke whenever she's asked how old she is.

Jo's claim that Barjo's attracted celebrities and politicians was quite true. In 1980, we seemed to have a succession of famous people as customers. In the spring, when California Gov. Jerry Brown was an Independent party presidential candidate, he stopped at Barjo's with dozens of TV cameramen and reporters.

His tour had taken him across the country from California to Maine. That morning he had made a speech at the local radio station, WOXO, on a call-in program called "Open-Mike."

After leaving the radio station, Gov. Jerry Brown came to Barjo's for a "whistle-stop" visit. His campaign entourage included the California television crew of "NBC Burbank." Jo had the restaurant crowded with people eager to meet him. Jerry Brown came into the kitchen, followed by TV cameras, to meet Jo. Standing by the counter where many of her pies—custard, lemon meringue, and berry—were on display, she welcomed the candidate to Barjo's.

Kidding her later, I accused her of making the lemon meringue just to decorate her pie counter. Like her famous custard pies, these are four-inch, deep-dish pies that are well-deserving of their local reputation.

"You were just trying to make a good impression on the Governor," I teased.

That evening, one of her Fogg cousins-in-law called Jo from California. "I couldn't believe my eyes when I saw you and your custard pie on the San Francisco Evening News!" she exclaimed.

Beryl Russell, a Barjo's customer, received a call from her son in northern California who said to her, "Mother, I saw you on the front steps of Barjo's shaking hands with Gov. Brown on the NBC Nightly News tonight. I can't believe that Barjo Restaurant has been publicized coast to coast today!"

Another call came in to Margaret from a relative from Arizona. "I just saw Jo and her custard pie on TV," she reported. "Barjo's has coast-to-coast exposure!"

Jo's custard pie was a famous delicacy at Barjo's. Over the years, one of the first questions many customers asked when coming in the front door was "Is there any custard pie left?" Or "Be sure to save me a piece of custard pie!"

One thing that made her pie special was the tender loving care with which she sculpted the shells. Another was the way she mixed the piecrust in a huge mixing bowl by hand using pure lard and an unbleached flour called "Flaky Crust." She worked the piecrust with her fingers so that it was over two inches above the pie plate. Her method was similar to the same way an artist sculpts clay for a statue.

Next, the filling for two pies was made with 22 eggs plus other ingredients that included a special formula of pure vanilla extract made for her by Schlotterbeck & Foss.[14] The pies were filled three-quarters full when she placed them in a 500-degree oven to set the crust and the filling. When the crust was set, the rest of the filling was added and the oven set to 350-degrees to cook for about an hour or until the pie was firm. Several customers told her the filling was over three inches deep, because they had measured it. Many customers took pictures of the height of her pies because they didn't think their friends would believe them if they didn't have proof.

In the early 1980's, after Cummings Brothers in Portland sold their wholesale business to the S. Prawer Company, the new company stopped handling Jo's favorite flour. Others she had tried didn't seem to produce the quality crust her customers were accustomed to.

One day, I searched out the address of the manufacturer and found out that the company, Minnesota Milling, had home offices in the Midwest. Jo had me call to find out if anyone in Maine still handled this product.

When I talked with the sales manager, he told me their nearest distributor was in Exeter, New Hampshire. He told us we'd have to order 1000 pounds (20 fifty-pound bags) and pick it up in Exeter ourselves. We placed the order.

"But now how can I get all that flour to Norway from Exeter?" Jo thought to herself.

At noon, when her nephew Edwin came in to dinner, Jo told him what had transpired.

"Well, you're in luck, Aunt Jo," he said. "I have a load of dowels going to Exeter from C. B. Cummings this afternoon. I'll be glad to pick up your flour on the way back."

That solved the immediate problem, but not for the long term. After another call to Minnesota Milling, Jo was able to contact the New England sales manager. Through him, she was able to buy Flaky Crust flour in 1000 pound lots from Thompson Baking Supply in Connecticut. Sanborn's Motor Express picked up the flour for her and delivered it to our Deering Street home where it was stored. Because of the quantity she was required to buy, our garage became the restaurant warehouse. We continued this practice until Barjo's was sold in 1991.

More noteworthy events were on the horizon for Jo. On an early spring day in 1980, State Police Officer Percy Turner called to tell Jo that Barjo's had been chosen for a visit by President Carter's son. Percy told Jo that an entourage of Secret Service officers and Maine State Police would be accompanying him. The Secret Service had selected Barjo's as the place where they would all eat lunch. Chip was on his way to a skiing excursion in the White Mountains.

"I knew that Barjo's was one of Percy's favorite spot to eat," Jo said. "What fun that he was bringing the president's son to eat at our place!"

When they came in, Percy brought Chip into the kitchen to meet Jo. She greeted him warmly and told him how glad she was to meet him. I had gone home for the afternoon and Bertha was helping Jo in the kitchen. She was peeling hard-boiled eggs by the sink on the other side of the kitchen. Jo turned to her and said, "Put up those eggs. Wash your hands and come meet the president's son."

Several hours later, Bertha asked Jo, "Who did you say that young man was?" She couldn't get it through her head that she had met President Carter's son, Chip.

With an astonished look, Jo said to her, "I told you—that was Chip Carter!

Bertha was dumbfounded and exclaimed, "No, you must be kidding me!"

Vickie Gay, who had graduated from high school with Jo's granddaughter, waited on the celebrity's entourage.[15] She was enchanted by the president's son and could hardly keep her mind on what she was doing.

Chip Carter was a very congenial young man and everyone was honored that his group had chosen Barjo's for lunch. While he was at the restaurant, he called his father at the White House from the dining room phone. Jo thanked Percy for his consideration and told him how much she appreciated her introduction to this famous young person.

More local customers also enjoyed Barjo's that year. On April 27, 1980, a restaurant critic from Portland made a visit. She had visited many restaurants in Maine and published an article every Sunday in the weekend edition of her paper.

The reviewer wasn't exactly a neighbor, but she learned about the restaurant from one of the customers. Neighbors in Norway knew that they were likely to meet friends at 210 Main Street. It's been that way for a couple of generations because Barjo's Restaurant is at that address.

All our regulars know they don't have to wait to be seated by a hostess. Many have a favorite waitress or table, so they seat themselves. Others prefer the comfortable booths along the wall with individual wall-boxes for the jukebox. This was an added attraction for the kids. Our Hitchcock tables sat large parties in the center of the dining room.

When the reviewer came, our menu included thirty sand-wiches that were served all day along with salad plates and din-ner entrees. At noon, a luncheon special, the "Businessman's Special" was featured to accommodate the business community.

That Friday night, we were serving homemade fish chowder, flavored with tiny pieces of salt pork and filled with potatoes and haddock. The restaurant critic praised the service, the atmos-phere and especially the potato salad and the chowder.

She wrote,

> The potato salad tastes as if it were prepared especially for my family. I enjoyed the firm potatoes, chunks of eggs, pep-pers, radishes and onions, and how it was attractively served with two large slices of beefsteak tomato on iceberg lettuce leaves.

Veda told her, "Everything hot at Barjo's is served on a hot plate—don't touch the dishes!"

When Veda told her that the pies were homemade, her party just couldn't skip dessert. She exclaimed over the custard pie. She couldn't believe how thick it was, the highest she'd ever seen.

After the meal Margaret waltzed her into the kitchen to meet Jo, then age 76. Entering the kitchen, she could tell that Jo's idle rolling pin hadn't been that way long. The pie board was dusted with flour and dozens of pies lined the shelves and the counter beside it.

After they left, Jo commented, "Well, that lady seemed to enjoy her dinner and guided tour of the restaurant. She came in unannounced, but I think she was pleased with Veda's service."

She certainly must have been, because she came back the next year. This time, she was writing profiles of restauranteurs for the newspaper. Jo fascinated her. She chose her as a subject for her new series of articles.

Jo has never been one to accept gifts with ease. She prefers to be the giver not the receiver. One summer day in the 1980's, Larry Sanborn, a member of the South Paris Police Department, caught her by surprise by showing up at Barjo's back door with huge trays of fresh strawberries.

"I can't accept all those berries you worked so hard to pick," Jo said to him. "You boys do too much for me now. How can I ever pay you back?"

"I picked these for you and I refuse to take 'no' for an answer!" Larry told her. "I didn't spend the afternoon in the hot sun just so you could refuse my gift. This is the only way I can think of to repay you for all you do for all of us police officers."

"Well, *I* feel that you fellows help *me* a great deal more than anything I can ever do for *you*," was Jo's reply.

Over the next several years, Larry picked over 100 pounds of strawberries each summer for Barjo's. He knew Jo would turn them into her famous fresh strawberry pies.

Because of the increase of crime in the area, the police were soon to be more involved that ever in Jo's life. Drugs and alcohol were becoming more common in the rural areas of Maine. Norway was no exception. This would soon become a factor at Barjo's as well.

---

[14] *This special formula of vanilla extract was created exclusively for Barjo's in the 1930's and was sold to her in 40-gallon batches (5 cases of 4 gallons each).*

[15] *For more stories about Vickie and her sister, Karen, see Appendix 1, "Stories of the Barjo's Family."*

Susie Olmstead and Veda Taker in the Barjo's diningroom, 1972.

below left: Jo mixes her famous piecrust with help from Emily in the Barjo's kitchen.

right: Jo's cherished dogwood china set for a Barjo's favorite—the 1976 NRA Top of the Table winning meal— Maine Lobster.

CHAPTER 34

The Modern World Catches up with Small Town Maine

Until the late 1970's and early 1980's, and except for a few sensational events, crime wasn't been a big issue in the small communities in Maine. But that would change. With alcohol and drugs much more prevalent, break-ins and robberies were about to hit the area. Gangs were beginning to roam the region.

One afternoon, Jo and Donald were discussing local issues.

"I honestly believe we have lived in the best years of this century," he said to her. "What do you think, Jo?"

"When we moved to Norway, no one thought about locking their doors or about people breaking into their homes," she answered. "Today that's all the newspapers and the television seem to talk about. What is this world coming to?! You can't trust people anymore. I wouldn't dare to go to bed at night if all my doors weren't locked."

Little did Jo know that Barjo's would soon be hit. Within a short time, Jo and I would experience some hair-raising episodes. Evidently some thought it was an easy mark.

Many nights after my recovery from the brain surgery, we would lie down to rest in one of the dining room booths for several hours before finishing cleaning and cooking for the next day.

In the early morning hours one day in June 1980, we had turned out the dining room lights and were resting. Suddenly, there was a sharp, thumping sound on the front door and at the back door, almost simultaneously. A gang of about 10 young men was trying to break into the restaurant! We recognized several of the boys. They were some of the kids that Jo had fed many times in the past. They were now full of drugs and alcohol, and we had no idea what they might do. They were banging on both doors with clenched fists trying to smash them in.

They kept at it—it seemed like forever—with a deafening noise. I hardly dared to try to reach the telephone for fear of revealing we were there. Finally, I crawled across the floor on my stomach to call the police. But the police didn't come—a cruiser merely drove by several times.

"Why do you suppose the cruiser is just driving around the block?" Jo whispered to me. "Do you think they're afraid to tackle those boys because they are outnumbered?"

It was hard to say. She might have been right, but we never did find out.

The next day, when Donald Guilford, one of Norway's officers and a Barjo's regular, came in, Jo told him what had happened. He listened intently, taking it all in, but he didn't comment before leaving the restaurant.

When he came back, later that evening, he said, "I don't think those boys will give you any more trouble. My son, Jeff, Keith Smith, and their friends found out whose gang that was. They met them at the Casco Bank in South Paris and stood them up against the brick wall. My son and his friends told those boys that if they ever harassed you again they'd have a score to settle with them! The gang knows that means a beating!"

It seemed the two gangs had a more effective method of controlling each other than the cops. In any case, Barjo's never had anymore trouble from that particular gang.

Later that same summer, at about 2:00 a.m., again while we were in the dining room resting, Jo and I heard a noise coming from the kitchen. It was a kind of scraping noise and, when I went in to investigate, I saw a young man with his head and shoulders inside the window by the stove in the kitchen.

"What do you think you are doing, Kelli?!" I exclaimed.

He was from a family Jo had been feeding for years. At night after we closed, we often packed up the day's leftovers and loaded them into my car to take to their house. There were six kids in the family and their mother got a government check, but Jo knew it wasn't nearly enough to feed a family that size.

Kelli backed out through the window and slid to the ground. By the time the Norway officer, Tom Collins, arrived, Kelli and his friends had run around the corner. Tom had several officers as back up and they rounded up the boys—all eight of them. One of them, whom Jo had also fed, was quite a lot older than the others, probably in his late twenties. He was the mastermind in the gang's attempted break-in.

The cops questioned them about what they were doing and why they were hanging around in back of the restaurant.

A quick thinker, Kelli claimed he had just fallen against the shelf at the back of Barjo's and knocked over some #10 cans. Of course, he had been using the shelf as a stepladder to reach the window, where I caught him!

"I don't know why you think that I was trying to break into the restaurant," he told the officers.

"How Kelli came up with that story was hard to believe when I could have touched him with my hand! He was half-way through the kitchen window when I saw him," I told the police.

Apparently the boys didn't know that Jo and I were in the store and thought they could steal the liquor and not get caught. Nothing came of it as the boys continued to deny their intent.

But local boys looking for trouble weren't the only menace as Norway grew and changed. One morning, in April 1981, Jo and I returned to Barjo's at 4:00 a.m. to clean and get ready for the day. Going to the head of the cellar stairs to turn on the lights, I noticed that the kitchen window screen had been cut corner to corner. I immediately told Jo what I had found.

"You better call the police," she said in a disturbed voice, "and don't you dare go down cellar—someone might be hiding there waiting for us!"

We had only been gone for less than three hours, but someone had come into the building through the window in the alley. By the time the Officer Ernie Dunham came, I had found a wallet on the ice cream cabinet in front of the kitchen window. Apparently the thief had lost it either coming in or going out. The area around the cash register in the front room was a disaster with the rubbish box under the desk dumped all over the dining room floor. The thief must have thought that we had hidden the money in this area of the restaurant.

The officer found that the wallet belonged to a man who was living in an upstairs apartment in the building across the street. He was going with the daughter of one of Barjo's former employees and his wallet contained love letters to her.

When Officer Dunham confronted him, he admitted to breaking into the restaurant, but he told him that all he had taken was a hi-ball. When he had been unable to find any money, he broke the lock on the sliding doors of the liquor cabinet in the kitchen. "I was already inside. I thought I might as well enjoy myself," he said, "so I made myself a cocktail."

He also told Ernie that for months he had been watching Margaret cashing up from his apartment windows. Being an undesirable character, he was sure he could find some easy money at the restaurant.

Back at the Oxford County jail, Ernie checked the man's record. The officers found that he had committed a wide variety of crimes, from petty larceny and forgery to armed robbery. He was booked on a felony charge. Jo had to appear before the judge in Oxford County District Court. The case was transferred to Superior Court because of the seriousness of the crime. The man's court-appointed lawyer was John Jenness of South Paris.

While Jo was testifying at the Superior Court trial, his attorney asked many very particular questions such as, "What side of the alley is the window on?"

Finally, after having heard enough of this kind of foolishness, Jo exclaimed, "I don't see what you are trying to prove! It makes a difference whether you are coming from Main Street or the back yard. That is what determines which side of the alley the window is on, whether you are *coming up* or *going down*!"

John Jenness also questioned Jo about the way the locks were installed on the liquor cabinet doors. He asked her repeatedly whether they were cabinet locks or locks of another style.

When she came back from court, Jo took the doors off the liquor cabinet and vowed never to use them again. She said, "If anyone wants the liquor that bad, why bother to lock it up!"

Because he had such an extensive record, the man was sentenced to serve five years at the Maine State Prison in Thomaston.

On cold winter nights, I often started the car to warm it up before going home. One night in the winter of 1981, Jo was finishing the kitchen floor as I went out to start the car. I came back into the kitchen to get our coats, and Jo went out ahead of me.

She turned around, surprised, and said, "Where is the car?"

Just minutes before it was right by the back door as usual.

"What do you mean, 'where is the car?'" I asked.

We were so astonished that we both looked again to be sure we weren't mistaken, but, sure enough, the car was gone. I called the county sheriff's dispatcher who radioed David Daniels, the Norway officer on duty.

Dave had just seen my white 1980 Ford Fairlane come out of the alley, onto Main Street with no lights on and only one person in it. He radioed the dispatcher for assistance, and she called the Oxford police. The officers set up a roadblock at the bridge to stop the car before it got out of town toward Portland. When the car thief saw the roadblock, he turned up Oxford Street and the police forced him off the road into a snow bank.

Shortly, the police called to tell us the car hadn't been damaged. They took the thief to the jail while Dave picked us up in the cruiser to retrieve my car.

Getting into the back of the cruiser, Jo looked at me with a laugh and said, "Now we know what it feels like to be arrested and taken to jail in the back of a cruiser—only this time it's to retrieve our own vehicle, not to be taken to jail!"

The thief evidently had been standing in the shadows of a next-door entryway watching me as I started the car. He had noticed a bank bag on the front seat and must have thought it was the day's receipts.

"He must have thought he had it made! I filled the tank this afternoon," I said to Jo. "He must have thought he'd have a head start on the cops by the time we discovered the car was gone."

This taught me a very good lesson: never start the car without locking the doors with an extra set of keys. It also taught me never to leave a bank bag on the seat, even if it was empty.

In the early fall of 1982, the parking lot in back of Barjo's needed paving, so Jo hired a local firm to do the job. Little did she realize this little job would lead to a big "job."

At that time, the restaurant was short of freezer space, so Jo had purchased an upright freezer, similar to the ones used to store bags of ice. The outside freezer was chained to the building and had padlocks on its door. All the 10 lb. boxes of frozen meat plus turkeys, lamb legs, frozen vegetables and fruit in #10 cans were kept there. I usually stocked the short order freezer, which we served from in the kitchen, from the upright about once a day.

When the paving crew came, they had to move this outside freezer and take all the food out. We moved some of the meat to the Country Way and the rest in a freezer at the house while the paving was being done.

Several months later, in January, on a very cold morning, I went to stock up from the outside freezer as usual. I found the padlock missing and everything but the liver and the blueberries gone. The thieves apparently had fussy taste! When an inventory was taken for the investigation, the total was almost $6,000.

Within a few days, some of our young regulars told us they had heard that the food had been taken and stored on the flat roof of the building next door. The temperature was well below freezing that night. It had then been distributed to several different people locally and in Oxford.

The police found some empty cans and boxes in the dumpster of the apartment house next door to the restaurant. They brought them into the restaurant for us to identify. It seemed the kids knew what they were talking about.

The suspected mastermind behind the robbery was one of the men on the paving crew. He had seen how much meat and other food was in the freezer, when they had moved it to do the paving.

"From what the kids told us," Jo stated, "he had a good time spreading his stolen food around the neighborhood."

Even though the police had many tips and leads about the thief, they never made an arrest or prosecuted anyone.

Jo was also a target for a thief at home. In 1982, several days before Christmas, Donald, gave her a gift of a collection of silver dollars. They were both avid coin collectors. The 26th of December was Jo's birthday and also the day of Barjo's annual Christmas party at the Country Way. The following day, we had an unusual experience at home.

With the restaurant open on Christmas Day, we had been too busy for any relaxation. So it wasn't until we came home after the party on the 26th that we opened all of our presents. We left our gifts on the sun porch, where we opened them, planning to take care of them the next day.

In the afternoon, we came home to rest for a little while.

Nick, Robbie's son, came to the door and said to me, "I want to come in."

"Nana Jo is resting, Nick," I told him."It's not a good time for company."

"How come John's already in there?" Nick replied. Jo's great-grandsons were seven years old and great pals.

I turned around, and to my surprise, John, Jody's son, was standing on the plant shelf in the back corner of the sun porch.

"John, how in the world did you get there?" I asked him.

"Look!" he said. "See? The window was already open! I just climbed up the tree and crawled in."

"Jo!" I hollered, "Come quick! John and Nick have discovered where someone has broken into the house."

The police, with the help of young John and Nick's spyglasses, found footprints around the backside of the sun porch. They also discovered that someone had chiseled out all the putty around two of the windows hidden from the street by the big evergreen at the corner of the house. Whoever had done this must have worked at those windows for a long time!

Originally, these windows opened on hinges, which were still intact. They opened out like a door and the person breaking in had climbed the tree and had easily come into the house. The police found footprints on some of the presents we had left on the sun porch the night before, but nothing seemed to be missing.

Jo figured that someone had seen Donald give her the collection of silver dollars the day before Christmas. Luckily, she had put the collection in the safe. Whoever had broken in knew the collection was valuable and was looking for it.

"When Donald and I were talking about crime a few months ago," Jo said to me, "I had no idea you and I were going to have so many wild experiences in such a short time."

"Well," I said to her, "the one thing we can be very thankful for is that neither one of us has suffered any harm. Things can be replaced, but lives can't."

Through all these incidents, Jo remained positive about helping others. When we had been in harm's way, we had often repeated a little prayer Norman Vincent Peale composed many years ago. It is in his book, *Imaging*, published by Guideposts of Carmel, New York. It goes like this:

> The light of God surrounds me.
> The love of God enfolds me.
> The power of God protects me.
> The presence of God watches over me.
> Wherever I am, God is!

The rest of the 1980's would hold many surprises for Jo, but these were of a much different kind. There would be sorrows as well. Margaret would soon be unable to help us at the restaurant. Donald would replace Margaret as the cashier and host at Barjo's.

In 1983, the seventh annual Christmas parade sponsored by the Merchants Association was held in November on the Sunday afternoon just after Thanksgiving. The parade had never had a grand marshal. The organizers asked Jo if she would be their "First Grand Marshal." She accepted.

Kenneth Kilgore of Bessey's Motor offered the association a brand new Dodge convertible for Jo to ride in with Kevin Swan of Swan's Supply as her chauffeur. Martha Holden, Jo's niece who owned Woodman's, made two bright yellow felt banners with red and green lettering honoring her as the grand marshal. These were attached to the sides of the convertible. Martha also made a yellow felt flag with "Barjo's" on it for Jo to wave from the beginning to the end of the parade route.

The merchants had Florence Cairns of Family Fabrics make a brilliant scarlet velvet cape trimmed with soft, white fur trim. I got her a fancy pair of snow-white mittens and a lovely white angora knitted cap. Jo laughed about the fact that the merchants had the cape made for her.

"I think they must have thought I was going to wear the pedal pushers I wear in the kitchen for the parade! They just wanted to be sure I was covered up!"

Back in the 1940's, Cliff Davis, who owned the grocery store across the street from Barjo's, and Merle Wade had bought her a pair of bloomers. To prove to them that she could take a joke, Jo had worn them when she washed the front windows in the dining room. I think these folks had the same thing in mind.

I served dinner with one of the school kids during the parade, while Jo entertained the community in her fancy get-up.

There were several thousand people along the parade route from the high school to Advertiser Square. Jo was greeted with cheers and shouts.

"Hello, Jo!"

"How 'ya doing, Jo!"

She sat up straight as a die on the back of the convertible and vigorously waved her flag to acknowledge all her friends and customers.

"I just love my red velvet cape," she said mischievously, "and I want you to know that no one else can ever have it to wear because it was made especially for me. I'm going to wear it when I'm buried!" she told me.

"I had a ball!" Jo exclaimed. "I saw hundreds of my friends and customers."

The misfortune of ill health would hit Jo's family again. This time it would be at Donald's home. Back in 1980, Mildred had suffered a stroke that affected her short-term memory. Donald seldom left her side now. He had his mail and groceries delivered to the house. Many times we took meals to their home to help Don out with the cooking.

One noontime in the spring of 1984, I got an unusual call at the restaurant from him. "Can you bring Margaret up to the house to stay with Mildred?" he asked. "I need to go to the hospital but I can't leave her alone."

"I'll be right there," I assured him.

I knew that it had to be an emergency for him to call. Turning to Jo, I explained. Stepping to the dining room door, I beckoned Margaret. She came rushing down the aisle and into the kitchen.

"Hurry up," Jo said in a worried voice. "Emily, don't you dare let Don drive if he is so sick he needs to go to the hospital."

When Margaret and I arrived, Don's face was gray and he was gasping for breath. He thought that he had passed out, but he wasn't even sure. As sick as he was, he still thought he could drive himself to the hospital, but I knew better.

I got him into my car and drove to the hospital just as fast as

I dared. I realized after I got to the hospital that the smart thing would have been to call the ambulance. But at the time, all I could think of was how fast I could get him there. He was so weak when we arrived that the nurses had to take him out of my car.

The doctors found that he needed to have a pacemaker, but he still thought he was going to be able to go right back home. They finally convinced him he had to stay in the hospital for the operation. We made arrangements for Margaret to stay with Mildred while he recovered.

After Donald's immediate health problems were solved, he was able to continue to care for Mildred at home. But that summer, on August 4, 1984, Mildred passed away at age 78, after having a massive heart attack.

That same year, Margaret had two back surgeries at Central Maine Medical Center in Lewiston. Her first surgery was in June. After that, she was still able to help at Barjo's, but on a limited basis. She continued to do the bookkeeping. After the second surgery in September, she had to use a walker. This made it impossible for her to work at the restaurant, but she still took care of all the banking and did the bookkeeping from her home.

After Mildred's death, Donald, who had retired as Norway's town manager eleven years earlier, offered to help at the restaurant. In September, he took Marg's place as host and cashier and continued until the restaurant was closed in January, 1991.

Jo's mother hadn't lived to see it, but things had come full circle. It had been a long time, but now her three children, Donald, Margaret and Jo were once again working together in the operation of the restaurant.

Every morning, Don went to the bank and picked up the night deposit bag for Margaret. She counted out the kitty for the day's business and then made out the deposit. We sent all Margaret's meals to her from the restaurant because it was no longer safe for her to go near the stove to do any cooking.

In the morning, I took her breakfast to her and helped her get ready for the day. Later, Donald brought her lunch from Barjo's and then took the deposits to the Norway Savings Bank. After he had his supper, he brought Margaret's to her. She still insisted on staying alone, which worried Jo. She realized it wasn't safe.

"It was a very sad day for us all when Margaret had to give up work at the restaurant. For the first time since 1942, she had to let the accountants help her with the payroll accounts," Jo said in a sad voice. "She was very disturbed that she could no longer do what she felt was her share. I missed Marg a lot and I knew how much the customers loved her and what an asset she was to the dining room."

In the summer of 1986, Norway celebrated its bicentennial. After Mildred's death in 1984, Donnie had returned home from Ann Arbor, Michigan, to be with his father. He took a two-year sabbatical from his hospital work as a chaplain to write several books on the history of the town of Norway. These books, *Bound by Memories' Ties, Norway in the Forties*, and an updated copy of the History of the Town of Norway, were published to coincide with the town's celebrations. Father Don was also co-chair of the bicentennial committee and helped organize all the events.

To do our part, Barjo's waitresses wore gowns of the 1700's with white pinafores and small caps of that time period.

During the bicentennial parade on Saturday, Barjo's closed so all of us could be in the parade. The entire Main Street was blocked off for the duration of the parade. Because it was over two miles long, the parade extended from Norway Lake to South Paris with hundreds of people participating. Many businesses and organizations made floats to depict the historical significance of Norway's past.

Jo, in her famous red velvet cape and sporting a new summer cap, rode along the parade route with Jerry Twitchell in his dune buggy. He was a former science teacher at Hebron Academy.

"I'd ridden with Jerry on the back of his motorcycle in the past," Jo exclaimed with a laugh, "but, that day he was crazier than ever. I thought he was going to drive us right into the crowd several times. He was one of Stony's classmates, so we'd been good friends for years. That day everybody had a blast!"

The entire Barjo's crew rode in the back of a pick-up truck, which sported two six-foot wooden road signs, designed especially for Barjo's, attached to the sides. The waitresses, all dressed in their floor-length, bright plaid gingham gowns and white pinafores sat in the back. I was the chauffeur and wore in a long-sleeved white shirt with a bright red bow tie, knickers with red, white, and blue suspenders, and a chauffeur's cap.

There was also a boat parade on Lake Pennessewassee so all the summer residents could participate. It was a wonderful week for every one in Norway.

During the 1980's, Jo continued to promote the restaurant industry and the National Restaurant Association. During

October, National Restaurant Month, everybody joined in the fun. Barjo's girls were dressed up with red aprons bearing the National Restaurant motto with sharp-looking Sailor hats with red and blue ribbons embossed with the NRA slogan.

Her policy of buying the 4-H lambs at the fair had grown to be a highlight of the fall season for the whole community. Several weeks before the fair, we often got a call or a letter reminding her of the date and time of the 4-H Lamb Auction.

"All the boys at Oxford Foods, Jordan's Meats, and Kirschner Foods wanted to be sure I was there," Jo commented. "They loved to bid against me, because they all knew that I'd buy the Grand Champion pen of lambs, no matter what the price. One year I paid $6.50 a pound live weight for that pen of three lambs."

On the third Sunday of October, 4-H Lamb Sunday had become an even larger event than Mother's Day, which is considered the biggest day of the year for the restaurant industry. The restaurant was mobbed from the time we opened at 10:30 a.m. until we closed in the evening.

Jo was 80 years old in 1984 when the parking lot was sold. She had also listed Barjo's with Maine Business Brokers, Mr. and Mrs. Willie Cameron who had sold her other real estate. They held several meetings with Jo, our accountants and me to go over the financial papers of the restaurant. After some discussion, we decided on a price of $250,000. Several offers were made, but raising the money to buy the restaurant seemed to be a problem for the buyers. The banks were not any more cooperative than they had been when I had tried in the late 1960's.

Some people from Connecticut offered to make a down payment of $50,000.00 and have Jo hold a mortgage herself for the rest. She knew nothing about these people and didn't want to get involved in that kind of an arrangement at her age.

Another young couple was from a local family. They wanted to buy Barjo's in the worst way. The girl was a manager at a restaurant in the Fryeburg area, and the young man was a cook there. Neither of them could borrow the money from the banks, but they both were excellent workers and probably could have been a successful team. Again, the problem was in the financing, and they wanted Jo to hold the entire mortgage.

"I would have loved to help them if I could have. But with my responsibilities to my own family and given my age, I knew that I couldn't. That was something even you never asked me to do," Jo told me.

Even though Donald was helping in the dining room, without

Margaret to share the responsibilities, I could see that everything seemed like a big challenge to Jo.

After having owned P. Y.'s cottage on Lake Pennesseewassee since the early 1930's, Jo decided it was time to sell. Barbara and Henry had built a home with a swimming pool on Crockett Ridge in Norway that they called the "Oslo." Her grandchildren were grown up and had families of their own. Because we were too busy at Barjo's, we hadn't been able to go there for many years.

In 1984, she sold the cottage with its 400-foot frontage on the lake to a Massachusetts couple for $78,000. The deep water in front of the cottage was a perfect place for them to land their seaplane when coming from their Massachusetts home.

"Did you have regrets about selling the cottage?" someone asked her.

"Well, of course I did. It was the one thing that P.Y. had been able to save when he ran into financial problems in the early 1930's. I always kept it for that reason," Jo said. And in her practical way, she added, "I thought the grandchildren would like it, but no one is using it. I am too old to enjoy it myself and I thought now was the best time to sell."

In the morning of the day the final papers were to be signed, Jo's grandson, Robbie, went to the cottage and took a bed out of one of the bedrooms. He wanted this memento of his childhood times at the cottage. Unfortunately, the bed caused some problems for the deal and for Robbie!

Even though the furniture there hadn't been mentioned in the legal papers, the people had assumed at it was part of the deal. At 5:00 p.m. that day, Donnie went to the lawyer's office as Jo's representative. He had to do some tall talking to convince the buyers that nothing wrong had been done by the bed being removed. Looking over the contract they found that he was right.

"I never told Robbie that he could take that bed, but the kids always thought anything I had they were free to take. They all knew that I never said *no* to them," Jo explained.

That day, the bed caused Robbie as many problems as it did Jo. He parked the pick-up at the back door of the cottage while he went upstairs to get the bed. When he came back down, the truck had rolled through the huge trees that surrounded the building and into the lake. He went running down the embankment to try to retrieve the truck before it sank into the deep water. He tried to tie a piece of rope around the back bumper to stop it from sinking from sight. As he ran, he tripped and broke his leg. Not wanting to upset his grandmother, he tried to crawl up the camp road to the Greenwood Road for help. The cottage was about five miles from Norway village off the Greenwood Road.

When Robbie had been gone longer than his friend Bob Brown thought he should have been, he went to look for him. He found him about half a mile from the cottage crawling up the camp road.

"When I found out what had happened," Jo said, "I told Robbie don't worry about the truck. That's a minor detail, but be sure you look after that leg."

She called a local wrecker and had them pull the truck out of the lake. It was completely submerged by the time they got there and was beyond repair.

Jo was invited to be the first Grand Marshal of the annual Merchants Association Christmas Parade in 1983.

In 1986, Jo was featured again, in the Fourth of July Parade. Shown here with Si Twitchell.

PART VIII

Horizons Beyond Jo's Wildest Dreams

*Jo's favorite Celtics player, Kevin McHale (kneeling), and Jo (standing at full height!),
February 1990, Boston Garden.*

Jo with her fellow 1989-1990 "Salut au Restauranteur" Award honorees.

March 1990, Wakulla Springs, Florida
Emily and Jo posed with the captain after their riverboat tour.

CHAPTER 35

Unique Experiences for Jo

Several exceptional events occurred for Jo in 1989 and 1990. The first came in 1989 when the Maine Restaurant Association named her the first "Maine Restaurateur of Year." Next, the local police officers gave her a trip to a Boston Celtics game on February 28, 1990. Then, she went on a trip to Florida in March to accept the prestigious "Salut Au Restaurateur Award" from Florida State University.

On April 3, 1989, Jo went to Portland to accept the "Maine Restaurateur of the Year" award at the Maine Restaurant Association's annual banquet. She closed Barjo's for the day so all of us could go with her. She also invited Mary Delameter, her favorite reporter from the Lewiston *Sun*, to accompany us on the trip. This required special permission, willingly granted, from the *Sun* and also the Portland *Press Herald*.

"I haven't been down here in 40 years," said Jo as she stood outside the grand ballroom of the Sonesta Hotel waiting for the ceremonies to begin.

The business she started in 1932 with Don and Margaret had kept her close to home. Barjo's was the longest-operating restaurant in Maine owned continuously by the same owner.

The Maine Restaurant Association tribute to Jo included a slide presentation, which showed the restaurant from the 1930's to the present day. When introduced to accept the award, Jo received a standing ovation from the audience.

Carl Sanford of the Maine Restaurant Association cited her "outstanding achievement, unselfish devotion to her community and the highest interests of her profession" as the reason for her selection for the award. This was the first time the Maine Restaurant Association had given this distinguished award.

Jo was more used to being behind the scenes than in front of an audience. After a brief thank-you and acknowledgment of her honor, she turned the microphone over to her nephew, Donnie, who introduced her family and employees seated in the room.

Shunning the limelight, she had requested to be seated not at the head table but with us.

Besides Donnie, other family members attending the event were Barbara and Henry; her three granddaughters: Andrea Tucker and her husband, Ben III; Joline (Jody) Paradis and her friend, Joe Baker; Darcy and her husband, Danny McCabe; and her grandson, Robert Paradis and his wife, Lynn. Unfortunately, Jo's brother, Donald, and her sisters, Margaret, Grace and Helen were unable to attend this festive celebration.

Jo also brought her employees to the ceremony. They included Veda Taker of South Paris, who had been employed at the restaurant since 1946, Gloria Day of Norway, a 20-year employee, Jeanne Morrissette of Harrison, Judy Ripley of South Paris, Christopher Brackett of Norway, Mike Webber of South Paris, Robert Hill of Norway and me.

"Jo can't ever remember missing a day of work," said Donnie.

"Try to keep up with her, that's all I can say!" put in Carl Sanford, the Executive Secretary of the Maine Restaurant Association.

"Over the years we've fed an awful lot of people, old and young people alike," Jo commented.

"Jo has a tender heart," Donnie said.

"It makes you feel good to help someone and see them help themselves," she replied.

"Aunt Jo has been a counselor and mediator for at least half of the kids in town," Donnie confirmed. "We used to call her 'Doctor Anthony.' Today that would be like calling her 'Dear Abby..'"

"And they have helped us as much as we've helped them," Jo quickly added.

"She's truly a benefactor to the young and the old," Carl Sanford commented.

Later that month, Oxford County Senator Donald Twitchell, accompanied by Representative Joseph Walker of Norway, on behalf of the Legislature and the people of the State of Maine (by Act of the Maine State Legislature), also recognized her achievement as the oldest restaurateur in the state. They presented Jo with a dark blue folder containing a Certificate of Special Recognition adorned with the Maine State Seal embossed in gold.

The annual publication, "Who's Who of Women Executives" honored Jo by including a resume of her life and accomplishments in the 1989-1990 edition. They sent her a wall plaque and a copy of the book, which were both displayed at Barjo's and are now at our Deering Street home.

In the fall of 1989, I received a call from Carl Sanford, telling me that Jo was being nominated by them for the "Salut Au Restaurateur" award at Florida State University. I was told that Department of Hospitality Administration Director, Walter Ashcraft, would call me with a list of guidelines and questions regarding Josephine Stone and Barjo's Restaurant.

I had to keep the entire process of the nomination a secret because I knew Jo didn't like being in the spotlight and would put an end to it if she found out what was going on. I didn't want to give her the chance to tell me "no!" Yet I felt strongly that Jo deserved recognition for her achievements and I loved the prospect of surprising her with a *fait accompli!*

Trying to keep all my telephone calls and exchanges of letters about this award from Jo was a challenge! It helped that she disliked answering the phone. So, at first, I worked with the executive secretary of the Maine Restaurant Association and his secretary by phone. That was the easy part.

When I collected the mail, I had to remove every letter from Florida before we looked over the mail together. There were quite a few exchanges of information before I learned that Jo had, indeed, been chosen as one of the seven businesspeople in the country who would be presented with the "Salut au Restauranteur" award the following March in Florida.

In the meantime, at our Christmas party in 1989, the local police had planned their own surprise. All the officers knew that she loved basketball. In the backroom of the restaurant, they had many discussions with her about their favorite team, the Boston Celtics, and their games.

"For years and years and years and years, Jo Stone has always been good to the cops—she's fed us as part of a benevolent society of her own for law enforcement," Larry Sanborn said, expressing his appreciation for her. "It's time to give her a treat she'll always remember!"

They knew, from having many discussions with her about their favorite basketball team, that Jo loved the Celtics. Kevin McHale and Danny Ainge were her favorite players, and the boys were forever kidding her because Larry Bird wasn't in her select group. She thought this star player lay on the floor in front of the bench too much and didn't play enough minutes in a game.

As a Christmas present, the local officers bought tickets for Jo and me to go to a game on February 28, 1990. The gift included the officers taking us out to dinner at the Hill Top Steak House on the way to the game as well as a guided tour of the city. The excursion was a gift from the officers of the Norway and South Paris police departments, which had benefited from her longtime tradition of feeding patrolmen while they are on duty. We were to be accompanied by Dane Tripp and his son, Shawn, Ernest Dunham, Larry Sanborn, Alan Afflerbach, and Paris Police Chief, Lloyd "Skip" Herrick who was also the driver of the van. It was a donation from Kenneth Kilgore of Bessey Motors in South Paris as his part in the festivities.

By the first of February, Jo had uncovered the plans I'd put in place for the 'Salut au Restauranteur' award. Up to this point, she had remained unsuspicious because she never expected recognition for her life's work.

One of the requirements for the award from Florida State University was that Jo must accept it in person. And she didn't want to disappoint the police officers who had gone to all the trouble of getting tickets to the Boston Celtics game to treat her. In order for us to go on these two trips, Jo made the unprecedented decision that the Barjo's would be closed from February 27 to March 16, 1990.

It would be Jo's first trip to Boston in 50 years. The last time had been a very sad occasion for her as she had gone to Deaconess Hospital to see P. Y. Fogg. She had been told that there was no hope for him to recover. By the time she returned home that day in 1940, she had to go to the railroad station in South Paris to meet the train bringing his body home for burial.

In 1990, the trip would be a much happier one.

"I've been wanting a long ride and I am sure going to get it today!" she said to me.

Officer Alan Afflerbach of Norway said he would always remember the moment they started out of town that Wednesday afternoon, when Jo turned to me excitedly and said, "Emily, we're *really* going!"

During the ride from Maine, Jo enjoyed seeing the major changes on the route—like how the former Howard Johnson's restaurants along the turnpike were now Burger Kings.

"Well, I'm telling you something," she said, "there are 5 million cars on each side of us! There are a million cars ahead of us! I don't think anybody lives *in* the city, they all get *out!*"

The officers chauffeured us around Boston during the afternoon to see hospitals, universities, the state capital building,

Fenway Park and the U.S.S. Constitution.

"You could get lost in there awful quick," said Jo.

Jo also got to see several historic sites—none of which she had ever seen—besides "Old Ironsides." These included the governor's house, Boston Common, the Public Gardens, the Old North Church and Haymarket Square. They even took us down through the slums and the Combat Zone. It was quite a tour.

When we got to Boston Garden, Jo's eyes were as big as saucers. Entering the lobby, we didn't know where to go. Turning to me, she asked, "Do you know where we are? *I* sure don't!"

"Right this way, Jo!" the boys said, leading us deep into the building. Suddenly, there outside the team's locker room, Jo's favorite Celtics player, Kevin McHale was waiting to greet her.

"Oh, my *goodness!*" Jo squealed (—"Just like a six-year-old!" Alan said later).

This meeting was a surprise. The officers had the arrangements all made with the Celtics trainer to take her directly to the locker room and had mentioned Jo's love for McHale and how unimpressed she was with Bird.

When McHale bent his 6-foot-11-inch frame to hug Jo, who stands just barely 5-feet tall, his first words were, "I hear you're the lady from Maine."

He told Jo, "My mother's called Josephine, so I'm partial to that name. I am also from 'the woods'—in Minnesota."

"Oh, he was *handsome*," Jo who had been a Celtics fan since 1950, said later.

While we were all standing there, Jo told the boys, "We can't be bothering him!" referring to McHale.

"Jo was important enough to us to bother him," Larry Sanborn said. What he admires in Jo, he added, is "the free spirit of giving, the constant giving, no desire for any self-recognition."

McHale signed a Celtics yearbook for her and presented her with a team shirt autographed by all the players while Dane Tripp and Alan Afflerbach took lots of pictures. McHale, though he was down on one knee beside her, was the same height as Jo!

Suddenly, Bird opened the locker room door and gave Jo a real hard time! He said, "I hear you're talking bad about me!"

Overcome, Jo turned all red and squealed with laughter.

"I got to admit that Bird looked handsome," Jo said. "He's got the best figure of anybody on the team."

We got to sit right in back of the Celtics bench during the game and saw their coach, Chris Ford, right up close. "I hope they fire him," said Jo, opinionated as ever when it came to her favorite game.

When we got home, the boys had a photo made up and framed as a surprise memento of her once-in-a-lifetime Boston trip. It truly was a memorable treat.

In March, Jo and Barjo's were recipients of the "Salut Au Restaurateur" Award at Florida State University in Tallahassee, Florida.

On a sunny morning, March 10, 1990, Donnie drove Jo and me to Portland Jetport where we boarded a Delta Jet to Tallahassee, Florida. It was an exciting and unusual day in the life of Jo Stone who, for nearly 60 years, had seldom left her restaurant kitchen!

Jo, Donnie and I were traveling first class and were only several rows behind the plane's kitchen facilities. Jo was fascinated by the way the food was served on the aircraft. She was too busy watching the flight attendants prepare meals and snacks to gaze at the puffy, white clouds beneath the jet. As I watched her, she seemed to be critiquing the food, the service and hospitality to see how the compact flying restaurant-type operation was done. When the stewardess served us breakfast, Jo was amazed at the efficiency at 40,000 feet in the air.

We flew over the Blue Ridge Mountains and into Atlanta International Airport where we changed to a smaller plane. As we shuttled across the airport, Jo could hardly believe the size of the place, which seemed like a city in itself.

"You get there before you start!" Jo said matter-of-factly of her first plane ride. "I didn't think about it beforehand. I made up my mind before I ever got on that plane that I was going to accept the idea of flying."

When we got into town, Donnie had already made arrangements for a rental car, so Jo and I waited in the lobby of the airport while he got our luggage and the automobile to go to the Radisson Hotel in downtown Tallahassee.

"What a unique way to unload our suitcases," she said of the conveyor belt that brought our luggage from the belly of the plane.

Shortly after we got to the hotel, Barbara and Henry met us there. They had driven up from their condo in Pompano Beach, about 400 miles away.

The Radisson reflected the warmth, grace and charm of the Old South while offering all the luxuries of today. Located in the heart of Historic Downtown, within walking distance of the State Capitol, it offered us a serene and elegant environment for our special trip.

Having been a hotel owner herself, Jo noticed many things at the hotel. The luxurious carpeting, furnishings and elegant foliage plants. The professional elegance of the rooms which had been designed with business executives in mind. The suites included room service, evening turndown service, a complimentary newspaper and wake up calls every morning.

Sunday morning, March 11, the five of us decided to do a little sightseeing. The first event at Florida State University wasn't until 6:00 p.m. that evening. We decided to take a trip to St. George Island in the Gulf of Mexico. It was a beautiful day and the long, narrow island of St. George Island State Park contained more than nine miles of undeveloped beaches and dunes. The park had forests of pines and oaks and a bay with sandy coves and salt marshes.

That evening, the Florida State University held a reception in a dining room that had been decorated to look like a tropical garden. After the reception, we ate dinner at an Italian restaurant. It was Henry's birthday and the restaurant had a team of singing waiters who serenaded him.

Two full days of activities were scheduled for the Maine delegation. Each "Salut Au Restaurateur" award recipient had been assigned a student host who would be our guide for all the festivities at the University.

"It was a lot different life than we were used to," Jo observed, "but I kept right up with them."

Monday was a full day of activities at the University. Our student host met us at 8:00 a.m. for a continental breakfast prepared by a student team. The tables were spread with many kinds of fruits, juices, breads of all varieties and many different kinds of coffee. The buffet table had a gorgeous ice carving of a basket filled with real fruit.

"Look at all the work these kids have done! They must have been up all night to prepare this beautiful smorgasbord," Jo said.

All the "Salut Au Restaurateurs" honorees participated in a panel discussion, "Share Your Success." Shunning the limelight as usual, Jo had asked Donnie to make the Barjo's presentation for her. She also asked me to stay by her side to help her answer students' questions during the panel discussion.

Donnie opened his presentation by noting that the restaurant had been started in the 1930's with only $300 working capital borrowed from Jo's life insurance policy. He told how she had made her own ice cream using cream from local farmers and native fruits in season and how it was frozen by hand using salt and ice. He described the many different ways chicken had been served during World War II because meat was scarce due to rationing, and how, during the 1940's, the Portland Pipeline crews had laid a pipeline from Portland harbor to Montreal and generated much needed business at Barjo's.

Donnie's talk included descriptions of changes in menu selections through the years and specific programs Jo had supported such as the 4-H Lamb Auction, followed by the Grand Champion 4-H Lamb Sunday at Barjo's during National Restaurant Month in October. The restaurant's participation in special events surrounding the Norway Bicentennial were also mentioned.

He mentioned the many school programs, such as the 20 years the Head Start children had been entertained by the restaurant and the students of OHHS Vocational Region XI who worked at Barjo's as a part of their curriculum at the school. He also cited her employment over the years of high school students who lived at the Hotel Stone and worked at the restaurant. He described what an integral part of the community Jo was and how she donated numerous banquets for area high school classes and clubs and had led the way in combining the two towns of Norway and South Paris as one region, paving the way for a regional school system. Donnie finished by telling how Jo had just been named the first Maine Restaurateur of the Year and was proprietor of the oldest restaurant in the state of Maine under the same ownership.

Students asked pertinent questions of each panelist about their business. Each restaurant had submitted copies of their daily, special occasion, children's and cocktail menus, as well as histories (biographies) of their professional careers with photos of their restaurants, both interior and exterior views. Each participant's materials also included lists of civic activities and services.

Because Jo was the oldest restaurant owner of the group, the other guests also asked many questions. One was, "How did you survive going into business during the Great Depression? Most businesses were failing while yours succeeded."

"I probably was in bankruptcy many times, but I didn't know it," she replied. "Back then, all I thought about was how I was going to be able to pay my bills. How I could continue to serve the public to the best of my ability was always my priority."

During a half-hour break we got acquainted with the other restaurateurs and viewed exhibits. Jo's student host gave us a tour of the University's Food Service Department.

After lunch, Jo and the other award recipients were inducted into the "Society of Hosts" established in 1857, a special honor for all restaurateurs. They came from all over the country, from

Maine to Florida, including Massachusetts, the Carolinas, Michigan, and Pennsylvania. Janet Finlayson of Belize was the only other woman inducted. Several honorees, from Tennessee and Wisconsin, were from the previous year, but had been unable to attend, so received the award with Jo.

The highlight event was the Monday night Awards Banquet featuring a ten-course banquet. It was a sumptuous meal and a fitting end to our exciting week. The menu included: Fresh Pea Soup, Scallops in Wine Sauce, Champagne Orange Sorbet, Snapper with Mustard Sauce, Asparagus with Hollandaise, Parsley New Potatoes, Spinach and Endive with Poppyseed Dressing, Peach Liqueur, Southern Pecan Coffee, and Poached Peach with Strawberry Mousse.

On Tuesday, March 13, we took the opportunity to do more sightseeing as we would return to Maine on Wednesday and Barbara and Henry would be driving back to Pompano Beach.

In the morning, we had breakfast in the hotel dining room and then decided to go to Wakulla Springs State Park where the "Tarzan" movies were all filmed. The tour included a boat ride.

Jo turned to our riverboat captain and said, "I would be honored if you would have your picture taken with me walking up to the board walk." He agreed. When we returned to the dock, he helped us from the boat and Jo and I had our picture taken with him. Then all of us had our pictures taken on the boardwalk by the Riverboats.

Our next stop was a visit to the Alfred B. Maclay Botanical Gardens in Tallahassee. Everything was in full bloom and the scenic view was marvelous.

When we got out of the car, Jo looked at me and said, "I don't know about you, but even if this is a beautiful place, I'm not really impressed with the idea of having to do a lot of walking."

I agreed. She wasn't used to walking outside and she was 86 years old. And after I had been paralyzed in 1979, my right leg wasn't very strong. Uneven ground like the footpaths of the gardens didn't look inviting to me either.

After a half-hour walk through the gardens, we came to the Maclay house. We were ready to rest while Henry and Donnie took pictures. Jo, Barbara and I sat on the porch, while Donnie and Henry took pictures of the park, the house and Lake Hall. Then we went together for a tour of the house.

Throughout the various paths in the Botanical Gardens and by the pools, many benches had been placed so visitors could sit and enjoy the different gardens with their unique designs. One thing that amazed us was how much of the flora and fauna was familiar to us from Maine. But we also found a different path and saw more exotic foliage and flowering shrubbery.

After walking on meandering flag stone paths for over two hours, we found a stone bench beside one of the pools. There we stopped to rest before finishing our walk back to the car.

As we left the park, we drove back to the hotel by a new route. We saw quite a different section of the northern Florida peninsula as well as the suburbs of Tallahassee.

That evening, we enjoyed an excellent dinner at the hotel dining room. Barbara and Henry were leaving early in the morning for their drive to Pompano Beach. We were taking a morning flight back to Maine.

On the flight home, our sightseeing continued as we flew over the U.S. Capitol, the White House, and the Pentagon. The late afternoon lights were beautiful and showed the buildings in all their grandeur. Jo had never seen the Pentagon or the Capitol Building and was truly amazed by their splendor.

"No wonder, the kids wanted me to see Washington!" she exclaimed to me as she peered out the window.

We flew into Boston in the early evening but the weatherman wasn't cooperating very well. A heavy fog was closing over the airport. Some planes were grounded and many were delayed. The tower allowed ours to leave Logan, but, after circling several times, it was the last one to land that night at the Portland Jetport. This was the only part of our trip that was rough.

"Well," Jo said to me as the plane finally touched down on the runway, "I survived that plane ride. But I think it will be my first, last and only one. Until an hour ago, it wasn't bad, but that landing was pretty bumpy."

"You're kind of funny sometimes," I said to her. "Remember when you sent me to Chicago when I was 19? I hadn't ever been on an airplane and I had to change planes three times. I've been right by your side all the way on this trip—quite a lot different from what you expected of me."

As we started our ride to Norway, the fog was thick. Thank goodness, Donnie had the responsibility of driving, not me.

"Aunt Jo, you were a real trooper and seemed to enjoy every minute of your trip," he said afterwards.

"Well, I had a wonderful time, but I'm glad to be back home!" she replied.

Jo was looking forward to reopening the restaurant Thursday morning, St. Patrick's Day. The girls decorated the dining room with shamrocks while she got right to work making pies and I peeled vegetables for the corned beef and cabbage, a Barjo tradition. By 9:00 a.m. we had everything ready for dinner.

"I was awfully anxious to open up. I got into the swing before we even opened the door," Jo said. "We were overrun with customers filing through the kitchen all day extending congratulations and welcoming us back home."

The customers were all very glad to see us back. My silver-haired friend with sparkling blue eyes obviously enjoyed having her red butcher's apron on again and greeting her customers after her exotic trip to receive the honor.

"We've always made fun out of having to work," she said, making light as usual of all the congratulations. "We always make everybody who comes through that door welcome, that's all."

At the Barjo's Christmas Party, 1988, held at the Country Way, Jo's great-granddaughter posed with her in front of the Christmas tree with Emily and Donald. Examining the photo later with Emily, four-year-old Katherine Tucker demonstrated that Jo's traits have been passed on. "I'm the manager, Nana Jo is the owner, you are the cook, and Uncle Donald is the cashier," she said. "That makes me the boss!"

Margaret in her customary position at the cash register at Barjo's. In later years she ran the cash and kept up the book-keeping even after she was unable to work the floor. Donald, who came back after Mildred's death, kept the restaurant in flowers like these magnificent gladiolas from his garden.

Jo's great-grand-children in 1988:

Jody's son, John, (L) Andrea's son, Ben and Robbie's sons, Scott (R) and Nick (sitting), and Andrea's daughter, Katherine.

CHAPTER 36

Sad Days Ahead

By 1990, Margaret was 81 years old and had been unable to work in the dining room at Barjo's for over five years due to her back problems. After her two surgeries in 1984, she used a walker. Even though getting about was difficult, Margaret insisted on living alone in her Deering Street home. She continued to do the bookkeeping for the restaurant, a tremendous help to Jo.

Two weeks after we returned from Florida, on April 2, 1990, Margaret fell in her home. Over the past five years, Margaret's beautician, Edwina, had come to her home regularly to do her hair. That Tuesday afternoon, Edwina had set her hair and seated Margaret in her dryer chair. She told Margaret she was going to do some errands while her hair dried and would be back shortly to comb it out. Always an immaculate housekeeper, Margaret noticed that the beautician had spilled some water on the kitchen floor. Because it was difficult for her to walk, Margaret tried to reach over the side of her chair to wipe up the water with a towel. In the process, she fell forward, then onto her side.

Fortunately for Margaret, Barjo's was closed on Tuesdays and Jo's home was nearby. Painfully, Marg crawled into the living room and reached the telephone.

"Can you come right over?" Margaret asked Jo. "I've fallen and I don't know how bad I have been hurt. I heard a crunching sound in my leg and hip as I hit the kitchen floor."

"Don't move," Jo told her. "We'll be right there."

As we hurried across the street to Margaret's, Jo turned to me and said, "You know I have expected something like this to happen. I never should have listened when Marg wanted to stay alone. I feel responsible because I didn't insist that she have someone living with her."

Margaret's home was a short walk, so we got there quickly. When we saw how badly she was hurt, we called an ambulance.

"While we were waiting for the rescue team," Jo said, "the only thing Marg asked for was a cigarette. I knew she must be in a lot of pain, but she didn't admit it. Maybe she thought the cigarette would help her relax." Margaret had smoked cigarettes for many years but Jo never had and thought it was a bad habit.

It has always puzzled us about that afternoon, for it was the last time Marg ever asked for a cigarette. After she got to the hospital and had surgery to repair her hip, she never again mentioned smoking.

When the ambulance came, the crew put her on a stretcher after examining her leg and hip. They told us they thought that her hip was broken and took her to Stephens Memorial Hospital.

Two weeks later, Margaret called her family to the hospital and told them she had decided to go to Ledgeview Nursing Home in West Paris. The doctor had told her she needed to receive around-the-clock nursing care. At the time, we all thought her stay would be only until her hip healed, but sadly, she was never able to return home.

Jo had been trying to sell the restaurant for several years. It had been listed with the Camerons who had sold the hotel lot, with Thatcher Turner of Maine Business Brokers, and most recently with Biz Realty of Norway. None of these brokers had been able to make a sale. Jo was sure that she could bring Margaret back home if she stopped working at the restaurant. She thought that she and I would be able to take care of Margaret.

But that was never to be, as Margaret's condition continued to deteriorate. We went to the nursing home to see her every Tuesday, but soon she wasn't able to remember who I was and she thought Jo was her mother, not her sister. Donald was given Power-of-Attorney so he could pay her bills at the house and the nursing home.

Of course, after her accident, it was impossible for Margaret to continue the bookkeeping she had done for decades. Austin Associates was hired to do the bulk of it. I was able to handle the cashbook and the bank deposits. Jo was never happy with this setup because she felt nothing was checked as thoroughly as when Margaret had done the books. But it seemed, at the time, to be the only alternative.

We went to Ledgeview to see Margaret every time we had a chance, and always on Tuesday evenings. Even though she seemed vague about who we were, it made us feel as though we were contributing to her care in a small way.

Although she didn't admit it, I knew that Jo was trying to overcome a health problem herself. Jo was 86 years old and even though her family didn't realize it, I knew that she was having trouble with her eyes. This was something she admitted to no one, but I knew that it was hard for her to walk outside without my help. She didn't want me to hold onto her, but the minute we stepped out the door, I would feel her hand on my arm. In the restaurant where everything was in its proper place, she was as confident as ever. There, Jo was doing her baking and handling the grill and fry pots just as she always had.

Since 1989, Jo had noticed that her vision was dimming, but had kept it to herself. By October 1990, it was becoming more apparent how hard it was for her to see.

"I could see just a little around the sides of my eyes and by looking down," Jo said. "Everything else seemed to be a blur and nothing had any color."

One afternoon in the fall, Donald Farr came in to see Jo. He had done a lot of work for her over the years, so he was well acquainted with many of her habits.

"Jo," he said to her, "don't you try to fool me. You are having trouble with your eyes. You need to see an eye doctor."

"Don't be foolish," she replied. "You know how I hate to go to the doctors. I'll be all right."

Another who noticed Jo's problem was Father Colpitts. One Sunday evening he came into the kitchen to visit with us.

As he came through the backdoor, Jo said to Richard, one of the kitchen boys, "Richard, here comes your mother. Are you ready to go home?"

Father Colpitts laughed. "Jo, it's Father not Richard's mother," he said. "What is the matter with you? Couldn't you see that it's me or did you really think I was Richard's mother?"

She laughed, but down deep she knew her secret was out. Father Colpitts didn't joke with her. She knew that he realized now how bad her vision had gotten.

Ben was helping in the kitchen then, and I know he realized that his great-grandmother was having a hard time, too. If he or his sister, Katherine, took her home instead of me, they walked her to her door, too.

Between us, we were finally able to convince her to see Dr. Tere Porter on Alpine Street in Norway. After examining her eyes, he told her that cataracts had formed on both of her eyes. It would require surgery. He sent her to Dr. Reed at the Maine Eye Clinic in Portland for an evaluation.

Dr. Reed told Jo that he would operate on one eye at a time. There would be a three-month waiting period between surgeries to allow the first eye to heal before doing the second. All the blood tests and her physical examination were to be done by her local doctor, Dr. James Eshleman, at Stephens Memorial.

She decided she would keep the restaurant open through the Thanksgiving and Christmas season and have the surgery in January. She would close on the 21st of January and reopen in the spring after her vision had been restored. Dr. Reed scheduled the first operation for January 22nd.

On the morning of the procedure, Jo wanted to leave home at 6:00 a.m. to get to the clinic.

"Why in the world do you want to start so early? Your surgery is scheduled for 8:00!" I said.

"Well, you know me," she replied. "I don't like to be late or to keep anyone waiting. Just maybe, the doctor can take me in early and we can get home sooner."

As usual, she was right. Dr. Reed took her in a half-hour early and started her surgery at 7:30 a.m. I watched the whole procedure on a monitor in the surgical care waiting room. From my vantage point, I could see the doctor making the incisions, removing the cataract, and then inserting the permanent lens in her eye. It took about an hour. After she rested for an hour in the waiting room, Dr. Reed told her to go home and come back the next morning for him to examine her eye. By 10:30 a.m., we were on our way back to Norway.

She turned to me and said, "See what did I tell you! By getting there early, I've had my surgery sooner. Now, we'll be home before noon."

The next day, the doctor told her the operation had been a success and gave her a video of the operation.

"You look like a pirate," I told her, referring to the black patch she had to wear for a week over her eye.

As her chauffeur, my only problem was how afraid she was when we drove on Route 295 going into and out of Portland. Because of her eye patch, she could see the traffic on just one side of the three-lane road. She thought I was going to hit every car on the other side of us. She really isn't a turnpike person! Though I assured her everything was fine, she still felt vulnerable.

In all, we made sixteen trips to Portland for her follow-up check-ups. After three months, Dr. Reed felt the first eye had healed sufficiently for her to use it, so in March, she had glasses fitted by Dr. Porter and was able to see well out of her left eye. Dr. Reed scheduled the second surgery for April 16.

In the meantime, Jo had many decisions to make. One thing that bothered her greatly was the fact that Margaret would never be able to do the bookkeeping again. She determined that her best decision, considering her age of 87, was to sell Barjo's

Restaurant. This was a difficult decision, as the restaurant was her life's work and she had never given any thought to retirement, though she had toyed with selling for years.

She had me call Bob Ivey, a good friend from Norway National Bank, who was now heading the Small Business Administration in Augusta. He had been Executive Vice-President of the bank and lived in Norway.

He suggested that, if she was serious about selling, a public auction was the best way to go. He knew she had been trying to sell Barjo's for several years, but that the realtors hadn't produced a buyer. He suggested two auction houses that worked closely with the SBA, and Jo decided on Dale Folsom of Folsom Auction Service.

First, there were still more decisions to be made. One was what Jo would like to do with Barjo's inventory, which was valued at about $50,000.

As was usually the case, Jo was thinking of how she could help someone else. She gave all the groceries that were of the sizes the Oxford Hills Food Pantry could use to them for needy families in the area. The rest she gave to Barbara and Henry for their inventory at Country Way. She gave supplies of paper goods, cookware, or anything they could use to some local organizations and churches.

But one big question still bothered her: what to do with the dining room china, all in the Syracuse China Dogwood Pattern.

These dishes had a lot of meaning to Jo because of the symbolism of the dogwood pattern. The petals of the dogwood flower are said to signify the cross of Jesus. The red indents in the petals denote the nail holes in Jesus' hands and the center of the flower represents the crown of thorns placed on His head.

The Barjo's dinner service contained enough dishes to serve 300 people. Some were just as they had come from the factory and had never even been unpacked. There was also glassware and silverware.

Donnie, who had been ordained as a Catholic priest in 1971, was serving as chaplain at Mercy Hospital in Portland and on the weekends said several masses at St. Catherine's in Norway. Several times, when the Norway church needed a priest, he had filled in until a new priest could be found.

One afternoon, Donnie and Father Colpitts of Saint Catherine's were talking with Jo. They happened to mention that the church's dishes for their suppers were mismatched. After the new church was built, there was no money left to buy dishes, so, each family in the church had donated a place setting from their own set. When the dining hall was utilized for functions of any size, the church had to use paper plates.

Jo thought to herself, "This would be a perfect place for Barjo's dinner service. The people at Saint Catherine's would truly appreciate the significance of the dogwood pattern, and they would be able to serve public suppers on china instead of having to use paper."

The next day, when Donnie came to see her, she approached him with the idea. He was thrilled! Father Colpitts was tickled to death. They both came with some of their parishioners to Barjo's on a Saturday and packed all the dishes carefully in boxes and moved them to the church.

Father Colpitts had Ray Courcy build beautiful hardwood cabinets at the church rectory. He wanted to be sure that no one could take any of the china as souvenirs of Barjo's and that they would be used only for functions at the church.

"I am keeping the dishes in locked cabinets where no harm can come to them," he told Jo. "You don't know how much I treasure your gift."

Using wholesale price-lists from Burbank, Douglass & Co., the restaurant suppliers in Portland, I recorded the prices for the restaurant quality dishes glasses and silverware. The Syracuse China Dogwood Pattern was the most expensive they sold. Jo's gift was valued at $25,000 and this figure was 80% of the original cost.

"On behalf of the parish family of St. Catherine of Sienna Church and myself," said Father Colpitts to Jo, " I want to thank you for your friendship and kindness to the parish and me. Your goodness will be remembered for many years to come. You have been a big part of Norway's history as you have touched many people with your generous support."

In a thank you note, he wrote, "May you and Emily enjoy the future years as blessings from God for your service. You have lived the Gospel Message, 'I was hungry and you fed me.' Your generous gift will live on in service to this community. We all wish you both many blessings."

In the meantime, Jo's great-grandson, Ben, and I had been working hard to have the place spotless before the auctioneer's inspection tour. We had cleaned everything from the cellar to the attic including all the equipment and the built-in walk-in refrigerator Because of the condition of her eyes, the doctor didn't want Jo around any dust, and when we were cleaning it was pretty dusty. I knew that she really missed coming to help us at the restaurant.

But in a way, it was good she wasn't there to see what was done with a lot of her treasures. Others didn't have the same feeling about her possessions as I did. The restaurant had been her life—and mine. I had misgivings about how many things were disposed of, but under the circumstances, I did my very best to protect her interests.

In late March 1991, Dale Folsom and his son, Matthew, came to see the restaurant and its equipment. After looking over the premises, they estimated it might bring an auction price of at least $150,000.

The closing of Barjo's was an event not just for us but for the town of Norway and the surrounding community. On April 4, I brought Jo to the restaurant so she could talk with John Powers from the local newspaper. When asked what her plans for the future were, Jo was adamant. "Let's get this clear: I'm not retiring. I'm going to do some community service, but I am not retiring."

When he asked about what she had done for others in the past, she said, "No one wants to hear about any of that stuff!"

Sitting in one of the red leatherette booths (complete with its now vintage juke-box selector), he asked Jo to tell him about her life and times. Her memories came flowing back.

She told him of her childhood in East Stoneham and about moving to Norway where her father was the night constable; about her years at Norway High, where, despite her small size, she was known as the most aggressive guard the school basketball team ever had—that's how she acquired her love of the game and became an ardent Celtics fan. She told him how it was working F.P. Stone at Stone's Drug Store where she learned to make ice cream.

When asked about the early days of the restaurant, Jo said, "We started as 'McAllister's' in the Newberry Block and, in 1935, moved to this location. When I took over alone, I changed the name to Barjo's. Margaret worked here for over 50 years. When she retired because of illness, Don came back as cashier and host in the dining room. It's been a family place always."

Her eyes sparkled as she talked about World War II. "It was exciting. The place was always crowded. We had to send the kids home at five so we could serve supper. By seven, they'd be back to spend the rest of the evening. The Opera House across the street was busy with basketball games and other entertainment. There were very few automobiles, so all the kids came to Barjo's afterwards because we were so close by. We'd just push back the tables and they'd dance to the jukebox. We had to send them home at five so we could serve supper. By seven, they'd be back to spend the rest of the evening."

Occasionally, as she talked with the reporter, I verified a comments, but Jo seemed to relish talking about the past. She had some words about the present and future, too.

"When they tell me the town is dying, it just makes me disgusted!" she told him. "Main Street needs people who believe in Main Street. Look at it! There isn't one drug store or grocery store here. I don't mind saying what I think and I let people know how I feel. But folks didn't listen. Maybe now they think I know something about it. This is a great town. It always was and always will be. But you can't be lazy and expect everything to fall into place with no work involved."

The reporter later commented, "I suspect the greatest rewards Jo Stone ever had were from the hearts of the thousands of people whose lives she touched over her many years on Main Street. Jo Stone is what Main Street America is really all about."

Jo's second operation would be done in the same manner as the first, although Dr. Reed used a different kind of lens implant for her right eye. She was a good patient and did everything the doctor told her to to ensure that her eyes healed.

With her surgery date in mind, I talked with the auctioneers. After going over all the details with her, I told Dale Folsom she was ready to sign a contract for the auction. It was set for April 19, just three days after Jo's surgery. I was glad the way things had fallen in place. I don't think Jo would have been able to watch them auctioning off the restaurant. It was better that she stay at home with Barbara and Donnie while Henry and I went to the restaurant with the auctioneers. Barjo's had been their home as children, and they both were upset to see it go on the auction block. As it was, it nearly broke my heart to hear the chanting of the auctioneers as they first offered Barjo's in its entirety and then the contents by numbered lots.

While Folsom was auctioning off the restaurant in its entirety as an operating business, Russell Nealey of South Paris who was the owner of Oxford Bowling bid $90,000. The room was still as no one raised the bid.

Folsom then accepted bids for just the property and then for all the equipment in the restaurant. At the end of that process, Nealey's $90,000 bid remained as the highest. No one showed interest in the property as real estate only. Folsom said that lot bids for the furniture and equipment only totaled some $15,000.

The auction halted while Henry went down to the house to ask Jo about the bid. He returned 10 minutes later with the news that she would not accept the $90,000 bid. Henry told Folsom that Jo wouldn't accept anything under $100,000 for Barjo's. Nealey declined to increase his offer. In the meantime, Ben had been talking with Cheryl Leach.

"Do you know what a good business this is?" he asked her. "You've been working in restaurants all your life. Why don't you buy Barjo's, and I'll help you get started. Andy and I have helped Jo cook, so we know the ropes."

"I had no idea of buying a restaurant today," she protested. "I just wanted to see what kind of a place it was and who was going to buy it. I've got my own job as a waitress at Market Square in South Paris."

"If you want to go into business for yourself, you'll never have a better chance," he said. "Make a bid—see what happens!"

When the auctioneer asked for bids again, she raised her hand with a bid of $100,000. The auctioneer asked once, then twice, for further bids. Cheryl looked around to see if anyone else was participating.

"Going, going, gone!" the auctioneer said as he pounded the table with his gavel. "Cheryl Leach of West Paris is the new proprietor of Barjo's Restaurant in Norway with a bid of $100,00!"

Shaking her head in amazement, and looking at Ben, she said, "I can't believe I let you talk me into buying Barjo's! It's like inheriting Jo Stone's 60-year legacy!"

"I was in disbelief at becoming Barjo's new owner. At first, I didn't feel anything! I just came to see who was going to buy it— I never expected I would be the highest bidder!" she told me.

But when she realized that she'd really bought the restaurant, she smiled and described herself as being "overwhelmed."

After the auction, I had the difficult task of handing over the keys of Barjo's to her. It was like tearing out a piece of my own heart. I had hoped that this day would never come and that when Jo left Barjo's I would continue in her place. But that wasn't to be. My brain surgery in 1979 forced me to take on a completely different itinerary for my life. Now my place would always be by Jo's side, though no longer at the restaurant.

The restaurant was nearly filled for the auction with many long-time acquaintances, customers and friends of Jo's.

"I can't believe Jo is selling Barjo's! Where are we going to eat now?" was a question asked by many of our regulars.

"How sad it is to see the restaurant go under the auctioneer's hammer," one man said to me. "You don't know how much I'll miss seeing you and Jo in the kitchen. It'll never be the same!"

"I wonder what Cheryl is going to do? Do you think she'll

reopen soon?" another couple asked me. "Do you suppose she'll serve the same kind of food?"

I had no answers to all these questions. All I knew was that Jo and I would no longer work those long hours. The restaurant would no longer be the focus and the center of our lives. Though I accepted the necessity of the sale, I was heart-broken and I knew Jo was, too. I knew Jo wasn't as strong as she would like to have everybody think. I don't think anyone gave it a thought that she was, after all, 87 years old.

After they talked with Cheryl, many old customers seemed relieved when they learned of her plans to reopen soon.

Among those who were at the auction to watch and remember were Joyce and Walter Bennett of Oxford, who had both worked at Barjo's, Joyce as a waitress, Walter as a kitchen helper.

Walter, who had worked in the restaurant for 15 years during the 1940's and 1950's, recalled how Jo had helped a lot of kids.

"You know that Jo brought us kids in from the street and gave us jobs," Walter said. "I also remember that around 1940, the upstairs of the building caught fire. When she was forced to close the restaurant that Monday morning, she treated all the neighborhood children to the ice cream in the freezers before it melted."

"I was a waitress at this Norway landmark for many years beginning in 1945," Joyce recalled. "My sister and I worked in the dining room with Barbara. She gave me a lot of responsibility when I was very young. I was taking cash when I was 12. This is one place where many memories have been made and they'll never be forgotten."

Other people sent letters, notes, cards and called our home to express their feelings about the loss of the restaurant.

The sale of Barjo's was concluded June 1st with the issuing of the warranty deed. In the interim, I came to the restaurant to check on things for insurance purposes every day until the final papers were signed.

Cheryl reopened the restaurant in the middle of June. She had decided to operate as a family restaurant for the "same loyal customers" who frequented Barjo's, and who had enjoyed weekday specials and relaxed Sunday dining.

Already this had been quite a year for Jo, but it wasn't over quite yet. While Jo was having her eye surgery and working on the sale of the restaurant, the Norway Merchants Association had been making some plans of their own. With the help of Sheriff Skip Herrick, they wanted to honor Jo in a special way, but they wanted to keep it a secret from her. They checked with me to see how her eyes were progressing and with Barbara to plan a special event when we thought she would be able to enjoy it. It was good to have something to look forward to as I faced this big transition in both our lives.

Main Street Merchants sponsored the celebrations. L—R: Jeanine Dale, Jeanine Stone, Jo, Gary Howe, Emily Foster.

Donald, who shared in many years of Jo's business and community involvement in Norway, joined over 1,000 others in congratulating his sister on Jo Stone Day. Jo lost her bet with him that no more than 50 people would show up that day!

Jo Stone Day 1991 included many of Jo's favorite things: horses, appreciative customers, friends, family wonderful food at Country Way. It was a great satisfaction to the organizers that the town-wide celebrations were kept secret nearly to the end!

The guest of honor was carried to the party by horse and carriage. She was chauffeured home in Bob Bahre's 1932 Chrysler Convertible.

CHAPTER 37

Jo Stone Day

In June 1991, the sale of Barjo Restaurant was complete. After nearly 60 years, Jo would no longer devote all her waking hours to the restaurant. Her eye surgery was behind her and she could now enjoy her surroundings. She loved to have me take her for a ride in the rural area surrounding Norway and South Paris.

"Emily," she said to me, "just see how green the trees are and the beautiful colors of all the flowering shrubs. I didn't realize how much I have been missing. Everything looked so dull and drab. My eyes must have been a lot worse than I thought they were. Now everything looks so fresh and bright!"

Because we always had worked such long hours at Barjo's, we hadn't seen all the changes taking place on all sides of Norway. On our afternoon rides, Jo couldn't believe all the new construction in the community. Many of the farms in the area were now housing developments. Numerous new roads had been built not far from us. As we explored, we were surprised that we had missed so much.

Of course, Jo's first priority in this new chapter of our lives was that we clean our house from top to bottom. Ben helped me do the initial work because of her eyes. After that, she quickly established a routine that included a certain day of the week for each room of the house to be cleaned. She still maintains this routine today.

Now we could enjoy our home. Even though Jo had owned the house since 1961, she hadn't had the opportunity to appreciate it fully. Instead of just sleeping there, now we could sit on the sun porch and watch television or visit with friends. Now I could read to her without having to meet the restaurant's deadlines. We had time to enjoy our Bible study together. Her deep faith in God had never wavered. But she wanted to learn more by having me read books to her to help us deepen our knowledge of the Bible. In 1979, God had saved my life, so I was an eager student and willingly obliged. We spent many pleasant days and evenings in our new, more relaxed routine.

After checking with me to see how Jo's eyes were progressing, members of the Main Street Merchants Association, with the support of Sheriff Skip Herrick, decided it was time to surprise Jo with a special public event. Jeannie Stone (no relation) of the Jack and Jill Shoppe, Jeannine Dale of Margo's, and Gary Howe, of J. J. Newberry worked hard to create a unique event that would honor Jo by creating a community-wide celebration.

"At first, we thought we might have a sit-down dinner," Jeannie told me. "But then we thought, where could be we possibly hold it so all Jo's friends could come?"

So many people knew Jo or had been associated with Barjo's that a "bang-up" party for everybody seemed a better idea. We decided it would be an open house.

I told them, "If you want to surprise Jo, you'd better do most of your business with Barb. Jo is pretty sharp about catching on if she starts thinking I'm up to something."

"We can use the banquet room here at Country Way," Barbara suggested when they met with her. "Why don't we have the party from 1 p.m. to 4 p.m. on a Sunday? That way anyone who works during the week can come."

By the first week of June, Jo was, indeed, getting suspicious about the many phone calls I was receiving.

"I know that you all are up to something!" she said to me. "Come clean and tell me. I want to know what is going on."

"Well, I promised not to tell you," I said. "But I know you. If I don't tell you, you'll refuse to go anywhere with me. Promise me that you don't say anything to anyone. Next Sunday, June 9, we're have a little party for you."

About that time Donald came in on his way home from visiting with Margaret at the nursing home.

"What do *you* know about next weekend?" Jo demanded.

"About what?" he asked.

"Don't play dumb," she said. "The party at Country Way. I think it's a stupid idea. Who would want to visit with an old woman? I'll bet you less than fifty people will show up!"

"I'll take that bet," Donald said with a laugh. "And you better be ready to pay up, Jo."

The next day, she said to me, "If you expect me to go to that party, I have to have something to wear. Will you take me to the city to get a new dress?"

"Of course I will," I answered. "I'll take you to J. C. Penney's this afternoon."

Her request came as a big surprise to me. Over the years, Jo had always sent Stony, Margaret or Barbara to Lewiston to choose her outfits for her. Sometimes this had meant several trips back and forth to Ward Brothers or Peck's department store before she made her selection.

In 1958, Jo had entered me in the Miss Maine Restaurant contest, in which I was first runner-up. Margaret and I had gone to Peck's to select an outfit for me to wear. I'll never forget the look on the salesclerk's face when Margaret signed Jo's name to the sales slip.

She looked Margaret in the face and said, "Am I finally going to meet Josephine Stone? I've helped her husband select her clothes for years."

Margaret laughed and said to her, "Sorry, not this time. I'm her sister."

To this day, she hesitates to go into any store. Perhaps she thinks she is still that bashful little girl from East Stoneham, uncomfortable whenever she is outside her own familiar world.

As we came out of J.C. Penney's, she said to me, "How do you like the dress that I picked out? Maybe some people will think it's too flashy for an 87-year old, but I don't want an old woman's outfit."

"I love to see you in bright colors," I answered. "You'll never seem old to me."

What I didn't know was that the very next day the publicity team was ready to put their plan into action. The Lewiston *Sun* and the Norway *Advertiser-Democrat* ran full-page ads inviting the public to attend the open house at the Country Way on "Jo Stone Day," June 9. If I hadn't told Jo about her party, she would have found out when we read the morning newspapers. The local radio station, WOXO, also helped with the publicity by running spots during rest of the week.

"I don't understand all this publicity," she said to me. "What does this full-page ad about "Jo Stone Day" mean? Don't you know that since I closed the restaurant, everybody forgot all about me?"

"We'll see who is right, you or Donald," I said with a laugh. "Remember what you said about how many people will show up. It'll cost you fifty dollars when you're wrong."

Red was Jo's favorite color and all the storefronts were clad with red bows and balloons. The local merchants added congratulatory signs for her to their front windows. After Jo found out about the party, I was free to decorate our home, too. I hung huge red bows around the front door and wrapped the front columns of the entrance with wide red ribbons.

In addition to the publicity, the Merchants Association committee, Barbara, Henry and I invited everyone we could think of including salesmen, former employees, senior citizens and all Jo's friends, family, and business associates so everyone could wish her well in her retirement, although she was still insisting that it was just a change in employment.

June 9th was a beautiful sunny day, a perfect day for the party. At noon, Jeannie Stone and Gary Howe came to our home to greet Jo and offer us a ride to the party. Never wanting to be late, Jo was ready and waiting when they arrived. I knew she was in for a huge surprise, as she thought we were going to go with them. But Jeannie and Gary's visit to our house was just a decoy.

They presented us both with beautiful corsages. Loving bright colors, Jo was wearing her cardinal red linen blazer over a light cotton dress with a kaleidoscope of bright flowers on a dark background. She wore two strands of pearls to add a touch of elegance to her outfit.

"My, my, don't you look sharp today," Jeannie said to her. "Are you sure you haven't got a new boyfriend?"

"I picked my dress out myself," Jo said.

Jeannie asked if she would be willing to wear the red velvet cape, which she had worn as the first Grand Marshal of the Christmas Parade. I knew that Jeannie was going to ask about her about it, so I had the cape all ready for her to put on.

Jo agreed with a chuckle, clearly enjoying the fuss.

About the same time, Ben Conant, chief deputy at the Oxford County Sheriff's department, showed up with his camera to take some pictures.

"What are you doing here?!" Jo asked him.

"Wait a few minutes and you'll find out," he said with a broad grin. "If you take a look down street, in a minute you'll see why."

Peering down Deering Street, to Jo's surprise, she saw a carriage with black fringe on the top drawn by two stately Belgian horses coming toward us. It pulled up in front of our house to take us to the party. Robert Bean, the owner of the horses was a former Central Maine Power lineman and had been a frequent customer at Barjo's. He helped Jo into the "surrey with the fringe on the top."

As the carriage made its way down Main Street in Norway, Jo looked at me and said, "Did you know about this, too? Who in the world thought about getting these beautiful horses and where did they find the carriage?"

"Well, I knew about it, but the ones involved in getting the horses were Helen, Margaret, Grace, and Donald," I told her.

"They know how much you loved horses as a kid and thought this was a perfect way for you to ride to your party."

"This certainly is some surprise!" she exclaimed. "That Donald was pulling my leg with that bet! He really knew what was happening all the time, didn't he?"

"He was a big part of it," I admitted.

As we rode down Main Street, Jo couldn't help but see the red banners, balloons and bows sported by all the stores in the village all in her honor. Big signs said, "Go Jo!" and "Best Wishes, Jo!"

Many friends were waiting on Main Street shouting greetings to her. As we drove by, cheers of "We love you, Jo!" and "Have a wonderful day!" rang out all along the route from our house to Country Way.

One little boy ran along beside the carriage, until Jo said to Bob Bean, "Let him ride with us. I know how much he wants to. I can remember when I was a kid and how much I loved horses." Bob reached down and helped him into the carriage.

A crowd of family, friends and business acquaintances were waiting for Jo's arrival under warm, sunny skies. The parking lot was full of people as we pulling into the yard. As the horses pulled up to the restaurant door, we heard boisterous cheers of "Hurray for Jo!" as the carriage came to a stop.

As Skip Herrick helped her out of the carriage, she smoothed out her dress, and gave me an inquisitive look. It was as if she was wondering to herself, "What's going to happen now?"

"Don't people have anything better to with their time on a Sunday afternoon," she said to me, still protesting. "What is this crowd of people doing here?"

"Looks to me like Donald was right," I said with a grin. "Well, Jo, I think you were mistaken about people forgetting about you."

"I haven't been to a party like this for a hundred years!" she exclaimed, clearly ready to enjoy the special event.

Jo was escorted into the banquet hall by her nephew, Father Donald. She might have had second thoughts at first sight of the huge crowd, but she didn't show it. She was the life of the party, greeting people and shaking hands with everyone.

As she entered the room, she saw Veda who had worked at Barjo's from 1946 to 1991, sitting at a table by the door with a guest book for everybody to sign.

"I can't believe how well organized everything is," Jo said to her. "You folks certainly put one over on me this time!"

In the banquet room, she was led to a queen-like high-backed chair. I was seated beside her with Margaret and Helen.

As she looked around trying to take in everything at once, Jo noticed that the room was decorated with red streamers and posters proclaiming "Jo Stone Day." Numerous large bouquets with red flowers adorned the banquet room, which also featured red ribbons. Red tablecloths covered the tables that were decorated with candles and balloons.

At a table on the left were all the awards and honors she had received over the years. On the wall behind it hung her Celtics jacket with Kevin McHale's number 32 on it, and an emblem from the Mid-Maine Motorcycle Club who had made her an honorary member in 1977.

"How did you get all of the awards out of the house without me knowing it," she asked me. "I can't believe my eyes! What a day this is going to be."

"I assure you it wasn't easy," I told her. "I brought them over here a few at a time so you wouldn't know what I was doing."

On the right side of the banquet room, a buffet table was filled with many kinds of fancy finger rolls and other delicacies with a punch bowl shaped like a fountain in the center. In the center of the room was a table holding an enormous cake adorned with red roses that said in green lettering, "Congratulations on Your Retirement, Jo!" This table also included napkins printed in red lettering that stated "Jo Stone Day—June 9,1991."

Donnie acted as the Master of Ceremonies. He introduced Town Manager, David Holt, who presented Jo with a plaque proclaiming "Jo Stone Day" in the Town of Norway. Dave led the dignitaries who spoke at the reception. "Jo, you're a real lady, you have a huge heart and a strong character," he said, before reading out the "Josephine Stone Day" Proclamation.

Everybody in the room clapped and cheered as she thanked him for this special recognition.

Jo looked at me in bewilderment and said, "I still can't believe what's happening. All these people, and declaring today 'Jo Stone Day' for me. It seems like a dream! It just can't be true."

Rick Bennett, the State Representative from Norway read a Proclamation by the State of Maine declaring June 9, 1991, "Jo Stone Day" in Maine. He made the presentation on behalf of Governor John McKernan. Everyone clapped and cheered for Jo. Rick commended Jo for her outstanding service to the state and for having the longest running restaurant under the same ownership in the history of the state.

In the background the Parisiens, a local orchestra, played all the old-time songs and dance melodies that Jo had known and loved throughout her lifetime.

During the afternoon, over a thousand people filed by Jo's

chair to greet her and extended their congratulations. She had a wonderful time greeting all her friends, former employees, business associates and family. Chet Jordan, president of Jordan's Meats, of Portland, was one of the first to greet her. Other guests included a former salesman for John Sexton, John Emery, wholesale grocers of Westwood, Massachusetts, and a jukebox official, Eddie Dresser, from Ferris Music, Madison, who had supplied the restaurant jukebox with records since the 1930's. Some guests were wearing red in her honor, they told her.

At intervals throughout the afternoon, more awards for Jo were announced. Walking up in front of her chair, Dick Hallee, president of the Main Street Merchants Association, was handed the microphone. He held up an engraved plaque for all to see.

"Jo," he said to her, "the Norway Merchants Association wants to present this to you for your dedicated service to the people of Norway. This plaque will stay on permanent display on the wall of the Norway Town Office for the entire community to see."

"I know how hard you all have worked to make this day a success," Jo exclaimed. "I can never thank you enough for everything that you have done for me."

This time I was in for a surprise, too. After presenting Jo with her award, Dick came over to me and said, "We wanted to honor you, too, Emily."

He presented me with a plaque that said, "To Emily Foster: For her dedicated service to Barjo's Restaurant and to the community. Presented to you by your friends, The Norway Merchants."

This time *I* was without words. I had no idea I was to be included in Jo's special day by my friends in the Norway Merchants Association. It was truly a great honor. I don't remember what I said to Dick, but I know that I told him how much I appreciated it.

At a table close to Jo, a large wicker basket decorated with red ribbon was placed for donations to a scholarship fund to be established in her name. Many of her friends made contributions.

This Josephine Stone Scholarship is presented annually to a high school student from Oxford Hills High School who will study culinary arts or some phase of the Food Service industry in college. The Scholarship Trust is administered by the Norway-Paris Kiwanis Charitable Foundation.

Norway's Fire Chief, Bob Butters, presented a check for the scholarship fund from the Norway Firemen's Association, saying "I hope that somebody will learn to cook as well as you do!"

On behalf of the Oxford Hills Technical School-Region XI,

Irvin "Duffer" Pendleton presented her with a plaque for "Outstanding Service" to the school and its students.

As he made the presentation to her, he said, "I only wish that all my students could have the opportunity to have you teach them how to work. What a difference you have made in so many young lives."

Then he reached over and kissed Jo on the cheek.

She looked pleased and said, "Thank you, Duffer, but I think you are exaggerating quite a bit."

For many years, Jo had given her own private scholarship of $100 to the technical school program for a deserving student. She still continues to do so. The goal of this scholarship is to help one student each year get a start in a career or new job from the training they have obtained at the Voc-Tech School.

Throughout the afternoon, Jo's well-wishers were interrupted periodically to allow for more formal presentations of plaques, citations, letters, awards and gifts. Today these are all on display at our Deering Street home.

Sgt. Ernest Dunham of the Norway Police Department announced the inauguration of the "Jo Stone Citizen of the Year" Award. He presented her with a lithographed scroll of the criteria for this award and a wall plaque engraved with her name as the first recipient of the honor.

The criteria established that this award is to be given annually in June to a Norway resident who is active in the community, devoted to the needs of others and to assisting young people, all attributes of the award's namesake.

The seven other living members of Jo's Norway High School class of 1923 joined her that day. They included four of the women who played with her on the Norway High School basketball team.

As Skip Churchill, a professional photographer, was setting up his camera to take group pictures of the basketball team and the NHS Class of 1923, many of them shared fond and funny memories of Jo.

"We all had a good time," said Helen Purington, who had played forward on the team. "Jo was real tough to play against. She held the floor and didn't let her opponent score any points."

"She would back them up against the wall with her arms flying and they couldn't do anything," said Alice Montpelier, the center. "Jo had 'em pinned right up against the wall."

Florence Hadley Conant and Marita Cushman Andrews also congratulated their high school basketball teammate.

Her classmates were asked about their recollections of their school days with Jo. They admitted they had some, but, "none that she'd want told," said Livy Gouin.

All of the Barjo's Restaurant employees gathered around Jo's chair for a group picture. Many had worked at the restaurant during the 1940's, 1950's and 1960's. All the police officers from the local, state and sheriff's department had a group photo taken with Jo, as well.

The Norway Merchants later presented Jo with an album of pictures as a memento of "Jo Stone Day." Ben Conant from the Oxford County Department, also, took a lot of the pictures and later gave Jo a complete set. And the Norway Historical Society had a video made to be kept at Norway Historical House on Main Street in Norway.

"I can't believe it," she said to me, pondering how hundreds of people had turned out to congratulate her. "This has been the most wonderful day in my life."

"Hasn't this been quite a party?" she asked her sister, Helen Grover, 93, of East Stoneham.

"It sure has," Helen answered. "You're going to be some tired tomorrow!" she added, ever the big sister.

"No, I won't!" Jo said, asserting her authority. "It'll do me good."

This exchange made me laugh! How many times had I heard Jo say that? "Tired" wasn't in Jo's vocabulary. She had never allowed any of the rest of us to use that excuse either.

When Jo was asked about her mode of transportation to the party, she said, "I was kinda glad. I loved those horses. It reminded me of my days in East Stoneham when I was driving our horse, Jack."

"Ever since she was real small she could drive horses," recalled her brother, Donald, age 84. "Why, once I remember when Jo drove Jack right through Cold Brook to beat Helen's boyfriend, Perle." His eyes twinkled with the memory. "Helen didn't appreciate that one bit," he added.

"We had a wonderful day. I just can't believe it," Jo said before leaving the party. She didn't know there was another surprise awaiting her.

"We're going to have one every year for somebody," she allowed.

As she was escorted to the door, I said to her, "How do you think you are going to get home, Jo? Donald just left."

"Well, I know you don't have your car, but probably Barbara will give us a ride home," she said to me.

About that time, someone said to her, "That's a pretty fancy automobile waiting at the door for you, Jo. How do you rate all this attention?"

The guest of honor was taken home in a chauffeur-driven restored 1932 Chrysler convertible, one of Bob Bahre's automobiles from his Antique Car Collection. After pictures were taken of her being assisted into the car, I joined her for our ride home.

Sitting on the sun porch that evening, she looked at me and said, "What an extraordinary day this turned out to be. I think everybody had a wonderful time. I have so many memories and I saw so many people I haven't seen in years."

"I'm so glad you had a good time," I commented. "We all wanted it to be the very best party you ever had and it was bigger and better than we ever imagined it could be."

The next day Donald came to see how she was doing.

"Well, Jo," he said. "I've come to collect my $50. Remember you bet me that less than 50 people would show up."

Jo certainly had to pay up, because there were over 1000 at the Country Way Restaurant for "Jo Stone Day." Later, as we looked over the guest book, she recognized many names of friends that she hadn't seen in years. For several months, cards and letters continued to come from all over the country congratulating Jo. Many reminisced about different things they remember either about Barjo's or about Jo herself. Some told stories about a funny incident they remembered.

Jo said to us, "I want you all to know that I had my funeral yesterday and I enjoyed every minute of it. I was able to greet all my friends, see all my flowers and enjoy the "Celebration of my Life." I want you to remember—no fanfare when I die. Just dig a hole to put my ashes in at Pine Grove Cemetery and have Donnie say a simple prayer."

Jo has always denied her acts of generosity to the people from different walks of life who came through the restaurant door at Barjo's, though many people have been the beneficiaries of her numerous acts of kindness and have not forgotten it.

Instead of looking for praise and recognition, Jo's attitude remains, "God has been very good to me and given me my health and strength, so I want to be sure that I always do my part and share with others!"

These are Jo's own thoughts about her life:

It has been a good race; it has been a good time to live, the best of times for me.

We have accepted the torch of this relay race from our predecessors and sped on, stumbling at times but never quitting, never losing faith.

This lap had brought us far. From gaslights and kerosene lamps to electric lights and neon lighting that makes the skies over cities glow at night. From slow-moving horses and buggies to luxurious automobiles, and speeding diesel trains and planes that streak across the skies. We have gone into outer space and put men on the moon to walk and discover many miracles for the benefit of mankind.

In my lifetime, communications have advanced from the printed newspaper to the radio and on to television that brings news, entertainment and education in our home around the clock. With the Internet age upon us, we can now transmit messages around the world with unbelievable speeds.

Medical discoveries have extended life expectancy. From the wood stove we have moved to gas, oil and electric heat to electronic systems controlling temperature and air quality in our homes. We have gone from the laundry tub and corrugated scrub board to the washing machine. A lively interest in the arts and crafts has been revived. This is good. Man does not live by bread alone. These are but a few of the achievements I have seen in my lifetime.

We as a generation have accomplished many things, but there is much more for you to do. There are many problems yet to be solved; human frailties make it so. Hopefully, we have laid some of the groundwork for you to go forward to find the solutions.

May you accept your torch with courage, strength, high ambition, confidence in your God-given gifts, and with the same faith that our forefathers passed on to us centuries ago.

God bless you all.

Jo Stone, *Norway, Maine, 2000*

With characteristic modesty and concern for her staff, Jo took the Barjo's crew
with her to the Sheraton-Eastland Hotel in Portland when she was awarded
the 1989 Maine Restauranteur of the Year Award.
front:Veda Taker, Jo, Emily; back: Gloria Day, Judy Ripley, Jeanne
Morrissette, Mike Webber, Chris Webber, Robert Hill.
(Mary Delameter photo)

Jo passed on her passion and her skills to successive generations of young people, including members of her own family. Here, in March, 1987, she is teaching two-and-a-half year old Katherine, her great-granddaughter, the art of making pies.

— EPILOGUE —

After Jo closed Barjo's for good, we made it a daily routine to visit Margaret at Ledgeview Nursing Home, but, in December 1992, I developed a seizure disorder and was unable to drive to West Paris. Donnie, Barbara and the kids offered to take us to see Margaret often—if not daily. After sixteen months, in May 1994, I was able to drive again and we resumed our schedule of daily visiting with Margaret.

Over the next several years, we made many quick trips to West Paris when the head nurse, Carrol Cone, would call to alert us but Margaret was made of tough McAllister stock and she always came back from these crises.

Then in the first week of October 1995, Grace, Jo and I stayed with her around the clock as it seemed that, this time, we would lose her. On the evening of October 9, we could see her slipping away before our eyes. Finally, at 1:15 a.m. on October 10, Margaret stopped breathing and the presence of God surrounded her as His angels took her home. Margaret was 84.

"I was saddened that Marg was gone," Jo said. "But it was a burden lifted from my shoulders knowing that all her terrible suffering and pain was over. Over the years, we had gone through many good times and bad together. I knew I'd miss her keen mind and quick wit. No one could wish for the torment she had gone through to continue. But it was a great loss to me to have her gone."

Of all the McAllister siblings who grew up together on the farm in East Stoneham, Margaret's death left only Jo and her youngest sister, Grace. Donald, Jo's brother, business partner, rival for their parents' support and finally, her co-worker and partner again at Barjo's, had departed after a short bout with lung cancer on September 4, 1992. Helen, who had suffered the humiliation of Jo's childish teasing and in later years came to rely on her generous participation in community projects, had passed away September 24, 1993. Gerald, "Jim", the oldest who had always led the way for the younger ones, had died back in 1981.

The lingering effects of my illness made us dependent on friends and family. Jo and I are grateful for everything they did for us when I was unable to drive for so many months at a time. Donnie made special trips from his work in Portland, to take me shopping and to do our errands during those months. God's guidance sustained us though these times of trial.

Again when I lost my license in 1995 because of seizures, Jo's grandchildren—along with Barbara, Henry and Donnie—all helped us with shopping and errands. We can never thank these people enough for all they have done for us.

Having God's hand on my shoulder through those many dark days, my hope is that I will be able to accomplish all the work that God has planned for my future.

Jo continues to be Jo—spunky, caring, intelligent—and her interest in life and the future remains unchallenged.

We look forward to hearing from our many friends who are reading this book.

For myself, I hope that Jo and her life will continue for generations to inspire people in our own and in other communities, those who have travelled far away or may never have met her.

Jo's influence on my life, and on the lives of several generations of people young and old, in the western foothills of Maine during the 20th century, is a story of spunk, endurance, savvy, and warmth.

It's the story of a certain woman in a certain time and place who made the most of her God-given talents and who spread her concern for the welfare of others in a far-reaching swath of generosity that emanated, always, from the big heart of that small woman in the kitchen of Barjo's.

— APPENDICES —

Jeannie Stone presented the Norway Merchants Association Award to Jo on Jo Stone Day, 1991.

Jo with the sizeable display of her National Resturant Association awards, 1989. Jack Shaner, of Shaner's, South Paris, looks on.

Among Jo's many patrons-become-friends over the years are Forrest Goulet of Lewiston, and Pat and John Gundry (below) of New Zealand.

Four generations of a restaurant family in front of the Country Way: L—R: Robert (Robbie) the current proprietor of Country Way, Andrea, Henry, Nick, Jo, Barbara, Joline (Jody), Darcy, and Katherine.

Appendix 1

Amusing Stories of Jo's 'Barjo's Family'

Over the years, as these pages have recounted, Jo helped many young people. There are amusing tales and some more serious in nature. Included here are some comical experiences that touch on Jo and the school kids. Some of the narratives tell what different young people were able to accomplish later in their lives. These stories cover a span of over fifty years—from 1940 until Jo closed Barjo's in 1991.—E. F.

■ ■ ■

The Kimball kids worked at Barjo's during the 1940's. They had lost their mother, and to the younger children, especially, Jo was like a foster mother. After Jo bought the Hotel Stone in 1949, some of the Kimballs helped on banquets there as well as at the restaurant.

One afternoon, Leona was washing dishes as Jo prepared the evening meal. Later when Jo looked over again to the other side of the room, Kathy, a younger sister, had taken Leona's place.

"Kathy, where did Leona go?" Jo asked.

"She wanted to go swimming, and I told her I'd take her place," was her reply.

Knowing they were all good workers, Jo said nothing. It was a busy afternoon, and Jo didn't watch Kathy too closely.

"It seemed she finished those dishes in a hurry, but I didn't think too much about at the time," Jo said.

Later, after Kathy left for the day, Jo went outside by the backdoor of the kitchen for a breath of air. There, lined up on the ground, she was surprised to find all the dirty tin dishes. Now she knew how Kathy had whizzed through her job so fast! Jo brought the dishes in and finished the work herself.

"Kathy was really too young to be working anyway," Jo said. "I felt sorry for those kids because no one had ever shown them any kindness. I knew Kathy had cut the job short to go off swimming with the others, but I never said a word to any of them about the dishes."

■ ■ ■

One day, Jo and Stony took Dickie, the youngest of the Kimball kids, to Lewiston and bought him a whole outfit of new clothes with shoes and the works.

When they got home, Jo said to him, "Now, Dickie, don't forget you have to help us with a banquet tonight. Don't you forget to come to work."

But when it was time, Dickie was nowhere to be found. The next day, Jo asked him, "Where were you last night? Didn't you remember you were going to work the banquet?"

"Oh, Jo! I went home and dressed up in my new clothes to show them off to my friends," Dickie replied. He had never had new clothes before and was proud of his outfit. Jo didn't scold him even though she knew she ought to. Dickie promised never to miss work again, and she forgave him because she knew he didn't mean any harm.

■ ■ ■

During the 1940's and 1950's, Barbara and Joyce McAllister waited on tables at Barjo's and also at the Hotel Stone. When I first started at the restaurant, Barbara was the shift leader. Working together, to meet the pace of the restaurant day after day, Jo and her employees were involved in each others lives in many ways.

While working at the restaurant, Barbara married Kenneth Lawrence, a likeable guy, who worked at the Feldspar Mill in West Paris. They eventually had two children, a son, Henry, and a daughter, Marjorie. After Barjo's, Barbara had several restaurant positions over the years, including manager of the banquet facilities at the Round House and at Rolandeau's Restaurant, both in Auburn.

After they were first married, Kenneth often had supper at Barjo's on the nights when Barbara worked. He always ate at the counter in the kitchen. It turned out that Ken was a drinker, and Barbara just didn't know how to deal with his alcoholism. When he came in from work, she'd pretend at first that everything was normal. Then her anger would get the best of her, and she would exclaim, "Ken, you're drunk again!"

One night, Jo turned around from the grill where she was cooking, and asked, "Why do you say that to him every night? You know he has had a drink!" Though she certainly wasn't defending Ken's habit, Jo thought Barbara's reaction wasn't solving the problem.

Barbara's retort was harsh, "Well, Jo, not everybody is as lucky as you and buries her husbands!"

Growing up with a grandfather who drank too much hard cider, Jo had been taught by her mother that drinking could only cause heartache. Marrying a man with a drinking problem didn't make any sense to Jo. Reforming an alcoholic never seemed to happen either.

■ ■ ■

Barbara's sister, Joyce, also worked at Barjo's. She married Walter Bennett and went on to have a very productive career in a different field. In 1968, she went to work for the Office of Economic Opportunity for Oxford County. From her office at 225 Main Street, she managed the food distribution center located in the old Rex Theater building.

In 1977, she went to work at Madison Avenue Association with offices located in Oxford. She became a Certified Housing Manager for Robert Bahre who owned the company.

While there, she wrote the specifications for the State of Maine winterization program. This program became a model for a federal one. Joyce also wrote the original Federal Housing Application for United States Housing Authority. The very first Section 8 Housing Unit in the whole U. S. was the Park Street Apartments in South Paris. The national media from California to Maine covered the opening of this unit.

At the time of her retirement, Joyce was managing six hundred rental housing units for Madison Ave. Associates. After a bout with cancer, Joyce passed away on May 1, 2000.

■ ■ ■

During World War II, Jack Smith waited on tables at Barjo's. After he graduated from high school, he enlisted in the military.

Afterwards, he came back to the restaurant. One day he told Jo, "When I was in the South, they treated me wonderful. I'm going to give up my job and go back down there and find work."

"Jackie," Jo said, "remember, when you were there, it was during the war. Everybody everywhere gave all the soldiers special attention. I think you should reconsider!"

"Don't try to talk me out of it, Jo," he said and off he went.

In less than a month, Jo got a telephone call from Jack. "Can you send me enough money to come home," he asked her sheepishly. "I should have listened to you, Jo. Everything you said was right. Nothing is the same down here as it was before."

Jo wired him the money and he went back to work for her. After staying in Norway for a while, he married and moved away. In later years, Jack settled in Florida where he and his wife became involved in a Christian school. He was given a special recognition dinner, March 31, 1994, from the county commissioners of Dade County, Florida, with an award for being a "True Humanitarian." It was truly a surprise to him as no one else had ever received this kind of award in the state of Florida.

Jack Smith gave Jo all the credit for guiding him to be compassionate to others. She had shown him, at an early age, how a little kindness and a helping hand could guide someone to have a productive life. Now in his seventies, he has always kept in touch with Jo over the years .

■ ■ ■

In 1954, Gerry and Arlene Bean came to work at Barjo's. They were happy-go-lucky girls who enjoyed a good time. Because they were identical twins, the customers were often confused as to which one was waiting on them. They made the most of it!

One of their favorite victims was George Cummings, a regular who ate lunch at Barjo's everyday. He was a brother to Elliot, who had married Jo's sister, Grace. The Cummings family owned the wood products mill.

George was a bachelor and lived alone in an apartment in the Merrill Block on the other side of Main Street. He didn't like to cook or to eat alone, so he came to Barjo's for lunch as well as after work for supper. He was a very nervous person and could easily get upset but he thought the twins could do no wrong. No matter how they teased him, he accepted it.

"George would get really frustrated with all the other girls. When the twins waited on him, he was all smiles," Jo said. "He was working at C. B. Cummings mill and had a short lunch hour, so we always had his meal on the table when he arrived at noon."

One day, the twins stuck his cup and saucer together with a suction cup. When he drank from the cup, the saucer came off the table with it.

"Was he ever flustered trying to figure out what was going on!" Gerry said. "We told him the cup and saucer must have been molded together."

"He trusted us so much he believed anything we told him—which only encouraged us to tease him more!" Arlene said.

Another time, when George ordered a dish of ice cream for dessert, the twins put toothpicks in it. When he complained, they told him a porcupine must have been near and the quills fell off.

"What a puzzled expression George had on his face!" Gerry said with a laugh. "But he made like he believed us."
Even though he must have known that they were pulling his leg, George never let on the girls were playing tricks on him.

During the busiest hours, one of the kitchen boys, David Card, had a habit of asking the waitresses to stop what they were doing and make him a Velvet (a milkshake with ice cream beaten into it).

One day he ordered a Chocolate Velvet from one of the Bean

twins. It was a bad mistake on his part. When they made it for him, they added a whole package of Ex-Lax to the Velvet.

"Boy, did David have a busy afternoon!" Arlene exclaimed.

Gerry got married before Arlene did and then the customers thought, for sure, they would be able to tell them apart. Things weren't that simple, though. If anything, it was little confusing. The wedding ring made it easier than ever for them to fool their friends.

"On Saturday night, when the guys came in from the dance, I gave my ring to Arlene. Brother, were they embarrassed the next day, when they found out we had fooled them again," Gerry said with a laugh.

Arlene married later. Interestingly, these twins both married twins, but not twin brothers.

"Those girls were real clowns," Jo said. "But the customers loved them. They made the days go faster with all their antics."

■ ■ ■

In the late 1950's, the Dunn sisters became part of our Barjo 's Family. I had seen their grandmother on Main Street one day, and she asked me if I thought Jo would be willing to hire them. I told Jo about my encounter and the next weekend Mary and Alice Dunn came to work for us.

The family lived on a dirt road off the main highway in East Waterford in a small, tarpaper building with no modern conveniences. Every week the girls gave their mother their paychecks to buy groceries. Their father was a woodsman, but worked very little. Many times when they went to visit, if one of the kids at home needed shoes or stockings, the girls came back barefooted.

The first Christmas they were with us, Mary and Alice bought a lot of gifts for the little ones at home. There were 15 children in the Dunn family, so Christmas gifts had always been scarce. Their grandparents had made them clothes, but with so many kids, they could provide little else. The girls wanted to share with their younger brothers and sisters. Having money in their pockets from tips gave them a chance to buy toys and games they had dreamed of having themselves. Even using ribbon and wrapping paper was a novelty.

"It was the first time we had money to buy gifts for our brothers and sisters," Mary, the oldest, said. "We bought things for Mother, Dad, and our grandparents, too."

"I'll never forget what a good time we had wrapping up presents for the little ones," Alice exclaimed. "We wanted to surprise the family. Jo and Stony helped us get a lot of goodies and candy, gifts, decorations and a tree."

On Christmas Eve, Stony loaded up the pick-up truck with all the presents, and took the girls to their home in East Waterford to surprise their folks.

■ ■ ■

In the fall of 1967, the Dunn sisters' cousin, Pamela Dingley, was a senior who wanted to graduate with her class though her family was moving to Connecticut. Pam asked Margaret if she could live with her until June. Margaret agreed.

"You don't have any idea what you are getting yourself into, Marg," Jo warned her. "I've had teenagers living with me for years. Your lifestyle will change dramatically."

Margaret's home was hardly the setting for a teenager and it proved to be some experience for both Margaret and Pam!

Margaret had never married and was a typical "old maid." To take on the responsibility of a teenager was certainly new for her. In addition, Pamela was a little on the "wild side." Hers was the extreme opposite of the life Margaret lived. They made it through the rest of year, but Pam found out what discipline truly meant.

Pamela learned to understand that Margaret meant exactly what she said. When she told her to be home at a certain hour, there were no ifs, ands, or buts about it! Pam quickly discovered that Margaret would be waiting at the door if she were even five minutes late.

Pam had to give up her habit of hanging out back in town after work. Margaret expected her to stay at home and study.

"Well, Marg, how did you like bringing up a teenager?" Jo asked her in June with a sly grin. "Don't you find things are a lot different than when we lived with Mother?"

"You were right! This is something I will never try again," Margaret said. "I love all my relatives, but living with a teenager at my age is a little too much."

After Pamela graduated from high school in June 1968, she rented an apartment from Jo in the barbershop building. She continued to work at Barjo's waiting on tables. She made friends with several of the cops who were regulars and got interested in a young, handsome state trooper who ate at the restaurant often. He was one of Jo's best friends and still keeps in touch with her.

He rented a room from an elderly landlady in Mechanic Falls. "Don't you ever try to call on me at my house because my landlady won't like it!" he cautioned Pam.

One evening, however, she went to Mechanic Falls to find him. At Christie's Restaurant, where a lot of young people met in the evening, she found out where he lived. Later that evening she found a way to sneak into the house and appeared at his room.

It happened that that same night there was a break-in at Mechanic Falls High School. Pam had left her car in the schoolyard, so that her friend, the trooper, would be surprised. Naturally, the first thing the local police did when they discovered the break-in was to write down the license plate of the "abandoned" car in the schoolyard.

"Before Pamela ever got back to Norway, the cat was out of the bag about what she was up to," Jo said. "When the Mechanic Falls officer asked for a check of the license plate, the other cops heard it on the radio. They knew right away whose it was and came into Barjo's and to tell us. They never let Pam forget it!"

Jo and Margaret tried to guide Pamela about how to be a responsible adult and taught her how to be a good waitress. Several years later, she left the restaurant and moved to Lewiston where she married and had two daughters of her own.

■ ■ ■

In 1968, Gloria Day was the winner of the Easter Bonnet Contest. Carl Broome, Membership Director for the National Restaurant Association, was a guest of the restaurant during the Easter season and sent a broom-shaped trophy to be engraved with the winner's name. Gloria was the lucky waitress to receive this special memento.

Soon after Jo sold Barjo's in 1991, Gloria died very suddenly of a heart attack. Everyone in the community, including the Barjo family, was saddened by her premature and tragic death.

■ ■ ■

In the spring of 1970, Terry Richards and his wife were working with his foster parents, Alma and Loren Gardner, as assistants to help the Head Start teacher, Joyce Rich. Terry was the son of Allie Richards, who worked for Jo back in the 1940's. Many Head Start children had never been in a restaurant. They were learning table manners and how to eat using the proper utensils.

"Jo," Terry asked, "would you be willing to treat the Head Start kids to dinner at Barjo's as a part of their program? A lot of these kids don't know what the inside of a restaurant looks like."

"Sure," she replied. "Just let me know when you're coming, and all the meals will be on the house."

Joyce Rich and her assistants brought a class every year for over twenty years. Each year Jo tried to do some little thing unusual, like a unique favor or a special toy for the kids to take home. Head Start had its 20th birthday party at Barjo's, too.

"For the birthday party, I had Gloria's mother make them miniature cupcakes with funny little monkeys on top," Jo said. "The waitresses put a birthday candle in each one, so each child could blow out his or her own candle."

On the next school day the kids always made a card for Jo as a class project. Some drew pictures while others tried to print their names. Their teacher always wrote a lovely note on the inside. Jo has all these pieces of the children's artwork packed away with all her other mementos of Barjo's.

■ ■ ■

In 1986, school kids continued to play a big part at Barjo's. The minister's wife, Karen Ellis, conducted a class in etiquette for her third grade class at Guy Rowe Elementary School. After the children had completed the course, Jo invited them to Barjo's to practice their new skills. Even though they were older than the Headstart children Jo had been treating for years, many were in awe as they sat down to be serve by a waitress.

Sometimes these trips also included a tour of the local newspaper office, the Advertiser-Democrat, or of C. B. Cummings dowel factory.

These kids wrote Jo their own notes of thanks that mentioned the thing that most impressed them about their dinner. Their reactions were very different. Some liked the tiny carrots. Others mentioned how kind and patient the waitresses had been with them. These notes, too, are all in Jo's scrapbooks.

One year, Karen asked Jo to come into the dining room after their dinner. The principal of the elementary school was there.

"I had no idea what Karen wanted when she asked me to come out front," Jo said. " The kids had been coming to Barjo's for a long time, and I loved to treat them. To see their happy faces and know that they were having a good time was all the thanks I needed."

Karen Ellis presented Jo with a "Special Achievement Award" from the Guy Rowe School on behalf of all the teachers and the students.

■ ■ ■

Over the years, Barjo's had many student workers from the General Trades Program at Oxford Hills Regional Vocational School. Many had learning disabilities. They needed the hands-on experience of a working environment. Mr. Pendleton, who was in charge, told Jo that many businesses kept his students for a trial period of six weeks, but never paid the kids for their work.

At Barjo's, Jo treated these students like other employees and paid them minimum wage. The students blossomed under her guidance and learned to accomplish the tasks assigned to them. In order to succeed, many just needed the one-on-one attention they couldn't get in school.

The kids worked in both the dining room and the kitchen, and it was amazing how well they responded to working with everyone in the Barjo family. Jo and Margaret made out evaluations for them each semester so they could get credits toward graduation. They were graded on their job performance, on how they related to other employees and on what kind of improvement Jo thought they had shown.

After Jo sold Barjo's, she established a scholarship for a deserving student in this program who was chosen by the school to receive this award at class night.

■ ■ ■

Several employees of the restaurant, including Vickie Gay and Freddie Morrissette, learned to make Jo's special dessert—her famous custard pie—by watching her through the serving window at the restaurant.

Vickie and her sister, Karen, worked at Barjo's while going through high school and then waited on tables weekends and holidays as they went through college. After leaving Barjo's, Vickie won the Miss Maine USA contest and represented the state in the national finals. She went on to the Portland School of Fine Arts and is now an illustrator.

Several years ago, Vickie wrote and asked for some of Barjo's recipes as she and a friend were planning to publish a cookbook.

Karen told us this story about her sister, Vickie, and the custard pie. Her father loved the pie, so Vickie was determined to learn how to make him one. She watched Jo intently to see how the crust was made. Then she tried baking one at home.

"Karen told me that her sister sat, for the entire time the pie was cooking, cross-legged in front of the glass door of her mother's oven so it wouldn't run over or the crust collapse," Jo said with a laugh.

Finally, she mastered the art and told Jo how much her father enjoyed his pie made from Jo's recipe.

In the 1980's, Freddie Morrissette, who worked in the kitchen washing dishes, was another kid who accomplished the art of making custard pie. He never let on that he watched how Jo made it or that he was practicing at home.

After he left Barjo's, he became a short-order cook for Tom's Restaurant in Bridgton. One afternoon, much to Jo's surprise, in came Freddie proudly showing off a piece of custard pie made by her recipe.

Appendix 2

Barjo's Customers Fondly Remembered!

Many customers celebrated their birthdays or wedding nights by having dinner at Barjo's and returned year after year.

Elmer Shortridge, from South Paris, came every year on his birthday. Jo treated him to fried clams, a restaurant specialty. Albert Raymond and his wife from Bethel came for over twenty years on their anniversary for fried clams on the house. This tradition continued until the restaurant was closed in 1991.

Dr. and Mrs. Richardson, from North Bridgton, were at the Christmas party the year the Celebration Barn Theater of South Paris provided entertainment. Mrs. Richardson was ecstatic. When she was a child in Scotland, a mime show was part of her Christmas tradition and she hadn't seen one since coming to America.

Dr. Richardson had had a very prosperous veterinary practice in Waterville. When he was thinking about retiring, he learned about two young men wanted to go into business for themselves, and he made it possible for them to buy his practice.

Unfortunately, after his retirement to North Bridgton, he had health problems. Often when he arrived home after being hospitalized, he would tell his wife, "We're going to Barjo's!"

Over his pajamas would go his pants and coat, and he and his wife would drive to Norway. His first words to the waitresses were, "Here I am for a real meal!"

He loved all of us at Barjo's and we were saddened when he passed away.

■ ■ ■

Mr. and Mrs. Jordan, regular customers from Portland, also came to our Christmas parties. Because their family had moved away, they were lonely during the holidays. When they came to Barjo's, they met acquaintances and it became a bright spot of their day. At Easter and Christmas, they often sent beautiful plants and floral arrangements to dress up the dining room.

After her husband died, Mrs. Jordan went to live with her son in California. The day they were leaving Maine, her son brought her in for dinner. She told all of us how much fun she and her husband had had at Barjo's and how much she would miss us.

■ ■ ■

One of Jo's daily guests was Pearl Cook Kilborn. She had been a local music teacher who had led the Norway Community Band. Her father was a barber and had his business, Cook's Barbershop, at 225-227 Main Street. After he retired, her husband ran the barbershop, and she taught music in a room at the back of the building.

When Jo's daughter, Barbara, was a little girl, Pearl had been her music teacher and Barbara was a part of her marimba band. They played at quite a few places including WCOU Radio in Lewiston.

After Pearl's husband died, she sold her home on Pleasant Street and moved into an apartment in the Merchant Block on Main Street. She spent many hours at Barjo's talking and reminiscing about old times with Jo and Margaret.

■ ■ ■

Molly May and her husband, Perley, owned May's Drug Store in South Paris. Over the years, they ate at Barjo's regularly after closing the drug store each evening.

During the 1960's and 1970's, coin collecting was just catching on as a hobby in the area. When it became apparent that Perley was too sick to continue dispensing medicine, Molly began selling coins. She got Jo and Stony interested in coin collecting.

"Molly was a great one to try to tell you that she was giving you the best deal in the world," Jo explained. "Still, Stony and I bought quite a few coins from her."

After Perley passed away, Molly came to Barjo's often. After selling her business and moving to an apartment on Danforth Street, she was lonesome. Knowing how much Molly enjoyed talking with people, Jo invited her to come to Barjo's for her meals. Molly, Margaret, and Jo had been friends for many years, going back to the Stone's Drug Store days.

Several years later, Molly became ill and her daughter, Joanne, moved her to New Hampshire to be nearer to her family. She died in a nursing home there.

■ ■ ■

Many customers, including Larry Martin and his family, came first as summer residents and then, after moving to Maine, as year-round patrons. Larry bought one the Shepard's Camps and made it into a year-round home. He came to lunch with his friends for the Businessman's Special at noontime and was always asking for strawberry pie. The rule with the noon special was "no substitutes" because it was such a busy hour.

Jo, who always liked to tease, would see that he got strawberry pie every day even if something else he liked better was being offered on the special. Because of this we all called Larry "Mr. Strawberry Pie." He loved Jo's lemon meringue, too, but we never served him a piece when he ordered the day's special.

■ ■ ■

Lyonsden, the home of Captain Harry Lyons, is on the Common on Paris Hill near the home of Abraham Lincoln's first vice-president, Hannibal Hamlin. In 1929, Lyons served as the navigating officer of the plane Southern Cross, which made the first trans-Pacific flight from the American West Coast to Australia.

As a regular customer first at Stone's Drug Store and later at Barjo's, he was well-known to Jo and Margaret and a real colorful character.

He later married Thelma Bradbury, one of Jo's high school classmates. He passed away in 1963, but memories of some of his wild antics live on. His wife ran the Lyonsden as a guest home after his death.

In the 1970's, John and Mary Lloyd bought Lyonsden. Whenever these new owners came to the restaurant, John would say to Jo, "Be sure to tell Margaret that Harry Lyons asked for her last night," referring to the local belief that Harry's ghost still walked the streets of Paris Hill, harassing his friends.

John was always looking for a good laugh. One night he hooked up strobe lights, a small motor and a timer in his attic. To anyone passing the house at night, it looked like Harry Lyons' ghost really was taking a stroll.

"John," Jo laughed, "what a commotion you must have caused in the neighborhood when the old ladies took their dogs for a walk or somebody drove by. I'd like to have seen the expressions on their faces when they looked up!"

"I certainly woke the town up for several nights," he grinned.

Whenever John Lloyd ordered his favorite menu entree, rainbow trout, he sent word to Jo to be sure to remove the tail from his fish. To cater to his wishes, one evening, Jo cooked his trout and then cut the tail off before serving it. What she did next, was the real surprise—she wrapped the fishtail in foil, put it in a doggy bag and sent it out with his dinner. She peeked through the serving window to see his reaction. As she watched, he opened the bag and threw back his head, laughing.

"You'd better keep that!" Jo exclaimed heartily. "You might need it!"

Many years later, John still mentions that night when Jo played her own practical joke on the joker. She took him by surprise, and he never got the opportunity to retaliate.

■ ■ ■

Since Barjo's has closed, several of our neighbors have shown Jo and me what being good friends is really all about.

One of them, Ashley Everett, has taken care of the walks at our home by snow blowing, shoveling and salting them when they were icy in winter.

Richard Kimball and his wife, Shirley, have brought us fresh vegetables from their garden as well as raspberries and strawberries they have picked. Many nights, we have heard a knock on the door in the evening, and there was Richard with a special treat he picked for us after getting out of work for the day.

Neighbors like these are irreplaceable.

It is not easy for Jo to accept the kindness of others because she has, over the years, always liked being the giver not the receiver. Because of all she has given to so many over the years, it's a joy to me to experience the warmth of friendship and caring coming back to her in these gifts of kindness both large and small.

In 1995, Jo's family gathered around her great-grandson Nick to celebrate his wedding. Surrounding Nick and his wife Becky are Ben Tucker IV, Ben Tucker III, Barbara Meserve Paradis, Andrea Paradis Tucker, Katherine Tucker, Scott Paradis, Henry Paradis, Danny McCabe, Darcy Paradis McCabe, Jo Stone, Robert Paradis, Lynn Paradis, John and Donna (Hobbs) Paradis. Not in the photo is Jody Paradis. Nick and Becky are the current proprietors of Barjo's Restaurant.

Appendix 3

Jo's Honors and Awards

The first award Jo received was from the National Restaurant Association. This is the wording of it:

The National Restaurant Association
Proudly awards this certificate to
JOSEPHINE A. STONE
In Appreciation
For whole hearted and loyal endorsement of the manifold activities of the Association; For your personal support through financial assistance in the form of membership dues; For your unselfish contributions of time, thought and effort to local, state and national industry affairs; And for your cooperation with other National Restaurant Association members, and allied industries,
to advance the restaurant business in the public interest.
We look forward to your continued and active participation in our expanding activities. And we congratulate you and extend to you our warmest personal greetings.

John O. Sabotes, President
Larry Hillaire, Vice President
Frank Diffler, Ex-Vice President
L.C. Langford, Treasurer
April, 1957

■ ■ ■

Barjo's and Jo have received many awards and expressions of recognition for her work over the years.

1958
■ Distinguished Service Award
—*Junior Chamber of Commerce*
■ Honorary Citizen of Boys Town
—*Father Flanagan*

1959
■ Appreciation Award—"June is Dairy Month"
—*National Dairy Council, American Dairy Assoc. and International Association of Ice Cream Manufacturers*

1960
    ■ "Recipe of the Year"
—*John Sexton Co., Wholesale Grocers*
for "Rice and Tomato Soup" by Henry Paradis, chef
Published in John Sexton Yearbook Westwood, MA
■ Dedication of School Year Book, *The Caduceus* to
Jo & Stony
—*Norway High School*

1963
    ■ Golden Host Award of Merit
"In recognition of outstanding devotion and achievement
in the Field of Civic Welfare"
—*Restaurant Management Magazine*
■ Operation ROSCO, NRA 400 Membership Drive
—*National Restaurant Association*
■ Operation ROSCO Special Achievement, NRA 400
—*National Restaurant Association*

1964
    ■ Silver Bowl Award for Outstanding Service, NRA 400
—*National Restaurant Association*
■ Operation ROSCO Two Time Winner, NRA 400
—*National Restaurant Association*

1965
    ■ Silver Spoon Society, Charter Membership
(40 outstanding members of NRA 400)
—*National Restaurant Association*
■ Outstanding Promotion of Maine Agriculture
presented by Maynard Dolloff, Commissioner
—*Maine Department of Agriculture*
■ Norway High School Alumnus of the Year
—*Norway High School Alumni Association*
■ Appreciation Award
"For Promotion of Maine Products in Menu Planning"
awarded during "Maine Potato Week"
—*Maine Department of Agriculture*
■ Senior Supper Award
presented by class president, Rusty Frothingham
—*Class of 1965, Oxford Hills High School*
■ Operation ROSCO, Three-time Winner Award
—*National Restaurant Association*
■ Appreciation Award
—*Oxford Hills Music Boosters Association*

1966
    ■ Senior Supper Award
—*Class of 1966, Oxford Hills High School*
■ Elected to the International Association of Hoteliers,

Restauranteurs & Caterers (HO-RE-CA), Zurich
Julian Françoisin, president, Paris, France

1967 ■ Senior Supper Award
  —*Class of 1967, Oxford Hills High School*

1980 ■ Appreciation Award
  —*Norway-Paris Senior Citizens Club*
  "In recognition of faithful service and dedication
  to the Norway Paris Senior Citizens"
  presented by Larry Tidswell, President

1971 ■ Certificate of Appreciation
  —*Oxford County Economic Opportunity Council,*
  Community Action Agency Anti-Poverty Program
  presented by Robert Reny, Executive Director

1973 ■ American Police Officers Hall of Fame
  —*National Police Officers Association*
  presented by Frank J. Schiva, Executive Director

1974 ■ Certificate of Appreciation & Service Award
  —*Head Start Program*
  presented by Charleen A. Lever, Director

1975 ■ Business Member Award
  —*United States Chamber of Commerce*
  by invitation of the Chamber's Board of Directors

1976 ■ Appreciation Award
  —*Norway-Paris Senior Citizens Band*
  presented by Evelyn Bonney, President
  ■ Honorary Chairman
  —*Stephens Memorial Hospital Fund Drive*
  Groundbreaking Silver Shovel presented by Robert Goodwin

1977 ■ First Community Service Award
  —*Oxford Hills Chamber of Commerce*
  ■ Honorary Member
  —*Mid-Maine Motorcycle Association of Auburn, ME*
  presented by Ollie Dore, President
  ■ Special Achievement Award
  —*Maine Restaurant Association*
  presented by Carl Sanford, Chairman of the Board

1978 ■ National Community Service Award
  —*Norway Grange No. 45*

Robert Barrows, National Grange Master
presented by Hattie Harmon, Lecturer

1979 ■ Appreciation Award
—*WCBB-TV Channel 10, Maine Public Television*
"For the interest and support given in advancing
the goals of Public Television"
presented by Bob Gardner, President

1980 ■ Commission of Honorary Captain
—*Maine State Police*
Signed by Colonel Allen Weeks, Maine State Police
and Governor Joseph Brennan

1986 ■ Special Achievement Award
—*Guy Rowe Elementary School*
presented by Karen Ellis on behalf of the entire school

1987 ■ Special Recognition & 20th Birthday Party
—*Head Start Program*
presented by Joyce Rich, teacher

1989 ■ Included in Who's Who of Woman Executives
(1989-1990 publication)
■ Maine Restauranteur of the Year
—*Maine Restaurant Association*
■ Recognition Award: Oldest restaurant
in Maine under the same ownership
—*Maine Restaurant Association*
■ Special Recognition Award
—Legislature of the State of Maine
presented by Donald Twitchell, Senator (Oxford)
and Joseph Walker, Representative, (Norway)
■ Special Recognition
—*National Restaurant Association*
presented by Jim Peterson, President

1990 ■ Josephine Stone and Barjo Restaurant featured in
The Congressional Record: Senate S 2686-March 9, 1990
presented by William Cohen, U.S. Senator (R-Maine)
■ 4-H Special Recognition Award
—*Oxford County Fair & 4-H Clubs*
for 40 years of Distinguished Service to 4-H
■ Framed portrait of Jo with Kevin McHale
at Boston Celtics Game at Boston Garden,
—*special tribute by the Local Police Officers*

presented by the officers of all the local departments
- Election to the Society of Hosts
—Florida State University, Tallahassee, Fla.
- 'Salut au Restauranteur' Award
—Florida State University, Tallahassee, Fla.

1991

- Proclamation declaring June 9, 1991,
"Josephine Stone Day" in Maine
—*State of Maine*
by Governor John McKernan
- Proclamation declaring June 9, 1991,
"Josephine Stone Day" in the Town of Norway
by Town Manager, David Holt
- First 'Citizen of the Year' Award
—*Town of Norway, Maine*
- Distinguished Service Award
"For Outstanding Support to Her Fellow Merchants"
—*Norway Merchants Association*
presented by Richard Halle, President
- Outstanding Service Award
—*Oxford Hills Technical School-Region XI*
presented by Irving "Duffer" Pendleton
- Citizen of the Year
—*Norway Police Department*
presented by Officer Ernest Dunham

Appendix 4

In the Words of Friends

When they learned about "Jo Stone Day," many of Jo's old friends sent notes recalling special things they remembered about Barjo's and Jo. The following are excerpts from a few of these treasured letters.

Remembering the 1950's
For all—the Cokes and gossip at noon!
For all—the giggles and French-Fries after school!
For all—the Fried Clams, long after midnight on Saturday night!
—Thank-you!
Remembering the 1960's and 1970's
For all—the food you fed us all!
For all—the years Andy, Jody and Robbie hauled our kids in for extras!
For all—the ice Brad ever borrowed from your basement!
—Thank-you!
Remembering the 1980's
For all—The Christmas Eve—Chicken Pies!
For all—the Businessman's lunches!
For all—the Roast Lamb Dinners!
For all—the Custard pies that I loved!
For all—YOU ARE!
—Thank-you!
—Brad and Carol Ann Raymond, *Norway*

If Barjo's hadn't been around—I wouldn't be here! My parents met at Barjo's when they were in high school. I'll never forget your amazing piecrust or meeting Ray Brown for lunch—he practically lived there for years.
You've meant so much to my family. Enjoy yourself now!
—Debi Irons, *Art Moves, Masonic Building, Norway*

I want to thank you for being so good to "Blackie and Alice", my mother and father, over the years. Dad always enjoyed going to Barjo's for dinner—Mom enjoyed it also, but Dad knew more people and there was always someone who went there to talk with him. You were so good to us children when we were small, too.
—Pauline Blacquiere Henderson, *Panaca, Nevada*

■ ■ ■

Capt. Josephine Stone, Retired
Barjo Restaurant
Dear Capt. Stone,

I want to take a minute to thank you for all the expert advice, supervisory assistance and of course, the excellent cooking you provided to me and my troopers while we worked in Oxford County. I could always count on you to tell my people they needed haircuts, needed to work harder or needed a good meal. I sincerely appreciate your continued friendship and look forward to seeing you soon. Please, any time you are in the Gray area, stop in to the Troop B Barracks. I'll give you a personal tour and stop for coffee, donuts or lunch. Don't hesitate to call if you ever need anything. You still have to teach me how to make your delicious tomato stew—you promised!

Have a long and *happy* retirement.

—Lt. Bradford S. Smith, *Commander, Troop B, Gray, Maine*

■ ■ ■

It has been with great pleasure that I read the wonderful celebration Norway recently put on in your honor. I'm so happy that both my husband and my youngest daughter had the opportunity to meet you in recent years.

The Easton families have always thought so much of you over the years.

May the Lord bless you and keep you in your retirement years and may you live them to their fullest.

—Elinor Easton Ives, *Happy Camp, California*

■ ■ ■

Dear Mrs. Stone,

Father Colpitts tells me that your visit to the hospital for your eyes was very successful and you have made an excellent recovery——I am very pleased to hear that news.

I wish to thank you for those wonderful meals you made available on Sunday evenings at your restaurant——I will always remember them and was pleased to have met you. I know Father Colpitts thinks the world of you. I can still savor the Roast Lamb and the Custard Pie.

Sincerely,
Reverend Monsignor Paul Gleason

—Saint Patrick's Church, *Lewiston*

■ ■ ■

Dear Rev. Mother Josephine,

Sincere thanks for your many kindnesses to me and your generous gift to the Saint Catherine Parish of the dishes, glasses, flatware and other useful items. It is a gift the parish will enjoy for many years. I will miss seeing you at the store. I slept better at night after I worked with you doing dishes. I hope you have many pleasant years in retirement.

With Love and Thanks,
Father "ABC"
—Father Albert Colpitts, St. Catherine's Parish, Norway

■ ■ ■

Do you remember me? I worked for you in 1937-38. I married Vert Edmunds—He died in 1951. I have two children—Everett is a Social Studies teacher in Guilford and Janet works at Brewster Academy here in Wolfeboro, NH. I live in Florida 9 months of the year and 3 months here to visit with the children and grandchildren. I brought up my children doing waitress work so you know how that was.

I remember the Central Maine Power Company men eating at Barjo's. Also the "Big Trial" that brought lots of business to town.

Hope you enjoy your retirement!

Elinor
—Elinor Bean Edmunds, Wolfeboro, NH

■ ■ ■

Dear Jo,

I just wanted to join your hundreds of friends in wishing you well as you enter a new chapter in your life. Over the years you and Barjo's have become a legend in Norway and, indeed, in all of Maine. I certainly hope someone will come forward who will want to keep your wonderful restaurant going.

Although no one will ever be able to take your place, I feel sure your example of compassion for those less fortunate and your willingness to hold out a hand, will be passed on to many you have touched over the years.

I will miss you and all that great cooking!! All my very best for a busy and happy retirement.

Sincerely,
Olympia J. Snowe, Member of Congress
—Olympia J. Snowe, *(then) 2nd District Representative, Maine*

■ ■ ■

Dear Mrs. Stone;
...I am Sergeant S. Coleman, better known as "Bud". My mother was the former Isma McKeen of Lovell and my aunts were, Winnie Bickford, Muriel Brown, Hester Mann, Hallie Harriman and Sarah Grover.

I worked my way through school, working in the summer resorts and for Mayford Mann in his shoe store during the school year. During those years, Barjo's was the "place in town" for the young as well as older people.

Jo, you did so much for the community as well as neighboring towns such as East Stoneham, cooking turkeys, pies, etc. You also contributed much to us working school children, giving us meals and jobs. My sister, Eudora, worked for you, as you'll recall.

I joined the service in 1941 and left Norway to serve in the South Pacific. I was fortunate and after 27 months came home for one month and then went back for 8 more months. During my leave I spent three weeks in Norway…At that time, when you dined at Barjo's and received a "red star" on the back of your bill, your meal was free. …I was most fortunate on several occasions.

I was discharged in 1945 and have lived in Florida ever since, visiting Maine …as often as I could, and always enjoyed visiting with you, Jo.

In 1953, I brought my wife, Ruth, for the first time and introduced her to you. I hadn't seen you in eight years. I went out to the kitchen and when you saw me I'll always remember what you told my wife.

I was home last summer and visited with you and had some Fried Clams and Custard Pie. I also visited with Margaret at the Ledgeview Nursing Home.

Jo, you are most deserving of "Jo Stone Day" on June 9, 1991 and I only wish I could have been there. You are loved and respected by many, especially me.

Sincerely,

"Bud" Coleman

—Bill Coleman, *Orlando, Florida*

■ ■ ■

After all these years, in the Advertiser, part of my past was once again cast on the "screen of life." The picture in the paper of us in our military uniforms was a complete surprise. Then, selling the restaurant and now "Jo Stone Day." Truly enough cannot be said for all you have done for Norway.

You always have been a wonderful person to work with and allowed me to put myself through Norway High School. The restaurant was my whole life for that period and thanks to you, it was fun and a real blessing. I could not follow in the footsteps of some of my brothers in alcoholism and thank God I was guided in another direction.

It was so much upon my heart to be there with you to celebrate "Jo Stone Day" and I'm sure it was wonderful. You have always been one not to allow people to praise you because you are a very humble person.

My wife and daughter were so happy to meet you that last time we were up home. I related all the fun I had working with you, and that you were more than an employer, you were as a mother that was proud of her son. You once said, "You are a self-made man!" Of course that pleased me beyond words.

After I went into the service, I went to the First Baptist Church of San Antonio, Texas.

There I opened my heart and life to the Lord Jesus Christ and accepted Him as my personal Savior. The Lord has led my life since and given to me the most wonderful wife and two children (now grown), two adorable grandchildren and a most wonderful daughter-in-law.

It's inconceivable to think of Norway without Barjo's, even if I have been away for a long time. Jo, have you ever thought of taking a trip to Florida? We would be so privileged to have you stay with us if you ever do. Tamarac is a part of greater Fort Lauderdale...

Much, much love and God's blessing upon you, dear Jo. In the Love of Jesus Christ, my Savior,

Jack Smith

—Jack Smith, *Tamarac, Florida*

▨ ▨ ▨

Dear Jo,

It's wonderful that a beautiful person, such as you, has been recognized in your efforts to be one of the best.

I am sure that you don't remember me, but back in the 1930's you bought extra Chase & Sanborn Coffee from me to help me over my sales quota. I won a trip to The New York World's Fair and beat every salesman in New England, including Bill Grady. (Maybe you remember him.)

It was always a pleasure to call on you and I guess every salesman in the State of Maine knew you.

It's been an honor to know you and I sincerely hope you have a long and happy retirement. You certainly helped to make this a better world against so many negative attitudes of the present.

Thanks for just knowing you,

—Jim MacNutt, *former Chase & Sanborn Salesman, Auburn*

▨ ▨ ▨

Dear Jo,

What a lady you are! I look back so many times and remember the good times I had at Barjo's. You and Margaret taught me a lot. You both were strict and wanted things done right. It molded me into a well-rounded person. I thank you both.

It was because of you that I have been successful. I am semi-retired now after 46 years in the restaurant business. Jobs I have had over the years include dining room manager, cashier, hostess; head waitress, customer service representative; trainer and training manager. I also opened four stores for Arby's (for the Raffle brothers) where I have been for 13 years.

Thank-you for teaching me at the age of 17-18, the right way to do things and to realize that hard work never hurt anybody.

God Bless You, Jo.

Edith

—Edith Davis Deegan, formerly of Bryant Pond, Maine

▨ ▨ ▨

Dear Jo,

Les and I want to extend our congratulations to you upon such an outstanding accomplishment, as well as for all of the other accomplishments which were mentioned in the paper. You certainly deserve every accolade that is forth coming. I know that the remaining members of your family, and the Town of Norway—as well—are very proud of you, and rightly so.

You have enriched as many lives made a multitude of people so happy over the years and I recall that when there were strategic decisions to be made with regard to town affairs you candidly and honestly expressed your opinion. A rare and admirable quality. I reiterate: "Congratulations!"

Our mutual hobby as Ham Radio Operators, which my husband and I have shared over the years and still enjoy, keeps us attuned with friends all over the world. A fulfilling hobby. One of our "Ham" friends (the late Virgil Thompson of Porter, Maine), was a great admirer of yours and he often spoke over the air, of going into Barjo's to have a piece of Jo's Custard Pie. If we get to Norway/South Paris this summer, we'd like to drop by and see you.

The two towns have changed so drastically...other than the folks we especially went to call on, we didn't see a familiar face on the streets!

Les joins me in best wishes for your good health and happiness.

Cordially & Love,

—Dot Marston MacGowan, Pittsfield

■ ■ ■

Dear Jo,

My main reason for writing is to thank you! I want to thank you for all of the wonderful memories you have given me and thousands of others.

For me, you were always *special* in that you were not just a restaurant owner out to make a buck, but a friend who always showed an interest in how I was doing and how the rest of the family was doing.

You were always so good to my Mom and Dad. I know they considered you a dear friend. I'm going to miss seeing you and Emily when I come home to visit. My son, Kevin, will miss your Strawberry Pie!

I'll never forget the days when I was in Little League and you always were so giving to all of us players. I know we appreciated it and we respected you for being so nice to a bunch of wild little kids. Thanks for being such a kind and giving person and for enabling me to have such wonderful memories to share with Kevin.

I hope that now you're going to find a new career and as usual, will continue helping people. Good luck in whatever you decide to do. Thanks again for all the wonderful memories of Barjo's!

Your Friend,
Tommy

—Tommy Gilford, *formerly of Norway*

■ ■ ■

Dear Jo,

Another news item about you, today. What a celebrity you have become!

How I miss coming to Barjo's. Betty Jones always reports to me when she goes there. She shares my love of both you and your cooking. Remember when all of us teachers used to come to the restaurant in the 1940's? Norway is still a favorite place for me. I was never happier than during the many years I spent there.

Remember me to Grace, and Margaret and Kudos to you.

—Daphne W. Winslow (Merrill), *former NHS Teacher ,Auburn*

Dear Jo,

I'll introduce myself. I am Helen McIntosh, 87 years old, who lives in Weymouth, Mass. My husband and I taught in Brookline, and spent our summers on Dillingham Hill, Auburn, Maine. We had two daughters and I can remember having a high-chair at Barjo's for Marjorie, who is now 52. With both my oldest daughter, Dorothy, and my husband now gone, I am alone with the help of two women, who alternate caring for me.

I still get to Maine and good friends take me to Barjo's often—a great treat. Two years ago, your brother, Donald, told me to use the back door as I am using two canes. I come, now, in the back way and have seen your Boston Celtics pictures. I am a Celtics fan, too, and have a little banner which goes up when they win and, sadly has gone down too much of late.

One of the other things I have told you about on one of my trips through your kitchen is my grandson, Scott Hamilton, the Gold Medal Olympic champion in Ice Figure Skating.

I wanted to tell you this interesting story, too. My husband and I and another couple stayed at Long Lake, in Harrison, and the men were playing golf. I drove them to the course and then my friend Martha and I would come over to Barjo's for lunch. One noon we had Lobster Rolls and the most delicious raspberry pie. Martha said, "I haven't had pie like that since my Mother died. Helen, would you eat a second piece?" Of course, I said, "yes!" That night, when the men got home, they said, "Let's go over to Barjo's for dinner." We didn't tell them we had already been there that day. So we went and had a lovely dinner, and my husband said, "I'm going to have a piece of raspberry pie for dessert." The waitress came back and said, "We've had a run on that kind today and we are all out." I didn't dare to look at my friend! This Barjo's story has been told many times since in our family!

I hope you think of all the friendliness and pleasure you have given others through the years. I remember your sister, too. You were quite a team'

Sincerely,
Helen McIntosh

—Helen McIntosh, *Weymouth, MA*

Appendix 5

The Congressional Record

Dear Josephine,

Upon reading the article about you in the February 20, 1990, Lewiston Sun Journal, I thought more people should learn of your work and your restaurant. For that reason I asked that the article be reprinted in the Congressional Record.

The Record, as the official account of Congressional proceedings, is read throughout the country. Now men and women throughout Maine and the rest of the country will be able to learn of your talents, already so well known to the people of Norway and Paris.

I've enclosed several copies of my statement and the article as they were printed in the Record. Please accept my congratulations on your recent honors and on your lifelong commitment to Barjo's and the people of your community.

With best wishes, I am,
William "Bill" Cohen,
United States Senator (R), Maine

■ ■ ■

S 2686—*Congressional Record*—Senate—March 9, 1990
JOSEPHINE STONE AND BARJO RESTAURANT

MR. COHEN: Mr. President, it has been said that diamonds are pieces of coal that stuck to their job. You will find few better examples of how persistence and hard work have resulted in the creation of a true gem than that of Josephine "Jo" Stone and her restaurant, Barjo's in Norway, Maine.

"Jo" is 86 and has not missed a day of work since the restaurant opened 58 years ago. She is as well known for her generosity as for her famous raspberry and custard pies and boiled dinners. She fed one poverty-stricken woman for 35 years and has given free meals to on duty area police officers for decades.

In recognition of her perseverance and kindness, the police officers of Paris and Norway, Maine, arranged for Mrs. Stone to travel to Boston to watch her beloved Boston Celtics basketball team last month. It was her first trip out of Maine since 1940. Stone was named the 1989 Maine Restaurateur of the Year and will be one of seven restaurateurs in the Nation to attend the 37th

Annual Salut Au Restaurateur of Florida State University in Florida in March. An article detailing the accomplishments of this remarkable woman appeared in the Lewiston Sun-Journal. I encourage all of my colleagues to visit this jewel in Norway, Maine, and I ask that this article be printed in the Congressional Record.

The article follows:

AFTER A HALF-CENTURY, NORWAY RESTAURANTEUR SET FOR SIGHTSEEING
By Mary Delameter

(Norway)—Josephine "Jo" Stone, 86, is going to hang up her apron next week and briefly close her landmark restaurant on Main Street to take two excursions out of state. She has not been outside of Maine since 1940, preferring instead to tend her business, Barjo's, that her family has owned since 1932. Stone's first trip will be to a Boston Celtics basketball game in Boston. The Feb. 28, trip is a gift from officers of the Norway and Paris police departments, who plan to chauffeur Stone and her restaurant manager, Emily Foster, to the Boston Gardens for the evening, with a stop for dinner along the way. The second excursion is all the way to Florida, where Stone will be one of seven restaurateurs in the nation selected to attend the 37th Annual Salut Au Restaurateur at Florida State University in Tallahassee. To get to the March 11 banquet, she'll be flying—for the first time in her life.

"Jo" admits she's apprehensive about leaving town and doesn't like being in the spotlight.

"I think it would be a good idea if someone else went," she said, but added that she accepted the university's invitation so that she could proudly represent "a little restaurant from Maine" in a prestigious national program. The university is one of the leading food service schools in the nation.

Stone was named 1989 Maine Restaurateur of the Year and accepted the award at a banquet in Portland, Me., a city that she had not visited since World War II.

Also last year, she was named in the "Who's Who of Women Executives", a listing of America's top women business leaders.

The trip to the Celtics game will offer Stone a chance to see the team she's cheered for since 1950. The 5-foot-tall former Norway High School guard will have an opportunity to see her favorite Celtic, Kevin McHale, the 6-foot-10-inch forward. Asked what she likes about him, she replied, laughing, "Oh, he's so handsome." If she were introduced to him at the game, she said, "I think I'd just faint away."

But the real reason for her admiration of McHale, she said, is his strong work ethic and unselfish style of play----character traits her admirers say she exemplifies. In the nearly 58 years she has been in business, she has closed Barjo's only once----for a two week renovation project in 1972.

Stone begins her workday at 4:00 A.M. with cleaning from the front door to the back, and making her famous raspberry and custard pies, homemade soups and boiled dinners. The restaurant, which until two years ago was open seven days a week, closes daily at 9:30 on a Tuesday through Sunday schedule.

Stone can't remember missing a day of work since the restaurant opened 58 years ago with her sister, Margaret McAllister, who still does the bookkeeping, and her brother, Donald McAllister, both of Norway. She took over the operation herself in 1936, serving mostly sandwiches and ice cream in the 2-1/2 story building constructed in 1804.

Stone has lost three husbands, and those tragedies, she said, caused her to fight for survival for her daughter and herself. "I would work harder and harder to overcome it," She said.

At the Florida banquet, which her daughter and son-in-law, Barbara and Henry Paradis, will attend, the businesswoman will participate in a panel discussion titled, " Secrets of Their Success". Asked what she will share, Stone gave the credit to her manager and staff.

"I couldn't have been here without Emily," she said of the restaurant's manager. "There's no question about it."

"We've been blessed with Veda Taker and Gloria Day," she added, referring to two longtime waitresses.

"We've had a lot of school kids, and they've helped us as much as I've helped them," Stone explained about her kitchen help.

Over the years, Stone has been known for her generosity. She had given free meals to many customers, young and old. She fed one poverty-stricken woman meals for 35 years. And she has made it a practice for decades to feed police officers while on duty; hence the reason for their gift to her.

"She's just a wonderful, kind woman who does so much," said Paris Police Chief Lloyd "Skip" Herrick. "She doesn't hesitate to give us her opinion on local issues, events and the Celtics."

"We fight all the time," Stone said of her banter with the officers about the basketball games.

"It's her strong character we admire," said Herrick. "If there's an opportunity to say thank you, we want to."

Dane Tripp and his son, Shawn, Larry Sanborn, Ernest Dunham and Alan Afflerbach will join Herrick on the Boston trip. A local automobile dealer, Kenneth Kilgore, is offering the use of a van.

■ ■ ■

Jo has a framed copy of the Congressional Record on display at her home. It was a great honor for Bill Cohen to have it published and they continue to be very good friends. He often stopped at Barjo's when he was in Maine and came to the kitchen to visit with her. William Cohen was appointed United States Secretary of Defense in January 1996.